By ORVILLE PRESCOTT

PRINCES OF THE RENAISSANCE

PRINCES
OF THE
RENAISSANCE

ORVILLE
PRESCOTT

LONDON
GEORGE ALLEN & UNWIN LTD
RUSKIN HOUSE · MUSEUM STREET

923.145
PRESCOTT
1.

PRINTED IN GREAT BRITAIN
BY JOHN DICKENS AND CO LTD
NORTHAMPTON

To four old friends of mine:

Niccolò Machiavelli, Francesco Guicciardini,
Baldassare Castiglione and Francesco Matarazzo

A*

Succeeding generations change the fashion of their morals, with the fashion of their hats and their coaches; take some other kind of wickedness under their patronage, and wonder at the depravity of their ancestors.

—Lord Macaulay in his essay on Machiavelli

❖❖❖❖❖❖ CONTENTS ❖❖❖❖❖❖

✠✠✠✠ ILLUSTRATIONS ✠✠✠✠

INTRODUCTION

JUDGED BY THE NUMBER of books written about it, the Italian Renaissance is one of the most perennially interesting of all historical periods. By universal consent it is also one of the most important. The great cultural revolution which swept over Italy in the fifteenth century transformed European civilization and the minds of men. In the liberating excitement of all the new ideas and new attitudes there was an explosion of artistic genius. The painters, sculptors, writers and architects of the Renaissance are the glory of Italy. The society in which they lived was dominated by the princes who ruled the many independent states. These princes were themselves profoundly important shapers of the political, cultural and moral climate of their time. Most of them are not nearly as well known as the artists they patronized, bullied or ignored.

And just as the artists expressed the ideas and ideals of the time, so did the princes. Since they were men of power, absolute lords in their petty domains, they enjoyed complete liberty to play their parts on the Renaissance stage as they saw fit. Their furious energy, their flamboyant individualism, their ostentatious magnificence, their deceit and cruelty and their cultivation, combined with moral corruption, were all part of the Renaissance world. It was a grim and gaudy world and the dukes, marquises, lords and despots were a spectacularly colorful lot.

A few were great men. All were involved in great events. Their lives were melodramatic. They were also full of psychologically interesting demonstrations of the use of power and of the way powerful men lived in an era of artistic triumphs and political anarchy. This book is a popular narrative about the lives, personalities and politics of extraordinary people. Most of them are unknown except to students of the Renaissance.

Biographies of a few of the characters in this book are available. Facts about the rest are widely scattered in many learned and obscure books, some of which have never been translated into English. Other important aspects of the Renaissance, such as economics, the revival of learning and the philosophy of the humanist scholars, which do not properly fit into this book, are authoritatively discussed in numerous scholarly works.

Ignoring the currently fashionable question of just when was the Renaissance, I have written about Italy only in the years usually considered incontestably Renaissance in that country—from 1400 to 1530. I have not included chapters on the two families whose names are best known to most readers—the Medici and the Borgias—although members of both families frequently appear in these pages. Many books about the Medici and Borgias are available. Some of them are listed in the bibliography. I have preferred to write about other princes of the Renaissance, all of them as interesting and some of them as important.

It is a pleasure to thank five people who have generously given of their time to help me complete this book, either by tracking down elusive facts or by reading the manuscript and making suggestions for improving it: Carlo Beuf, biographer of Cesare Borgia; Serge Hughes, Professor of Italian at Hunter College; Paul Reynolds; Lilias Prescott, my wife; and Peter S. Prescott, my son. I am, of course, solely responsible for all sins of omission or commission. I also wish to thank the kind people who courteously provided me with books from the following libraries: the New York Public Library, the Society Library of New York, the library of the Century Association, the Bodleian Library at Oxford, the Bridgeport Public Library and the New Canaan Public Library.

PRINCES OF THE RENAISSANCE

THE BEGINNING
OF THE END

"THE WINES OF ITALY were sour this year, and therefore not at all agreeable to the French, any more than the excessive heat of the atmosphere." The year was 1494. The French were the soldiers of King Charles VIII, invading Italy on their way to the conquest of the Kingdom of Naples. The writer was Philip de Commines, Lord of Argenton, a Flemish diplomat and bureaucrat who had served Louis XI for many years and had also served Louis's feckless son. Charles's long march from Lyons to Naples and his long retreat back again is one of the key events in European history. It marked the end of an era and the beginning of another, the end of the independence of the separate states of Italy in which the Renaissance had flowered and the beginning of the domination of Italy by foreign powers and the ravaging of Italy by French, German, Spanish and Swiss troops.

No royal warrior was ever less qualified to command an army than Charles. No military expedition was ever more casually planned. Nevertheless, its initial success was spectacular, humiliating to the Italians and wonderfully inflationary to French arrogance and French complacency. It is not surprising that Commines, who was usually a cynical and skeptical observer of politics and princes, concluded that "this whole expedition was a mystery conducted by God himself."

Commines was not the only one who saw God's hand in the matter. There had been much prophesying of the wrath to come. Long before Charles left France, several priests and hermits predicted that he would not only succeed in enforcing his dubious claim to the Kingdom of Naples but that he would conquer the empire of the Turks and become the universal monarch of the world.

In Florence the fanatical and fiercely eloquent Dominican friar Savonarola had long been prophesying disaster, invasion and reform forced by an agent of God's wrath. Savonarola was certain that Charles was the mortal embodiment of his apocalyptic visions. "Lo, the sword is come, the prophecies are verified, the scourging has begun. Lo, the Lord leads these armies. Oh, Florence, the time of singing and dancing is over; now is the time to weep for your sins with torrents of tears. Your sins, Oh Florence, your sins, Oh Rome, your sins, Oh Italy, are the cause of these afflictions."

What kind of man was this parrot-nosed young monarch with his wispy red beard, so obviously miscast as the scourge of God? What kinds of people were the ruling princes of Italy into whose circumscribed but highly civilized world Charles burst, leading his medieval, semibarbarous army? Charles's invasion profoundly influenced the destinies of the princely families of Renaissance Italy which are the principal subject of this book. The story of his invasion is in itself an introduction to many of those families.

Charles VIII was the only son of Louis XI, the Spider King, who by force and fraud, guile and dissimulation, had done much to unify France and to forge a national state. When Louis died in 1483 he left behind him a standing army, the first in Europe since Roman times, and a sickly, mentally backward son of thirteen.

As an infant Charles was small, weak, with spindly legs, protruding eyes and an abnormally large head. His anxious and disappointed father decided that the boy's education should not include Latin or any other fatiguing mental effort. Instead, he was to devote himself to hunting and other kinds of exercise. Louis declared that Latin (then the universal study of the few educated men) was useless for a king. He even pretended that his own erudition had been an embarrassment to him. But after

CHARLES VIII, *King of France*

"This parrot-nosed young monarch with his wispy beard, so obviously miscast as the scourge of God ..."

Louis's death Charles did study a little Latin. He never learned to write properly, however, and had difficulty signing his own name. He read in French many romantic tales of medieval chivalry. These filled his head with dreams of glory and conquest. In 1490, one year before he freed himself from the regency of his sister, Anne of Beaujeu, Charles was twenty. The Venetian ambassador wrote: "His Majesty the King of France is small and ill-formed in person, with an ugly face, large lusterless eyes, which seem to be short-sighted, an enormous aquiline nose, and thick lips which are constantly open; he stutters and has a nervous twitching of his hands which is unpleasant to watch. In my opinion—it may well be wrong—he is not of much account either physically or mentally; however, he is generally well-spoken of in Paris as being a good hand at tennis, hunting and tilting—pursuits to which, whether for good or ill, he devotes much time."

Commines, who knew Charles well, said that he was equally destitute of political and military capacity. Yet Commines added his belief that Charles "was so good that it is not possible to imagine a better man." Since Charles was not good in any usual sense of the word, being irresponsible, self-indulgent, promiscuous and indifferent to cruelty, Commines probably meant that Charles had a sort of simple-minded innocence, an appealing naïveté. In fact, Charles was so anxious to please and to be liked that he was called "the Affable." Charles was so incapable of refusing personal favors that one Neapolitan jokingly said to him that, had he been a woman, his desire to please everybody would have gravely imperiled his chastity.

Charles's decision to conquer Naples dismayed his more cautious advisers. Commines said that "neither his exchequer, his understanding, nor his preparations were sufficient for such an important enterprise." But there were many reasons why the campaign was waged. In addition to his claim to the throne of Naples, Charles had precedents for interfering in Italy. The French had ruled Sicily briefly and Naples for nearly two hundred years. Charles's own father, while dauphin, had led an army into Italy. France had the largest, best-equipped and best-disciplined army in Europe. Some use had to be made of it. After all, kings were supposed to wage war and were scorned if they did not. And Charles had dreams.

He dreamed not only of flying the fleur-de-lis banners over Naples. He dreamed of driving the Turks out of Greece, of conquering Constantinople and of redeeming Jerusalem. Naples would be only the jumping-off place for a crusade. Charles had a medieval mind—as did most Frenchmen in the late fifteenth century. The French first took serious notice of the Renaissance when Charles led them into Italy.

The French claim to Naples dated back to the thirteenth century, when the papacy had conferred its feudal fief of Naples on Charles of Anjou, younger brother of Louis IX. But the House of Anjou had been driven out of Naples by King Alfonso of the Spanish kingdom of Aragon in 1442. The royal House of Aragon may have had disaffected barons at home and embittered exiles abroad; but it was firmly established in Naples by right of conquest and in 1494 it had reigned there for more than fifty years. And Naples was far away, hundreds of miles down a mountainous peninsula divided into many states. Of these, not one could be counted on as a trustworthy ally of France.

But Charles was convinced of his right to rule Naples. He was certain also that nothing could be more fun than to cross the Alps as Charlemagne had done before him and to ride in triumph throughout Italy. The noble young lords who led his incomparable heavy cavalry boiled with an equally joyful bellicosity. And besides, hadn't Charles been invited by numerous Italians to undertake this "enterprise of Naples"?

Such invitations to France to intervene with armed might in Italy were almost traditional. Venice and the papacy had both tried to enlist France in their support before. And now when Charles established his court at Lyons in March of 1494 in order to be conveniently situated for his departure, he was bombarded by a steady cannonade of Italian eloquence.

A half-dozen noble Neapolitan exiles, who had supported the Angevin cause against King Ferdinand I of Naples, were in Lyons, urging Charles to get on with his enterprise against Ferdinand's son and successor, Alfonso II. Whether they would find life more to their liking under the House of Valois than that of Aragon was doubtful; but they were anxious to exchange the royal family they knew for one they did not. Most persuasive of these exiles was Galeazzo Sanseverino, the most famous of several warrior brothers who belonged to the most important of the Neapolitan noble families. Galeazzo was handsome, charming and the best jouster in Italy. He was the son-in-law and intimate friend of Lodovico Sforza, Regent of the Duchy of Milan, and he was the commander of the Milanese armies.

Lodovico had been reluctant to allow Galeazzo to go to Lyons. But Charles had demanded his presence. Since Lodovico had persuaded himself that his position as ruler of Milan depended upon Charles's giving a good scare to Alfonso II of Naples, he consented and sent off his glittering courtier. Lodovico's fear of Alfonso had good grounds. Alfonso was furious with Lodovico because of his treatment of Alfonso's daughter, Isabella, who was married to Lodovico's nephew, Gian Galeazzo Sforza, Duke of Milan. Lodovico ruled Milan as if he were Duke, and his wife flaunted her social leadership at court, which was rightfully Isabella's. Alfonso snarled and even threatened war against Milan.

On April 15, 1494, Galeazzo Sanseverino arrived in the outskirts of Lyons, too late in the day to make his grand entrance into the city. But the official Milanese astrologers had designated April 15 as propitious by the conjunction of the stars, so Galeazzo made a preliminary secret entry into Lyons. Disguised as a German knight, escorted by only four lesser knights, he entered the city incognito, enjoyed a personal interview with Charles and then left the city.

The next day, dressed in his war armor (he had left his jousting armor in Milan), Galeazzo led his cavalcade formally into Lyons. With him Galeazzo brought presents: for "The Most Christian King," war horses, Spanish jennets, armor and armor for horses, and perfumes for which Charles had a passion; and for the Queen, a Spanish dress of great magnificence. The crowds cheered. Charles rode out to meet Galeazzo, and this exiled soldier of fortune was received with unprecedented honors.

While at Lyons Charles, according to his usual custom, kept with him a bevy of pretty mistresses. How well Galeazzo succeeded in his mission not only to settle military details but to charm Charles may be seen in this paragraph from a dispatch sent to Lodovico in Milan by his regular ambassador at Charles's court:

"His Most Christian Majesty, having retired into his own quarters with a few of his most intimate friends and several of his mistresses, caused the said Lord Galeazzo to be introduced. After a little agreeable conversation, he (Charles) took one of these damsels by the hand, saying that he would like to give her to him as his mistress, then he chose one of them for himself, and each remained talking to his companion for a couple of hours."

Lodovico was delighted with his son-in-law. That Galeazzo was taken to the King's private apartments and "associated with him in all his domestic pleasures" seemed to Lodovico a triumph of diplomacy.

A more fiery champion of French intervention in Italy arrived in Lyons on June 1—Giuliano della Rovere, cardinal of San Pietro in Vinculi. Della Rovere was also an exile, from Rome because of his venomous feud with Pope Alexander VI. Two years before, the blunt and imperious Della Rovere and the suave and crafty Rodrigo Borgia had been rival candidates for the papacy. Borgia's bribes and promises had easily defeated Della Rovere's frank ambitions.

That was maddening enough because Della Rovere despised Borgia. But also provoking was the Pope's new alliance with Naples, only recently Della Rovere's own political ally. The Roman earth seemed to be quaking beneath Della Rovere's feet. As an open enemy of Alexander he had not thought it prudent to remain near the papal court where the very air was sinister with possibilities of violence. So the cardinal of San Pietro in Vinculi had fled to his fortress of Ostia and thence to France.

In Lyons he vehemently exhorted Charles to proceed with his enterprise. If Naples was an ally of the Pope, why then Della Rovere was an enemy of Naples. More important, he hoped that Charles would intimidate Alexander and that he could be persuaded to call a church council which would depose the Pope. Always a man who cherished his hatreds, Della Rovere was more insistent that the French march on Naples than even Lodovico Sforza. Lodovico had qualms and worrisome second thoughts. Della Rovere had none. He never did.

Considering his own enthusiasm for the "Enterprise of Naples" and all the encouragement he was receiving, Charles was astonishingly dilatory in getting started. He dallied in Lyons while spring turned into summer. Was he considering calling the whole thing off? What delayed him? One cause of delay was a neat little conspiracy hatched by several supporters of the King of Naples and opponents of the rash enterprise.

They employed a young woman of obvious charms and approachability, instructed her that the one thing she must not do was to surrender to Charles' easily aroused ardor, and then introduced her to the King. Charles was usually bored by too easy conquests. Now he was far from bored; he was infatuated. He spent his days in the house of a fortuneteller where the woman lodged. He took his meals there. He discussed matters of state there. When urged to depart he found implausible excuses. The Milanese ambassador embarrassed him with eloquent tirades.

Finally Charles left Lyons in late July, but he loitered for three more weeks in Vienne. Was the young woman there with him? It is not recorded. Charles did not reach Grenoble until August 23. Six days later when he mounted his horse to leave that city he was approached by André de la Vigne, a poet, who presented him with a ballade. In bad verse it reproached Charles for neglecting Mars while he was preoccupied with Venus.

Indifferent to the harsh realities of war, he let the summer campaigning season drift by, dismayed his allies, encouraged his enemies and increased his expenses. He crossed the Alps over the Mont Genevre Pass, reached Turin on September 5 and Asti on September 9. That town was a French outpost. It belonged to Louis, Duke of Orléans, Charles's cousin and brother-in-law, who had inherited it from his grandmother, Valentina Visconti, whose dowry town it had been when she married a French prince.

How large an army Charles brought to Italy is not known. In the fifteenth century no one was seriously concerned about statistics. Contemporary chroniclers and modern historians have made estimates which vary from 25,000 to 50,000. The most important units were the heavy French cavalry, the best mounted force in Europe; a contingent of Swiss mercenary infantry, armed with long pikes; and the French artillery. This consisted of thirty-six bronze cannon, eight feet long. They fired lead balls as large as a man's head; each was drawn on a wagon by a team of thirty-six horses. In addition, there were a number of smaller-caliber guns.

Charles's army was the first in history to take a wagon train of cannon on a long march. More powerful than anything the Italians had ever seen and far more easily transported, his cannon could batter breaches in massive stone walls in a few hours. Fortified castles were no longer capable of withstanding sieges. The Italians were horrified by such monstrous weapons.

A generation later the great Italian poet Ariosto lamented the introduction of firearms: "How did this infamous and ugly invention ever find a place in human hearts? Because of it the glory of war is destroyed and the profession of arms is without honor; valor and virtue are so debased that evil often seems better than good, and boldness and daring can no longer be put to the test in the field."

Charles's army also included archers, crossbowmen and arquebusiers. Wagons, horses and pack mules carried supplies and equipment. A horde of indispensable noncombatants included carpenters, farriers, teamsters, muleteers, grooms, cooks, servants and the members of the King's household staff. In addition, several hundred prostitutes accompanied the army to comfort the soldiers and help maintain their morale.

With their lances, pikes and pennants, their war horses and baggage animals, their gleaming armor, their plumes and many-colored costumes, the soldiers of King Charles filing down the passes of the Alps and onto the plain of Lombardy must have made a gorgeous spectacle. From afar they could be recognized as French by their white silk banners bearing the arms of France and the motto *Voluntas Dei* and *Missus a Deo*.

Charles himself went to war in royal state. As an annointed king his necessities were luxurious beyond the imaginations of modern millionaires on safari in Africa. His personal baggage included furniture and equipment for his bedchamber, chapel, wardrobe, pantry and kitchen. His staff included heralds, physicians, chamberlains, maîtres-d'hôtel, kings-of-arms, butlers, singers, boys of honor, keepers of the wardrobe, valets of the chamber, squires of the kitchen, waiters, pantlers, ushers-at-arms, ushers of the chamber, ushers of the hall, ushers of the kitchen, porters, clerks of supplies, buglers, trumpeters, sackbuts, drummers, harpers, oboe and cornet players, crack swordsmen, jousters, marksmen with the arquebus and culverin, and acrobats.

As the King approached the town of Asti he was met by Lodovico Sforza, the powerful Regent of Milan, and by Ercole d'Este, Duke of Ferrara, who was Lodovico's father-in-law.

The two Italian princes had arranged a grand ceremony of welcome. Its most novel feature to the French was the performance of an eleven-year-old girl who declaimed an oration of welcome in Latin. The French nobles, most of whom were illiterate, were dumfounded.

Two days later Lodovico's young wife, Beatrice d'Este, arrived at the nearby castle of Annona, bringing with her a choir of singers and musicians and eighty Milanese ladies chosen for their beauty. Charles, whose appearance may have been dismaying but whose manners were excellent, advanced cap in hand and kissed Beatrice, then Lodovico's bastard daughter, Bianca, the wife of Galeazzo Sanseverino, and then all eighty women. Beatrice wrote to her sister, Isabella, wife of the Marquis of Mantua: "I assure you no prince in the world could have made himself more agreeable. He desired to see my ladies dance, and then begged me to dance before him, which seemed to give him great pleasure."

The French were much impressed by the Italian ladies and by the elegance of their clothes—as Lodovico had intended. A member of Charles's suite wrote a letter to the King's sister, Anne, containing this description of Beatrice:

"When she arrived she was on a horse with trappings of gold and crimson velvet, and she herself wore a robe of gold and green brocade, and a fine linen *gorgerette* turned back over it, and her head was richly adorned with pearls, and her hair hung down behind in a long coil with a silk ribbon twisted round it. She wore a crimson silk hat, made very much like our own, with five or six red and gray feathers, and with all that on her head, sat up on horseback as straight as if she had been a man."

So enduring was the impression made on the French by the Italian ladies that a hundred years later the French courtier and memoirist Brantôme wrote: "Our women at that time were clumsy in their dress and not as attractive as they are today and as the women of Italy were then."

At Asti there was another delay. Charles came down with a mild case of smallpox which immoblized him for more than two weeks. When he could travel again, he rode with Lodovico and Beatrice to their summer palace at Vigevano, where he was munificently entertained. This was one of Lodovico's three principal residences. The others were a great castle-palace in Milan built by his father, Duke Francesco, and a magnificent palace at Pavia built by his maternal ancestors, the Visconti. Lodovico contrived to divert Charles from his capital city of Milan. He could not divert him from Pavia.

At Pavia Lodovico showed Charles the celebrated library collected by the Viscontis and the Sforzas and took him hunting in the enormous deer park. But Lodovico was not able to prevent Charles from calling on his nephew, Gian Galeazzo Sforza, and his wife, Isabella of Aragon, daughter of Alfonso II, King of Naples.

Gian Galeazzo was the titular Duke of Milan, a weak-minded young man who had never been interested in anything except dogs and horses. He had been content enough to let his uncle Lodovico rule the duchy, but now he was dying and he worried that Lodovico would usurp the ducal throne from his infant son. To make it all the more embarrassing, Gian Galeazzo and Charles were first cousins. Their mothers were sisters, princesses of the House of Savoy.

Isabella of Aragon was a strong-willed, unhappy young woman with a grievance. Married to an ineffectual weakling, she had known the double mortification of watching her husband's uncle rule Milan as if he were its rightful duke, and of being forced to play a subordinate role to Lodovico's high-spirited and aggressive wife. When Charles called on the young couple in Gian Galeazzo's sickroom, Lodovico came, too, which made it difficult for either the Duke or Duchess to speak frankly.

Nevertheless, Gian Galeazzo managed to request Charles's benevolent support of his son as duke. And Isabella tearfully pleaded with Charles not to deprive her father of the throne of

Naples. This evidence that one person, his daughter, cared for Alfonso is interesting because nearly everyone else in Italy detested him. Charles was noncommittal in replying to Gian Galeazzo. To Isabella he regretted that events had gone so far that the conquest of Naples had to be concluded.

The next day Charles left Pavia and went to Piacenza where his army was waiting for him. Between the French and the Kingdom of Naples lay only three Italian states: the Republic of Florence, which ruled most of Tuscany; the smaller Republic of Siena, which ruled southern Tuscany; and the Papal States, which was ruled in theory, but in theory only, by Pope Alexander VI.

In Florence confusion reigned and Piero de' Medici, eldest son of the great Lorenzo, dithered. Although Florence was still nominally a republic, Piero was the fourth member of his family to be its de facto ruler. Unfortunately, unlike his astute great-grandfather, Cosimo, his capable grandfather, Piero, and his brilliant father, Piero was a fool.

Lorenzo had understood Piero. When his three sons were still boys, Lorenzo said that one (Piero) was foolish, one (Giovanni, the future Pope Leo X) was clever, and one (Giuliano, the future cultivated dilettante) was good.

In 1494 Piero was twenty-three. Brutal, arrogant and tactless, he ruled Florence as if he were its hereditary tyrant. In fact, he was only the city's political boss and on sufferance at that—granted his chance because of his family position. He was a fine horseman and the best player of *pallone* in Italy. Francesco Guicciardini, the Florentine historian, suspected that Piero was a murderer, saying that he "had found himself at the death of a man or two by night."

Piero antagonized the Florentines by his crude and irresponsible behavior. He alarmed them by his politics. He abandoned Florence's traditional friendship with France and made an alliance with the much less powerful Kingdom of Naples. And he took no steps to meet the emergency of Charles's approach.

Piero's claim to be officially neutral was not very convincing, coming from an ally of Naples. But Piero made no agreement with Charles permitting the French to cross Florentine territory. Early in October the French army reached the Florentine frontier, and Charles sent envoys to Florence to request a safe-conduct and permission to continue his march.

For five days Piero kept the envoys waiting while he failed to make up his mind. Then the angry envoys left. Charles was furious. He threatened to sack Florence, at once crossed the frontier, captured the Florentine fortress of Fivizzano and massacred the entire garrison.

Piero was appalled. He knew that he had bungled everything and that he lacked the power to resist the French. He remembered how his father in an earlier crisis had journeyed to Naples, risked his life in the hands of the perfidious King Ferdinand and returned in glory with a peace treaty. So Piero hurried to the French camp. But once there, he did not negotiate for the best terms possible. He groveled before the King and gave him, not only the safe-conduct, but also several key fortresses, permission to occupy Florence and the promise of a large subsidy. The French, who would have been satisfied with much less, laughed at Piero behind his back.

The Florentines did not laugh. They raged. France may have been a traditional friend, but such incompetence in their ruler was intolerable. When Piero returned to Florence he found himself barred from the municipal palace and in danger of his life. Florence was through with the Medici for a while, determined once again to be a republic in fact as well as in name. Piero fled and for the rest of his short life was known as Piero the Exile.

In the meantime the French army occupied Pisa. That port city had been subject to Florence for nearly a hundred years. Now was the heaven-sent opportunity for which the Pisans had long waited. They declared their independence of Florence and asked Charles to guarantee their freedom. Charles did not commit himself. Before he could resume his advance an envoy from the newly reorganized Florentine republic arrived in Pisa. His name was Savonarola.

The dynamic prophet and reformer was no ordinary envoy. He could speak French and he was the leading personality in Florence. But Savonarola was not interested in the usual negotiations of diplomacy. Long ago he had predicted Charles's invasion and he was prepared to find in the grotesque little King the elect

B

of God who would do just what Savonarola thought God's agent should do. He did not hesitate to tell Charles what his predestined role was:

"Most Christian King, you are an instrument in the hands of the Lord, who sends you to relieve the afflictions of Italy, as I have for years foretold, and to reform the Church, which lies prostrate in the dust. But if you are not just and merciful, if you fail to respect Florence, its women, its citizens, and its freedom, if you forget the mission God gives you, He will choose another to fulfill it. He will harden His hand and chastise you with terrible afflictions. These things I say to you from the Lord."

Charles may have been surprised by these words, but if he made any comment it has not been preserved.

The French army moved on and entered Florence with a grand display of military might, Charles riding with his lance in hand in the traditional manner of a conqueror. When the diplomatic talks began, Charles demanded everything Piero had offered, plus French occupation of Pisa until the war was over, plus the restoration of the Medici.

A Medici restoration was too much for the Florentines. They rejected it angrily. There was so much tension that Charles broke off one bargaining session with a threat: "We will blow our trumpets," which meant that his soldiers would be called to arms.

Piero Capponi, the Florentine negotiator, replied with a reckless courage entirely uncharacteristic of the cautious Florentines: "We will sound our bells," which meant that the male population of the city would be called into the streets with their weapons.

Charles temporized. He insisted on continuing his occupation of Pisa, but he swore a solemn oath to restore Pisa to Florence when he left Italy. He demanded and got a large subsidy. He gave up the idea of a Medici restoration. He accepted an honorary title, Protector of Florentine Liberties, and resumed his march. As was only to be expected, his men had thoroughly looted the Medici palace.

The next stop on Charles's grand peregrination of Italy was Siena. The Sienese entertained Charles with banquets and helpfully made available facilities for some spectacular debauchery.

But not all the French army was quartered in Siena. A detachment estimated by a contemporary chronicler at twelve thousand was camped at Mercatello near Monte Ubiano, not far from Perugia, the principal city of Umbria. And in Perugia swarmed the beautiful and bellicose sons of "the high and mighty Baglioni."

That family of aristocratic warriors ruled Perugia as absolute lords, although the city acknowledged a vague allegiance to the papacy and maintained its republican forms of municipal government. Two young Baglioni cousins, the fiercest of the entire pride, decided to strike a blow for Italian military honor. The French had marched from the Alps to within striking distance of Rome unopposed except by two Florentine fortresses which did not get word to surrender in time. Gianpaolo Baglioni, who was only twenty-three, and Astorre Baglioni, who was not much older, rode out from Perugia at night.

"They rode," said Francesco Matarazzo, "with their warrior brothers and their soldiers and certain of their friends to fall upon them [the French] and plunder them and break them and scatter them; and when they had so devised, without leave or counsel of their fathers they set out on their way toward the enemy. But when their elders the High and Mighty Guido and Ridolfo heard of this they at once sent messengers after them with orders that they should turn back and leave the adventure they had taken in hand; and this they must do forthwith making no question but obeying. And the messengers rode and came up to them, following hard one on the other, with orders to return. They had almost reached the place where the Frenchmen lay, yet at the last to obey their elders they turned back that same night. But the Frenchmen when they heard this forthwith plucked up their standard and without further stay took themselves off. This thing was told to the King of France, and he was astounded at the great hardihood of the young men." As he had cause to be, for the young Baglioni on short notice could not have called out more than one or two thousand men. Such rash courage was not characteristic of most Italian warrior princes. Nor was it of Gianpaolo Baglioni when he grew older and became one of the most famous of Italian condottieri.

As the French army neared Rome, Pope Alexander VI was as worried as Piero de' Medici had been a few weeks earlier. He was officially an ally of the King of Naples, the only ally Naples had left. But the new King, Alfonso II, did not seem anxious to fight the French. His father, old Ferdinand I, had died in January, bravely defying the French but gloomily foreseeing the worst. The Pope's troops were entirely inadequate to oppose Charles. And Alexander knew that he was not exactly beloved by Charles. Hadn't he sent him a papal bull in the spring threatening him with excommunication if he crossed the Alps? And wasn't Della Rovere constantly at the King's side, suggesting no one knew what dreadful ideas to him?

And then came news that the Pope's beautiful young mistress, Giulia Farnese Orsini, Giulia's sister and Giulia's mother-in-law had been captured by a party of raiding French cavalry. The gallant young commander, Yves d'Allegre, treated the ladies with great respect. Nevertheless, a messenger was dispatched to the Vatican with a demand for a ransom of three thousand scudi. Ransoms were usual for prisoners in the fifteenth century, but a pope's mistress was not a usual prisoner.

No one could have sent off a ransom faster than did the Borgia pope, who loved Giulia with passion. Charles promptly sent the ladies on to Rome and followed soon with his entire army. On December 31 Charles rode into Rome in another great display of pomp and power.

For two weeks King and Pope negotiated through intermediaries. Charles had the power. Alexander had only the mysterious majesty of his role as the vicar of Christ on earth. Twice it looked as if Charles would order his cannon to fire on the castle of Sant' Angelo—just to encourage Alexander. But Charles revered the papacy too much to use such crude methods of persuasion. When the two men finally came to terms, it was apparent that Alexander was no longer an ally of Naples.

Among the points agreed upon were: permission for the French to cross papal territory and to occupy several towns; an understanding that the Pope's son, young Cardinal Cesare Borgia, would accompany Charles for four months as papal legate, actually as a hostage; and the surrender to Charles of Prince

Djem, younger brother of the Turkish Sultan Bajazet II. That luckless young man had lost a rebellion he led against his brother, had fled to Rhodes, had been sold by the Knights of Rhodes to Louis XI and had been sold again by Louis to Pope Innocent VIII. Now he was dear to Alexander's heart because Bajazet paid him an annual allowance of forty thousand ducats to keep Djem prisoner and thus incapable of starting new revolts. Bajazet had even suggested that if his good friend the Pope would arrange a quiet murder he would be rewarded with three hundred thousand ducats, payment to be made when the body was delivered.

Charles evidently thought he could use the allowance. Whether Alexander considered earning the three hundred thousand ducats is not known, nor whether Charles had such a possibility in mind. All that is certain is that shortly after the French entered Naples Djem died, probably of natural causes. But in that suspicious age it was rumored that Djem was poisoned by the Pope.

The French left Rome on January 28, 1495. The next day at Marino Cardinal della Rovere came to Charles with news. Alfonso II of Naples, after a reign of little more than a year, had abdicated and fled the country. He was succeeded by his son, Ferdinand II.

At Velletri three days later Cesare Borgia escaped. He passed quickly through Rome and proceeded to the more salubrious haven of Spoleto. Of his personal baggage train of nineteen covered carts seventeen were left behind him at Velletri. All were empty. The two which had been loaded were missing.

Charles fumed and demanded explanations of the Pope. Alexander blandly insisted that he had no idea where Cesare was. "What dirty dogs these Italians are," said Charles, "and the Holy Father is as bad as any of them." Charles had forgotten that Alexander was a Spaniard.

As the French approached Neapolitan territory two heralds were sent to demand the surrender of the fortress of Monte San Giovanni. The heralds also demanded the food supply of the fortress. For their impudence the commander cut off their noses and ears and sent them back to Charles in the optimistic belief that he was safe inside his strong walls with his large garrison. The unfortunate man had not heard what the French cannon could do.

A few days later Charles watched while his cannon battered two breaches in the walls and his troops massacred every soldier in the place. Nearly nine hundred men were put to the sword or thrown from the battlements. This example of French methods of warfare proved marvelously effective in encouraging the surrender of Naples. "I fancy," said Charles, "that they have paid rather dearly for putting me to the trouble of looking them up."

The Neapolitan army melted away and on February 22 the French entered Naples in triumph. Pope Alexander, glumly contemplating the French parade through Italy, remarked, "The French have conquered Italy with a piece of chalk." He was referring to the quartermasters who without opposition marked houses and barns where their troops would be quartered and their horses stabled. Commines, remembering how easy it had all been, said that the French met with "so little resistance that our soldiers scarce ever put on their armor in the whole expedition."

Although crowds in Naples had cheered the French as deliverers, two castles on the waterfront of the Bay of Naples held out briefly for the young King Ferdinand II, who had escaped to the island of Ischia. In the great medieval Castel Nuovo a subordinate commander defied the French. After a warning bombardment the French demanded the surrender of the castle within twenty hours. His reply was heroic: "Not in twenty hours, not in twenty days, not in twenty months, not in twenty years! Never!" He was then threatened with a general massacre when the fortress should be taken by assault. With an even finer gesture he replied, "King Charles is welcome to put me to death, for I am determined to force him to kill me."

Unfortunately, the messenger who relayed these gallant words to the French arrived at evening and supplemented them with the news that before sunset the commander had fled by water to the Castello dell' Ovo, which the French had not yet bombarded. From that castle he sailed across the bay to join Ferdinand on Ischia.

In Naples, said Commines, "We spent our time in gaiety, entertainments, dancing and tournaments, and grew so insolent and vain, we scarce considered the Italians to be men." Charles punctiliously attended Mass every morning, and seemed to consider that nothing more was necessary to conciliate public opinion. He enjoyed the climate, admired the view, wrote home about the beauty of Neapolitan gardens and dallied with several complaisant ladies. He did nothing to organize his conquest properly.

Ignoring all business matters, Charles let subordinates distribute lands and jobs to deserving Frenchmen. His Angevin supporters were outraged. They were treated little better than supporters of the defeated House of Aragon! And in Naples itself the French government was incompetent and corrupt. The French soldiers behaved in the traditional manner of conquering armies, that is, they were brutal, arrogant and woman-crazy. The French were demonstrating a national characteristic which became even more conspicuous a few years later during the Italian conquests of Louis XII and Francis I—they could conquer, but they could not govern.

Charles's easy expansion of French power annoyed his fellow monarchs and alarmed the Italians. So on March 31, 1495, not quite five weeks after the French entry into Naples, an anti-French alliance was signed in Venice. Its members were Maximilian, Emperor of Germany; Pope Alexander VI; Ferdinand, King of Spain; the Republic of Venice; and Lodovico Sforza, now Duke of Milan. The League of Venice was instigated by Lodovico, Charles's principal Italian ally. Its only militarily active members were Venice and Milan, the two states which dominated northern Italy. French communication with France might soon be cut, and also with a detachment left at Asti under the command of the Duke of Orléans.

Such a possibility did not unduly disturb Charles and his advisers. After all, they did not take the Italians seriously. So they lingered on the lovely shore of the Bay of Naples and during the last week of April held a tournament every day. Charles did not take part personally, but he did touch many people to cure them of scrofula, "the King's evil." William Roscoe, first English biographer of Lorenzo and Giovanni de' Medici, commented: "Thus prone have the sovereigns of the world generally been to disregard those calamities which they might have alleviated, and to attempt the relief of those which are beyond their power."

Still untroubled by the storm clouds gathering in the north, Charles on May 12 celebrated his conquest and his claim to the title of King of France, Naples and Jerusalem with a ceremonial procession of great magnificence. Assembling at Poggio Imperiale, French princes and barons and Italian nobles faithful to Charles formed into a splendid procession and paraded into Naples. Charles wore an imperial mantle and a crown upon his head. In his right hand he held a golden ball symbolizing empire and in his left a sceptre. Neapolitan nobles held a canopy over him. As he entered the city he was met by a delegation of Neapolitan lords and ladies with their sons, aged eight to sixteen, whom Charles graciously knighted. He then proceeded to the cathedral for further ceremonies and more oratory.

It was all very grand. But the threat of the League of Venice could not be ignored indefinitely. On May 20 Charles left Naples to return to France. Behind him he left half his army to garrison his newly won kingdom. As the retreating French approached Rome Alexander VI fled. The former ally of Naples, the very recent friend of France and the present member of the League of Venice did not think it wise to await Charles's arrival in Rome. He hurried first to Orvieto and thence to Perugia, taking with him twenty cardinals, the papal court and a small army.

Charles proceeded north via Siena to Pisa. There a deputation of leading citizens pleaded with Charles to keep Pisa under his protection and so safe from reconquest by the Florentines. When his reply was equivocal they sent their wives and daughters, dressed in mourning and walking barefoot, to unnerve Charles with their tears and lamentations. Charles did not promise Pisa freedom; but he broke his oath to Florence that he would restore Pisa to Florentine rule. And he left a garrison in Pisa, making it impossible for Florence to try and recapture Pisa without attacking France.

Before starting the difficult march over the Apennines Charles consented to the request of Cardinal Giuliano della Rovere that he be allowed to detach a small force and attack Genoa, then subject to Milan. Della Rovere as a native of the Genoese republic was certain that the population would rise to support him. He was mistaken and the diversion was a failure. It was also a violation of sound tactics. Charles needed all the troops he could muster to face the army of the League.

In the village of Pontremoli just south of the Apennines some of the Swiss pikemen provoked the inhabitants to attack them and thirty or forty of the Swiss were killed. Enraged in their turn, the Swiss massacred the population of the town and burned it to the ground. The flames consumed supplies of great importance to the French. To atone for their guilt and demonstrate their repentance the Swiss harnessed themselves in teams of a hundred and more and dragged with their own hands and backs Charles's heavy cannon over a steep and dangerous mountain track.

When the bedraggled and exhausted French army with its numerous noncombatants and camp followers and its baggage wagons, loaded with loot, descended from the mountains, they emerged into the valley of the river Taro, a small tributary which flows north between low hills to the Po. On the right bank of the Taro a road went north to Parma. And on the right bank lay the Italian army of the League of Venice. So the French decided to march north along the left bank. Although they scorned the Italians and rejoiced at the prospect of a real battle, their chief object was to make good their retreat to France. The Italians hoped to prevent that retreat and to destroy the French army.

The combatants in the French army have been estimated at nine or ten thousand. The Italians may have numbered fourteen thousand. Some scholars have even estimated thirty thousand, which is most unlikely. The army of the League included a Milanese contingent, but most of Lodovico's army was busy elsewhere, besieging the Duke of Orléans who was holed up in the Milanese town of Novara. So the army was mostly Venetian.

This did not mean that many Venetians were present. Far from it. It meant that Venice had raised the troops and sent them to fight the French; that Venetian ducats paid the wages of the mercenary commanders and their soldiers. Fully expecting to be attacked, the French rose early on the morning of July 6, 1495 and prepared to march north until battle action should stop them. Charles was tense with excitement and elated with chivalrous enthusiasm. He was conspicuous and gorgeous in a white and violet tunic worn over his armor. White and violet plumes nodded from his helmet. A noble young officer rode up to him: "Sire, I have often heard you say that your great desire was to take part in a fine big battle. Behold, your wish is fulfilled!" "You speak truly," Charles replied. "They outnumber us by ten to one; but we must force our way through the midst of them. Today I shall learn who are my friends, and with them I go forth to live or die."

Commanding the Italian army was Francesco Gonzaga, fourth Marquis of Mantua, then twenty-nine years old. A professional soldier like most of his ancestors and relatives before him, the short, popeyed, snub-nosed Marquis had a reputation for courage. Four or five other members of the Gonzaga family were with him, including his experienced uncle, Rodolfo. Francesco Sanseverino, Count of Caiazzo, elder brother of Galeazzo, commanded the Milanese contingent.

Three other princely families, celebrated in Renaissance history, were represented at Fornovo by members employed by the Venetians as condottieri. They were Antonio da Montefeltro, bastard half brother of Guidobaldo, the reigning Duke of Urbino; Annibale Bentivoglio, one of the brutal and bloody-minded sons of Giovanni Bentivoglio, de facto but not de jure Lord of Bologna; and Pandolfo Malatesta, the degenerate and vicious Lord of Rimini, the son and grandson of famous soldiers.

It had rained hard during the night. The Taro was swollen. Rain and thunder continued intermittently during the battle, which began with a random shot from an Italian gun. The French cannon replied. The Italians soon launched a general attack which was impeded by the muddy water of the Taro. One of the famous battles of Renaissance history, Fornovo was the bloodiest fought in Italy for two hundred years. But the next few decades were to see several bloodier still. At the time, both sides claimed the victory, both with some justice.

A day or two before the battle Francesco Gonzaga wrote his young wife, Isabella d'Este: "Here I am at the head of the finest army Italy has ever seen." The army of the League of Venice may have been fine by Italian standards, but its performance at Fornovo was poor.

The blame was partly Gonzaga's. As commander in chief he could have fortified the foot of the mountain track and bottled up the French, so that they could not attack in any strength. Instead, he allowed the French to file out unmolested and he chose to attack them across a river. He had given orders which required transmission by particular officers. Some of these were killed and there was much confusion. To make matters worse, several Italian units fled in panic and several did not fight at all. Last but not least of the Italian failures was the desertion of the Venetian stradiots, light cavalry recruited in the Balkans, who preferred looting the French wagon train to attacking the French rear.

But Gonzaga himself and his personal following charged the French center with great courage. Three Gonzaga cousins were killed as well as the Marquis's uncle Rodolfo. Throughout the battle the French knights proved their superiority to the Italian men-at-arms. When the battle was over, the French were able to resume their march toward Asti without fear of an Italian attack in force. They had achieved their purpose and consequently claimed the victory. But the Italians had possession of the field and of the French baggage train. So they, too, boasted of victory. However, since the Italians outnumbered the French, since too many of their number had not even fought, and since they had suffered dreadful casualties, their boasts of victory were hollow indeed.

Only two hundred French were killed. Some thirty-five hundred Italians were killed—mainly by French teamsters, servants and camp followers who rushed onto the field and murdered the wounded and fallen Italians. They slaughtered their helpless victims with axes and knives, ignoring their screams and giving no quarter. Commines wrote: "And hard they were to kill, so heavily were they armed, and I saw none of them killed where there were not three or four to do it."

The day after the battle Gonzaga tried to ransom his uncle and cousins. He naturally supposed that they were alive because the Italian military custom was to spare prisoners for their ransoms. But his relatives were all dead, murdered by the French ghouls of battle.

Discouraged by their losses and none too sure of their claims to victory, the Italians took comfort in the spoils of the French camp, which were valued at a hundred thousand ducats. The loot included two royal standards, several royal pavilions, a sword and helmet "said to have belonged to Charlemagne, a silver casket containing the royal seals, a set of rich hangings and altar plate, a jeweled cross and reliquary which held a sacred thorn and a piece of wood from the true cross, a vest of Our Lady and a limb of St. Denis."

Gonzaga returned many of these to Charles, and the King sent back to Gonzaga his favorite white horse captured by the French.

Two contemporary Italian chroniclers recorded a curious item found in the French king's pavilion. "There was found a book," wrote Bernardino Corio, "in which at various times and places had been depicted many naked women raped by the French in many cities and he (the King) had brought it with him as a souvenir."

Alessandro Benedetti, a Venetian doctor, claimed to have seen it himself: "I saw a book in which were depicted pictures of prostitutes painted at various times and places. It contained sketches of intercourse and lasciviousness in each city. These sketches the King had brought with him so that later he could remember them." The two chroniclers only disagree on the question of rape versus professional activity.

On the same day on which he had tried to ransom his relatives the Marquis of Mantua wrote a letter to his wife in which he admitted the failures of the Italians:

"The chief cause of the disorder was the disobedience of the Stradiots, who gave themselves up to plunder, and in the hour of danger not one of them appeared. By the grace of God we and this army have been saved, but many fled without being pursued by anyone, and most of the foot soldiers, so that few of these remain. These things have caused me the greatest sorrow which I have ever known, and if by ill chance our enemies had turned upon us, we must have been utterly destroyed."

After a day's rest, the French army set out for Asti, which they reached in an eight-day march of unspeakable hardship. For a hundred and twenty-five miles the tired, filthy, hungry men tramped over roads turned into quagmires by torrential rains, with little food, no water fit to drink, no place to sleep except the mud. Yet there was no collapse of morale or of discipline. Not a cannon or a cannonball was left behind. The Italian army followed at a respectful distance and did not even threaten an attack.

Louis of Orléans was no longer at Asti. In June he had marched out and seized the town of Novara. And there he had stayed while Galeazzo Sanseverino, commanding Lodovico Sforza's army, besieged him in a rather perfunctory manner. Louis had bungled. He should have done more or less. As a claimant through his Visconti ancestors to the ducal throne of Milan he might have marched on the city with a fair chance of success. He certainly had the minimum duty of keeping open Charles's line of communication and retreat. Instead, he sat sullenly in Novara while famine decimated his troops and the population of the town. Louis had quite unnecessarily immobilized and endangered an army of eight thousand or ten thousand men.

When Gonzaga and the army of Fornovo arrived outside the walls of Novara on July 19, he at once made sure that the siege lines around the city would be complete. Then he cut off the city's water supply, the vital water which turned the mill wheels which ground the flour for the people's bread. Heavy rains continued. People and soldiers starved. Epidemics broke out. The streets of Novara were full of dead and dying men.

Although the French had defeated, or at least tied, the Italians at Fornovo, Charles made no effort to relieve Novara by attacking the Venetian and Milanese army. The Italian army was miserable, too, and vulnerable to any attack. Soldiers were dying of dysentery and malaria, many of them muttering mutinously. Perhaps Charles's army was no better off. At any rate, he did nothing and the horrors inside Novara multiplied.

In August, Lodovico Sforza and his wife, Beatrice, arrived at the Italian camp. Lodovico composed a difference of opinion between Gonzaga and Galeazzo, went away and returned in late September to take charge of peace negotiations with the French. Charles had failed to obtain reinforcements from France and so was prepared to make peace. Lodovico wanted only to get the French out of Italy. So he signed the Peace of Vercelli, a separate peace about which he did not consult his great ally, Venice. Lodovico thus increased his reputation for faithlessness and for successful guile. The Italians of the time did not much mind the first and enormously admired the second.

When Louis of Orléans' troops marched out of surrendered Novara on September 24, they left behind them in the dreadful city two thousand dead comrades. The survivors were in so emaciated and pitiful a condition that many more died on the roads. Charles led his weary men back over the Alps in late October and reached Lyons on November 7. He had been gone from France for fifteen months.

The French were gone and the Italians rejoiced. The Enterprise of Naples had been mortifying, no doubt. It had caused much alarm and trouble. But no one in Italy seemed to worry that the French might come again. They did—in exactly four years. In October of 1499 that same Louis of Orléans, who had behaved so incompetently at Novara, rode in triumph into conquered Milan as King Louis XII. The long series of Italian wars which Charles began was in full spate.

Contemplating the miseries and disasters which Charles's Enterprise had begun, Guicciardini, the Florentine statesman and historian, wrote: "It began not only the mutation of states, overthrow of kingdoms, desolation of countrysides, ruin of cities, cruel massacres; but also new habits, new customs, diseases until then unknown, new and bloody methods of war."

From the distance of five centuries it seems obvious that most of those disasters would not have happened—at least not so soon or so horribly—if the various Italian states had stood together; if they had been able to recognize their common peril and their common nationality; if they had combined for Italy instead of intriguing and betraying for Venice, Milan, Florence, Naples, the Papal States, Mantua and Ferrara.

But national patriotism was unknown in Italy in the fifteenth century. Local city-state patriotism was intense and that was all. Even in the newly unified states of England, France and Spain national feeling was only just beginning to emerge. So in Italy between the departure of Charles VIII in 1495 and the arrival of Louis XII in 1499 the Italians continued business as usual. This meant that Florence fought Pisa; Florence fought Siena; Venice and Milan helped Pisa fight Florence; Pope Alexander VI fought the Orsini, a family of powerful Roman lords; the Colonna, another family of powerful Roman lords, fought the Orsini; Piero de' Medici, aided by Virginio Orsini, made an ineffectual attack on Florence; the Baglioni of Perugia fought a faction of Perugian exiles and also fought several neighboring cities; Milan, switching sides, helped Florence fight Pisa; and in the Kingdom of Naples the Neapolitans, aided by the Spaniards, fought successfully to drive out the French garrisons of Charles VIII.

II

PRINCES, POTENTATES AND POWERS

 IN 1494 when the French burst into Italy they entered a new world, the world of the Renaissance. The Renaissance itself can be compared to an army slowly conquering the minds of men, an army subdivided into independent but affiliated units. Among its major brigades were the rediscovery of Roman and Greek literature and a wave of enthusiasm for classic civilization; an explosion of genius and of new ideas and techniques in art, literature, architecture and scholarship; a secularization of life which emphasized the joys of this world and the capacities of individual men in contrast to the medieval belief in the miseries of life on earth and the supreme importance of the life to come in heaven or hell.

These and other related ideas are generally considered the prime movers of the Renaissance. But the Renaissance cannot be neatly defined. It cannot even be dated without controversy or localized without dispute. Some scholars have insisted that there was no such thing as the Renaisssance, only a continuation of ideas and trends dating back to the twelfth century. Nevertheless, it is plain that those cultural changes we have mentioned were first widely noticeable in Italy during the fifteenth century and the first half of the sixteenth. During the fourteenth century some precursors of the Renaissance mentality appeared, and some of the first shoots, which later bloomed so brightly.

The city-states of Renaissance Italy had grown naturally out of the Middle Ages. In some respects they looked medieval. They were surrounded by walls. In many, rich citizens had built tall towers as forts in times of civil strife and as symbols of conspicuous wealth. Contemporary chroniclers claimed that there were as many as seven hundred towers in Lucca, seven hundred in Perugia and nine hundred in Rome. In Bologna the towers clustered so closely together they were said to be less than five feet apart. And the city of Pisa boasted with wonderful effrontery that its towers numbered between ten thousand and sixteen thousand! Fourteen of these towers still stand in little San Gimignano. They all were witnesses to the endemic and unceasing violence of medieval Italy.

The handsome municipal buildings, churches and palaces of the great reflect the wealth which, throughout a period of wars, grew rapidly and made northern and central Italy the most comfortable and prosperous region in Europe, except for the Netherlands. Italians prospered as bankers, international traders and manufacturers of textiles. And each city was a deadly rival of its nearest neighbors.

These furious rivalries were inflamed by the long conflict between the papacy and the Holy Roman Empire for temporal control of Italy. Cruel wars were fought by leagues and alliances. And absurd but cruel wars were fought by small towns only a few miles apart. Many Italian towns were republics in their form of government, but the franchise was so strictly limited that they were not democracies in any sense. Most of these lost their independence to local lords and despots.

Too committed to factional struggles within and too weak to face dangers from without, inefficient and corrupt, the towns surrendered their liberty in return for strong leadership and the justice and order imposed by a warrior. Often the new prince seized power by force and was subsequently elected lord by a grateful or subservient people.

So by the fifteenth century a tradition two centuries old supported despotic governments. Some princes ruled by terror. Giovanni Villani, the Florentine chronicler, said of Francesco degli Ordelaffi, Lord of Forlì: "With a mass of violent threats he urged the citizens to be his faithful and loyal friends."

But most princes recognized that their chances of remaining in power and founding a dynasty would be better if they maintained justice, fostered the economy, won wars or discreetly avoided wars, and increased their city's fame and glory. A prince who could do all this—identifying himself and his family with the welfare and reputation of his city—could hand on his lordship to his son. A number of the princely families ruled for many generations.

The risks were great. No Italian prince was supported by the religious sanctions and traditional, ceremonial anointing as a ruler authorized by God which made kings almost sacred in the rest of Europe. The princes of Italy ruled by power, personality and political craft. Defeat in war could bring conquest or revolution. Factions were always conspiring. Exiled leaders of rival factions congregated in nearby enemy cities and urged war to obtain power for themselves and to turn the rascals out. Assassinations were frequent. And in spite of the strong family feeling which made some states seem almost like family domains rather than personal despotisms, murders within ruling families were frequent, too.

In the fifteenth century five Italian states dominated the peninsula. Venice, with its colonial empire in the eastern Mediterranean and its vast international trade, was much the strongest. The Duchy of Milan ruled over a number of subject cities. Rich with trade and the best agricultural land in Italy, Milan provided a firm base for the political ambitions of the Visconti and Sforza dukes. Florence was a republic in name, ruled tactfully through political manipulation by the Medici. Although Cosimo de' Medici coined the cynical aphorism "You cannot govern a state with paternosters," the Medici were never tyrants. They had no private army and depended upon popularity for their influence. Florence was rich because of its preeminence in banking and textiles; its preeminence in the arts made Renaissance Florence immortal.

The Kingdom of Naples controlled the largest area and the

poorest, most backward population in Italy. Under the House of Aragon Naples seemed stronger than it was. A cultivated court ruthlessly collected taxes which supplied funds for employing mercenaries, and success in war made the Kingdom of Naples glitter. From a distance the Neapolitan tinsel looked like gold.

The papacy, an elective monarchy ruled by elderly men, had declined as a spiritual force. Dedicated to the proposition that its survival depended on temporal power exercised over as large a territory as possible, the papacy was ruled lke the other Italian states, no better and sometimes less efficiently. Its spiritual authority was still respected by most Italians. But the political unscrupulousness of the Renaissance popes and the vice and avarice of popes, cardinals, priests and monks had disillusioned most intelligent Italians about the Church as an institution. They distrusted and scorned the popes, but they had to deal with them. The popes could hire large armies, too. So the more powerful princely families hoped to have a member elected pope and often had a member in the College of Cardinals.

The most important Italian states of the second rank were: Ferrara, ruled by the Este; Mantua, ruled by the Gonzaga; Urbino, ruled by the Montefeltro; and Bologna, a republic in form ruled by the Bentivoglio. There were dozens of lesser princely states. Perugia under the Baglioni and Rimini under the Malatesta controlled considerable areas. Some states, such as Camerino, Fermo, Piombino and Citta di Castello, were just dots on the map.

Absolute power is the key word to the princely states of Renaissance Italy. A minor prince might rule over one small town and a small agricultural area around it. He might be so poor he had to spend his life as a condottiere in the service of larger states. He might fear his neighbors, suspect his subjects and know that he was helpless to resist if one of the larger powers attacked him. Nevertheless, at home in his fortress-palace he was an absolute monarch. His word was law. He could exile or have killed anyone who displeased him.

Such opportunities for self-indulgence and total individual liberty have been enjoyed by few men in history. The rulers of Italy had standards of pride and culture and social conduct, but few ethical standards. They conformed to the rituals of the Church but ignored its moral teachings, as did many of the clergy. Some of the local despots indulged in every vice, committed any crime.

Others were moderate in their sins and immoderate in their patronage of art and learning. The courts of Milan, Mantua, Ferrara and Urbino were major centers of Renaissance culture. As willful and fierce a despot as Sigismondo Malatesta delighted in supporting poets, wrote poetry himself and employed the great Alberti as his architect. Even the warrior Baglioni were proud to be the patrons of Perugino.

Although most of the princes tried to rule well, their motives were always their own pleasure and glory. And if their conception of glory or of their personal rights required that they do so, they would wage prolonged wars which impoverished states and brought ruin or death to many persons. Most of these wars were fought by an aggressor to obtain control of another city, more agricultural land and more taxable subjects. The defender fought to prevent the dismemberment of his state. Some of the wars were civil, fought to replace one ruling family by another. Frequently alliances of several states fought each other.

The Italian wars of the fifteenth century, fought before the expedition of Charles VIII, are famous for their moderation. Usually fought only in the summers, with few pitched battles and much leisurely maneuvering, they were conducted like chess games. When a commander was out-maneuvered he retreated. The gentlemen men-at-arms in their heavy armor were seldom killed. The condottieri, or mercenary commanders, prided themselves upon their skill as tacticians, on their bargaining power with their employers and on their ability to keep common soldiers faithful to them. They knew that success meant an improvement in their reputation, higher wages and better contracts.

But they also knew each other. Today's enemy might be tomorrow's comrade in arms. Since war was their profession a prolonged, indecisive war was ideal.

The professional condottiere philosophy was never put more eloquently than by Jacopo Piccinino, a commander fighting for the exiled House of Anjou in Naples, when he rode into the camp of Alessandro Sforza, a commander fighting for the reigning House of Aragon in Naples. To Sforza he said: "Why do you wish to conquer me? It is I who bring you glory, riches, pleasure—all that you enjoy. Because I took up arms and overthrew the peace of Italy, you, who were lying idle at home, were called to the field. Will you do any good by taking me prisoner? Who wants peace? No one, save priests and merchants, the Roman Curia, and the traders of Venice and Florence. Peace in Italy brings them all they want, and leaves us nothing to scrape together. In peace we are despised and sent to the plough; in war we become mighty, and may follow the example of Francesco Sforza, who has raised himself to a dukedom. Our policy is to refuse to conquer, and prolong the war, the end of which is the end of our gains."

Niccolò Machiavelli, a minor Florentine diplomat with a major interest in politics, was so disgusted by the lack of bloodthirsty earnestness of mercenary soldiers that he persuaded himself that armies of citizen militia would be better. He was mistaken. Conscripts lacked the skill and the courage of the professionals. But recognizing the excessive caution of most condottieri, Machiavelli wrote: "Wars were commenced without fear, continued without danger and concluded without loss." Machiavelli exaggerated. A theorizer about, as well as a participant in, war and politics, Machiavelli sometimes exaggerated in order to support his theories as strongly as possible.

Pope Pius II felt much the same way about Renaissance Italian methods of conducting war: "It would be difficult for us to call on our captains to fight in a foreign country. Here war is carried on with no danger to life, and for high pay." The Pope's sarcastic remark was true about the commanders; less true about the soldiers; and not true at all about the true victims of war, the peasants. It was always the custom to burn villages, destroy crops, cut down fruit trees and massacre any poor villagers who got in the way or dared to object.

No one in Renaissance Italy objected to war in theory. It was part of life. All the popes maintained armies and used them regularly. War and successful warriors were glorified. Just as it was expected of courtiers and the members of ruling families that they should understand Latin, enjoy poetry and if possible write it, so the soldiers were expected to be brave and at least competent. Several of the ruling princes ranked with the best soldiers of the time: Alfonso of Aragon and of Naples; Federigo da Montefeltro of Urbino; Alfonso d'Este of Ferrara; and the most successful of all, Francesco Sforza, who began life as a condottiere and ended as the reigning Duke of Milan.

The Renaissance Italian prince differed greatly from his medieval ancestors, and resembled them, too. He was likely to be far more cultivated and civilized. Often he had received a strenuous education in Latin, Greek and classic literature. Often he was sincerely interested in art. He may have used art and artists to glorify himself and his court, demanding of a great painter that he design stage costumes and the interior decoration of palaces; but he truly enjoyed and appreciated art. Leonardo da Vinci was court painter to Lodovico Sforza for seventeen years. Mantegna was court painter to the Gonzaga for a lifetime.

Others than princes were major patrons of artists. Popes, cardinals, churches, monasteries and the government of Venice all commissioned works of art. Commenting on this, Giorgio Vasari, painter, architect and author of *Lives of the Most Eminent Architects, Painters and Sculptors of Italy*, wrote:

"The stimulating effect produced on talent by reward is known to every man who has been well paid for his work. He who can expect honor and reward feels no inconvenience, suffers no pain, admits to no weariness. . . . It is true that merit is not always fortunate in finding those able to appreciate it. . . . It cannot be denied that the liberality of princes is a great stimulus to the energy of those who toil for art."

The prince often liked music also. The Este of Ferrara were famous for their skills as musicians, many members of the family being expert on one or more instruments. Several princes were great book collectors, most notably Alessandro Sforza of Pesaro, Federigo da Montefeltro of Urbino and Cosimo de' Medici. Many gave large sums to universities and hospitals. Many prided themselves on being cultivated gentlemen, masters of courtesy and the art of conversation.

The importance placed upon good manners and seemly etiquette during the Renaissance in Italy inspired a worldly archbishop and papal nuncio, Giovanni della Casa, to write his celebrated *Galateo, or The Book of Manners*. This popular volume stressed that gentlemen should not only avoid social crudities but should also shun any behavior which could possibly be understood as being critical of others.

"Good manners depend upon consideration of other people's wishes instead of our own pleasure," wrote Della Casa. And he repeatedly insisted that the essence of good manners was social conformity. "It is better to be wrong in the company of others than to be the only one to be right."

From such Chesterfieldian generalizations Della Casa easily switched to practical details. "When you have blown your nose, you should not open your handkerchief and inspect it, as though pearls or rubies had dropped out of your skull. . . . It is not polite to scratch yourself when you are seated at table. You should also take care, so far as you can, not to spit at mealtime, but if you must spit, then do so in a decent manner."

In some unpleasant ways Renaissance princes even resembled several of the Roman emperors. Many combined cultural refinement with cold-blooded ferocity and calculated treachery. Gorgeous and sinister, charming and deadly, they were as dangerous as tigers, purring softly at one moment, killing as a matter of policy or in a sudden fury at the next. Some were murderers or even mass murderers according to modern ideas and no one thought the worse of them for that. Many of them were as sexually promiscuous as alley cats, and quite a few were fond of sodomy, a vice that was common in Italy, although it is difficult to distinguish personal abuse and political vilification from fact. Never before or since has the art of slander been more strenuously cultivated than during the Renaissance.

The small value put on human life was also essentially medieval. It was natural in an age when pestilences, famines and unceasing violence made all life uncertain—in the palace as well as in the hovel. Also medieval (but late medieval) was each prince's conception of his own absolute power. In this respect they all agreed with Bernabò Visconti, who in the fourteenth century shouted at a humbly kneeling archbishop: "Do you not know, you fool, that here I am pope and emperor and lord in all my lands and that no one can do anything in my lands save I permit it—no, not even God." Absolute power not only tends to corrupt, it also breeds cruelty. Most of the Renaissance princes were not as cruel as their medieval predecessors. But some inherited a blood lust and psychopathic savagery which made them infamous.

The general atmosphere of violence was not confined to men of power. Bandits, highway robbers, professional murderers, thugs and thieves flourished everywhere. Both Niccolò Machiavelli and Baldassare Castiglione complained that it was unsafe to go out alone in Rome by night. Benvenuto Cellini, sculptor, silversmith and autobiographer, murdered three people and tried unsuccessfully to kill another. And yet Cellini, who feared nothing on earth, said that so many armed robbers lay in wait on the outskirts of Naples that it was safer to leave the city by night than by day—the idea was to slip by in the darkness.

Ariosto, the great poet, who served as governor of a remote district in the Apennines, complained to Alfonso d'Este, Duke of Ferrara, that if he burned down the house of every criminal the place would become a wilderness of no value to the Duke.

And in Rome in 1492 there was an average of fourteen murders a day, a figure which we are privileged to doubt but which suggests that there was a horrendous lot of murders.

When we consider the prevailing political philosophy of the Renaissance we must make sure not to regard it as sharply localized in time or space. It was a time of cynicism, of duplicity, of ruthless expediency. But these qualities have always distinguished the art of government. They were particularly conspicuous during the Renaissance because of the frankness of the age. Princes could lie with bland skill and betray with smooth aplomb. But they were not hypocritical; they did not pretend to be virtuous. The one quality they most despised was simple-mindedness or gullibility. Guile was the indispensable tool of the ruler. If it could be combined with courage, leadership, astute judgment and luck, so much the better. Skill in war, while desirable, was not absolutely essential. Lorenzo de' Medici and Lodovico Sforza were not soldiers, but their artful diplomacy made them immensely influential. Some aspects of the fifteenth century often considered typically Italian were in fact European. Nobody could have been less trustworthy than three of the most celebrated kings of the century: Richard III of England, Louis XI of France, and Ferdinand the Catholic of Spain. Louis coined the maxim that he who knows how to dissemble knows how to rule. Ferdinand was so habitually deceitful that he frequently deceived his own ambassadors. When his secretary told him that Louis XII of France had complained that Ferdinand had twice deceived him, Ferdinand exclaimed: "The drunkard lies. I have cheated him upwards of ten times."

All governments put one purpose before all others—to survive. To do so, all governments frequently violate standards of morality to which most individual men pay at least lip service. Recognizing these truths Niccolò Machiavelli expressed them bluntly in two celebrated books, *The Prince* and *Discourses on the First Ten Books of Titus Livius*. Few books have provoked as much controversy and discussion as these. One reason for the unceasing debate is that Machiavelli had a split personality. At times he was a romantic reformer who yearned for virtue and morality; who idealized the peasants, who, he thought, would make fine soldiers; who believed in a republican form of government. He was deeply shocked by the corruption of the Church.

At other times Machiavelli was a tough-minded observer of politics and power, a man who could take considerable relish in the brutal methods and artful schemes of the ruling princes. So some of his remarks reflect the hurt and dismay of the disillusioned idealist, some the realistic awareness of the dispassionate student of things as they are.

Looking bleakly at the highly unsatisfactory state of the world, Machiavelli reached two basic conclusions: that human beings are weak, stupid and prone to evil; and that the essence of politics is power based upon violence.

"How we live is so far from how we ought to live, that he who abandons what is done for what ought to be done will rather learn to bring about his own ruin than his preservation." This remark applies to everybody, but particularly to princes. To attain power and keep it, "a prince, and especially a new prince, cannot observe all those things which are considered good in men, being often obliged, in order to maintain the state, to act against faith, against humanity, and against religion." The ability to rule depends on the ability to wage war. "War is the only art that is necessary to one who commands, and it is of such virtue that it not only maintains those who are born princes, but often enables men of private fortune to attain to that rank." This was sadly true in Renaissance Italy, but Machiavelli failed to mention that the ability to wage war depends upon money. Soldiers were hired and the money came from taxes. So successful war required continuing trade and agricultural production at home and the destruction of the trade and agriculture of the enemy. That is why the condottieri-commanded armies spent so much time burning crops and destroying orchards and vineyards. It was effective and much safer than fighting pitched battles.

Machiavelli is an important witness to the nature of a Renaissance prince. He admired the craft and ferocity of Cesare Borgia. He hoped that someone, perhaps Lorenzo de' Medici the younger (the son of Piero the Exile), might arise who would create a large Italian state and keep the barbarians out of Italy.

Another valuable witness, much less politically minded, thought that too many princes trusted far too much in craft and force and were not the honorable men they ought to be. This was Baldassare Castiglione, courtier, diplomat and friend of one of the few incontestably virtuous princes of the Renaissance, Guidobaldo da Montefeltro, Duke of Urbino. In his celebrated The Book of the Courtier Castiglione wrote:

"Never hearing the truth about anything at all, princes are made drunk by the great license that rule gives; and by a profusion of delights are submerged in pleasures, and deceive themselves so and have their minds so corrupted—seeing themselves always obeyed and almost adored with so much reverence and praise, without ever the least contradiction, let alone censure—that from this ignorance they pass to extreme self-conceit, so that then they become intolerant of any advice or opinion from others. And since they think that to know how to rule is a very easy thing, and that to succeed therein they need no art or discipline save sheer force, they give their mind and all their thoughts to maintaining the power they have, deeming true happiness to lie in being able to do what one wishes. Therefore some princes hate reason or justice, thinking it would be a kind of bridle and a way of reducing them to servitude, and of lessening the pleasure and satisfaction they have in ruling if they choose to follow it, and that their rule would be neither perfect nor complete if they were obliged to obey duty and honor, because they think that one who obeys is not a true ruler."

The princes of the Italian Renaissance, like all rulers, devoted much of their time to matters other than affairs of state. They cultivated their pleasures with imagination and without restraint. Most of them had many casual mistresses and a number of semi-permanent ones. Some—Francesco Gonzaga was one—fathered so many bastards that crude jokes were made about their efforts to increase the population of their states. But bastardy in itself was little handicap in the Renaissance.

Pius II remarked, "Most of the rulers of Italy in the present day were born out of wedlock." He was referring, among others, to Ferdinand I, King of Naples; Francesco Sforza, Duke of Milan; Borso d'Este, Duke of Ferrara and Federigo da Monte-feltro, Duke of Urbino. Later in the fifteenth century other distinguished bastards included: Cesare and Lucrezia Borgia; Caterina Sforza, Countess of Forli; Giulio de' Medici, who became Pope Clement VII; Lorenzo de' Medici, the younger, who was made Duke of Urbino by his uncle Giovanni, Leo X; Alessandro de' Medici, ruler of Florence until his assassination; Cardinal Ippolito de' Medici; and Leonardo da Vinci.

The Este family of Ferrara was famous for its numerous bastards, all of them brought up as important members of the ducal family.

Hunting was the favorite amusement of many princes. The rulers of the larger states had large game parks, stocked with deer, boar and hares. Some maintained menageries; the Sforza, Este and Gonzaga had famous ones. Even the warrior Baglioni kept lions in the courtyards of their palaces in Perugia.

Like most rich and powerful people the princes conformed to fashion and to cults. Three cults of major importance were those of revenge, ostentatious magnificence and beauty.

Revenge was an obligation and a pleasure. Traitors were tortured and slaughtered. Unfaithful wives were beheaded and their lovers tortured and killed. Personal enemies were murdered personally, or more often by hired killers called *bravos*. Highly respectable people stressed the duty of revenge.

Pope Pius II in one of his letters praised Philip the Good, Duke of Burgundy, above all his contemporary princes because of his anxiety to avenge his father.

And Guicciardini commented on revenge with cold-blooded detachment: "Revenge does not always spring from hatred or ill-nature, but it is sometimes necessary because from one example others learn not to harm you. It is proper that one should take one's revenge and yet not feel rancor against the enemy on whom it falls."

In the Renaissance mind, revenge was inextricably confused with justice. Criminals, traitors and suspects against whom nothing had been proved were tortured and killed, sometimes in public. It was the universal custom to hang the bodies of the executed from the windows of palaces and the battlements of fortresses. In the year 1500 during the reign of Pope Alexander VI a pilgrim in Rome said that he did not like to cross the bridge of Sant' Angelo because of the stench and horror of the long line of corpses hanging from the battlements of the castle.

Revenge inspired numerous assassinations of rulers. Churches were favorite sites for such murders. Revenge was one of the chief motives for waging feuds. Giulio Cesare Varano, Lord of Camerino, murdered his brother. He had a good precedent—his father had murdered two of his brothers.

Giulio de' Medici, Pope Clement VII, an intelligent but indecisive man, had no trouble deciding what he wanted to do to a political enemy who had provoked his desire for revenge. He had the man, who was a monk, shut up in a cell in the castle of Sant' Angelo and by reducing his food ration daily slowly starved the poor wretch to death.

Revenge was the privilege not only of the mighty. City mobs took fearful revenge on people who had displeased them. In 1435 a mob in Genoa rebelling against the rule of Filippo-Maria Visconti, Duke of Milan, murdered the Milanese governor, cut up his body into many pieces and scattered them about the city. Ten years later another mob in Bologna pursued the assassin of the city's popular lord, Annibale Bentivoglio, dragged him out of his hiding place in a grain bin, killed him and then dragged the body through all the principal streets before burning it. Revenge was a major element in the general climate of violence.

The cult of ostentatious magnificence inspired princes to build enormous palaces and to sponsor plays, concerts, pageants and tournaments, all of them as fancily dressed as possible. It required weddings to be turned into public festivals, which lasted for days. It meant that the princes wore gorgeous clothes and dressed their wives in equal finery. The men dressed in silk and were partial to sable capes. A long gold chain around the neck was customary for important lords.

Some men wore their hair short, many in long bobs falling onto their shoulders. Men were clean-shaven throughout most of the fifteenth century, but in the 1490s beards became fashionable. The women wore magnificent dresses with elaborate patterns which were sometimes symbolical. They experimented with new hair-dos and often dyed their dark hair a fashionable golden blond. They wore rings on their fingers, necklaces around their necks and on their heads pretty little caps ornamented with large jewels. In the first half of the fifteenth century women shaved the hair just above their foreheads, but stopped that unbecoming fashion in the second half of the century.

The most conspicuous expression of the cult of ostentatious magnificence was parades. They were held on every possible occasion and were the chief source of amusement for the common people. A military victory, the arrival of a bride, the departure of a warrior prince, the reception of an ambassador or of another prince—anything at all would do as an excuse for a parade. Triumphal arches would be erected. Choirs would rehearse songs of welcome. Boys and girls would prepare to recite appropriate verses in Latin. Brightly colored cloths would hang from every window on the route. And then the trumpets would sound, and the long array of beautiful horses ridden by men in handsome livery and by lords and ladies, gaudy as peacocks, would file past.

The people loved parades, and so did the princes.

The cult of beauty was an integral part of the Renaissance. Princes strove for beauty in their surroundings, in paintings and sculpture and the antiquities and works of silver and gold they collected. Nobody could have enough beautiful things. Sometimes they pretended to own more than they really did. It was customary to borrow tapestries and dinner services from a friendly court in order to impress a really important state visitor.

Beauty mattered in every way. It was sought in good manners and smooth social contacts. Physical beauty was admired in men as well as in women, and it was an immense asset to the fortunate men who were judged to have it. The Sanseverino brothers, the Baglioni, Cesare Borgia and Leonardo da Vinci were all famous for their beauty.

The beauty, magnificence, individual license and power which were part of the lives of Renaissance princes have fascinated modern romantics like Miniver Cheevy, hero of E. A. Robinson's poem, who "loved the Medici, albeit he had never seen one." But the threat of violence which was omnipresent in the Renaissance was not the only reason why a citizen of the twentieth century would heartily dislike being transferred by a time machine to the fifteenth, even if he found himself lord of a princely state. The palaces were big and grand; but they were cold, drafty, dirty and crowded. Food was abundant for the rich and powerful; but famines were frequent and many poor people were hungry much of the time.

Comfort, as we think of comfort today, was unknown, even for dukes. Beds had no springs. Transportation was by horse or mule back, litter or crude, springless cart. Cities smelled. Filth was dumped in the streets. Natural disasters made life hard for everyone—droughts, storms, floods and prolonged rains ruined crops. And two sources of solace in an unsatisfactory world which comfort modern men were unknown: tobacco and whiskey.

Entertainment was far more limited than it is today. It was largely confined to hunting, conversation, listening to oratory and poetry, watching pageants, parades and tournaments, playing crude or cruel practical jokes and in a few of the most cultivated courts attending performances of Latin plays and salacious modern comedies. Books were few, mostly medieval romances, classical or theological works.

Numerous Renaissance customs have disappeared from the world, others seem curiously modern. Most men of the upper classes went armed; even their servants wore swords. But local laws often regulated weapons. In the Duchy of Milan it was forbidden to carry arms after dark. In Florence after the restoration of the Medici in 1530 a law required swords to be tied into their scabbards so that they could not be used; they could be untied outside the city walls.

To bite one's thumb at anyone was a challenge or an insult. Spectacles with magnifying lenses were used throughout most of the fifteenth century. Branda Castiglione, Cardinal of Piacenza, did not need spectacles until he was past ninety and then wore them only at night to help him read by candlelight.

The Visconti had an indoor swimming pool, "a covered building of white marble with large windows," at their palace at Pavia.

Tipping was a problem. Commines complained that when he journeyed as French ambassador to Venice through the cities of Brescia, Verona, Vicenza and Padua, he was extended munificent free hospitality, but that he had to tip so many people he could not save much.

And occasionally traffic was a problem, too. Vespasiano da Bisticci, describing the jubilee year of 1450, wrote:

"The roads from Florence to Rome were so full that, looking at the people who traversed them, it seemed that they must be ants: so much so that on the bridge of Sant' Angelo there was a crowd of people of all ages, packed so close that they could move neither one way nor the other. For this reason when each one strove to go his own way, there arose so fierce a struggle between those who came and those who were there already, that more than two hundred men and women were killed. When Pope Nicholas heard of this most grievous accident he was greatly displeased, and provided that the like should never happen again; moreover, he built at the foot of the bridge two chapels in memory of this slaughter, and he caused all the victims to be buried."

The lords and ladies of the Renaissance, who seem so wordly and sophisticated in many respects, were in many others ignorant, credulous and superstitious. They all believed firmly in astrology. Popes and dukes, bankers and condottieri, all tried to arrange their lives in accordance with the conjunctions of the stars. All the larger courts employed resident astrologers who were regularly consulted. The universities had chairs of astrology. Cosimo de' Medici and his grandson Lorenzo de' Medici, two of the most astute statesmen of the entire Renaissance, both took astrology seriously. In 1478 during the Pazzi war the Florentine government of Lorenzo waited for a propitious day selected by astrologers before proceeding with the formal ceremony in which Ercole d'Este, Duke of Ferrara, was made commander of the Florentine troops.

Lodovico Sforza considered himself an expert on astrology and tried to do nothing of any importance except on days chosen by his astrologers. One of the very few skeptics about astrology was Guicciardini, who was skeptical about most things. He wrote, "The astrologers do not know what they say. They are right only by chance."

But even Guicciardini could not be consistently skeptical. He believed, as did everyone else, that the air was full of spirits which sometimes communicated with the minds of men. Witches, devils, necromancers abounded. The great humanist scholar and poet Poliziano in 1483 delivered a lecture on women who could change themselves into serpents. Pope Pius II was sure that "witches are very numerous in Savoy" and Pope Nicholas V was equally certain that "the dreams of rulers often come true." Popes Innocent VIII and Alexander VI both formally denounced witches.

Cellini never doubted that he had seen regiments of fiends and devils summoned to the Roman colosseum by a necromancer, or that angels had visited him in prison. When Pope Paul III died, it was widely rumored that he had been strangled by an evil spirit which had escaped from its prison in one of his rings. When Alexander VI died an even better story was circulated.

Francesco Gonzaga, Marquis of Mantua, was in Rome at the time and wrote at once to tell his wife, the brilliant Isabella d'Este, all about it:

"Most noble lady and beloved wife, in order that you may know all concerning the death of the Pope Alexander VI, we shall tell you what follows: when he fell ill, he began to wander like someone losing his reason; yet he was perfectly lucid, and this is what he said: 'It is right, I am coming, wait a little longer.' Those who know his secret then revealed that after the death of Pope Innocent VIII, during the conclave, he had made a pact with the devil, to whom he sold his soul in exchange for the Holy See. And among the other agreements, there was one which said that he was to occupy the Holy See for twelve years, which he did, with four days in addition. There are persons who declare that when he gave up the ghost, they saw seven devils in his room. After his death, the body began to boil and the mouth to foam like copper over the fire, and this lasted as long as it was on the ground. It became so swollen that it no longer had a human form, and was as broad as it was long."

The prevailing credulity of the age continued unabated the medieval reverence for the most improbable holy relics. In Rome were the heads of St. Peter, St. Paul and St. Andrew. The bones of Mary Magdalene were also treasured there. In Venice were the body of St. Mark, an arm of St. George, an ear of St. Paul, some of St. Laurence's roasted flesh and some of the stones which killed St. Stephen. The cities of Siena and Perugia once nearly went to war over the dispute concerning the rightful ownership of the wedding ring of the Virgin.

But much the most unpleasant aspect of life in the Renaissance was the fearful prevalence of deadly diseases and the dreadful things the ignorant doctors of the time did to their helpless patients.

The Black Plague, which reduced the population of Europe by one third in the middle of the fourteenth century, returned regularly to Italy throughout the Renaissance. All the major cities suffered terrible outbreaks of plague. In Florence it raged in 1479, 1496, 1497, 1527 and 1528. In the last two years mentioned, thirty thousand people are said to have died in Florence from the

C

plague, which would be about a third of the city's population.

In 1488 in Milan fifty thousand people are said to have died of the plague, and in 1524 between eighty thousand and a hundred thousand more are reported to have died there. Both estimates must be gross exaggerations, but they reveal the terror caused by the plague. Between 1434 and 1486 there were eight serious outbreaks in Perugia. And yet, since nothing could be done about plague, some people tried to ignore it.

In 1503 Machiavelli wrote from Rome: "The plague is doing its duty well, and spares neither the houses of the cardinals nor any others where it can find victims, and yet no one here makes any account of it."

Among the great personages who died of plague were Cardinal Ascanio Sforza, (brother of Lodovico), Titian and Giorgione.

Diseases which destroyed armies were malaria, dysentery and typhus. Much the most fashionable ailment was gout. Since the art of diagnosis was primitive indeed in the Renaissance, gout may have been a term which also included arthritis, bursitis, displaced spinal disks, and other painful ailments. Gout was hereditary among the Medici. Cosimo, Piero and Lorenzo were all its victims. So were five popes: Eugenius IV, Nicholas V, Pius II, Sixtus IV and Julius II. Guidobaldo da Montefeltro, Duke of Urbino, suffered acutely from gout from the age of twenty. Louis XII and Lodovico Sforza also complained of gout. So did Columbus.

The most celebrated Renaissance disease is syphilis. It was unknown until 1494, and its origin is still unknown, but a popular theory has it that syphilis was brought to Europe from America by Columbus' sailors. However that may be, in an age of sexual promiscuity syphilis spread rapidly. "In Rome," wrote Cellini, who suffered from syphilis himself, "this kind of illness is very partial to the priests, and especially to the richest of them."

The list of prominent victims of syphilis is nearly as distinguished as that of gout: Pope Julius II, Cardinal Ascanio Sforza, Alfonso d'Este, Duke of Ferrara, the marquis Francesco Gonzaga, Cesare Borgia, the condottiere Vitelozzo Vitelli, and Lorenzo de' Medici, the younger.

Although medicine was a serious study taught in Renaissance

universities, the treatments prescribed by doctors for any illness were likely to be wild, wonderful, repulsive and absurd.

Vespasiano da Bisticci in his *Lives of Illustrious Men* described two medically interesting therapies. When Nicolao degli Albergati, Cardinal of Santa Croce, fell gravely ill with a kidney stone, "the physicians could only think of one remedy for him—a dangerous one—which was to drink a beaker of the blood of a he goat." The Cardinal had the good sense to refuse.

When Cardinal Jacopo di Portogallo, who, at the age of twenty-two was celebrated for his singular virtue, "ruptured a vein in his chest," a Florentine physician "tried to induce him, as an extraordinary experiment, to submit to a remedy revolting to him, and hurtful to his spiritual welfare. According to what this man said it would be advantageous to the Cardinal's health if he slept with a young girl, and that no better remedy than this could be found." The young cardinal refused with indignation.

Pope Pius II in his *Commentaries*, which he wrote in the third person, described his experience at the sulphur baths of Petriolo: "For twenty days the Pope had the warm waters poured through a pipe onto the crown of his head; for the physicians said this would be beneficial since his brain was too moist."

Lodovico Sforza sent to the dying Lorenzo de' Medici his personal physician with a miraculous medicine of dissolved gold and pearls, which, he said, had been used with great success on his father, Duke Francesco. This was kind and thoughtful, but Lorenzo died anyway.

After the death of Pope Alexander VI Cesare Borgia was desperately ill, probably with malaria. For five days his physicians struggled to save his life. Carlo Beuf in his biography of Cesare describes their efforts: "They bled him until his heart almost stopped beating. They made him swallow enormous quantities of the most potent emetics. They plunged him up to his neck into a jar of ice water from which he emerged practically skinless; and in an effort to sweat the malaria out of his system, they packed him into the still pulsating entrails of a mule." Cesare lived, but he was exceptionally strong.

It is small wonder that Guicciardini was not favorably impressed by Renaissance doctors: "The doctor, because of the ambition and jealousy which exist among his kind, is a very vicious animal without conscience and without respect. And, safe in the fact that his mistakes are hard to prove, either to promote himself or discredit his colleagues, every day butchers our bodies."

ALFONSO THE
MAGNANIMOUS

 DURING THE RENAISSANCE the Kingdom of Naples was ruled by five kings of the House of Aragon. The first, Alfonso the Magnanimous, was a great man and in the opinion of his contemporaries a good king. The second and third kings, Ferdinand I (called Ferrante) and Alfonso II, were cruel and treacherous tyrants feared by their subjects and hated by their fellow princes. The fourth, Ferdinand II (called Ferrantino), died young and so what kind of monarch he might have been cannot be known. The fifth, Federigo, was gentle and amiable, but was soon robbed of his kingdom by the treachery of more powerful rulers. Two good men (well, reasonably good), two vicious men and one question mark. The average is not high, but perhaps it is no worse than that of many royal dynasties.

When Alfonso V of Aragon conquered Naples in 1442 and became Alfonso I of Naples, he added a seventh kingdom to the six he already ruled: Aragon, Catalonia, Valencia, the Balearic Islands, Sicily, and Sardinia and Corsica. Born a prince of a junior branch of the Castilian royal house of Trastamara, Alfonso became a prince of Aragon in 1412, when his father became king. Four years later Alfonso succeeded his father and soon demonstrated the astute political judgment he was to display often thereafter. To conciliate his most important subjects, the Catalans, to a foreign dynasty he made Catalan the language of his court.

Conquering Naples was an old and popular custom. Independent Norman adventurers had done so in the eleventh century. Charles of Anjou, brother of Louis IX, had done so in the thirteenth century. Eight years after Charles's conquest of Naples Alfonso's nephew, Ferdinand the Catholic of Spain, in alliance with Louis XII of France, was to conquer Naples yet again and exile Alfonso's grandson, King Federigo.

For fifty years we anxious citizens of the twentieth century have feared wars and have regarded wars of aggression as evil. But to understand any century prior to our own we must momentarily forget our modern terrors born of the horrors of the age of science and accept the ideas of the past. The simple and praiseworthy motive of all those Neapolitan conquests was always the same—to become a reigning prince or to become a greater prince by conquering somebody else's kingdom. Conquest was meritorious. It was a means to glory as well as to more power and more taxes. So it was natural, almost inevitable, that an able, ambitious, energetic and clever man like Alfonso should devote his life to military conquest.

He began in 1420, when he was thirty-five, by circumnavigating the island of Corsica with a large fleet of war galleys and imposing his rule on every coastal town save one. Thirty-eight years later when Alfonso died in 1458, he was still planning further conquests.

This tireless commander, who never went to war without taking with him a copy of Caesar's *Gallic Wars*, looked like a ruler of men. His nose was arrogantly curved, his eyebrows heavy, his chin firm. His expression of confident command may be seen in the portrait medallion made by the famous artist Pisanello. Alfonso wore his hair in a short bang on his forehead, down over and well past his ears in back. During his lifetime he was famous for his kindness, generosity and magnanimity, and also for his guile and ambition.

Waging wars never occupied the whole of Alfonso's time and attention. A great patron of scholars and poets, a lover of classic literature, a profoundly religious man in an era of unthinking religious conformity, indifference or skepticism, Alfonso was one of the most notable Renaissance princes of his time. Francesco Sforza, a better soldier, also conquered a state; but he was a less cultivated and a less religious man than Alfonso. Cosimo de' Medici was as great a statesman and a far more cultivated man; but he was not a soldier and Alfonso was a good one. The two outstanding attributes of this medieval Spaniard who became a Renaissance Italian were his adaptability and his charm. Alfonso had no trouble whatever adjusting himself to fifteenth-century Italy, to its condottiere methods of warfare, to its subtle and intricate politics and to its newly awakened enthusiasm for classical civilization. His charm, always controlled by his shrewd intelligence, was an enormous asset. It won Alfonso the liking and respect of humble subjects only recently conquered as well as of courtiers and scholars. It made it easy for several of those scholars, who were generously paid for their works, to write chronicles of Alfonso which cast him as a paragon of romantic chivalry. Their perhaps mercenary flattery has, to a certain extent, obscured Alfonso's occasional deeds of savage brutality and of unscrupulous trickery. Alfonso, a good king, was only good within the conventions of his time and of princes.

When Alfonso conquered Corsica it meant that he went to war with Genoa, which never surrendered its claim to the island. It was while Alfonso was fighting Genoa in 1420 that he received an invitation which changed the history of Italy. It came from Queen Giovanna II of Naples.

This elderly and depraved woman had inherited the kingdom on her brother's death. Without morals or scruples, she let her current lovers rule her kingdom and anarchy convulse her state. Naples was never far from anarchy anyway, and would remain near it for years to come. A fossilized medieval kingdom, it resembled France in the eleventh century more than the rest of Italy in the fifteenth. Its feudal nobles retained their power and ruled numerous semi-independent domains of their own. Naples was in theory a fief of the papacy and the popes never tired of interfering in the affairs of the kingdom. And, just as it is today, the south of Italy then was poor, backward and ignorant compared with the north.

Giovanna was in danger of losing her throne to a pretender, Louis, Duke of Anjou, whose turn it was to try to conquer Naples. To divert this threat Giovanna offered to adopt Alfonso as her heir to the kingdom if he would come to Naples and drive out Louis. Alfonso could not resist such an opportunity. He dispatched fifteen galleys to Naples at once and, in June of 1421, arrived there himself.

Several of Alfonso's advisers tried to persuade him not to become involved in rescuing the notorious queen of Naples. One of his court poets and authorized biographers, Antonio Beccadelli, known as il Panormita, quotes Alfonso as saying: "I see quite well that this war which we are about to undertake is hard and grim, but for all that, it will be more glorious yet, for no great aim or deeds can be achieved without much travail or danger." The style is suspiciously florid and sounds more like Panormita than Alfonso; but Alfonso was still young and no doubt thrilled by the prospect of a great adventure.

For two years Alfonso fought and schemed in the kingdom. At first he was much in the Queen's favor. But then mutual suspicions raised their ugly heads. Giovanna believed, quite rightly, that Alfonso was impatient and planned to seize her throne while she still lived. Giovanna's lover, Giovanni Caracciolo, conspired to have Alfonso murdered, and Alfonso responded by throwing Caracciolo into prison. Alfonso even tried to capture the Queen herself, failed, and besieged her in a Neapolitan castle. This effrontery by a Spaniard caused rioting crowds to threaten Alfonso, who barely escaped with his life.

Giovanna in her fury with Alfonso decided that Louis of Anjou, her former enemy, was preferable to her new enemy and made a new will which named Louis heir to her throne. Thus things were going badly for Alfonso when word came that his younger brother, Juan, needed help in fighting against the King of Castile. Alfonso admitted temporary defeat and sailed for Spain.

Sailing with his fleet along the coast of Provence (in those days ships seldom ventured far from land if they could help it), Alfonso came to the city of Marseilles, chief port of Louis of Anjou's state of Provence. Alfonso may have been magnanimous, but the temptation was too great to strike a blow at his enemy. Twice he tried to set the town on fire. Twice rain put out the flames. Should it rain a third time, Alfonso told his soldiers, he would acknowledge it as a divine sign and sail away. It did not rain and Marseilles was burned to the ground.

Bartolomeo Fazio, another of Alfonso's chroniclers, wrote: "Once the city was taken, Alfonso, bearing in mind the chastity of women, ordered that no harm come to any of them finding refuge in churches; and he had trustworthy men stand guard around them so that they would not be humiliated by soldiers. And when the women in gratitude sent him a great amount of gold and jewels he refused to accept it but had it returned to them, and gave them their liberty, instructing them to send for their husbands and relatives to come and get them, for they had survived the fire."

Alfonso did not take the gold; but he did steal the bodies of three saints, including that of Louis IX, and took them back with him to Spain. Sacred relics were prime targets for looters throughout the Middle Ages and the Renaissance.

After Alfonso's departure from Naples Queen Giovanna, aided by Filippo Maria Visconti, Duke of Milan, succeeded in reestablishing herself upon her throne. Alfonso fought a campaign in Spain and another in North Africa and then settled down in Sicily to wait for a better opportunity to conquer Naples. It did not come until the winter of 1434-35 when Louis of Anjou died. Soon after his death Queen Giovanna connived in the murder of her lover, Caracciolo. And soon after that the vicious old queen herself died. But before her death she had replaced Louis as her heir with his brother Réné. Alfonso, naturally, preferred her old will in favor of himself. He invaded the kingdom and the Neapolitan barons sympathetic to the Anjou cause opposed him.

Alfonso captured the city of Capua and laid siege to the important port of Gaeta. The siege was prolonged and the city began to suffer from famine. The "useless mouths," old men, women and children, were driven outside the city walls. In similar circumstances only sixteen years earlier Henry V, England's hero-king, had refused to let the "useless mouths" of besieged Rouen pass his lines and they all had died of starvation or disease. Al-

C*

fonso allowed the "useless mouths" of Gaeta to pass through his lines instead of forcing them to stay at the foot of their city's walls, where their pitiful presence would put heavy pressure on the town to surrender.

He told his protesting generals that he would rather fail to capture the city than to be without humanity. He did fail to capture Gaeta, but his merciful gesture did much to help him win the affection of the Neapolitans. It was during this siege that Alfonso tried another method to secure victory. He sent Panormita, the humanist scholar and poet we have already quoted, to try to secure by formal rhetoric and polished eloquence what arms could not obtain—the surrender of the city. Panormita did his best, but Gaeta stubbornly refused to surrender. Alfonso did not hold Panormita's failure against him and continued to honor and befriend the poet until his own death.

In the same year Alfonso's old enemy, Genoa, a city subject to the Duke of Milan, sent a fleet to support Gaeta. The Genoese decisively defeated Alfonso's fleet. Alfonso, one of his brothers and many of his nobles were captured. It might have been the end of a great career, for to be a prisoner of Filippo Maria Visconti was never an attractive prospect—particularly when the sinister Duke of Milan had cause to fear the power of his prisoner. The Genoese were commanded to bring Alfonso and his brother to Milan without passing through Genoa.

Filippo Maria Visconti, son of the great Gian Galeazzo, was almost as crafty and almost as successful as his father. Repulsively ugly and grossly fat, he had deformed feet and legs and was so weak he had to lean on a staff or a page to rise from his seat. Nearly blind, with a receding chin, snub nose, projecting brows and a bull neck encased in coils of fat, the monstrous Visconti was cruel, treacherous, cowardly and superstitious.

He wore fancy clothes, but was always dirty. He slept in three different beds a night, always sideways across the bed. He dreaded death and screamed with terror at the sight of a bare sword. During electrical storms he was so afraid of lightning that he hid under the bedclothes. He trusted no one and was amused by nothing.

Yet, this psychopathic creature was extremely able. He reigned for thirty years and waged many successful wars, without ever seeing a battle. He employed the best generals and knew how to hold their loyalty. He could be kind and gracious to courtiers, and if he wasn't cruel to prisoners he could be kind to them, too.

Although Filippo Maria had fought to prevent Alfonso from conquering Naples, he received Alfonso and his brother courteously, saw much of them himself and arranged that their captivity was not unpleasant. One contemporary story has it that the two Trastamara brothers won fifteen hundred gold pieces from the Duke in a game of cards! But Alfonso won from the Duke a much bigger prize than that. By charm, logic and eloquence Alfonso convinced the suspicious tyrant that it would be a disaster for him if René of Anjou became king of Naples. With French might established in Naples, all Italy would be subject to French pressure and Milan would be in danger of conquest.

But if Alfonso were king of Naples his chief enemy would be the French whom he had driven out. If the French should attack Milan, it would be much to his interest to fight at Milan's side. Alfonso and Filippo Maria were natural allies!

The Duke of Milan released his Aragonese prisoners, made an alliance with Alfonso, ordered Genoa to give him back his captured ships—and lost his rule over Genoa by his generosity. That city was enraged by this sudden reversal in favor of its bitter enemy, revolted and drove out the Visconti garrison. Alfonso, by personality and intellect alone, had turned defeat into victory in a triumph of personal diplomacy.

Alfonso returned to Naples and continued campaigning in a desultory war against René of Anjou and the troops of Pope Eugenius who supported René. The war dragged on for years and Alfonso ruled a large part of the kingdom, but not yet the city of Naples. René grew discouraged and challenged Alfonso to a duel which would settle once and for all the question of who should reign in Naples. Alfonso, who was no longer young, replied with typical Renaissance realism that no one but a fool would risk his life for a prize that was certain to be his. Finally, in 1442 after a fierce siege, Alfonso captured Naples and René fled home to Provence.

During the siege Alfonso's brother Pedro was murdered. A prisoner of the Genoese who were supporting Réné, he was shot from the mouth of a cannon in the tower of a church.

"When the King first heard the bad news," wrote Fazio, "overcome by fraternal love, he began to weep; then, having given vent to his grief, leaving his tent he went to the Church of the Magdalene where his brother's body had been brought. And opening his brother's breastplate he kissed his bare chest and said: 'My brother, you who were with me at my side in all my trials, may you rest in eternal peace.' Having said these words and having praised him for his valor, he added that in that day the flower of knighthood had died. And because he saw all the soldiers downcast and especially those who had fought with his brother, he began to console them and distribute among them his brother's arms, urging that the death of one man should not make all lose heart but should make all think only of winning the war."

To celebrate his final victory Alfonso had a large breach knocked out of the wall of Naples and entered the city in a triumphal parade riding in a gilded chariot like a roman imperator. Magnificence, not modesty, being a princely virtue, he had the great gateway into the medieval Castel Nuovo rebuilt with a triumphal arch in Renaissance style. Inscribed upon it were these words: *Alfonsus Rex Hispanicus Siculus Italicus Pius Clemens Invictus*, which can be translated as "Alfonso King of Spain, Sicily and Italy, Pius, Merciful and Unconquered."

For the next sixteen years Alfonso divided his time and effort between warfare and reigning over Naples as a cultivated Renaissance prince. He fought against Pope Eugenius and for him, for Pope Pius II against Sigismondo Malatesta of Rimini, against Florence and Siena, briefly in Greece. He even aspired to the throne of Milan and claimed that Filippo Maria, who had no son and only an illegitimate daughter, had made a last-minute will in his favor. If one will had been helpful in acquiring Naples why not another for Milan? Whether the will was genuine is doubtful, but in any case nothing came of it.

Alfonso the Magnanimous was faithless in politics, artful in concealing his emotions and intentions, woefully extravagant. He taxed his Spanish subjects heavily as well as his Italian ones to support his wars and his luxurious court. He was not cruel. He knew better than any Italian prince of his generation, save Federigo da Montefeltro, how to reign as an approachable monarch beloved by his subjects. Many stories were told about him.

It was the scholars and poets who made Alfonso's court at Naples famous. Panormita spent much of his time reading Latin authors aloud to Alfonso. He says that Alfonso took such intense pleasure in listening to him read Quintus Curtius' *Life of Alexander the Great* that he was cured of an illness. Alfonso placed great trust in Panormita, making him his secretary and tutor to young Ferrante, his illegitimate son and heir. That Panormita made an ideal tutor is doubtful. He was a notorious homosexual and the author of *Hermaphroditus*, a collection of elegies in explicit praise of homosexuality. Although Pope Eugenius forbade anyone to read this work on pain of excommunication, it was widely read and highly praised by scholars, poets and princes. Alfonso had few prejudices.

Fazio, Alfonso's other principal biographer, was treated with exceptional generosity. While writing his chronicle in ten volumes Fazio had been paid five hundred florins. But the project took so long that when it was completed Fazio was broke and asked if he could have two or three hundred more florins. Alfonso paid him fifteen hundred more florins.

The most distinguished writer at Alfonso's court was Lorenzo Valla. This poet, literary critic and bellicose foe of the papacy was invited by Alfonso to join his court in 1437, when he had not yet completed his conquest of Naples and was at war with Pope Eugenius. Valla had already eloquently denounced the ideal of virginity, which he considered an intolerable torment that no one should be asked to endure. This opinion naturally did not please the Church. While serving Alfonso, Valla wrote his treatise on *Constantine's Donation*. This celebrated work exposed an ancient forgery which purported to justify the Church's temporal power in Italy on the ground that the great emperor had presented vast territories to the early Church. That the Church should repudiate Valla was natural. But that Pope Nicholas V should employ Valla as an apostolic writer was extraordinary. Nicholas evidently admired Valla's scholarship more than he objected (if he objected at all) to his ideas.

To support the scholars at his court Alfonso paid in the last part of his reign twenty thousand florins a year. Alfonso's orthodox piety was beyond dispute. "His favorite haunt," wrote Burckhardt, "seems to have been the library of the castle at Naples where he would sit at a window overlooking the bay and listen to learned debates on the Trinity." But piety did not prevent war against the Church as a political institution or an attitude of sarcastic anticlericalism.

Alfonso Borgia, who came to Italy from Spain with Alfonso and owed his election as Pope Calixtus III at the age of seventy-seven to Alfonso's influence, did much to annoy the king with the papacy. In return for his aid Alfonso demanded that Calixtus hand over to him the March of Ancona. Calixtus, who was so feeble that he spent most of his time in bed, refused to oblige his old friend: "Let the King of Aragon govern his kingdom, and leave to us the administration of the Church." Alfonso had a favorite saying: "Blows have a better effect on priests than prayers." Once in an argument about the origin of harpies Alfonso said that "harpies used to live on islands and now many have come to live here in Rome." He could be equally sarcastic about courtiers: "They are like sea gulls who follow the wake of a ship for food, and once they have it they fly off."

Vespasiano da Bisticci in his life of Alfonso wrote that he heard Mass three times a day and "every Holy Thursday he would wash the feet of as many poor men as he had years of life, washing them in proper fashion: drying them afterward and giving to each of the poor men a white garment, a pair of shoes, an Alfonsino, a Carlino and I know not what other money besides. Afterward on the same day he caused a dinner to be spread, and made the poor men sit down thereto; and, having directed the cook what viands should be sent up, the King stood at the table with a napkin round his neck and a girdle. As soon as the eatables came from the kitchen the King set them before his guests, together with wine and all else needful with most humble carriage. His majesty, indeed, was unwilling that they should be served by any other hand than his own. Every day he repeated without fail the office of Our Lord with great devotion, and he never failed to rise during the night, remaining on his knees for some time: this custom he observed as long as he lived."

Many tales were told about the King's casual deeds of kindness to his subjects. So confident was Alfonso of the affection of his subjects that he regularly walked about the streets of Naples without an escort. When his courtiers protested he replied: "What has a father to fear among his children?"

Panormita, who told how Alfonso never drank wine and denounced gambling as a pernicious custom, said that Alfonso was "a very gay man, witty, elegant, graceful and clear-headed." He also commented on Alfonso's habitual facial control: "Face to face with prosperity or adversity or with the unpredictable, the King always looked the same. In his dress, in his speech, in gentleness and humaneness and clemency, he was always constant." Panormita describes a scene where Alfonso had to have a dangerous growth removed and the wound cauterized. The king refused to let himself be tied and with stoic bravery endured the pain "without making a single sudden move or outcry."

Alfonso was so much a part of his time that he wasted a hundred and fifty thousand florins entertaining the Emperor Frederick III when he visited Italy in 1452. He was so great an enthusiast for antiquity that he was a bit of an archeologist himself. When the people of Gaeta told him that they had found the tomb of Marcus Tulius Cicero, Alfonso went to Gaeta. There he studied the lettering and pointed out that the name was not Marcus Tulius but Marcus Vitruvius, concluding that "the people of Gaeta have inherited olives from the goddess Pallas but not wisdom."

In an age of frequent poisoning and of exaggerated fear of poisoning, Alfonso was refreshingly sensible. When Cosimo de' Medici sent Alfonso a present of a copy of Livy, several of Alfonso's courtiers warned him not to read it lest it be poisoned. Alfonso laughed and told them not to talk like fools. Another time a Florentine exile offered to arrange the murder of Cosimo, but Alfonso refused and ordered the would-be assassin to leave his kingdom at once and not to return unless he could make a nobler offer.

One of the best stories about Alfonso was told by Baldassare Castiglione in his book *The Courtier:*

"Once King Alfonso I of Aragon gave one of his servants weapons, horses and clothes, because the fellow said that he had dreamed the night before that His Highness had given him all these things; and then, not long afterward, the same servant said that he had dreamed that night that the King was giving him a goodly sum of gold florins; whereupon the King replied: 'From now on do not believe in dreams, for they are not true.'"

Another story which sounds less likely was told by a Florentine writer of humorous anecdotes, Niccolò Angeli dal Bucine.

"Niccolò d'Andrea Giugni was ambassador of the Florentines to King Alfonso of Naples at the time when His Majesty was in love with Lady Lucrezia, a Neapolitan noblewoman. Out of his love for said lady, the King had held many feasts and other entertainments, always stating that he loved her for her high qualities and that he had never sinned with her.

"It so happened that one day when King Alfonso was riding with messer Niccolò, they met Lady Lucrezia who, in most charming and gracious manner, curtsied to the King. Later, while talking of this lady, Niccolò said, 'Your Majesty has certainly made an excellent choice in loving this lady, for she is a true paragon and mirror of beauty; but I was sorry to hear that there is a serious blemish on her body.'

"The King, who had been greatly pleased by the first words of Niccolò, was very much disturbed by his last statement and said immediately: 'What did you hear about her?'

"Giving the impression that he was loath to mention it, Niccolò said, 'I have heard that she is very hairy, and that her body is covered with unusually long hair.' Whereupon the King said, '*Per cap de Dieu* [By God], it's not true.'

"And Niccolò countered, smiling, '*Per cap de Dieu*, Your Majesty has slept with her!'"

True or not, the story suggests that Alfonso was no tyrant and that ambassadors might have dared to make impudent jokes at his expense.

Lucrezia was the love of Alfonso's old age. Other chroniclers believed she never was Alfonso's mistress. Pope Pius II wrote in his memoirs:

"She was a beautiful woman or girl, the daughter of poor but noble Neapolitan parents (*if there is any nobility in poverty*), with whom the King was so desperately in love that in her presence he was beside himself and could neither hear nor see anything but Lucrezia. He could not take his eyes off her, praised everything she said, marveled at her wisdom, admired every gesture, thought her beauty divine. He had made her many presents, had given orders that she was to receive the honors of a queen, and at last was so completely dominated by her that no one could get a hearing without her consent. Marvelous is the power of love! A great king, lord of the noblest part of Spain, obeyed by the Balearic Islands, Corsica, Sardinia, and Sicily itself, who had subdued many provinces of Italy and defeated the most powerful generals, was finally conquered by love and like any captive of war was a slave to a weak woman! He had no intercourse with her (if report is true) and they say she used to declare, 'Never with my consent shall the King ravish my maidenhood! But if he should attempt force, I shall not imitate Lucrezia, the wife of Collatinus, who endured the outrage and then took her own life. I will anticipate the outrage by my death.' But noble acts are not so easy as noble words nor did her afterlife bear out her protestations. For after Alfonso's death she went into Piccinino's the condottiere's camp, where she had no reputation for virtue; indeed it was common talk that she was his secretary's mistress and had a child by him. But Alfonso thought there was nothing in the world more divine. Though wise in everything else, in regard to this and hunting he was stark mad."

Alfonso was married to Margaret of Castile and had no children by her. How many bastards he had is unknown. But his heir, Ferrante, was thought to be the son of a court lady named Margaret de Hijar. The queen, in a fit of mad jealousy, arranged the murder of Margaret de Hijar. Instead of having his wife beheaded as many of his contemporary princes would have done, Alfonso sent her back to Spain. From the moment he heard of the murder he never spoke to her or even looked at her again.

There were several rumors that Ferrante was not Alfonso's son. Since Ferrante was cruel and vicious and universally detested and Alfonso was kind and widely beloved, it is not surprising that doubts circulated about Ferrante's parentage. But if Ferrante was not his son, one wonders why Alfonso made him his associate in the rule of Naples, arranged his legitimization and made him his heir. Would he have done all that for another man's bastard?

Alfonso the Magnanimous died in 1458 after an illness of forty days. Pope Pius II wrote that "the King died in sanctity, for he confessed his sins like a Christian and received the sacraments before he passed to the other life." Pius, who, like most of his contemporaries, admired the King of Naples, had dedicated a book he was writing on the history of Bohemia to Alfonso. No gesture could have been more appropriate to honor the magnanimous soldier-prince whose personal emblem was an open book.

FERRANTE,
KING OF VILLAINS

ALFONSO LEFT his hereditary kingdoms in Spain and the Mediterranean to his brother Juan and his newly won kingdom of Naples to his illegitimate son Ferrante. Both Pope Eugenius IV and Pope Nicholas V had recognized Ferrante as the heir to the kingdom. But frail, old Calixtus at the age of eighty still cherished his feud with his former patron, Alfonso, and extended it to his former pupil, Ferrante. A few days before Alfonso's death Calixtus wrote: "Since Alfonso has come into possession of Naples the Church has had no peace; he has been a constant torment to Pope Martin, Eugenius and myself. Therefore when he dies, I will do my utmost to deliver my successor from such bondage by preventing the succession of Don Ferrante, the King's illegitimate son."

On the day Alfonso died, Ferrante, according to the custom of the time, rode through the streets of Naples to receive the cheers of the people. When Calixtus received a letter from Ferrante announcing his father's death, the peevish octogenarian exploded with rage because Ferrante referred to himself as king. "The little bastard," said the Pope. "This boy, who is nothing, calls himself king without our permission. Naples belongs to the Church." So Calixtus published a bull which claimed Naples for the Church as a lapsed fief. He was invoking an old legalism which had had no practical validity for years.

FERDINAND I, called Ferrante, King of Naples

"He was cruel, avaricious and vindictive personally. But he was intelligent, clever, persistent and successful. Ferrante could smile and smile and be a villain."

Ferrante had the messengers who dared bring copies of the bull into the Kingdom of Naples soundly beaten. It was an inauspicious start to a violently troubled reign. Fortunately for Ferrante old Calixtus died that summer. Before the conclave which elected his successor, Pius II, Ferrante's ambassadors in Rome lobbied strenuously for Pius, who returned the favor by recognizing Ferrante as King of Naples.

When Ferrante became king he was thirty-four years old. His reputation was bad. It grew steadily worse during the thirty-five years of his reign. Ferrante was not only unscrupulous and treacherous in politics. He was cruel, avaricious and vindictive personally. But he was intelligent, clever, persistent and successful. Ferrante could smile and smile and be a villain. His son, Alfonso, the Duke of Calabria, was even more wicked, but crudely and blatantly so. Alfonso was a passable general, but he was not clever and he did not smile. Both men were feared and hated. Ferrante was respected. Alfonso was not.

Ferrante married twice. His first wife, Isabella of Taranto, was the daughter of one of the leading Neapolitan barons. She bore him four children who lived: Beatrice, who married Matthias Corvinus, King of Hungary; Alfonso, who reigned briefly as Alfonso II and married Ippolita Sforza, the daughter of Francesco Sforza, Duke of Milan; Federigo, who became the last Aragonese king of Naples; and Eleonora, who married Ercole d'Este, Duke of Ferrara. Ferrante was married a second time to Juana, a sister of King Ferdinand of Spain. She bore him one daughter, Giovanna, who is remembered because she married her nephew, Ferdinand II, who was Ferrante's grandson.

The honorable estate of marriage was as confining to Ferrante as to most of the ruling princes of Renaissance Italy. There were numerous women in his life, some of them the wives of his noble subjects. How many illegitimate children he fathered is unknown.

When Commines was in Naples with Charles VIII, he became fascinated by the evil reputation of Ferrante and Alfonso and inquired about them among their former subjects. Writing of Alfonso he said: "Never was any prince more bloody, wicked, inhuman, lascivious or gluttonous than he. Yet his father was more dangerous, because no man knew when he was angry or pleased."

Although Commines had spent many years in the service of Louis XI of France, who also was cruel and treacherous, he still was profoundly shocked by the two bad kings of Naples. "This Ferrante had nothing of tenderness or compassion in him, as I have been informed by his nearest friends and relations, nor was he ever known to take the least pity of his own necessitous subjects in relation to their taxes. The whole trade of buying and selling he engrossed to himself all through his kingdom. He delivered hogs to his people to feed, and required them to make them fat, that they might fetch a good price; and if any of them chanced to die the people were forced to pay for them. In Apulia and other countries which are plentiful in olives, he and his son bought up all the oil, almost at their own price; the same they did with their corn, buying it at a cheap rate before it was ripe, and then selling it again as dear as they could; but if the price of any of their commodities happened to fall in the meantime, they obliged the people to take them off their hands; and whilst they were disposed to sell, nobody durst buy of anyone else."

Commines was particularly shocked at the lack of any pretense of conventional piety in the two kings. "Both father and son had ravished several women; they made no conscience of sacrilege, nor did they retain the least respect or obedience to the Church. They sold their bishoprics, as that of Taranto, which the father sold for thirteen thousand ducats to a Jew for his son, who the Jew pretended was a Christian. He gave abbeys to falconers and others for their children, telling them, 'You shall keep me so many hawks, and mew them, and keep me such a number of soldiers at your expense.' The son never kept Lent in his life, nor so much as pretended to do it; and for many years he never was at confession, nor ever received the Sacrament of the Lord's Supper. In short, it is scarce possible that any prince could be guilty of greater villainies then these two were."

Ferrante had enjoyed the best of humanist educations. Panormita, Lorenzo Valla and Alfonso Borgia (the future Pope Calixtus III) had all been his tutors. Alfonso himself had set him an instructive example in the arts of war and kingship. But the fat-faced Ferrante, with his heavy jowls and double chin, lacked his father's charm, personal magnetism and pleasure in pleasing. He often spoke Spanish, which annoyed Italians. He wore gorgeous clothes in contrast to Alfonso's simple black. He did not care if he was unpopular.

He did care about keeping his throne and maintaining his autocratic power. To do so he was forced to wage two prolonged wars against his rebellious barons. He was involved in several foreign wars. He was both an ally and an enemy of several popes, regularly switching his policies, regularly breaking his promises. Even to outline the intricate complexities of Ferrante's wars and diplomacy would boggle the mind. I shall summarize heroically and omit much.

Within a year of Ferrante's accession to the throne many of the Neapolitan barons revolted. They wanted to exercise feudal, almost independent power. Ferrante wanted royal power solely for himself. It was as simple as that. The barons offered the crown of Naples to Réné of Anjou, whom Alfonso had driven out, and invited his son Jean to come and fight with them as the Duke of Calabria, or heir to the throne he would inherit after his father's death.

This baronial cum Angevin revolt lasted for five years, from 1459 to 1464, and gave employment to some of the leading condottieri of the time. Ferrante finally won it.

For the next decade Naples was more or less at peace. Ferrante presided over a cultivated court, whose chief ornament was the Latin poet Giovanni Pontano, who developed a literary academy of great fame. Pontano, poet, philosopher and diplomat, served as Ferrante's prime minister. His Latin poems included one on astronomy and one on the proper cultivation of oranges. Ferrante cared little for literature, but Alfonso's example had taught him the publicity value of patronage of poets and scholars. Once when Pontano entered his tent the King made all the courtiers present rise, saying in the surprised silence, "*Ecco il maestro.*"

Pontano complacently recorded this honor. And yet it was Pontano who put into circulation one of the worst stories about his royal master's villainies. Pontano said that Ferrante kept a private museum in which were preserved the embalmed bodies of his enemies, dressed in their favorite costumes. Ferrante, according to Pontano, had enjoyed gloating over the misery of his enemies when they were confined in dungeons and starved. He liked to continue his gloating after their deaths.

Since Pontano, although greatly talented, was vain, sycophantic and treacherous himself, it is impossible to know whether the mummy story was an imaginary atrocity. But it is believable, because Ferrante was naturally cruel and did conciliate many of his enemies, pretend friendship, entertain them at dinners and then imprison or execute them. Pontano's last appearance in history was after Charles VIII conquered Naples when he made an eloquent speech of welcome to the French king in which he vilified the wicked king who had honored him.

Ferrante became a major belligerent in the Pazzi war because of a strategic alliance he concluded with the brutal and arrogant Pope Sixtus IV. It was a regular policy of Ferrante's to make alliances with popes, break the alliances by refusing to pay the agreed-upon tribute, and even wage war against the papacy. When Ferrante went to Rome in 1475 to conclude his alliance with Sixtus he was struck by the facilities the ancient city offered to citizens interested in rioting or rebelling against the popes. He cautioned Sixtus that it would be prudent to widen streets and tear down towers, loggias and balconies. "You will never," he said, "be master of Rome while the women, by throwing down stones, can put to flight your best soldiers." Ferrante and his numerous suite stayed in Rome for only three days. It was long enough for Infesura, the diarist, to record with some surprise that "the number of falcons which the Neapolitans brought with them completely cleared the city and all the neighborhood of owls."

The Pazzi war was waged by Pope Sixtus and Ferrante against Florence. With the connivance of the Pope himself, Sixtus' contemptible nephew, Girolamo Riario, had organized a conspiracy to assassinate Lorenzo de' Medici and his brother Guiliano. Lorenzo was only slightly wounded, but Guiliano was killed. Sixtus was furious with Lorenzo for not being killed, too, and for imprisoning a cardinal implicated in the conspiracy. He excommunicated Lorenzo, put Florence under an interdict and went to war against Florence with Naples as his active ally. The war was not fought energetically by either side, although Ferrante's son Alfonso, the Duke of Calabria, won a great victory over the Florentines in 1479. When Florence began to suffer from famine because Alfonso had ravaged her territory and destroyed her crops, Lorenzo made his famous journey to Naples to negotiate a peace. It was certainly a bold decision. An enemy once in Ferrante's power had good reason to worry about his fate. Would Lorenzo's be impossibly harsh peace terms? Prolonged imprisonment? Poison or the knife? When Pope Sixtus heard that Lorenzo was at the court of Naples, he was dismayed. Ferrante reassured him. He swore that he would rather lose ten kingdoms and his crown than let Lorenzo go free without securing the terms Sixtus desired. As usual, Ferrante was lying. His own terms imposed on Lorenzo were surprisingly reasonable. Ferrante concluded a separate peace with Lorenzo and demanded only a substantial indemnity and several small territorial concessions. The fact that Lorenzo had two admiring friends in the royal family of Naples, Ferrente's younger son, Federigo, and his daughter-in-law, Ippolita Sforza, Alfonso's learned wife, probably did not influence the coldly calculating king. But the presence of friends must have comforted Lorenzo during the prolonged tension of the negotiations.

The following year was terrifying for Ferrante and all Italy. In August of 1480 the Turks captured the Neapolitan city of Otranto. More than half of the town's population of about twenty-two thousand were tortured and killed and the rest were carried off into slavery. According to their usual custom, the Turks encouraged other unbelievers by publicly sawing in half the local governor and the archbishop.

Fearful that this was the start of a major invasion of Italy, Ferrante assembled his troops to confine the Turks within Otranto. Alfonso arrived with reinforcements. And then in May of 1481 providence seemed to intervene directly to help the House of Aragon. The Sultan Muhammed died. Most of the Turkish troops left for Constantinople. Alfonso enrolled some of the remaining Turks in his own army and received credit for a glorious victory.

Ferrante's separate peace with Florence had enraged Pope Sixtus and broken their alliance. Ferrante joined a league with Milan and Florence. Sixtus allied himself with Venice. The brutal old pope intended to conquer Ferrara, give it to Venice, or give it to Girolamo Riario, or divide the duchy between them. He also intended to destroy Ferrante. The war of Ferrara broke out in 1482, and the new league came to the aid of the hard-pressed duchy.

Alfonso, the Duke of Calabria, marching north to reinforce the defenders of Ferrara, where his beautiful sister Eleonora was wife of the Duke, invaded papal territory. Sixtus screamed for help and Venice sent him the best condottiere in the signory's employ, Roberto Malatesta, who soundly defeated Alfonso in a swamp near Rome.

Establishing a treacherous precedent, which his nephew, Pope Julius II, was to emulate in reverse a generation later, Sixtus suddenly switched sides, deserted Venice and joined the league against Venice. Alfonso was made Captain-general of the league, and the war dragged on until the summer of 1484. As far as Ferrante was concerned, it stopped just in time. He was soon busy suppressing the second revolt of his barons, known as the Barons' War.

It was Ferrante's insufferable son, Alfonso, who was responsible for the outbreak of the Barons' War. In the autumn of 1485 he had been sent in state to Rome to negotiate with the new pope, Innocent VIII, and instead of acting diplomatically had blustered and threatened and arrogantly demanded the incorporation of several papal towns into Neapolitan territory. Innocent refused and Alfonso snarled that "before long he would make the Pope beg for the annexation of his own accord." The weak, stupid and cowardly Duke of Calabria had quite unnecessarily made certain that Innocent would be an enemy of the House of Aragon.

Alfonso began the new war by persuading his father to make a sudden attack on a group of disaffected barons. Pope Innocent at once joined the war as an ally of the barons and so did Genoa. Milan and Florence aided Naples. Alfonso won a great victory over papal forces and twice led his army close to the walls of Rome.

It was an odd war because nobody could tell when it was over. In 1486 Ferrante and Innocent made a peace and Ferrante acknowledged papal supremacy and agreed to pay his back tribute. And Ferrante promised an amnesty to his rebellious barons if they submitted. But within a month Ferrante had murdered the Pope's representative in the town of Aquila and had broken his promise to the barons. He arrested them, their wives and children, threw them into prison and confiscated their estates. One wonders why the barons trusted Ferrante's promises; for years they had been known to be worthless.

Two years later Ferrante was busy fomenting revolts within the Papal States, and two years later still the bellicose old villain was threatening to enter Rome in arms. And always Ferrante refused to pay tribute. But in 1492 Ferrante and Innocent suddenly reached an apparently amicable agreement; Ferrante blandly promised to pay tribute and to cement the new alliance of old enemies. Ferrante's grandson was betrothed to Innocent's niece, Battistina.

But in the same year Innocent died and Rodrigo Borgia became pope as Alexander VI. Ferrante furiously opposed him and eloquently denounced him for his many sins. And then as the threat of Charles VIII loomed over them both, the two old sinners concluded an alliance. After Ferrante's death Alfonso's bastard daughter, Sancha, was married to Pope Alexander's bastard son Joffre.

When Ferrante of Aragon died in January of 1494 he was seventy years old. During his long reign he had regularly displayed his skill in dissimulation, treachery and survival. A master of short-term expediency, he lacked the vision to recognize that the welfare of his dynasty depended in the long run on the welfare and trust of his subjects. Ferrante despised public opinion, inspired no loyalty in his subjects and so insured the collapse of the House of Aragon. But he could be so shrewd that it almost seems as if he could have been, had he cared to be, a true statesman. A few days before his death Ferrante wrote like a prudent elder statesman: "When disturbances and wars come, distress and danger are the lot of all, for when fire has once been kindled and grown into a conflagration, it spreads to places where it is neither expected nor feared; and it has often happened that he has been the first to suffer who thought that he would merely fill the spectator's role."

FERRANTE WAS instrumental in establishing the silk industry in Naples. He built new walls around the city. He was a generous patron of the university. He continued to support poets and writers, although not as munificently as his father had done. He foresaw the danger to all Italy, not only to Naples, in Lodovico Sforza's encouragement of Charles VIII's invasion.

The court of Naples during Ferrante's reign was a dismaying combination of high Renaissance culture and low Renaissance corruption and intrigue. The examples set by the King and by Alfonso were horrible. Nevertheless, Ferrante's other legitimate children escaped infection. Eleonora, who married Ercole d'Este, Duke of Ferrara, was renowned for her virtue and kindness as well as for her beauty. Federigo, who became the last Aragonese king of Naples, was not a forceful character, but he was amiable, well-intentioned and completely free of the cruelty and treachery which made his evil father and brother notorious.

In addition to his legitimate children, Ferrante had at least six bastard sons and several bastard daughters. In this respect, he conformed to the traditional practice of most ruling Renaissance princes.

Two examples of Ferrante's smiling cruelty particularly impressed his contemporaries and have survived in the chronicles, where, presumably, lesser deeds of infamy went unrecorded.

The first was the murder of Jacopo Piccinino, a condottiere who had fought against Ferrante in the first revolt of the barons. Later Jacopo had played a treacherous part in the confused fighting for the rule of Milan which followed the death of Duke Filippo-Maria Visconti. Francesco Sforza had won the prize and become duke. He did not forget that at one point in the campaigning Jacopo had betrayed him, nor that Jacopo was dismayingly popular among the nobles of Milan.

Nevertheless, a marriage was concluded between Jacopo and Francesco Sforza's bastard daughter Drusiana. Shortly after the wedding Jacopo left for Naples, where Francesco had arranged with Ferrante that Jacopo would be hired as commander of the Neapolitan forces. Drusiana was sent to the town of Selmona, there to await her husband.

Ferrante welcomed Jacopo cordially and entertained him with banquets and festivities for twenty-seven days. Then without warning or provocation he arrested Jacopo and had him strangled. Ferrante had avenged himself on an old enemy in the smiling, hypocritical fashion he liked best. Poor Drusiana returned to Milan, bore a son and disappeared from the stage of history.

But had Francesco conspired with Ferrante to murder his son-in-law, who was also an old enemy of his? Historians have argued both for the defense and for the prosecution. Machiavelli believed Sforza was guilty. Sforza was not usually revengeful; but he was cynically unscrupulous, according to the customs of the time described and recommended by Machiavelli in *The Prince*. Perhaps he didn't much like Drusiana and considered her happiness expendable. Perhaps he thought it would be comfortable to have a popular soldier whom he disliked and distrusted gainfully employed at the other end of Italy. Perhaps he had no advance knowledge of the murder, but, knowing Ferrante's reputation, considered such a possibility likely and let events take their course.

Francesco Sforza's innocence has been argued because he sent strong protests to Ferrante and delayed the marriage of his legitimate daughter, Ippolita, to Ferrante's son Alfonso for two months. This is equally plausible. So, whether Francesco was a guilty accessory to the murder of his daughter's bridegroom remains one of the mysteries of history.

Just as calculated in its cruelty and far more elaborate in its plotting was Ferrante's betrayal of the barons who thought they had made peace with him. While the less suspicious barons were agreeing on terms of surrender with Ferrante, the Duke of Salerno, who knew the worth of Ferrante's promises better than did the others, fled to France. Nailed above the gate of his palace he left the message "*Passero vecchio non in caggiola,*" which may be translated as "An old sparrow does not walk into the cage."

Soon afterward Ferrante combined a festival of conciliation with the marriage of his niece to the son of one of the leading rebel (now reconciled) barons, the Conte di Sarno. The grand bridal dinner was held in the great hall of the Castel Nuovo in Naples, the hall which, ever since, has been called the Sala dei Baroni. Without warning, in the midst of the gaiety, soldiers of Ferrante rushed into the hall and arrested every baron present, including the bridegroom. Even the women and children of the baronial families were rounded up and imprisoned. And all the estates of the trapped barons were confiscated with all their property, including even their mules. For this grand treachery Ferrante bore the responsibility, but rumors said that the inception of the scheme was Alfonso's.

Several of the most prominent barons were publicly executed, but the fate of some twenty others remained unknown. For a while food was regularly sent to the cells where they were confined. But when it was noticed that the executioner was wearing the gold chain which had belonged to one of the Sanseverino princes, hope was given up.

The imprisoned barons were never heard of again. But it was widely believed that Alfonso was responsible for their mass murder five years later on Christmas Day, 1491, a day of such terrible storms that they were considered appropriate for the terrible crimes ordered by Alfonso. This was three years before Ferrante's death in January of 1494, a lapse of time which seems not to have been noticed by Commines, who thought that Alfonso ordered the murders after his own accession to the throne. So whether the barons, who had received an amnesty, were murdered in 1491 or in 1494 is uncertain. Commines wrote:

"Alfonso ordered all the prisoners to be removed to a small island not far from Naples called Ischia and put them all to death after a most barbarous and inhuman manner. I inquired very carefully how they were so cruelly murdered (because many people believed them alive when the King entered Naples) and I was told by their principal servants that they were horribly and villainously knocked on the head by a Moor of Africa, who, immediately after their execution, was dispatched into Barbary, that no notice might be taken of it. I was informed that he did not even spare those ancient princes, some of whom had been kept in prison for five-and-thirty years."

·   ·   ·

KING FERRANTE ALWAYS lived in great luxury and in great splendor. When the French captured the Castel Nuovo, wrote the chronicler Sanuto, "There was found the wardrobe which had been left by the King, since he could not take it away; it comprised much cloth of gold and many silks, to the value of 200,000 ducats, so that the French, who had been clad at the first in broadcloth after their fashion, began one and all to array themselves in silks."

The French were flabbergasted by the riches found in the castle: wines, foods, "more drugs than ever had been seen in Paris," fabrics, textiles, tapestries, tents and pavilions, leather goods, harnesses, bits, bridles, three armories full of weapons and armor, artillery and ammunition, vases and furniture of alabaster, marble, gold and silver, Venetian glass and Venetian pottery. "And I verily believe," wrote an astounded Frenchman, "that at the time of King Alfonso's departure the place was the richest and best furnished in the world, and that all the possessions of the King, M. d'Orléans, and M. de Bourbon added together would not be as valuable as the contents of this castle."

THERE IS no doubt that Ferrante was one of the great villains of the Renaissance. But he has had, if not his defenders, his reluctant sympathizers. François Delaborde, distinguished author of *L'Expédition de Charles VIII En Italie*, wrote: "When one considers the unceasing activity, the incessant efforts made by the old king during his last days, one cannot help feel some commiseration, even sympathy, for that man who, after thirty-five years of struggle, after having recaptured Naples from King Réné, after never having hesitated from treason and massacre to fortify his throne, saw that throne menaced again by the most powerful prince in Europe. One forgets that Ferrante was only a bastard elevated to a throne contrary to all the laws divine or human, one forgets Piccinino murdered, the survivors of the revolt of the barons slaughtered after five years of captivity, to admire the obstinate energy of the old man."

THE FALL
OF THE HOUSE
OF ARAGON

 IT WAS this energy and stubborn persistence which were lacking in the pusillanimous Alfonso, who seated himself on the throne of Naples with ostentatious splendor and abandoned it twelve months later in cowardly panic.

Alfonso II of Aragon, the brutal, arrogant soldier who had been widely considered one of the capable Italian commanders, was an incorrigible coward. He had won several important victories in his military career, but when Roberto Malatesta defeated him in the marshes south of Rome Alfonso deserted his troops in the middle of the battle and fled in panic. His short reign ended when he panicked once again, terrified by the advance of Charles VIII.

During Ferrante's reign the Aragon-Sforza alliance had been marked by Alfonso's marriage to the Duke of Milan's daughter, Ippolita. The alliance was supposedly strengthened again when Alfonso's and Ippolita's daughter, Isabella of Aragon, was married to her cousin, Gian Galeazzo Sforza, the third Sforza duke of Milan, but a duke in name only.

Lodovico Sforza's regency and his determination to keep all

power to himself enraged Alfonso. His daughter was married to a duke and the Duke was a negligible weakling. And Isabella's letters of bitter protest to her father made Alfonso angrier still. He began to talk about making war on his father's ally, Milan.

Isabella sent a famous letter to Alfonso which reads suspiciously as if a scholarly hand had written it for her:

"It is now several years, my father, since you arranged for me an alliance with Giovanni Galeazzo, with the idea that he should, on reaching a proper age, govern his state as his father Galeazzo, his grandfather Francesco, and his ancestors, the Visconti, have done before him. He has now attained the requisite age, and is already a father; yet his authority has been completely stolen from him. Only with difficulty can he obtain the necessities of life from Lodovico and his ministers. Lodovico manages everything as he pleases, decided upon war or peace, makes laws, confers diplomas, exempts from taxes, imposes taxes, distributes favors, appropriates treasures—all according to his pleasure. We, on the other hand, deprived of all assistance, and without money, lead the life of private persons; Giovanni Galeazzo does not appear as the lord of the state, but Lodovico stations the prefects in the fortresses, surrounds himself with soldiers, augments the Council, and usurps all the exclusive privileges of the ruler. Not long ago he became the father of a son, who, according to the popular belief, is destined to be Count of Pavia, and later to succeed as duke. Meanwhile, the mother is honored as though she were the duchess. We and our children are despised, and are indeed not without risk to our lives under his rule, so that one day, in order to bring to an end the hatred which is openly and on all sides manifested to us, we may be swept out of the way, and I can already imagine myself an inconsolable and deserted widow. And yet I still feel in me courage and strength. The people love and sympathize with us, while they hate and abhor our tyrant, who has sucked their blood in order to satisfy his avarice. But I bow beneath the unequal weight, and submit to the ignominy which is laid upon us.

"If thou hast any bowels of compassion, if thou dost cherish a vestige of affection for me, if my tears can move thee, if there is in thy heart a spark of generosity, so let me entreat thee to free

D

thy daughter and thy son-in-law from cruel bondage, insults, and death, and raise them to the throne. But, carest thou nothing about our fate, better would it be for me to take my own life than that I should continue to bear the yoke of tyranny and suffer every reverse under the eyes of my rival."

It was the letter of a proud, bitter and angry young woman who knew she could receive no help from her weakling husband. From Isabella's point of view it was more humiliating to take second place to her "rival," her cousin, Beatrice d'Este, wife of Lodovico Sforza, than to see her husband regarded as a nonentity. Isabella had all the pride and courage of her maternal ancestors, the Sforzas, and of her Aragonese ancestors, Alfonso I and Ferrante. Young Gian Glaeazzo had none of the pride and courage of the Sforzas or of his Visconti ancestors.

Ferrante vetoed war against Milan in behalf of Isabella. But Alfonso, when king, went to war against Milan when it was too late.

Alfonso II was not crowned King of Naples until May 7, 1494. The coronation was performed with great ceremony by Cardinal Giovanni Borgia, a nephew of Pope Alexander. Soon afterward, to strengthen the alliance of the papacy and Naples against the threat of Charles VIII, a marriage was arranged between another of Alfonso's daughters, a bastard, Sancha, and the youngest of Pope Alexander's bastard sons, Joffre. Joffre was only thirteen, Sancha seventeen. At sixteen she was already a famous beauty, with black hair, a dark complexion, sea-green eyes and prominent eyebrows. Considering her later reputation for promiscuity (she was simultaneously the mistress of both her brothers-in-law, Cesare Borgia and his elder brother, the Duke of Gandia), Sancha could not have been entirely satisfied with the husband chosen for her.

Although Sancha was only a teenager and Joffre only a child, the wedding was celebrated according to the customs of the time, ribald customs more suitable (if that is the word) for a more mature couple. Joffre had a new house not far from the Castel Nuovo. He went there ahead of his bride, who arrived soon afterward, accompanied by King Alfonso and Cardinal Borgia. Preparations were made by Sancha's attendants. Giggling girls or elderly women—who they were is not known. But they undressed the young couple, put them to bed with the covers turned down, leaving them naked as far as the waist. Then the attendants left the bridal chamber and the King and the Cardinal entered. They made numerous jests they thought appropriate to the occasion before the Cardinal blessed the nuptial bed. Then they left in a heavy rainstorm.

WHEN SANCHA arrived to take up her residence at the Borgia court in Rome, she brought with her six jesters.

Alfonso, who knew that Charles VIII would soon be knocking at his door, squandered vast sums to cement the useless Borgia alliance, including a dowry of two hundred thousand ducats for Sancha. He broke off relations with Milan, Charles's ally, and prepared to go to war with Milan before Charles could arrive to help Lodovico. In his desperation Alfonso even sent a messenger to the Turkish sultan, Bajazet, warning him of Charles's vague crusading plans to conquer the Ottoman Empire (after he had conquered Naples) and asking him for aid.

While he was preparing to fight Lodovico Sforza, Alfonso, with the treachery habitual with him and his father, tried for a last-minute reconciliation with Lodovico. But Lodovico's ambassador in Naples wrote to warn him to beware of assassins and poisoners because he knew that "the new king had paid large sums of money to several Neapolitans of bad repute, who had been sent to Milan upon some evil errand." It might have been only a rumor, but Alfonso was not the man to shrink from such methods of conducting affairs of state. It wasn't only outraged subjects who murdered or tried to murder ruling princes during the Renaissance. Pope Sixtus had connived in the Pazzi conspiracy. The seigniory of Venice had tried in vain to poison Filippo Maria Visconti, Duke of Milan. And Lorenzo de' Medici himself had encouraged conspiracies against Girolamo Riario, Count of Forli and Imola, who had only just failed to arrange Lorenzo's own sudden demise.

As Charles VIII marched triumphantly south across the Italian peninsula, Alfonso II of Naples completely lost his grip on the realities of politics and power. He could have surrendered before superior force. He could have fought a delaying action in the hope that something unexpected, such as Charles's death, might turn up. At first he had wanted his ally, Pope Alexander, to join him in sending the combined forces of the papacy and of Naples to fight the French and Milanese in Lombardy. But Alexander was so apprehensive about the possible action of the Colonna family, who were sympathizers with the French, that he refused to send any troops out of Rome.

So Alfonso made matters worse and hastened his certain defeat by disastrous strategy. He divided his army into three parts. He diverted a small force to help keep an eye on the Colonna near Rome. He himself held a larger command, which never left Neapolitan territory. And Alfonso sent his young son, Ferdinand II, called Ferrantino, north to attack the Milanese and a detachment of the French that Charles had sent into the Romagna. The inexperienced Ferrantino was easily outmaneuvered by the competent French commanders and soon retreated into Neapolitan territory. Not long afterward Charles succeeded in detaching Pope Alexander from his alliance with Alfonso, and then marched out of Rome on the way to Naples.

Alfonso, the veteran general and ruthless destroyer of his enemies, chose this moment to collapse into gibbering panic. Unable to sleep, overwhelmed by the prospect of defeat and disaster, he was suddenly smitten with remorse and guilt for his many crimes and cried out nightly that he was haunted by the ghosts of his starved and strangled victims. And in the darkness of the night he shouted that he could hear the tramp and clangor of the approaching French troops and that even the stones and trees were threatening him with cries of "France! France!"

Sovereignty was not worth such terrors. Alfonso summoned into his presence his brother Federigo, several of the chief barons of his kingdom and his secretary, the poet and scholar Pontano, and then dictated to Pontano the text of his abdication which made his son Ferrantino the fourth Aragonese king of Naples. Alfonso's stepmother, Ferrante's widow who was a sister of Ferdinand the Catholic of Spain, and Ferrantino both loyally pleaded with the broken king not to abdicate. Several courtiers hypocritically threatened to throw themselves out of a high window if Alfonso did abdicate—better be on the safe side in case he should not.

But no persuasions availed. Alfonso declared that he wanted to consecrate the rest of his life to expiating his sins in a monastery. Four galleys had been prepared. Alfonso boarded one of them, taking with him his jewels, his finest tapestries, his library and a selection of his finest wines. His pious resolution did not mean that he intended to embrace the simple life. The galley took him to Sicily and safety under the protection of the crown of Spain. In the village of Mazzara he established himself in a monastery, and before the year was out he died. It is probable that no one in Italy sincerely grieved for him except his unhappy daughter, Isabella of Aragon, who was already mourning the untimely death of her weak and feckless husband, Gian Galeazzo Sforza.

Alfonso's departure seemed to some of the people of Naples a suitable opportunity to pillage the Jews. Ferrantino began his reign by energetically suppressing the riot. He then abolished several unpopular taxes, released certain barons who were still prisoners and sent off appeals for help. These went to Venice, to Spain and to the Sultan of Turkey, who had already made vague and meaningless promises to Alfonso.

Ferrantino was young, twenty-six, innocent of the crimes of his father and grandfather, courageous and energetic. He was also the first king of the House of Aragon since the death of his great-grandfather, Alfonso the Magnanimous, to be at all popular with the people of Naples. But he became king at the eleventh hour. With the French on his frontier, his own armies deserting or going over to the enemy, and the people indifferent or even ready to welcome the conquerors from beyond the Alps, it was too late.

With no chance of victory Ferrantino still prepared to fight. He collected a small army, entrusted its command to an exiled Milanese condottiere, Giangiacomo Trivulzio, and planned to make a stand at the city of Capua, some twenty miles from Naples. But Ferrantino learned that a rebellion in favor of the French had broken out in Naples. Leaving Trivulzio to face the French, he rushed back to Naples to suppress the revolt. As soon as Ferrantino had left the walls of Capua behind him, Trivulzio went over to the French and surrendered the city. His treachery was one of the most disgraceful in the history of the condottieri. Even before the French troops could enter the city, Neapolitan soldiers had begun to sack it. Ferrantino's army was lost to him. Rebels were rioting in the streets of Naples. Ferrantino retreated to the island of Ischia, taking with him his uncle Federigo, the widow of his grandfather Ferrante, and her young daughter Giovanna, who was Ferrantino's aunt although she was younger than he was. While his galley crossed the Bay of Naples Ferrantino sat in the stern, quoting to himself with philosophical composure, "Unless God keep the city, the vigils of the keepers are vain."

On Ischia the lieutenant in command of the royal castle there, one Guisto della Candina, refused to admit Ferrantino and his party. He was already in traitorous communication with the French. After some talk he consented to admit Ferrantino alone, probably intending to capture him and make his fortune by turning him over to Charles. The gates were opened. Candina appeared. Ferrantino walked in alone, drew a carbine from under his cloak and shot Candina dead on the spot. The garrison surrendered and Ferrantino took possession of his own castle.

Ferrantino was now king of one small island. But he would not surrender. Charles tried to negotiate a peace, offering, if Ferrantino would give up his crown, to grant him a fief in France and to provide for Federigo and the other members of the royal family. Federigo, who served as Ferrantino's representative in the negotiations, said that he knew his nephew well enough to be certain that he would never surrender his crown, that he was determined to live and die a king. The negotiations collapsed, and Ferrantino sailed to Sicily where he had a brief interview with his father and began preparing an invasion to recover his kingdom. He himself was, to use our modern phrase, a government in exile.

Ferrantino was an athletic young man noted for his skill in running, jumping and horsemanship. He had, said Castiglione, a habit of raising his head and twisting his mouth to one side, the result of some illness from which he had recovered. No one ever doubted his bravery, but as a military commander he was to prove hasty, rash and impetuous. When he returned to Neapolitan territory to drive out Charles's garrisons, he was immeasurably aided by the greatest soldier of the time, the Spaniard Gonzalo Fernandez de Cordoba. Ferdinand of Spain had sent Gonzalo to Sicily with a small force to support Ferrantino. Together they reconquered the kingdom of Naples in a series of brilliant battles and campaigns, for which Gonzalo rightly won most of the credit.

Ferrantino sometimes acted unwisely against Gonzalo's advice. "The King," wrote Gonzalo, "is the kind we expected from the information we had before coming here. If he himself determines something, he insists that that course is best. Often he will make a decision and later change from it, though it be good and advisable. The result is that he is almost always off target."

This was a technical military judgment by the soldier best qualified in the world to make it. Others, less informed about the details of the successful campaign to drive the French out of the Kingdom of Naples, were much impressed by Ferrantino's character. Guicciardini wrote: "He won the highest respect for his courage and ability, the nobility of his mind and the royal virtues which shone out of him."

Ferrantino, with few soldiers and almost no money, desperately needed help to reconquer his kingdom. That is why he begged for help from Spain. King Ferdinand sent Gonzalo and thereby secured a foothold in the Kingdom of Naples which enabled him later to betray his relatives in the House of Aragon and to seize Naples for himself.

Shortly after his triumphant reconquest of Naples in 1496, young Ferrantino died. Two interesting stories were told about his tragically youthful death at the summit of his fame and success. One was about the cause of his death. He had recently married his aunt, Giovanna, and according to the story had so enjoyed the lawful pleasures of matrimony with that near relation that he died of sexual exhaustion. This unlikely tale reveals more about the minds of Renaissance chroniclers than it does about Ferrantino, who had recently been campaigning in some of the most insalubrious regions of Italy. It is a good guess that the cause of his death was malaria.

The other story suggests that the young hero may not have

been as virtuous a king as many supposed and that if he had lived he might have resembled his father, Alfonso II, and his grandfather, Ferrante, more than his great-grandfather, Alfonso the Magnanimous. The poet and scholar Pietro Bembo, who as a young man loved Lucrezia Borgia and as an old man became a cardinal, wrote that Ferrantino while lying on his deathbed ordered the execution of a bishop who was his enemy. And he had the bishop's severed head laid on the foot of his bed so that he could see with his own eyes that his vengeance had been properly carried out.

Such bloodthirstiness was never felt by his amiable uncle Federigo, who now became the last king of Naples of the House of Aragon. A kind, agreeable, well-intentioned man, Federigo was better fitted for private life than to be a Renaissance prince in a period of perpetual crisis. Neither skilled as a politician nor as a soldier, he was celebrated for his benevolence and his concern for justice. Unquestionably the most decent and virtuous member of his royal house, Federigo often did the morally right thing when the morally wrong thing would have been more expedient.

In gratitude to Gonzalo for his indispensable aid in driving the French garrisons out of the kingdom Federigo granted him the Neapolitan duchy of San Angelo. Gonzalo, a Spanish general, thus became a vassal of the King of Naples. When in 1501 King Ferdinand of Spain and King Louis XII made their infamous pact to conquer Naples and divide it between them, Gonzalo, who was in command of the Spanish army ordered to attack the kingdom, offered to return his duchy to Federigo and also asked to be relieved of his feudal obligations of homage and fealty to him. Gonzalo, who conspicuously failed to keep his word on several occasions, was on the whole an honorable man with medieval ideas about his duty. Federigo gladly relieved Gonzalo of his feudal obligations. But he insisted that Gonzalo keep his duchy, which, Federigo said, was an inadequate compensation for his past services. Such a chivalrous gesture was almost unknown in the Italy of the Renaissance. It makes Federigo seem to resemble the Knight of La Mancha more than his contemporary princes.

A year or two earlier Federigo had made another royal gesture of great generosity and some risk. Cesare Borgia, the unfrocked cardinal and brutally ambitious son of Pope Alexander, had offered himself as a husband for Federigo's daughter, Carlotta. That sensible young lady persistently refused to marry the sinister Borgia, and Federigo firmly supported her in her refusal. Since the Borgia power was great and the Borgia politics impossible to foresee, Federigo could not know what menace he might provoke by offending Cesare. His fatherly concern for his daughter was not shared by most of his fellow rulers who, in the ordinary way of foreign policy, regularly married their daughters to scoundrels.

Louis XII, who had conquered Milan in 1499, joined Ferdinand of Spain in 1501 and the two kings together conquered Naples. Although the Italian enterprise of Charles VIII had begun the Italian wars which were to last for more than forty years, this cynical appropriation of foreign territory provided a gruesome example of the bloody way in which the subsequent wars would be fought. Capua, which had been sacked in 1495, was sacked again by the French. In their enthusiasm the French slaughtered seven thousand persons.

Like his nephew Ferrantino before him, Federigo fled to the island of Ischia. But unlike his nephew, Federigo did not continue to resist. He recognized that defeated Naples, with no powerful friend to help her, could not fight the two strongest states in Europe, France and Spain. So he surrendered his throne and went into an honorable and comfortable captivity in France, where King Louis gave him the duchy of Anjou. He had reigned for only five years. Three years later, in 1504, Federigo died. He was the last, best and least capable monarch of the royal House of Aragon; and also the least known of the five kings of that house who ruled the Kingdom of Naples from the time of the conquest of Alfonso the Magnanimous in 1442 to the joint conquest by France and Spain in 1501.

That joint conquest, of course, insured further wars. Naples was divided and almost at once the two predatory powers were fighting each other over the spoils. Largely because of the military genius of Gonzalo de Cordoba Spain won and drove the French out of the kingdom. But Spanish rule did not bring peace

D*

and tranquility to the harried and miserable people of Naples.

In the sixteenth century, after the Spanish dominion was firmly established, the most famous of the Spanish viceroys was Don Pedro de Toledo, Marchese di Villafranca (1532–1554), who was always called the Great Viceroy. Don Pedro ruled with harsh severity and did his very best to stamp out brigandage. But, he complained, although he had executed eighteen thousand persons, brigandage was as prevalent as ever. So, although there were no more semi-independent barons and no more devastating civil wars, it is not surprising that some melancholy citizens of Naples looked back to the days of Ferrante, as well as to those of the first Alfonso, with sad nostalgia.

THE MAN WHOM FORTUNE LOVED

 It was only a little battle, but as usual Muzio Attendolo was winning it. He had driven the enemy back from the north bank of the Pescara River where it flows into the Adriatic Sea and had forded the flooded river with most of his cavalry. But the water was high, the wind gusty and several squadrons hesitated on the south bank. The fifty-five-year-old condottiere beckoned for them to cross. When they still did not dare, he plunged his horse into the water and started back to lead them personally.

Halfway across, his page, who was carrying Attendolo's helmet, fell from his horse and began to sink. "Poor boy!" shouted the old soldier, "will no one help you?" He leaned far out of the saddle and clutched the page's hair. But his frightened horse reared, the would-be rescuer was thrown into the water, and weighed down by his heavy armor he sank from sight. Twice his steel gauntlets, clasped as if in prayer, appeared above the water, but his body was never found. So on January 4, 1424 died the founder of the Sforza dynasty, which played so spectacular a part in the history of the Italian Renaissance.

Attendolo (called Sforza for his great strength and his forceful personality), who had fought for four popes and four kings, was one of the most successful soldiers of his day. His son Francesco

Sforza, was the most successful condottiere of all, a mercenary soldier who made himself Duke of Milan and arbitrator of the peace and politics of Italy. Francesco's eldest son, Galeazzo Maria, was an able prince but a psychopathic monster. Francesco's son Lodovico was the subtle, clever, self-destroying hero of a tragic drama which could have provided Shakespeare with a theme worthy of his genius. And Galeazzo Maria's bastard daughter Caterina was a warrior princess whose courage and cruelty made her name ring throughout all Italy. These are only the most important members of an extraordinary family, which included other able soldiers, a flamboyant and scheming cardinal, a lady of awesome learning and several feckless princes incapable of holding their thrones amid the violent tumult of the Renaissance.

Muzio Attendolo was born in 1369 in the village of Cotignola, in the northern part of the Romagna, into a family which ranked just a bare cut above the peasantry. He could hardly count, could not read and signed his name with a cryptogram. While still in his teens he joined a band of mercenary soldiers and within a few years became a mercenary captain with a band of his own. A bold fighter, a magnetic leader of men and a ruthless and treacherous commander whose fidelity could never be counted upon, the first Sforza won many victories, became high constable of the Kingdom of Naples, a queen's lover, and the proprietor of six towns in Neapolitan territory granted him as his personal fiefs. But he did not always prosper. Twice he was cast into dungeons and once he was tortured. While he was in prison he claimed that the Holy Virgin appeared to him and comforted him. Muzio was a religious man.

He was so religious that he forbade gambling and swearing in his military camps. His advice to his promising son Francesco is interesting. "I wish you to be assiduous in your observance of justice to everybody. When hereafter you come to rule over people, it will not only recommend you to the favor of Heaven, but it will make you especially popular among men. Take particular care not to offend any of your subjects by the commission of adultery. This is an injury which both the wrath of God and the bitter anger of men punish with the greatest severity."

Was this an old soldier speaking? In the Renaissance when a man's part in adultery was not even regarded as a peccadillo, much less a sin? Muzio himself had thirteen children (six of them illegitimate, including Francesco). Needless to say, Francesco paid no attention to this good advice and continued to commit adultery throughout his life, including the last night before his death at the age of sixty-five.

Muzio offered a bit of more practical advice to his favorite son: "Do not look at the wife of a friend. Do not beat anyone, or if you have beaten him, make your peace with him and send him far away. Ride no horse that has a hard mouth or a tender heel."

It is not worth our while to unravel the tangle of Muzio's intricate military and political career. But as a general he was known for his preference for battle action, in contrast to the cautious maneuvering and evasive action of his rivals. He was also famous for his harsh discipline. Any soldier who stole forage was dragged at a horse's tail. Traitors were hanged on the nearest tree. Soldiers who allowed spots or rust to deface their weapons were whipped. Those who failed to decorate their helmets with handsome plumes were mocked.

Muzio attended mass every day. He did not admit unbelievers, madmen or jesters inside his house. What did they have in common? Frivolity? Muzio was a serious character and a respected one. It is possible that he bore a burden of guilt and tried to appease his conscience.

When the first great Sforza drowned in the Pescara River, his son Francesco immediately appealed to his father's troops for their loyalty, promised them a glorious future if they would be faithful to him. He was twenty-three years old. He had been a soldier since he was twelve, had fought in his first battle at fifteen and had already won twenty-two battles. His courage, his military skill and his ability as a leader of men were well established.

Only the preceding year Francesco had demonstrated his rare combination of an astute gift for politics with mercy when mercy was expedient. Detached from his father's army he was serving in Calabria. Several experienced and able condottieri, whom Muzio had sent along to assist Francesco, announced their intention to desert to the enemy. Francesco persuaded them to stay until after the battle, which he won. He then arrested the traitors.

Muzio sent Francesco a peremptory order to execute his prisoners without delay. Francesco was shocked and surprised. His father was not usually cruel or vindictive. So Francesco asked the messenger how his father had looked when he gave the order. He was told that Muzio had been boiling with rage. Francesco decided that words spoken in an explosion of temper need not be regarded as a serious order. He had the captive condottieri brought before him and announced that both his father and he granted them a free pardon and permission to continue with the Sforzas or to depart. The traitors reenlisted. The Sforzas regained their useful services and also acquired a reputation for mercy.

When Muzio heard of Francesco's expedient generosity, he "exclaimed with tears of joy that his child was a much cleverer man than himself." It was an understatement. Francesco was cleverer than any other condottiere or prince in Italy.

Francesco Sforza was an athlete who could run faster and jump farther than anyone else, and so exceptionally strong he could lift weights of stone or iron as if they were made of wood. He ate abstemiously, drank little, required little sleep and never had trouble sleeping in a crowded, noisy army camp. Always calm, confident and judicious, he was famed for his patience, prudence and persistence—and also for his guile and ruthless determination. He could be treacherous and cruel. But he was careful not to be treacherous too often and acquire a reputation for treachery as did his contemporary Sigismondo Malatesta and his son Lodovico.

When Francesco grew older he became bald and wore the hair which grew on the sides and back of his head carefully waved in artificial curls. He was clean-shaven. His charm was great, and his eloquence and powers of persuasion were proverbial. He began life as a talented soldier ambitiously searching for an opportunity to acquire a state of his own. After he made himself Duke of Milan, he proved that his skills as a diplomat, administrator and statesman were as great as his ability as a general. He was one of the three greatest political figures of his time, along with Alfonso the Magnanimous and Cosimo de' Medici. Many of his contemporaries believed he was greater than either of those talented men.

Pope Pius II met Francesco Sforza in the autumn of 1459, when the usurping Duke of Milan was fifty-eight years old. Here is the way the scholarly pope described him:

"He sat his horse like a young man; he was very tall and bore himself with great dignity; his expression was serious, his way of speaking quiet, his manner gracious, his character in general such as became a prince. He appeared the only man of our time *whom Fortune loved*. He had great physical and intellectual gifts. Unconquered in war, he came from a humble family to a throne. He married a lady of great beauty, rank and virtue, by whom he had a family of very handsome children. He was rarely ill. There was nothing he greatly desired which he did not obtain, *and did not allow the stars which at birth (they say) he had found so propitious to be found false.* Some misfortunes however did befall him. His mistress, whom he loved passionately, was murdered by his *madly* jealous wife; his comrades in arms and old friends, Troilo and Brunoro, deserted him for Alfonso; another friend and comrade, Ciarpellone, he convicted of treason and hanged; he had to bear the treachery of his brother Alessandro, who went to France and tried to rouse the French against him; he had to imprison his son Sforza for plotting against him."

Machiavelli, writing fifty years after Francesco's death, said of him: "He was not restrained from treachery either by fear or shame; for great men consider failure disgraceful—a fraudulent success the contrary." Here in one sentence Machiavelli condensed the essence of his thinking about princes, politics and power in the Renaissance. Since Francesco Sforza was so triumphantly successful and Cesare Borgia was a failure, one might think that Machiavelli chose the wrong man as the inspiration for *The Prince*. His reason, however, is obvious. Machiavelli knew Borgia personally and never got over the impact of his sinister charm.

Francesco's charm was not sinister and it was irresistible to many. It won him the loyal devotion of his soldiers and the affectionate admiration of soldiers employed by his rivals and

FRANCESCO SFORZA, Duke of Milan

"The bastard son of an illiterate condottiere . . . endeared himself to his soldiers by remembering the names of their horses."

enemies. His magnetic presence was a guarantee of victory, in the opinion of the enemy as well as his troops. Stories were told of enemy soldiers laying down their weapons when they saw the great condottiere, uncovering their heads and saluting him as "the common father of men-at-arms."

Such personal influence is an innate gift, with which only a few soldiers are blessed. But those who have it often cultivate it with cold calculation—as did Marshal Bernard Montgomery and General George Patton in the Second World War. The one wore a black beret, and the other pearl-handled revolvers. Francesco Sforza achieved a similar picturesque touch. He never wore a helmet. And he endeared himself to his soldiers by remembering the names of their horses!

He could express his thoughts with a pithy kind of peasant wisdom. "There are three difficult things: buying a good melon, choosing a good horse, and picking a good wife. When a man wants to do one of these things, he should commend himself to God, pull his cap over his eyes, and fling himself head first into the adventure."

Like his father's before him, Francesco's military career is too intricate a tangle, too full of victories, reverses and intrigues, to be worth sorting out in detail. He served Duke Filippo Maria Visconti of Milan with distinction and success. But the pathologically suspicious tyrant threw Sforza into prison in 1428 and kept him there for two years. It wasn't the best way for an employer to inspire loyalty in his employee. But Sforza was the best condottiere available. The Duke continued to employ him for many years—even after an interval in which Sforza fought against him. When Filippo Maria released Sforza from prison, he sent him to help the city of Lucca in Tuscany which was in danger of being conquered by the Florentines.

Francesco defeated the Florentines and then accepted from them a bribe of fifty thousand ducats to go away. But he was obviously embarrassed by the flagrant dishonesty of this deal. He arranged that the bribe should be called money which the Republic of Florence had owed his father and was only now repaying. Machiavelli commented truthfully: "With mercenary soldiers, when force is insufficient, corruption commonly prevails."

Undiscouraged by this lack of energy in his service, Duke Filippo Maria tried to bind Francesco to him more securely. An engagement was announced between the condottiere and the Duke's only child, Bianca Maria, a bastard then aged eight. Sforza was thirty-one. The Duke proclaimed that Bianca Maria was his heiress. He called Francesco his adopted son, made him Count of four towns and authorized him to display the Visconti arms—a viper and a naked child—on his standard.

So Francesco's future prospects were bright indeed. But there was no way of knowing how long Filippo Maria would live. Francesco wanted to rule a state of his own as soon as possible. So, since the Duke did not require his services at the moment, Francesco marched south to carve out a state for himself in the March of Ancona.

The March is a district along the Adriatic Sea, northeast of Rome and just south of the Romagna. Like the Romagna, the March was theoretically part of the papal territories but was actually ruled by many petty despots. At this time Pope Eugenius IV was trying to enforce his claim to rule the March through a papal legate, whose cruelties incensed the population. A number of citizens appealed to Sforza for help.

Within twenty-three days Francesco Sforza conquered the entire province except for one town, Camerino. He drove out the legate. And instead of restoring the March to its local lords he seized it for himself. The Duke of Milan may have connived at this usurpation, perhaps optimistically believing that the March would be added to his own dominions to be inherited by Francesco after he was married to Bianca Maria and Filippo Maria had died. In any case, the Duke's threatening attitude intimidated Eugenius.

So, to make the best of a bad situation, the Pope made Sforza marquis of the March and commander of the papal forces. It was understood that the March would remain a fief of the papacy and that Sforza would drive out several lesser condottieri who were scheming to establish states for themselves elsewhere in papal territory. This was in 1433. Sforza ruled the March for the next fourteen years. During that time he fought with skill and success for the Duke of Milan and against him.

Eight years after his conquest of the March, Francesco Sforza and Bianca Maria Visconti were married. The Duke had tried to postpone the wedding, but he needed Francesco's help too much. The bride was seventeen, the groom forty-one. Bianca Maria was well educated, courageous, fiercely loyal to her husband. As the last surviving member of the ducal house of Visconti she was popular in Milan and enormously important as the source of Francesco's claim to succeed Filippo Maria Visconti as duke "by right."

The marriage was happy. Giovanni Sabadino referred to the "inexhaustible matrimonial love" between Bianca Maria and Francesco. And Sforza himself "thanked God for having honored him with a wife who had not her equal in the world."

Long before, when he was campaigning with his father in the Kingdom of Naples, Francesco had been married, but his wife died young, leaving him one daughter. Bianca Maria bore him eight children; and Francesco fathered eleven illegitimate children. So the grand total of his children was twenty.

Bianca Maria was a good mother and cannot be blamed for the behavior of her sons. Their Sforza-Visconti heredity and the amoral customs of their time account for many of their crimes and misdemeanors. Bianca Maria insisted that her children receive a good education according to the best humanist ideas of the Renaissance. She supervised what they were taught. She told their learned teachers, "We must remember that we have to train princes, not literary intellectuals." Bianca Maria carefully divided the children's days into hours fixed for study, for gymnastics and for training in the use of arms. Several ladies of the court were assigned to teach the children good manners.

Few powerful men united by a marriage alliance and by a community of interests have distrusted each other more than the Duke of Milan and the Marquis of the March. Filippo Maria had thrown Francesco into prison, had regularly suspected him of treachery and later organized an alliance to drive Sforza out of the March. Francesco in his turn had failed, in the customary manner of condottieri, to fight as hard for Filippo Maria as the Duke thought he should, had established a state of his own which the Duke wanted for himself and had insisted on marrying

Bianca when the Duke would have preferred to postpone the wedding indefinitely.

So it was not surprising, Renaissance war and politics being what they were, that in 1439, two years before he married Filippo Maria's daughter, Sforza should have accepted the command of the armies of Florence, Venice and the papacy in a war against Milan. Nor is it any more surprising that in 1442, the year after the wedding, the Duke of Milan should persuade Pope Eugenius, his recent enemy, that the time had come to drive his son-in-law out of the March of Ancona. An alliance was formed which proved too strong for even Sforza's military talents to resist. Its four principal members were the Duke of Milan (Francesco's father-in-law), the Lord of Rimini, Sigismondo Malatesta (Francesco's son-in-law, who had married one of his bastard daughters), Alfonso the Magnanimous of Naples and Pope Eugenius.

The war dragged on for five years with Francesco losing town after town. Filippo Maria tried to persuade one of the Marquis' best lieutenants to desert to him. Sforza did not want to lose an able man who knew too much. Nor could he any longer trust him. There was only one thing to be done: he hanged the potential deserter.

But Florence and Venice were fighting Milan. Suddenly the Duke shifted from hatred of his son-in-law to humble pleas for help. Venice was defeating him. Please come and help your poor old father-in-law, nearly blind, in danger of defeat, a defeat which will rob you forever of any chance of inheriting Milan. At first Francesco coldly refused. But his own desperate situation in the March persuaded him to change his mind. Sforza made stiff terms; he demanded 240,000 gold florins to pay his army and the right to rule the Duchy of Milan in the Duke's name as his commander in chief.

His demands were a bluff. He had lost every town in his own state save one, which he now sold to the Pope. Both Pope Eugenius and King Alfonso gave Francesco supplies to encourage him to go away. It was the low point (except for his imprisonment) and the turning point of Sforza's career. But his self-confidence never wavered. He was convinced that he was the only man who could defeat Venice and save Milan.

Marching north with four thousand men-at-arms and two thousand infantry, Sforza had reached Cotignola, his father's birthplace when news reached him that Filippo Maria Visconti, Duke of Milan, had died of a combination of malaria and dysentery in his castle of Zobbia. So seldom had the fifty-eight-year-old duke been seen by the people of Milan that when his body was brought to the city for the funeral crowds gathered to see what the grotesque tyrant looked like. His death meant freedom for the Milanese, a dismaying setback to Sforza, who had lost his employer who would have paid his soldiers.

The last Visconti duke died on August 13, 1447 without having arranged for a successor and without leaving an authenticated will. The result was a political explosion. The great Visconti citadel in Milan was torn to the ground as a symbol of tyranny. A committee of twenty-four "Captains and Defenders of the Liberty of Milan" took over the government, burned the tax records and proclaimed the Golden Ambrosian Republic (Ambrose was the patron saint of the city). Many of the towns formerly subject to Milan revolted. Venice continued the war. And the city of Pavia accepted the rule of Francesco Sforza in preference to acknowledging that of Milan—and this at a time when Milan and Sforza were negotiating to employ him on the same terms he would have had from the late duke. It was the beginning of a three-year period of bloody warfare, astoundingly intricate treachery and ultimate triumph for Sforza.

Although it is plain that Sforza intended to make himself duke of Milan at the first opportunity, he did save Milan from the Venetians and he won many minor engagements and two major triumphs. The greatest of these was his capture of the city of Piacenza, which had called in the Venetians rather than submit to Milanese rule. Piacenza was strongly fortified, well supplied and bravely defended. It was thought impregnable, but Francesco captured it after a prolonged siege and then allowed his soldiers to sack the wretched city for forty days. Thousands of people were tortured and murdered. Women and girls were raped.

Houses and churches were plundered of so much loot that rafts were used on the Po River to float the booty away. The people were robbed not only of their money and valuables but of their bedding and furniture. Many were sold as slaves. The sack of Piacenza was the most atrocious war crime perpetrated in Renaissance Italy until the horrible sacks of Capua, Brescia, Prato and Rome in the sixteenth century. It is the worst crime on Francesco Sforza's record, and it was particularly dreadful because he was usually merciful and often tried to prevent looting. Some historians have tried to excuse Sforza on the grounds that his soldiers would have deserted if they were not promised the reward of sacking the beleaguered town. This is unreasonable. The ablest and most loved and admired general of his time could have held his army together or could have recruited another. He made a deliberate choice, won great applause for his victory and hardly any blame for the sack. War in the "moderate" period of the Renaissance could be as cruel as at any time.

Sforza's other great victory over the Venetians took place in an autumn heat wave near the town of Caravaggio. The battle was something of a Sforza family affair. The Venetians were commanded by Francesco's uncle, Michele Attendolo. Francesco was greatly aided by his brother Alessandro. The heat was so severe that many horses died of heat prostration. Francesco and Alessandro captured 10,500 cavalry, 3,000 infantry and huge quantities of cannon, armor, gold, silver and grain.

The prisoners, according to the custom of the time, were stripped of their weapons, armor and outer clothing and then released. Only the officers were held as prisoners for ransom. Machiavelli tells a good story about one of the Venetian prisoners, a commissary, "who, in the course of the war and before the fight, had spoken contemptuously of Sforza, calling him 'bastard,' and 'baseborn.' Being made prisoner, he remembered his faults, and fearing punishment, being taken before Sforza, was agonised with terror; and, as is usual with mean minds (in prosperity insolent, in adversity abject and cringing), prostrated himself, weeping and begging pardon for the offenses he had committed. Sforza, taking him by the arm, raised him up, and encouraged him to hope for the best. He then said he wondered how a man so prudent and respectable as himself, could so far err as to speak disparagingly of those who did not merit it; and as regarded the insinuations which he had made against him, he really did not know how Sforza's father and Madonna Lucia, his mother, had proceeded together, not having been there, and having no opportunity of interfering in the matter, so that he was not liable either to blame or praise. However, he knew very well that in regard to his own actions he had conducted himself so that no one could blame him; and in proof of it he would refer both the Venetian Senate and himself to what had happened that day. He then advised him in future to be more respectful in speaking of others, and more cautious in regard to his own proceedings."

Here we have Francesco being merciful again; and also being smug and self-righteous as if he had never been responsible for Piacenza.

The two great victories frightened the unstable, increasingly radical government in Milan. If Sforza became too powerful, would he turn on his employers and try to make himself duke? So now began the most extraordinary example of the triple cross in the entire history of war and politics.

Sforza was besieging Brescia as a Milanese commander, hoping for an early surrender. And Milanese agents were secretly encouraging the Brescians to hold out, telling them that Milan had proposed peace terms to Venice which might soon end the war, and if this failed, Sforza would be ordered to take his army elsewhere.

While Milan and Venice were secretly negotiating peace, Venice (not intending peace) was secretly negotiating with Sforza, offering to make an alliance with him, to help him make himself duke of Milan and to employ him as the Venetian commander.

And Sforza was protesting to the Milanese that they did not trust him and did not support him adequately. While he protested Sforza made his plans, accepted the Venetian offer and then publicly pronounced that he was the rightful duke of Milan through Bianca Maria's inheritance and his adoption by Filippo Maria, and that he would enforce his just rights by arms.

Milan, of course, was deeply shocked by such treachery. The government which had tried to betray Francesco was itself betrayed. So the war continued. Instead of defending Milan against the Venetians Francesco now led Venetians against Milan. And soon he established a blockade of the city. The Milanese resisted furiously. All classes joined in denouncing the unscrupulous condottiere who had betrayed them. An extreme faction came to power and published an edict which announced that anyone who spoke favorably of Sforza would be executed. It also proclaimed a struggle to the death and promised that if Milan could not be defended successfully it would be surrendered to the Sultan of Turkey or to the Devil himself.

Suddenly a new treachery, as unexpected as the preceding betrayals of trust, brought hope to the desperate city. The Venetians, who had so persistently fought the Milanese, decided that they didn't like the prospect of Sforza's becoming duke of Milan, after all. So Venice switched sides, allied itself with Milan and the two states fought Sforza. Each city had an army larger than Francesco's.

But not even this reversal could discourage the patient, indomitable soldier. Sforza tightened his siege of Milan. The inhabitants starved. Rats, cats and dogs were eaten. The Venetians accomplished little.

Finally the famished city could resist no longer. In March of 1450 Milan surrendered to Francesco Sforza. As soon as peace terms were agreed upon, enormous crowds poured out of the city to meet the triumphant conquerer and to beg bread from his soldiers. The people who had sworn eternal hatred now welcomed Sforza with admiration and seemed to regard him as their deliverer from famine and from the total incapacity of their own government. Some cried out in Latin, quoting a sentence from the Psalms they had often heard in church: "This is the day which the Lord made, and let us rejoice in it."

Francesco Sforza rode in triumph into the miserable city of Milan. Giovanni Simonetta, his biographer, described Sforza's reception:

"Men pressed upon one another, anxious to seize his hand, or in any way to touch him. So great was the throng that for some little way his horse appeared to be carried on the shoulders of the citizens. All this time the dignity of his appearance was almost more than human; his countenance was both composed and cheerful; his words were seasoned with wonderful suavity. There was not less reverence than amity in their mode of receiving him, and he in his turn deported himself with a facility of manner and graciousness that was perfectly astounding."

Always careful of religious observances, Sforza rode to the Church of Santa Maria and entered it on horseback because the crowd was so tightly packed around him he could not dismount. There he gave thanks for his success. The next day in the great piazza the brilliant usurper was proclaimed duke of Milan by the acclamation of the crowd. Rarely in history has public opinion changed so violently; rarely have the conquered so rapturously hailed their conqueror.

The bastard son of an illiterate condottiere had achieved his life's ambition. Now he was the ruler not only of his own state but also of the state which, after Venice, was the most powerful in Italy. Most of the cities which had been ruled by the Visconti accepted his rule. But Sforza was still at war with Venice, and that war dragged on for four more years. Shortly before it ended, Venice offered a reward of a hundred thousand ducats for the assassination of the new duke of Milan.

Francesco Sforza began his reign by announcing that he intended to rule as a prince and not as a tyrant. This promise he kept. Within three days of the surrender he had enough food brought into Milan to end the famine. The taxes he imposed were not heavy. He built a great hospital, the Ospedale Maggiore, where any sick person could stay. He built a new and grand fortress-palace to replace the Visconti citadel which had been torn down by the mob. And he continued the construction of the enormous Milan Cathedral and of the Certosa of Pavia which had been begun under the Visconti.

One of his first steps combined a suitable reward for his most faithful followers with a gesture which expressed his own pleasure in the privileges of sovereignty. He created a new order of knighthood and with it honored a hundred and fifty of his officers and supporters.

From 1454, when peace was established, until his death in 1466 Francesco Sforza avoided wars and was instrumental in maintaining peace in Italy. There was no genuine, general peace, of course, but what wars there were were small. With the diplomatic astuteness which had marked all his life Sforza established friendly relations with Louis XI of France. Louis, who had plenty of problems at home, made Sforza a gift of his city of Savona near Genoa and of his claims to Genoa itself.

As usual, Genoa was torn by factional strife and had to be subdued by a slight demonstration of force, but Francesco went to vast trouble to make it appear that the Genoese wanted him to take over the rule of their city. This acquisition consolidated his rule over a large part of northern Italy and gave his landlocked state control of a major port.

Francesco Sforza was always liked and admired by many people. But he had few close friends. Of these the greatest and most helpful was Cosimo de' Medici. The two brilliant men trusted and liked each other. Cosimo lent Francesco large sums of money which made it possible for him to wage his campaign for Milan. In gratitude Francesco presented to Cosimo a site in Milan on which was built a branch of the Medici bank. Sforza was always extravagant. Cosimo, with a banker's respect for thrift, reproved Sforza for his improvident ways; Francesco replied that he would rather die than be stingy. Such an attitude has always been conventional among princes. But as a condottiere Sforza had often known what it was to be hard pressed for money. Evidently he preferred to forget those days. He forgot them so completely that when he died he owed the Medici bank more than 115,000 ducats. He had also had to pawn some of his jewels.

The great duke died of dropsy on March 7, 1466, at the age of sixty-five. His eldest son, Galeazzo Maria, was in France helping Louis XI fight some of his rebellious barons. Duchess Bianca Maria dispatched a messenger to summon him home at once and sent letters to the other princes of Italy announcing her husband's death and the accession of his heir. She then collapsed into the luxury of histrionic grief.

For two days she refused to allow the body to be moved. On the third day, when it was beginning to decompose, she repeatedly kissed the decaying face. She then made an eloquent speech in which she expressed her bitter regret that she had ever quarreled with her husband or had ever in any way annoyed him. Turning to her ladies-in-waiting, Bianca Maria said, "You who are married, I entreat you, by the Great God, be not troublesome to your lords. For, if you yourselves could but feel what I am now suffering in consequence, there is not one of you who would not henceforward be the most complacent of wives."

ACTS OF MADNESS AND THINGS THAT CANNOT BE WRITTEN

GALEAZZO MARIA was twenty-two years old when he became duke of Milan. As a boy he had been a pretty and precocious child. In 1452, when Frederick III journeyed to Italy to be crowned emperor in Rome, he stopped at Ferrara, to which Duke Francesco sent a delegation to offer diplomatic courtesies to him. It was headed by Galeazzo Maria, then aged eight, under the watchful eye of his uncle Alessandro, Lord of Pesaro and a famous condottiere in his own right. The boy delivered a Latin oration to Frederick "as long," wrote his proud uncle back to Francesco, "as two chapters of St. John's Gospel. One would have thought that he was listening to a practiced orator of thirty, and he is but eight years old."

Seven years later, when Pope Pius II went to Florence, Galeazzo Maria was sent to meet him there. Pius wrote:

"This handsome youth was not yet sixteen, but his character, eloquence and ability were such that he exhibited a wisdom greater than that of a grown man. In his expression and bearing there was the dignity befitting a prince; his extemporaneous speeches could hardly have been equaled by another after long preparation; there was nothing childish or trivial in his conduct. It was astounding to hear the sentiments of an old man issuing from the lips of a lad and to a beardless boy giving utterance to the ideas of a graybeard. His father had sent him with a splendid and magnificently accoutered escort of five hundred horsemen from Milan to Florence and thence to meet the Pope. Encountering Pius at the third milestone a little beyond the Certosa, Galeazzo dismounted and kissed the holy feet according to custom."

The second Sforza duke, so promising as a child and as an adolescent, reigned for only ten years—his short life ended by the daggers of assassins. His character was a tragic combination of good and evil, with the evil predominating. Intelligent, cultivated, a generous patron of artists and scholars, Galeazzo was a capable adminstrator, a reasonably good politician, popular with most of his subjects. But he was consumed by vanity. His unbridled sensuality and his ferocious cruelty seem to have been inspired by a deranged mind.

Much more extravagant than his father, Galeazzo lacked his father's military ability, his astute good sense and his moderation. Galeazzo's nose was curved like a hawk's beak. His feverish eyes were coal-black. His hands were too well cared for. He did not oppress the population of his duchy. Instead, he inflicted monstrous cruelties on selected individuals, many of them members of the Milanese nobility.

Galeazzo was engaged to Dorotea Gonzaga, the congenitally deformed daughter of the Marquis Lodovico of Mantua. But Galeazzo broke the engagement and married Bona, a daughter of the Marquis of Savoy. This marriage made him a brother-in-law of King Louis XI of France, who married Bona's sister.

In 1469 Lorenzo de' Medici went to Milan to attend the christening of Galeazzo's oldest son, Giovanni Galeazzo (called Gian Galeazzo), and to stand as the child's godfather. Lorenzo wrote home: "We gave the Duchess a gold necklace with a large diamond worth about three thousand ducats. The result was that the

Duke wished me to stand for all his future sons."

Three years later the Duke and Duchess of Milan returned the visit and went to Florence in such ostentatious state that it seemed excessive to the more sophisticated among the Florentines. Galeazzo's vanity carried the Renaissance cult of magnificence to an almost ludicrous extreme.

Galeazzo was accompanied by a bodyguard of a hundred men-at-arms and five hundred foot soldiers. There were fifty chargers for the Duke and fifty palfreys for the Duchess—all of the horses decorated with cloth of gold. There were five hundred pairs of hounds and many falcons. Some two thousand mounted courtiers were necessary to display the majesty of the Duke. The humblest servants were dressed in silk and velvet. The visit lasted for eight exhausting days. Machiavelli commented glumly:

"Upon this occasion the city witnessed an unprecedented exhibition; for, during Lent, when the Church commands us to abstain from animal food, the Milanese, without respect for either God or His Church, ate of it daily. Many spectacles were exhibited in honor of the Duke, and among others, in the Church of Santa Spirito was represented the descent of the Holy Ghost upon the apostles; and in consequence of the numerous fires used upon the occasion, some of the woodwork became ignited, and the church was completely destroyed by the flames. Many thought that the Almighty, being offended at our misconduct, took this method of signifying His displeasure. If, therefore, the Duke found the city full of courtly delicacies and customs unsuitable to well-regulated conduct, he left it in a much worse state."

As a ruling prince Galeazzo imposed some unpopular taxes, drafted forced labor to work on his estates and issued some arbi-

---

GALEAZZO MARIA SFORZA, Duke of Milan

"He did not oppress the population of his duchy. Instead, he inflicted monstrous cruelties on selected individuals, many of them members of the Milanese nobility."

trary and tyrannical decrees, such as the following—"To the Podesta of Pavia: No one in this city may dance after one o'clock at night on pain of his life." He was seriously concerned about the economic welfare of the state, built canals and reformed the coinage. He sponsored a printing press and maintained a choir for his private chapel. Once Galeazzo wanted to hear a popular lutist and a viola player perform. "Tell them that tomorrow they must not be drunk, but that for the rest of the year we give them leave to do as they please, so long as they are sober tomorrow."

The two other sons of Francesco Sforza who played important parts on the Renaissance stage, Lodovico and Cardinal Ascanio, were immoral and untrustworthy according to the general custom of their time. Galeazzo's crimes were psychopathic. An anonymous Ferrarese diarist wrote, "He was a man who committed acts of madness and things that cannot be written."

Galeazzo delighted in seducing or raping the wives and daughters of the nobles of Milan. He was said to take pleasure in letting their husbands or fathers know what he had done. It was even rumored that he sometimes gave up his victims to a life of prostitution.

Far more terrible than his crimes of lust were Galeazzo's crimes of sadism. Once, a priest who was also an astrologer predicted that Galeazzo would not survive the eleventh year of his reign. The Duke had him shut up in a dungeon with a loaf of bread, the wing of a capon, a glass of wine and a note saying that was all the food the victim would get. He died after twelve days.

On another occasion Galeazzo ordered a poacher who had illegally caught a hare to eat the animal whole—skin, bones and entrails. The wretch died.

A man who had been a favorite of the Duke was nailed up inside a chest. Galeazzo was said to have enjoyed listening to the dying man's moans. He also enjoyed torturing and mutilating with his own hands and sitting beside corpses in vaults.

Whether such atrocities were exaggerated by the men who recorded them it is impossible to know. But we do know that similar and worse crimes were attributed to several of Galeazzo's Visconti relations and ancestors. Galeazzo's great-great-grandfather Bernabò Visconti and his great-uncle Giovanni Maria Visconti were notorious for their abominable cruelties.

Galeazzo's mother, Bianca Maria, tried in vain to persuade her son to give up his crimes and to reform. So horrible was Galeazzo's reputation that when Bianca Maria died he was accused of poisoning his mother. But rumors of poisoning were constant during the Renaissance. It is doubtful if Galeazzo's crimes included matricide.

On the morning of St. Stephen's Day, January 26, 1476, the Duke of Milan was expected to attend Mass at the Church of San Stefano, according to his custom. Galeazzo dressed carefully. He put on a steel breastplate and then took it off, thinking it made him look fat. He wore a crimson cloak lined with ermine. His left stocking was brown, his right white. This color combination was a Sforza privilege granted to others only as a special honor. The weather was cold. The streets were slippery with snow and ice. Unfavorable omens had been observed, and the Duchess had had bad dreams. Like Caesar's wife upon the Ides of March, Bona begged her husband to stay home. Galeazzo decided to defy the weather, the omens and female premonitions. He kissed his sons good-by, mounted his horse and rode to church. There three young men, their nerves taut with excitement, were waiting for him.

All three were drunk with dreams of the glory of tyrannicide. They were disciples of a disreputable rhetorician, Cola da Montana, whom the Duke had once had publicly whipped. What his offense was is not recorded. But Cola instigated the young men with tales from Plutarch and patriotic appeals to rid Milan of a brutal tyrant. The young men did not need much urging because they were personally motivated.

Carlo Visconti's sister had been one of the Duke's victims. Andrea Lampugnano was a penniless adventurer who had been condemned to death by Duke Francesco but pardoned by Galeazzo. He resented being deprived, unjustly, of course, of a church sinecure. Girolamo Olgiati was a poet and a fanatical idealist, intent on immortal fame.

The three murderers, wearing breastplates and armed with long daggers, flung themselves on Galeazzo just as he entered the

E

church door. Lampugnano thrust his dagger into the Duke's belly and then into his throat. Olgiati stabbed him in the chest, the throat and the wrist. Visconti struck him three times from behind. *"Oh, Nostra Donna!"* cried Galeazzo and fell dead. Lampugnano tripped over a woman's long skirts and was immediately slain by a Moorish servant of the Duke. Visconti was also killed. But Olgiati fled to his father's house.

His horrified father refused to let him in. Olgiati then fled to a friend's house. There he heard the yammering of a mob, went out to satisfy his curiosity and found that the body of Lampugnano was being dragged through the streets. Olgiati was recognized, arrested and tortured frightfully. On the rack, while the skin was peeled from his body, he refused to repent and dictated an account of his pure motives. He concluded:

"And now, Oh Holy Mother of Our Lord, and you, Duchess Bona, I entreat you to provide for the safety of my soul. I petition only to be left enough consciousness and strength to confess my sins, and then I am ready to undergo my fate. I have been a great sinner and deserve far worse torture for other sins; but the righteous deed that I have done is a solace to my conscience. Far from esteeming it a sin, I believe that the Judge of all will pardon me my other offenses thereby. No ignoble motive actuated the deed, only the desire to remove an insupportable tyrant. So far from repentance am I that could I come back ten times to endure the same tortures, and consecrate every energy and every drop of blood to so noble an end, I would not hesitate to do so."

Olgiati was only twenty-two. When the executioner began to cut open his breast with a blunt knife, he cried out, *"Mors acerba, fama perpetua!"*—"Death is sharp, fame ever-lasting." Parts of his body were hung over the gates of the city, and his head was exposed on a tower.

The body of Galeazzo Maria Sforza, Duke of Milan, was wrapped in a robe of cloth of gold sent to the church by Duchess Bona and was buried in the cathedral without much ceremony.

But Bona was worried about the soul of her wicked husband. She wrote to Pope Sixtus IV, asking if he could be granted posthumous exemption from the pains of purgatory. Bona admitted that Galeazzo had committed many crimes, which she itemized, but said that "after God" she had loved Galeazzo above all else. She said that Galeazzo was "versed in warfare, both lawful and unlawful; in pillage, robbery and devastation of the country; in extortion of subjects; in negligence of justice; in injustice knowingly committed; in the imposition of new taxes which even included the clergy; in carnal vices; in notorious and scandalous simony and in various and innumerable other crimes."

And yet, Bona loved the man! The capacity of women to love scoundrels is one of the abiding marvels of the world. Pope Sixtus suggested that he might be able to do something for Galeazzo's soul if a large contribution to the defense of the Church was forthcoming. Bona paid.

THE LADY OF
FORLI

 THE ASSASSINATION OF Galeazzo Maria Sforza left the
Duchy of Milan to be ruled by his foolish and emotional
widow, Bona of Savoy, who became regent. The murdered duke left four legitimate children: Giovanni Galeazzo (always called Gian Galeazzo), now titular duke, aged seven; Ermes;
Bianca Maria and Anna. Galeazzo Maria had also found time to
father illegitimate children, of whom one, Caterina, became one
of the most famous members of the Sforza family and the second
most famous woman of the Italian Renaissance who was exceeded
in enduring celebrity only by Isabella d'Este.

There is no record of the time or place of Caterina's birth. But
she was probably born late in 1462 or early in 1463 and so was
about fourteen at the time of her father's murder, old enough to
be horribly shocked. Her father had legitimized her, and she had
been brought up in the ducal palace with his legitimate children.
Her mother, Lucrezia Landriani, was a compliant lady, who
seems to have had children not only by her husband and by the
Duke but by others as well.

Caterina was tall, slim, blond and handsome. When she was
about nine years old, she was engaged to Girolamo Riario, a
gross, uncouth, brutal and cowardly young man, who was always
called Pope Sixtus' nephew but who was believed by many to be

his son. Girolamo was the grandson of a poor fisherman of Savona near Genoa. As a very young man there, he peddled oranges and raisins in the streets and worked as a clerk in the customs house. But the election of his uncle Francesco as Pope Sixtus IV opened up a new world of wealth and power to the loutish Girolamo. Sixtus made him the count of Bosco and also the papal vicar of two nearby towns, Imola and Forli, in the Romagna.

The couple were married by proxy in February of 1477, and the fourteen-year-old bride departed for Rome, where her twenty-nine-year-old husband controlled so much military and ecclesiastical power that he was called "the Arch-Pope."

Caterina was welcomed with great ceremony and with a twenty-two-course banquet, which lasted for five hours. Between courses children recited verses, classical tableaux were staged, dancers performed a ballet and six children dressed in hunting costumes brought Caterina a variety of cooked game "all served in their natural forms."

Such splendors and the colossal expenditures of Girolamo's equally worthless older brother, Cardinal Pietro, showed where some of the papal revenues went and how far the family had come. Some authorities say that Pope Sixtus' father was so humble that he had no last name, others that his father was named Della Rovere. In any case, the name sounded aristocratic and there was an aristocratic family of that name. Sixtus kept it. Girolamo's name of Riario came from his obscure father, who married Sixtus' sister, that is, if he really was the Pope's nephew.

Soon after Girolamo was summoned to Rome to share the family fortunes, Sixtus made him Captain General of the Church and commander of the Castel Sant' Angelo, although he had no military experience or ability. Fat, lazy and arrogant, Girolamo was suspected of numerous murders and was the terror of Rome. He was so hated that he did not dare go out on the streets without an armed escort.

It is unlikely that Caterina loved such a man. Girolamo certainly did not love her. But Caterina was a tough, proud, stormy-tempered teen-ager with a strong sense of the feasible and expedient. She delighted in Girolamo's power and rank and so put up with his offensive character. Caterina was also extremely sensual.

Her first child, a daughter named Bianca, was born in the spring of 1478, when Caterina was fifteen. In the next nine years she and Girolamo had six more children. In addition, she had one son by each of her two other husbands. And in the gaps between the two lovers, whom she eventually married, Caterina was to enjoy well-publicized love affairs with at least three men who have been identified.

Only a year after their marriage Girolamo, in alliance with the Pazzi family of Florence and with the blessing of Pope Sixtus, organized a conspiracy to murder Lorenzo de' Medici and his brother, Giuliano. The conspiracy may have seemed a good idea to Girolamo because Lorenzo disliked the idea of his ruling Imola and Forli. The Romagna was to the rest of Italy then what the Balkans were to the rest of Europe in the nineteenth century. Venice, Milan and Florence all had spheres of influence. The papacy was the nominal overlord of all the petty independent states. Imola and Forli had formerly been under Florentine influence. If Lorenzo was murdered, a possible threat to Girolamo's security would be eliminated, and in the general confusion perhaps Girolamo could expand his state at Florence's expense.

As the daughter of a murdered prince, Caterina probably viewed quite calmly her husband's conspiracy to murder the Medici brothers. Political power was not pursued or held long by those who prized security more than the pleasure of ruling. She was to survive the assassination of two husbands and the natural death of a third.

Count Girolamo's incapacity and irresponsibility as a military commander were well demonstrated during the War of Ferrara when Alfonso, Duke of Calabria, intended to march to Ferrara across papal territory. Girolamo did nothing, kept the papal troops just outside the walls of Rome, sacrilegiously shot dice on the altar of San Giovanni in Laterano and gambled away the money which was supposed to pay the soldiers' wages. So it was disgust with Girolamo as well as fear of Alfonso which made Pope Sixtus appeal to Venice for help. Roberto Malatesta came and conquered, and Girolamo, who took no part in the battle, tried in vain to claim part of the credit for winning it.

When Pope Sixtus died in 1484 and Rome was beset by the violence and anarchy customary after the deaths of popes, Caterina personally seized control of the Castel Sant' Angelo in the name of her absent husband. The garrison obeyed her. When a cardinal wanted to negotiate with her for the castle's possession she exclaimed, "Ah! This man would try to outwit me! Does he not know that I am Duke Galeazzo's daughter and have his brains in my head?"

It was then that an admirer wrote of her: "Wise, brave, great, with a beautiful face; speaking little. She wore a tan satin gown with two ells of train, a black velvet hat in the French mode, a man's belt whence hung a bag of gold ducats and a curved sword; and among the soldiers, both horse and foot, she was much feared, for that armed lady was fierce and cruel." And this was about a girl of twenty-one, a girl who was seven months pregnant at the time! Caterina held the Castel Sant' Angelo for thirteen days, until she learned that her husband was not supporting her and that the game was up. She then surrendered the fortress to the cardinals and marched out.

The Count and Countess went off to the Romagna and took up residence in Forli. They built a palace and strengthened and enlarged the *rocca*, or fortress, of Ravaldino. The Count tried to make himself popular with his subjects by lowering taxes and rebuilding convents and churches. He paid his soldiers highly. But he soon ran out of money, forgot about popularity, raised taxes, cheated some of his subjects and confiscated property. So nobody liked him or trusted him. And many hated and feared him. He was suspected of being a poisoner. Caterina, who seldom feared anything, was afraid of the Count. "You cannot imagine the life I lead with my husband. It has often caused me to envy those who die."

Caterina may have detested her husband, but she never doubted for a moment his and her right to rule over Imola and Forli. In September of 1487, while the Riarios were in Imola, a few foolhardy men tried to raise a revolt in Forli, failed and were captured. The Count was not well, so the Countess rode to Forli to see that justice was done. "In the name of God," wrote an eyewitness, "the Countess had the heads of six malefactors struck off in the square, and their bodies quartered." The bodies were left on the ground until evening. Then they were hung up on one of the city gates, one of the churches and from the battlements of

the Ravaldino. Caterina had made it clear that those who dared
conspire against Riario authority did so at their peril. A few
hours later Caterina had the dismembered bodies removed and
the lesser conspirators released.

This bungled conspiracy was only a forerunner of events to
come. In 1488, when the Riarios had been settled in Forli for only
four years, the bell tolled for Count Girolamo. Two brothers,
Cecco and Lodovico Orsi, organized a new conspiracy to murder the Count and to liberate Forli from his tyranny. One of the
assassins remarked, "Better to do so to him than that he should do
it to us"—a sentiment which expresses the motives of most political assassins and tyrannicides so neatly it might well serve as an
epitaph to be carved on their tombstones.

On the evening of April 14 Cecco Orsi, captain of the Count's
guard, and two accomplices entered Girolamo's private room in
the palace. The Count was leaning on the window sill and chat-
ting with two friends. He was unarmed. "How goes it, my
Cecco?" he asked. Orsi offered Girolamo a letter, and when
Girolamo raised his hand to take it he struck under his victim's
arm with a dagger, stabbing him in the breast. The Count's two
friends fled. Orsi's friends finished off the Count, stabbing him
many times.

Count Girolamo Riario was forty-five when he was slain. His
worst crimes had been committed in Rome. His rule in Imola and
Forli had been mild. But he had made many enemies, most notable among them being Lorenzo de' Medici. Since revenge was
important to fifteenth-century Italians, it is possible that Lorenzo
had some connection with the murder of the man who planned
his own murder and succeeded in arranging the murder of his
brother. But this is speculation.

One of the horrified witnesses ran to Caterina with the dreadful news. Knowing that she and her children were probably also
marked for death, Caterina had the door to her room blocked
with heavy furniture and ordered her women servants and children to scream from the windows: "Help! Help! They have
murdered the Count! They are trying to murder Madonna!
Help! Help!"

No help came. The Orsi and their party ruled the city. They
broke into Caterina's room and took her and her children to their

own house. But somehow Caterina had managed to send a message to the fortress of Ravaldino, which held firm for the Riario, and a courier left to seek help in Bologna and Milan.

The palace was sacked by the excited mob and Girolamo's body was thrown out of a window into the town square. There it was stripped naked and mutilated. It was essential to the Orsi to obtain control of the fortress. But Caterina's secret messenger had instructed the commander, Tommaso Feo, not to surrender, no matter what happened or what she said. So when Caterina and her six children (two infants still in arms) were brought before the Ravaldino, the following dialogue took place:

"Surrender the fortress to these people to save my life and the lives of my children!"

"They can take me from here in pieces," said Feo, "but I will not yield an inch."

"They will murder me!"

"Whom will they murder? They have too much reason to fear the Duke of Milan."

A second time Caterina was brought before the castle wall, and this time Caterina persuaded her captors that if she was permitted to enter the castle she could convince Feo that he must surrender. After some debate and a reminder that her children were hostages for her good behavior, she was permitted to enter the fortress for three hours.

When the time was up, Caterina did not return. What happened then is a matter of dispute and of several legends. The best story has it that Caterina appeared on the rampart, denounced the traitors and threatened to punish them when help came from her half-brother, the Duke of Milan. The Orsi are then supposed to have held knives to the throats of Caterina's children. With furious scorn Caterina is then quoted as saying that if they murdered her children she could always make more, raising her skirts to display "the mold for casting more."

Some version of this gaudy tale was told all over Italy and was repeated by various historians, including Machiavelli. But Caterina's most learned biographer, Count Piero Desiderio Pasolini, insisted that the legend was false. Two residents of Forli who wrote at length about the Orsi conspiracy never mention the rampart anecdote, and they certainly would have done so if they

E*

had heard of it. It's too bad. One of the most famous stories of Renaissance Italy is no more to be believed than that of Washington and the cherry tree.

While the Orsi party vainly besieged the fortress, Andrea Orsi, a man over eighty, arrived in Forli from his country house and said to his sons, "What have you done?"

"We have done well," replied one of the leading conspirators. "For did not the preacher say, 'Who will be the mouse that will bell the cat?' We have belled the cat and freed the poor mice."

The old man was weak from a recent illness, but he possessed in full the cynical wisdom of the Renaissance.

"My sons," he said, "to my mind you have neither done well nor done bravely, but have rather done ill twice over. First, since you had killed the Count, you should have finished the others or have penned the whole family alive and kept them prisoners. Then you have let Madonna into the fort, to wage deadly war with you. . . . God help you! I would not have been drawn into it! You have behaved like driveling infants and will repent and suffer for it; would that others need not suffer, nor I, who am old and ill. I foresee where you will end!"

And then the old man repeated his charge: "Since you have killed the Count you should have finished them all."

As the Orsi might have expected, help came from both Milan and Bologna. When the relief force neared Forli, the principal conspirators fled. Cecco and Lodovico Orsi, with two married sons, two cousins and a brother-in-law, all scurried off. Behind them they left their wives, children and old Andrea. As soon as the flight of the Orsi was known, the people of Forli rejoiced and cheered for Caterina. But aged Andrea with his daughters-in-law and the daughters-in-law of his sons tried to find safety in the church of San Domenico. The monks said later that Andrea hid in an empty grave, lamenting, "Accursed children, whither have you brought me?" Why he did not accompany his sons in flight is not recorded. Perhaps his presence would have delayed them.

As soon as possible Caterina sent out patrols to arrest as many of those implicated in the conspiracy as possible. And, according to the senselessly destructive custom of the time, she ordered the houses of the principal conspirators destroyed. She also hung up in the piazza an edict which threatened to hang anyone who did not restore what he had plundered from the Riario palace. So frightened were the citizens that everything was brought back except what the fugitives had taken with them. Many of the lesser conspirators along with their wives and children were imprisoned in the dungeons of the fortress. Old Andrea Orsi was arrested, spat upon, beaten and thrown into a dungeon. And then in a day of horror many of the victims were tortured and executed in the piazza. "Oh, reader," wrote an eyewitness in his diary, "they who named that square the Lake of Blood told no lie!"

Before his own execution Andrea Orsi was forced to witness the destruction of the Casa del Orso. He was then cruelly tortured in the piazza before he was executed. "One of those dogs of soldiers," wrote the diarist, "tore the heart from the body, put his teeth to it, and having bitten it like a dog, threw it into the square." The fragments of the body were scattered about and only several hours later removed. On the same day the miserable women of the Orsi family were released.

The mad ferocity of such cruelty to the innocent as well as to the guilty was repeated by Caterina's orders on a subsequent occasion. Judged even by the terrible customs of the time, there was no excuse for it and no explanation except Caterina's own bloodthirsty hysteria. Perhaps this part of her character was hereditary. Caterina, whose courage and pugnacity were so great that she was admiringly called a *virago* (a woman of masculine force), was a brutal tyrant.

She was also, like her grandfather Francesco and her uncle Lodovico, a usurper. Her eldest son, Ottaviano, was the rightful Riario lord, and Caterina was only regent. But when Ottaviano, who was fat and lazy like his father, grew older, Caterina did not hand power over to him. She liked to rule too much herself and suspected that Ottaviano was incapable of doing so. She sent him off to serve Florence as an incompetent condottiere. And she remained the only ruling princess in Italy, known everywhere as "the Lady of Forli."

At this time Caterina in her spare moments was collecting a book of recipes and prescriptions which she kept with her to her death. Its beauty preparations included items to preserve smooth complexions, to dye hair blond, a wash of rose-water to keep her blue eyes beautiful, and a special cream (made partly of the lard of a male pig) to keep her large breasts smooth and lovely.

The medical prescriptions included treatments for asthma, toothache, headache, sciatica, plague and leprosy. There was a recipe to cause abortions, another which recommended roasted mouse or lion meat to cure frenzy, and a panacea made of thirty different ingredients which would cure anything! There were prescriptions for poisons also. And, since this was in the fifteenth century, there were magical formulae of great potency. One was for exorcising devils and demons, and one would transmute base metals into gold.

Caterina could rule like a man. She couldn't live without one. She was soon infatuated with a young man named Giacomo Feo, younger brother of the Tommaso who had valiantly held the fortress for her. She took Feo as a lover and then secretly married him. Cobelli, the diarist of Forli, described him: "He was a youth of twenty years or a little more, fair, beautiful and good to look upon. Now when Fortune beckoned him, he followed, and Madonna made a knight of him—captain of all her men-at-arms, vice-regent of Imola and Forli, so that he may make or mar as if he were indeed lord. And now when he rides abroad, it is with a goodly company a hundred strong, armed with partisans, lances and pikes. . . . Truly, Fortune has exalted him into the heaven of Venus and Mars. . . . There be those who say that Madonna has committed an enormity in taking her poor servant for a husband."

One contemporary wrote of Caterina's love for Giacomo Feo: "She would rather bury her sons, her relatives, and her possessions, abandon her soul to the Devil and her state to the Turk than give up Giacomo."

Feo, like other favorites raised from obscurity to power and privilege, was insolent, arrogant and much resented. He liked to wear scarlet satin and cloth of gold. One diplomat who interviewed Caterina and Feo jointly wrote: "In beauty they were like two suns."

As Feo's arrogance increased, so did the anger of numerous

courtiers and the rage and jealousy of Ottaviano. At sixteen he was old enough to rule, but he had to endure the condescension and contempt of his mother's secret husband. One day Ottaviano lost his temper and viciously insulted Feo. In return Feo struck Ottaviano in the face. Caterina stood by, and said and did nothing; she could not bring herself to defend her son against her favorite. The result was murder and massacre.

On September 27, 1495 Caterina, Feo, Ottaviano and his sister Bianca and his brother Cesare rode back into Forli from a hunting party. They were waylaid. Feo was speared, dragged from his horse, stabbed again and mutilated. Still alive, he was thrown into a pit, where he prayed for his sins to be forgiven before he died.

Caterina galloped to the fortress. So did Ottaviano and Cesare, but they did not enter, fearing that their mother would regard them as accomplices, which they probably were.

Cobelli, the diarist, went into a church where Feo's body had been taken. "Oh! The pity and the cruelty of it! Oh, reader, I never saw the like of that face that had been so beautiful. It looked like a pomegranate that had been torn open and hacked. I could not refrain from weeping, remembering him so fair and white and clean, who now lay hideous in his clotted blood, wrapped in his bedraggled coat of cloth-of-gold."

The chief murderer, Gian Antonio Ghetti, shouted to the crowd that Caterina and Ottaviano had ordered the crime. It is possible that he believed this. If Ottaviano had suggested the murder, Ghetti might have felt certain he would not have done so without his mother's connivance. Ghetti himself was killed in the turmoil. His wife and two small children were dragged to the Ravaldino fortress and there were thrown down a spiked well.

Caterina's vengeance for Feo's murder was far more terrible than for Riario's murder. The first was a matter of bloody politics. The second was politics plus the raging fury of a bloodthirsty woman avenging her lover. More than forty persons, innocent as well as guilty, were killed. A priest who was one of the accomplices was tortured by fire until he revealed the names of other guilty persons. These and their wives, mistresses and children were tortured and killed. Others were only imprisoned.

The only crime of two of these unfortunates was imprudence. One was a peasant who said in a shop that the murderers were foolish not to have killed Caterina when they killed Feo. The other was a guest at an inn who speculated about the reasons why Caterina might have been killed, too. Both were jailed on the charge of inciting sedition. One survived and was eventually set free. The other died of his sufferings in a filthy dungeon.

The torturing went on in the Ravaldino for several days. Ottaviano himself was confined there for a while. And it was widely believed that the Lady of Forli took pleasure in the sufferings of her victims.

The day after Feo's funeral Caterina announced that she had been married to him. She had a son by him, Bernardino, who was five years old at the time of his father's death. Perhaps an official announcement was intended to make sure that the child would be legitimate.

There was a third man important in Caterina's life. A handsome Florentine, only twenty-eight years old, he came to Forli as a rich businessman and speculator in grain. Giovanni di Pierfrancesco de' Medici was a member of a younger branch of the great family, a personal enemy of Piero the Exile. In short order he became Caterina's lover, political adviser, the unofficial ruler of her state and her second secret husband. Caterina, who ruled with such brutal efficiency, when in love liked to let her men rule for her. Only a year later Giovanni died a natural death. His and Caterina's son lived to become Giovanni delle Bande Nere, the greatest Italian soldier of his generation. And his son, Cosimo, lived to become the first grand duke of Tuscany and the most successful and cynically adroit Italian ruler and statesman of the sixteenth century.

Caterina was again a widow and still Lady of Forli. And she was still a cruel tyrant. Peasants slow in reporting to be drafted into her army were severely whipped. One murderer who killed Caterina's current lover was tracked down by her soldiers. Whether they killed him is not known, but they brought back his right hand and presented it to Caterina as a trophy. It was all right for Caterina to commit murder, but not for anyone else. This theory of justice was subscribed to by most Renaissance princes, including most popes.

In 1499 Cesare Borgia began his long-planned scheme to carve a state for himself out of the many petty states of the Romagna. He began by attacking the Lady of Forli. Financed and backed by Pope Alexander, supported by King Louis XII of France who lent Cesare a large force of French, Gascon and Swiss soldiers, Cesare had an army variously estimated by historians at nine thousand to fifteen thousand men. He was far more powerful than the widow who prepared to defend herself with stubborn courage and a garrison estimated between nine hundred and two thousand.

Realistically appraising the odds against her, Caterina took extraordinary measures. She tried to poison Pope Alexander VI. But the agents she sent to Rome talked too much and bungled the job. They were arrested, thrown into the dungeons of the Castel Sant' Angelo and were never heard of again. The Pope was furious and denounced Caterina as "a daughter of perdition." Caterina did not bother to defend herself or deny the poisoning attempt. At an earlier date she had expressed her political philosophy: "One cannot defend a state with mere words."

Her preparations were thorough. She sent her children and jewels to safety in Florence. She garrisoned the Ravaldino fortress and stocked it with arms, ammunition and food. She had all the buildings within a quarter mile of the city wall of Forli torn down and all the trees and shrubs within a mile cut down. She reduced some taxes to stimulate loyalty in her subjects, and she erected a gallows on the piazza to remind them of the penalty for disloyalty. She took hostages from prominent or possibly hostile families. And then she wrote a letter to the Marquis of Mantua:

"The Pope, without a semblance of Justice, persecutes Us, so that he may give this State to his son; but We, knowing ourselves to be blameless, cannot believe that God and man will withhold compassion from Us. On Our side, we despair not, but shall defend our own as long as We can, so that perchance they may find the enterprise less easy than they persuade themselves."

The "blameless" Caterina, who so rarely showed compassion to others, did not doubt that she herself deserved compassion.

First the city of Imola meekly surrendered to Borgia. Then Forli surrendered also, and Caterina in her fortress raged with contempt. Twice she refused to surrender the Ravaldino when

Borgia courteously demanded it. Then Cesare announced a reward of ten thousand ducats for Caterina dead or alive. Caterina responded with an offer of ten thousand ducats for Cesare alive, but only five thousand for him dead.

The siege began December 19, 1499. It lasted for twenty-four days in miserable winter weather. Cannon battered the fortress, and cannon in the fortress replied. Caterina, wearing armor, fought personally on the ramparts.

Finally a breach was made, the enemy swarmed in and Caterina was captured. The Ravaldino was brutally sacked. The French, Gascon, Swiss and Italian soldiers of Borgia's army slaughtered nearly seven hundred of the defenders and wounded and tortured more. Some even ripped open the bellies of the wounded in an effort to find coins or jewels they might have swallowed.

Caterina's heroic defense won general admiration—except from those who had good cause to hate her.

Cesare Borgia treated the captive "Lady of Forli" as he treated other women. He raped her, and on the next morning boasted to his companions that Caterina had defended her fortress with more determination than she had defended her virtue. He repeated his crime several more times and then took Caterina to Rome and shut her up in the Belvedere palace in the Vatican gardens. But after an escape attempt was discovered, Caterina was transferred to a cell in the Castel Sant' Angelo. Although the Riario claim to Imola and Forli was based entirely on their papal appointment as vicars of the Church, Alexander and Cesare thought that Borgia rule would be more secure if Caterina would renounce her claim—really Ottaviano's claim—to the two towns. They demanded that she do so, and Caterina stubbornly refused. After she had spent four months as prisoner in the Belvedere and a whole year in a damp and filthy dungeon, French pressure secured her release. When the Lady of Forli emerged, she was thin and haggard from insufficient food and nervous strain. Her hair had turned white. Bowing to the superior force arrayed against her she formally renounced her lordship. An argument that influenced her decision was her recognition that her sons, Ottaviano and Cesare, cared far more about money than about their mother and far more about being bishops than being petty princes.

Caterina went to Florence, where she lived the next eight years of her life. She refused to talk about her imprisonment. Her only known references to it were two. She wrote that her sufferings might be a punishment for her crimes against innocent persons after Feo's murder. And she said to her Dominican confessor, "Could I write, all the world would turn to stone." She had unquestionably endured severe hardships, but she had not been treated as cruelly as she had treated others.

During her comparatively quiet years in Florence Caterina was engaged in two lawsuits against her last husband's brother, who tried in vain to secure possession of Giovanni de' Medici's property. She grew fat, and died on May 28, 1509 of a liver ailment plus peritonitis and pleurisy. She was forty-six years old.

A PRINCE
OF VERY RARE
PERFECTION

 AFTER THE MURDER of Galeazzo Maria, Duchess Bona ruled Milan as regent for two years and eight months. She was a foolish and stupid woman called a *dame de petit sens* by Commines. During her regency actual power was held by Cecco Simonetta, former secretary to Francesco Sforza and the brother of Francesco's biographer, Giovanni Simonetta. This situation did not please the late duke's brothers.

There were five of them. The eldest, Filippo, was a nonentity, content to remain obscure in private life. The next oldest, Sforza (Sforza Sforza, what a name!), and the youngest, Ottaviano, died. That left the ambitious and crafty Lodovico and the ambitious and wily Ascanio, already a priest, to intrigue and wage a sort of guerrilla war against Bona and Simonetta. Neither loyalty to the child duke, Gian Galeazzo, nor respect for Simonetta's lifetime of faithful service to the Sforzas could divert the brothers' drive for power.

In September of 1479 Lodovico Sforza, then twenty-eight years old, secretly entered Milan and was admitted to the Sforza castle by a postern gate. No one knows what arguments Lodovico used or what magnetic spell he cast during his fateful interview with his sister-in-law. But a reconciliation was effected, and Lodovico persuaded Bona that he, and not Simonetta, should be supreme in Milan. The shrewd old man, when told by Bona of the new state of affairs, warned her not to trust Lodovico. "I shall lose my head, and before long Your Serene Highness will lose your state."

Cecco Simonetta was too experienced a politician and had too many enemies to be left at large for long. Lodovico had him arrested and imprisoned at Pavia. Simonetta's money was safe in a Florentine bank; even under torture he refused to sign it away, insisting it belonged to his rightful heirs. Soon after, he was beheaded. He was seventy years old. This act of needless cruelty is the only one of its kind charged to Lodovico Sforza, who was kind and merciful by the standards of his age.

Lodovico swiftly concentrated his power. He had his young nephew crowned duke and himself made guardian, and soon afterward regent. He exiled Bona from Milan. And he even sent Ascanio away. Lodovico wanted to be sole ruler without the embarrassing presence of a brother as able and as unscrupulous as himself. Ascanio became an influential cardinal, drew a large income from Milan and loyally helped the Sforza dynasty interests. Even so, Lodovico wrote him: "Monseigneur, pardon me if I do not trust you although you are my brother."

It was not a tactful remark, but it was a frank expression of an attitude common among Renaissance princes. Strong family feeling was frequently found among the ruling families; but rivalry, jealousy and murder were frequent, too. Cesare Borgia is believed by most historians to have murdered his elder brother. Cardinal Ippolito d'Este ordered thugs to blind his halfbrother. Carlo Gonzaga led an army against his brother Lodovico, Marquis of Mantua, in the hope of seizing his state. Family ties were never a guarantee against treachery and violence.

Lodovico Maria Sforza, regent and later duke of Milan, usurped the rule of the duchy first from his sister-in-law and then from his nephew. The most splendid and powerful of Renaissance princes, he blazed across the Italian skies like a comet, fascinating everyone by his brilliance, his magnificence and his

LODOVICO MARIA SFORZA, Duke of Milan

"Like a tragic hero he was destroyed by fatal flaws in his own character . . . In some respects he resembled Macbeth, a sovereign with a flawed title to his crown brooding over his lack of official legitimacy as a ruling prince."

good fortune before he plummeted to ignominious disaster. Lodovico was greatly talented and of high estate. But like a tragic hero he was destroyed by fatal flaws in his own character: hubris, vanity, self-doubt and cowardice. In some respects he resembled Macbeth, a sovereign with a flawed title to his crown, brooding over his lack of official legitimacy as a ruling prince. In other respects he resembled Richard III, a monarch who benefited from the death of his nephew, the rightful ruler. Richard, most historians believe, was at least morally responsible and probably directly responsible for the murder of the little Princes in the Tower of London. Whether Duke Gian Galeazzo Sforza died of poison or of illness and dissipation is unknown.

Many of Lodovico's contemporaries believed that he poisoned the simple-minded young man. Rumors of poisoning were a staple of Renaissance gossip. But was Lodovico, the hesitant intellectual who shunned violence, capable of poisoning his own nephew? If he was not, others were. Could some underling have arranged a poisoning to further the interests of his master? Unanswerable questions. So Lodovico, like Duke Francesco before him, marches down the long perspective of history under a shadow—the possibility of his responsibility for the murder of an inconvenient relative.

The new ruler of Milan had an aquiline nose, small but expressive brown eyes, a fat face and a double chin. His complexion was dark. His dark hair was cut in a bang just above his eyebrows and fell thickly down over his short bull neck. His lips were sensual and his mouth was small. He wore a ruby ring incised with Caesar's head and a handsome gold chain. He liked gorgeous clothes and was fond of robes of ducal red. His favorite motto was: I will treat you as you do me.

Throughout Italy Lodovico Sforza was called *il Moro*, the Moor. This was not because of his dark skin, as has been often reported. One of Lodovico's names was Mauro; as a child he was called Il Moro in the nursery and the nickname stuck. When Lodovico was five, the name Mauro was officially changed to Maria in honor of the Virgin. As a child Lodovico displayed the same precocity as did his elder brother Galeazzo Maria and his learned sister Ippolita. He had a remarkable memory, spoke Latin fluently, was genuinely interested in art and literature, had a head for figures, was an excellent administrator and an adroit diplomatist. He could dissemble and betray as expertly as any prince or monarch of the fifteenth century. Cynical, amoral, wildly extravagant, bemused by a dream of his own glory and magnificence, childishly vain and boastful, Lodovico Sforza was a bundle of contradictions. He could be eloquent. He was often charming. Women loved him; he had many mistresses and was always kind to them. He was polite and never lost his temper. He was not cruel and rarely condemned even convicted criminals to death.

With an intricate network of alliances, with subsidies for minor princes, with secret agents as well as ambassadors everywhere, Il Moro was influential and superbly well informed. But some observers had their doubts about the magnificent ruler of Milan. In 1489 the Ferrarese ambassador wrote from Pavia: "He is a great man, and intends to be what he is in fact already—everything. And yet who knows? In a short time he may be nobody."

And Lodovico, who was certainly clever, thought that he was cleverer than he was, cleverer than anybody else. He misjudged individuals and by his arrogance antagonized and aroused jealousies. One of the great nobles of Milan and one of the finest soldiers in Italy was Gian Giacomo Trivulzio, who had loyally supported Galeazzo Maria. Lodovico passed him over and made his handsome and charming favorite Galeazzo Sanseverino commander of the Milanese armies. Trivulzio, an older and far abler general, was mortally offended. He went into exile and nursed his hatred for Lodovico. When the French army of Louis XII conquered Milan in 1499, its commander was Trivulzio. A year later, after Lodovico had reconquered his state, had been defeated a second time and captured, the two men met again. The distinguished prisoner refused to humble himself before his triumphant enemy and summed up their enmity in a scornful question: "Who can tell why he loves one man and hates another?"

IN JANUARY OF 1491 Beatrice d'Este, the younger daughter of Ercole d'Este, Duke of Ferrara, was married to Lodovico

Sforza, Regent of Milan. The bride was fifteen, the groom thirty-nine. Ten years before, Lodovico had offered himself as a husband to Beatrice's elder sister, Isabella. Ercole had replied that Isabella was engaged to Francesco Gonzaga, heir to the Marquis of Mantua. Would Beatrice do, instead? She would. Beatrice became engaged at the age of five. But when the time for the wedding came, Lodovico kept finding excuses for putting it off. He was in love with his current mistress, a noble Milanese lady named Cecilia Gallerani, who was as famous for her learning as for her beauty. Cecilia spoke and wrote Latin fluently, wrote sonnets in Italian and entertained the theologians and scholars who visited her by delivering Latin orations. Cecilia, who was pregnant at the time of Lodovico's wedding, bore him a son, who was christened Cesare. Leonardo da Vinci painted her portrait. (Years later, after Beatrice's death, her sister Isabella wrote Cecilia a cordial letter asking if she could borrow the Leonardo picture. She wanted to see an example of Leonardo's portraiture.)

When the wedding could be postponed no longer, Lodovico arranged to make it a double one by marrying his niece, Anna Sforza, to Ercole's heir, Alfonso d'Este. The preparations were elaborate. Il Moro dispatched a circular letter to all the cities of the duchy, ordering their best painters to come to Milan to paint decorations for the wedding festivities. There would be profit and honor for the artists who came; those who failed to come would be fined twenty-five ducats and incur his displeasure! The painters came and covered the walls of the state ballroom, a hundred and sixty feet long, with frescoes depicting Francesco Sforza's victories. The ceiling was painted blue with gold stars.

So many guests planned to attend the double wedding bringing with them so many attendants that Lodovico felt compelled to ask them to reduce the size of their suites. Isabella d'Este, still a teen-ager herself but now the wife of Francesco Gonzaga, was much annoyed that she had to limit herself to only fifty people and thirty horses instead of the hundred and fourteen people and ninety horses she had intended to bring with her.

The wedding procession which rode into Milan on an icy-cold January morning was long and grand according to the most exacting standards of Renaissance magnificence. Lodovico himself wore a shining golden costume. The gorgeously dressed riders on their gaily decked horses filed through the Via degli Armorai where, in honor of the bridal couples, the celebrated Milanese arms makers had lined both sides of the street with samples of their wares. Swords, lances and shields shone brightly in the winter sunlight. Complete suits of armor, with the visors of their helmets lowered, were propped on armored horses—wooden ones presumably.

The young bride from Ferrara was no beauty. Her childish face can still be seen in the superb portrait bust by Cristoforo Romano now in the Louvre. Plump cheeks, round forehead, small mouth and petulant expression suggest Beatrice's immaturity. They convey no motion of the intelligence, rash courage and emotional high tension she would soon display.

Since princely marriages were diplomatic alliances not arranged to suit the fancies of the brides, most Renaissance princesses did not expect to love their husbands or to be loved by them. They were reasonably content if they were treated with respect and kindness. It was Beatrice's misfortune to love her husband. She forgave him his past mistresses, who did not concern her, became a close friend of his bastard daughter Bianca and furiously resented his current mistress.

Lodovico was miffed. What conceivable cause had Beatrice to be upset and angry? Didn't all princes keep mistresses? He confided to the Ferrarese ambassador that he still enjoyed Cecilia Gallerani's company because Beatrice was being so disagreeable.

Beatrice d'Este, who married at fifteen, died at twenty-one. In those few years she established herself as a woman of fierce ambition, ostentatious pride and capricious willfulness. Lodovico learned to love her sincerely, although he never remained faithful to her. He valued her advice and in his frequent moments of indecision depended upon her for guidance.

Probably because she was young and insecure, and unhappy about her husband's infidelity, Beatrice was determined to dominate the court, and the court included the nominal duchess, her first cousin, Isabella of Aragon, wife of Gian Galeazzo Sforza. The feud between the two young women was grim. Beatrice won it and enjoyed flaunting her finer clothes, her grander jewels and her social leadership.

BEATRICE D'ESTE SFORZA, Duchess of Milan

"Her childish face can still be seen in the superb portrait bust by Cristoforo Romano now in the Louvre . . . a woman of fierce ambition, ostentatious pride and capricious willfulness."

To divert herself and to disguise her unhappiness Beatrice kept herself furiously busy—designing clothes, sewing, hunting, dancing, gambling. In the course of the year 1494 Beatrice won three thousand ducats at cards. She would ride for thirty miles without dismounting. She narrowly escaped injury in encounters with a wild boar and with a frightened stag and took neither danger seriously. Only two years after her wedding Beatrice had in the Sforza summer palace of Vigevano, four hundred and twenty-four dresses! How many she had left behind in the Rochetta at Milan is not recorded.

Beatrice was short and plump. Her sister Isabella wrote of her, somewhat waspishly: "Some day she will be as fat as Mother." She wore jewels always—pearls, rubies, emeralds and diamonds—and wore them even when she went hunting. Her favorite costume was the *camora*, a full dress which fell to her feet. It had a low, square bodice laced in front, with sleeves of a different material and color from the rest of the dress. She often wore her hair in a Milanese fashion called the *cuazzone*. This was a long pigtail, which fell down past her hips, in which the hair was wrapped up in a white cloth and bound with a black cord in a criss-cross pattern of repeated x's.

Beatrice and her many ladies-in-waiting usually wore dresses of different kinds, but occasionally they all appeared in identical dresses like girls in a school uniform. They often wore garments with embroidered, decorative designs—mottoes, heraldry, emblems, and even notes of music on their dresses. Beatrice was fond of ribbons, gold cords, slashings—of anything, in fact, that was decorative, fancy and expensive.

She could gratify any caprice, any whim. In the first year of her marriage she wrote to Isabella: "I must tell you that I have had a whole field of garlic planted for you, so that when you come here, you may have your favorite dish in abundance." We can only hope that this was a joke. It would be dismaying to think that garlic really was Isabella's favorite dish.

Frivolous, excitable, sometimes almost hysterical though she was, Beatrice had an inner core of cold good sense. Lodovico trusted her so much that he sent her as an envoy to the Venetian Republic, where she delivered a much admired diplomatic oration.

Beatrice and Lodovico had two sons: Ercole, whose name was later changed to Maximilian, and Francesco.

Late in November of 1496 Lodovico's daughter Bianca, the wife of Galeazzo Sanseverino, died, to the great grief of Beatrice who lost her best friend. Beatrice was pregnant again and had still another cause for grief. Lodovico had taken one of her own ladies-in-waiting, Lucrezia Crivelli, for his new mistress. The lady was beautiful and her husband was cooperative. She, too, was pregnant by Lodovico. Lodovico was so infatuated with her that he had Leonardo da Vinci paint her portrait.

Beatrice was desperately unhappy. On the afternoon of January 2, 1497 she gave a party in her suite in the Rochetta and danced furiously and recklessly. A miscarriage followed, and early the next morning Beatrice died.

"And when the Duchess Beatrice died," wrote the poet Vincenzo Calmeta, "everything fell into ruin, and that court, which had been a joyous paradise, was changed into a black inferno."

Lodovico Sforza, knowing how miserable he had made the wife he loved in his own inadequate fashion, was overcome with remorse and guilt. Early the next morning he wrote to the Marquis of Mantua, husband of Isabella d'Este:

"Most Illustrious Ally and Very Dear Brother,

My wife was seized with sudden pains yesterday at eight o'clock. At eleven, she gave birth to a dead child, and half an hour after midnight yielded her soul to God. So premature and cruel an end has filled me with such bitter and indescribable consternation that I had far rather have died myself than lose what I held dearest and most precious in the world. In the great and excessive pain that I feel beyond all measure, and knowing what yours will be like, I feel I must tell you myself, on account of the brotherly friendship that exists between us. I beg of you to send no one to offer me consolation, as such would only renew my grief. I have not wished to write to the Marchioness and leave you the duty of breaking the news to her as seems best to yourself, knowing full well that her grief will pass all bounds. . . ."

To appease his conscience and to dramatize his grief Il Moro shut himself up in a room hung with black, dressed in a long mourning cloak and took all his meals standing. One hundred candles were lit daily around Beatrice's stone sarcophagus in the Church of Santa Maria delle Grazie, and Lodovico came every day and prayed beside her tomb. "The Duke has become very pious; he attends Mass every day, fasts and lives in chastity," reported the Venetian ambassador.

There was something histrionic and insincere in such extravagant demonstrations of sorrow. They did not, however, last very long. When Lucrezia Crivelli gave birth to a son, named Gian Paolo, Lodovico rejoiced at what seemed to him a sign of divine forgiveness of his sins. He gave Lucrezia a handsome present, resumed his normal routine of life and even considered marrying again.

Two years before Beatrice's death, just after Charles VIII had left Pavia and gone to Piacenza to join his army, the pitiable Gian Galeazzo died. Lying on his deathbed in the great palace at Pavia, he summoned the only living creatures whom he loved and who loved him—his hounds and horses. The animals were brought into his fetid chamber. Gian Galeazzo patted them affectionately. The pale, weak, depraved young man, whose only interests were hunting and gluttony, had been a total failure as a husband to his unhappy wife, Isabella of Aragon. He would have been a total failure as a duke if Lodovico had allowed him to rule as well as reign. Nevertheless, Isabella mourned him passionately. Her grief was probably not so much for the dead man as for her son and for herself. She knew that Lodovico would never acknowledge the child as duke and that she would never be regent or the mother of a duke.

Gian Galeazzo died on the night of October 20th, and that very night messengers galloped off in the darkness with a letter for Il Moro marked *cito, cito, cito,* the traditional token of urgency written on all letters reporting death. They found Lodovico with Charles in Piacenza. Lodovico immediately hurried to Milan.

He arrived there before the news did and called a meeting of the Grand Council in the castello. With suave hypocrisy he proposed that the legitimate heir be recognized as duke. But Lodovico had made sure in advance that his supporters on the council should object that "the circumstances of the state are such that a small child cannot be entrusted with this dignity." The ducal crown was thrust upon him, and Lodovico accepted it. He then rode in triumph through the streets of Milan as the new duke. Gian Galeazzo's death had certainly been convenient. By an outmoded medieval legalism, Milan was an imperial fief, just as Naples was a papal fief. Francesco Sforza and Galeazzo Maria had never received imperial investiture as dukes of Milan and so ruled only as de facto dukes and usurpers. This troubled them not a whit; nor did it trouble other ruling princes. But Lodovico yearned to be a legitimate duke, with all the trimmings. He explained. He argued. He protested too much when he should have kept quiet.

Once King Ferrante's ambassador, blandly ignoring the fact that Ferrante's granddaughter was married to Gian Galeazzo Sforza, suggested to Lodovico that, since the young duke was good for nothing, lazy and mentally backward, Lodovico might as well assume the title as well as the duties of the Duke. Telling the Florentine ambassador about this suggestion, Lodovico insisted that this would be a crime of which he would never be guilty. "If I were to attempt such a thing, I should be infamous in the eyes of the whole world." This fine moral position was the peak of hypocrisy. Il Moro certainly planned to be duke sometime.

While Gian Galeazzo was still alive, he made a deal with the Emperor Maximilian. Young Bianca Maria Sforza, Gian Galeazzo's equally simple-minded sister, was married by proxy in great splendor to Emperor Maximilian, a widower. Her dowry was 400,000 ducats. The impecunious emperor was not interested in Bianca Maria, but so huge a bribe was irresistible. In return he promised to invest Lodovico as duke, which he did the following year after the death of Gian Galeazzo. To appease his hankering for legitimacy Lodovico had squandered more than half his annual revenue to obtain a nearly worthless confirmation of a title he had already assumed.

THE COURT of Milan under Lodovico was a major center of Renaissance culture and elegance. Even its menagerie was larger than that of other princely courts. Lodovico had so many lions he gave some of them away. The court's influence was felt across much of Italy. Some writers have even claimed that this glittering, splendid, cultivated and amoral court was Lodovico's most important achievement, although he was an effective ruler and a subtle diplomat. But his rule ended in conquest by the French and his diplomacy failed. While it lasted, his court was a triumphant success. There, among others of great talent, Bramante, the greatest architect of his generation, labored in Lodovico's service.

In 1482, when Lodovico Sforza had ruled in Milan for three years, he received a letter from a Florentine artist applying for a job. The artist was Leonardo da Vinci. He was thirty years old and he stressed his talents as a military engineer rather than as a painter:

"Most Illustrious Lord, having now sufficiently seen and considered the proofs of all those who proclaim themselves masters and inventors of instruments of war, and finding that their invention and use of the said instruments does not differ in any respect from common practice, I am emboldened without prejudice to anyone else to put myself in communication with your excellency, in order to acquaint you with my secrets, therefore offering myself at your pleasure effectually to demonstrate at any convenient time all those matters which are in part briefly noted below:

"1. I have plans for bridges, very light and strong and suitable to be carried very easily, with which to pursue and at times flee from the enemy, and for others, solid and indestructible by fire or assault, easy and convenient to transport and place in position. Also plans for burning and destroying those of the enemy.

"2. When a place is besieged, I know how to cut off water from the trenches, and how to construct an infinite variety of bridges, mantelets, and scaling ladders, and other instruments pertaining to the said enterprise.

"3. Also, if a place cannot be reduced by the method of bombardment, because of either the height of its glacis or the strength of its position, I have plans for destroying every fortress or other stronghold, even if it is founded upon rock.

"4. I have also plans for making mortars, very convenient and easy to transport, with which to hurl a tempest of small stones, causing great terror to the enemy by reason of the smoke, and great loss and confusion."

Leonardo went on through five more paragraphs itemizing his virtues as an inventor of warlike engines and only in his tenth and concluding paragraph mentioned that he was also qualified as an architect, sculptor and painter. It is plain that he thought that the usurping lord of Milan would be more interested in the arts of war than of peace.

Leonardo got the job. In Milan he was Lodovico's court painter, military and civil engineer, producer and designer of theatrical shows, interior decorator, and architectural adviser. With serene equanimity and seemingly equal interest Leonardo painted "The Last Supper" and designed tournament costumes for Galeazzo Sanseverino. He even designed Galeazzo's stables! Leonardo lived like a lord himself, dressing like one and with manners as lordly as those of any prince in Italy. And in his private notebooks Leonardo drew sketches of everything: animals, anatomical drawings, faces, tanks and airplanes, an ingeniously designed brothel with three entrances and an improved toilet seat.

His major project was to create a memorial to Francesco Sforza which he hoped would be the finest equestrian statue ever made. For years Leonardo worked intermittently on the clay model, which was always called the *cavallo*—the horse. When it was finally completed, it was regarded as a work of genius, but it was never cast in bronze. Lodovico, who was pressed for funds, sent the hundred and fifty thousand pounds of bronze which were intended for the horse to Ercole d'Este in Ferrara to be made into cannon. Leonardo was philosophical. He wrote to Lodovico: "Of the horse I say nothing, for I know what the times are like."

When the French conquered Milan in 1499, Gascon archers shot arrows at the horse for fun or in practice and damaged it, but not severely. The following year Ercole tried to buy the clay model but was refused on the grounds that it was now the property of King Louis XII. What became of it is not known.

Lodovico did not always pay Leonardo his salary. While Leonardo was decorating several small rooms in the Rochetta for Lodovico's young wife, Beatrice d'Este, he was not paid. He wrote to Il Moro somewhat plaintively: "Perhaps Your Excellency has given no order to Messer Gualtieri in the belief that I have money." Later, when he was still unpaid, Leonardo wrote again: "It vexes me greatly that having to earn my living has forced me to interrupt the work which Your Lordship entrusted to me." He went on to say that he had not been paid for three years' work!

Lodovico was rich, but extravagant. In the great age of art patronage one of the world's supreme artistic geniuses had to plead to be paid. But the arrears must have been made good because prince and painter were reconciled and Leonardo was commissioned to decorate the wall of the refectory of the Dominican monastery of Santa Maria delle Grazie. He began work on "The Last Supper."

When the great picture was well on its way to completion, the prior of the monastery came to Lodovico and complained that it lacked the two key figures, those of Judas and Christ. Lodovico took the matter up with Leonardo, who said:

"What do the monks know of an artist's work? Can they paint? It is quite true that I have not been to the monastery for a long time. Nevertheless, not a day passes but I devote at least two hours to the work."

Lodovico asked how Leonardo could do that if he did not go to the monastery.

"Your Excellency is aware that Judas is missing. I cannot find features fit for so abandoned a character. I have been going every day, morning and evening, for more than a year to the criminal quarter, in which the scum of humanity live; but I have not yet found what I want. If I continue to search in vain I shall have to use the prior's head. It would serve well for the purpose. I have only hesitated to do this out of consideration for his feelings."

Lodovico was so amused that he repeated the story and Leonardo's joke became a widely believed story that the prior had unknowingly served as the model for Judas.

In addition to "The Last Supper," Leonardo painted on the

opposite wall of the refectory a picture of Lodovico, Beatrice and their two sons. It has disintegrated, leaving only shapeless stains. In April of 1499 Lodovico purchased a vineyard just outside the wall of Milan and presented it to Leonardo. Il Moro said that Leonardo could build a house on the property and so "strengthen the bonds which already unite him with our person."

So it was that for seventeen years Leonardo da Vinci served Lodovico and went his enigmatic way, creating immortal masterpieces, designing ephemeral costumes and stage effects, keeping the fantastic journals in cipher which contained the speculations and theories of the most versatile mind the world has known. Leonardo remained longer at Lodovico's court than he did anywhere else—perhaps the most important evidence that there was more to the paradoxical prince than his deviousness and egoism.

On the whole, Lodovico Sforza was a generous patron to Leonardo. Yet, after the French conquest of Milan, Leonardo left the city and dryly commented on Lodovico's tragic fate in his notebook: "The Duke has lost his state and his possessions and his liberty, and has brought none of his works to completion." No suggestion of pity or friendship. Leonardo was a genius, but his detached indifference to the woes of others seems inhuman.

ONE OF Lodovico's major faults was his boastfulness. He especially enjoyed inviting guests to inspect his treasures stored in an inner room of the castello in Milan. This was not only vulgar ostentation; it was politically foolish. It aroused jealousy and cupidity. It was no doubt harmless to display his wealth to Isabella d'Este, his sister-in-law and wife of the Marquis of Mantua. But to invite the French ambassadors to inspect his treasures did more than impress them—it spread abroad tales of the fabulous wealth of Milan which made that state seem an even more attractive goal to be won by the conquering might of France.

The Ferrarese ambassador wrote back to Duke Ercole:

"In the Silver Room spread on the ground were carpets about sixteen yards long and three yards broad, and thereon lay a great many bushels of ducats, the total of which was estimated as between 650,000 and 800,000 ducats. Then there were long tables

F

on which were laid out the jewels, chains and golden collars of their Highnesses—a very beautiful and valuable display. There were sixty-six silver *sancti* all around the walls of this room, together with three or four beautiful crosses loaded with precious stones. Then there was the Annunciation and Coronation of Our Lady, with great decoration of angels and other saints, that was not the least beautiful of the treasures there. Finally, in a corner of the hall, there was so much silver money, piled in such a great heap that a stag could not leap over it. There were also silver candelabra, of the size of a man or thereabouts. At last we were admitted to the place where the silver of greater value was kept. The whole treasure was valued at 1,500,000 ducats."

While his affairs prospered, Lodovico's pride and arrogance were so blatant that he almost seemed to be challenging the vengeful gods. He boasted that he was "Fortune's child." He encouraged the circulation at his court of a jingle: "God only and the Moor foresee the future safe and sure." And in a moment of mad intoxication with his own glory he said, "The Pope is my chaplain, the Emperor my general, the seigniory of Venice my stewards, and the King of France my courier." Megalomania could go no further.

And yet, this same man was timid in adversity, always apprehensive, ridden by self-doubts and full of the need to justify himself.

THE STATE which Lodovico Sforza ruled for twenty years, from 1479 to 1499, was the second richest and the second most powerful in Italy. Only Venice was greater. It included numerous subject cities, among them Pavia, Piacenza, Parma, Como and Genoa. Its annual income from taxes was 650,000 to 700,000 ducats a year, "which is absolute tyranny and makes the people prone to revolution," wrote Commines. This was an exaggeration. The Milanese did not love their Sforza rulers, but they admired their magnificence and endured their rule passively.

Toward the end of the fifteenth century Milan itself had a population of about a hundred thousand, the duchy about a million. The capital city was an important center of the silk industry and of banking, and it manufactured the finest armor and weapons in Europe. Other trades were those of the goldsmiths, ironworkers, woodcarvers, enamelers, embroiderers, perfumers, tapestry-weavers, potters, glass workers and makers of playing cards.

The rich merchants and the nobles lived in fine palaces. And so many citizens of Milan were rich that at a time when the first carriages were just coming into use there were sixty four-horse carriages in the city and many times as many two-horse carriages. In Paris then, there were only three families who owned carriages. No wonder the French were impressed by the riches of the duchy they conquered so often but could not hold!

The great Sforza castello in Milan built by Francesco to replace the Visconti castle razed by the mob was half castle, half palace. A huge square structure of red brick which weathered to pink, it was surrounded by a moat crossed by sixty-two drawbridges. Swans floated in the moat. Inside the great wall was the square ducal palace, and inside its square courtyard was a smaller palace called the Rochetta. There were cloisters and ballrooms, huge halls and smaller chambers, rich hangings, fine furniture, murals and paintings, a fine library. Five hundred guards protected the castello. Eight hundred courtiers and servants swarmed in it, and five hundred horses and mules were quartered in its stables.

It was in the Rochetta that Lodovico lived in state and it was there that he kept his treasure room. Gian Galeazzo lived in the larger ducal palace when he was not living in the other great Sforza palace at Pavia. Here in the castello of Milan Lodovico Sforza presided over the most luxurious and magnificent court in Italy. Here scholars and artists enjoyed his generous patronage and wasted much of their time on frivolous pursuits. Here the ladies and gentlemen of the court watched pageants, danced at balls, feasted at banquets and delighted in ritualized tournaments.

After the retreat of Charles VIII to France in 1495 Lodovico Sforza knew four years of power and glory. He did not seem to fear that the French would return, and until too late took no steps to resist them if they should. He lavished large sums on the model farm he maintained at Vigevano. He patronized astrologers as generously as he did artists and appointed four of them professors at the University of Pavia. Like most of his contemporary princes, he played crude practical jokes. Once while the court was staying at the summer palace at Vigevano, Lodovico collected foxes, wild cats and other animals by paying a ducat a head to the local peasants, and had them all let loose inside the house of the Ferrarese ambassador, a timid soul named Trotti. Terrified by this invasion, Trotti fled back to his house in Milan. That wasn't enough for Lodovico. He had the animals carried to Milan in sacks and let loose again in Trotti's garden.

Except for Beatrice's death, nothing seemed to go wrong for the great duke of Milan. "All that this man attempts succeeds," wrote a contemporary, "and all that he dreams of during the night comes to pass during the day. In truth, he is esteemed and respected throughout the whole world, and considered as the wisest and happiest man in the whole of Italy. Everyone fears him, for he is Fortune's favorite in all he lays his hand to."

And then in the summer of 1499 the French came again and the army of King Louis XII commanded by Trivulzio easily defeated the Milanese army ineptly commanded by Galeazzo Sanseverino, who was a fine soldier but a totally incompetent general. Almost in a day the mighty fell and the power and glory departed. In his extremity the proud Il Moro was reduced to making a speech in the piazza of Milan appealing to the citizens for their support. Guicciardini (in the quaint Elizabethan prose of Fenton's translation) summarized part of Lodovico's futile address:

"They had lived many years under him in great tranquility, & by that benefit their city raised into a wonderful estate & majesty of riches, reputation and glory, as was well expressed in the aspect of so many pomps, glories & honors, with the multiplication of almost infinite sciences and inhabitants: benefits, wherein the town & Duchy of Milan, doth not only give place, but doth exceed all other Climates & regions of Italy: That they should remember that, that he had governed them without blood & cruelty, & with what affability & readiness he had heard everyone, & that he only (above all the Princes of his time) without bearing respect to the pains & travails of his person, observed the days appointed for public audience & always had given to every one a ready expedition & upright justice: That they should bear respect & remembrance to the merits & gracious behaviors of his father, who had governed them rather in an affection of children, then in the property and condition of subjects: and withall to set before their eyes, how hard & grievous it would be for them to bear the proud & insolent yoke of the French, who, for the neighborhood and nearness of the realm of France (if they once came to command over the state of Milan) would plant there their perpetual dwelling, & chase out the inhabitants."

It did no good. The Milanese felt no affection for Il Moro who had taxed them heavily. They were sure that the French would triumph. They rioted in the streets and prepared to welcome them.

On August 31 Lodovico sent his and Beatrice's two sons to Como on the way to safety and exile in Austria under the protection of Emperor Maximilian. In their train went twenty mules laden with baggage and a wagon covered by a black canvas drawn by eight horses. In the wagon were what remained of Lodovico's jewels and 240,000 gold ducats.

Three days later Lodovico left Milan bound for Como and Austria. That same day the French entered the city. There they found the castello prepared to withstand a siege. Il Moro had given its command to a soldier called Bernardino da Corte, who was loud in his protestations of loyalty to the Sforza. A garrison of some three thousand soldiers was well supplied with food and ammunition.

But on September 13 Da Corte surrendered the castello to the French, bribed by a share of its treasures and a promise of an annual pension of two thousand ducats. The French despised him, and Da Corte died within a few days, supposedly of shame and guilt. Cardinal Ascanio Sforza, who accompanied Lodovico to Austria, had recommended taking along Da Corte's children on their flight as hostages for his loyalty. Lodovico refused. When he heard of Da Corte's treachery, Lodovico, who had often been treacherous himself, was deeply shocked and hurt. "From Judas to this day there has been no worse traitor than Bernardino da Corte," he said.

Five months later Lodovico Sforza returned in triumph to Milan at the head of an army of mercenaries he had hired in Austria. The Milanese, disgusted by the arrogance, cruelty and filthy habits of the French, welcomed Lodovico back as fervently as they had welcomed the French so short a time before. His restoration was brief. In April, outside the walls of Novara, which Lodovico was besieging, the Swiss mercenaries in Lodovico's army refused to fight their fellow Swiss in the French army and chose to march back to Switzerland.

To escape capture Lodovico disguised himself as a Swiss pikeman and marched with them. But a Swiss captain named Turmann recognized his employer and betrayed him to the French. Turmann was promptly executed by his countrymen, who were ashamed that such a traitor should disgrace them. The great duke of Milan was taken to France to live out the rest of his life in captivity.

For four years he was confined in the fortress of Lys-Saint Georges at Berry and for four years more in the great medieval castle of Loches in Touraine, where he died on May 17, 1508. He was not treated badly. Louis XII sent him his own doctor, allowed him to receive letters and even permitted one of Lodovico's dwarfs to come from Milan to amuse him.

And so, in the obscurity of a distant French captivity, perished the last of the great Sforzas. Seldom has the proverb about pride going before a fall been so aptly illustrated. Could this powerful and clever man have avoided his dismal end if he had been more prudent, more farsighted, more humble? Probably not. The French would have marched into Italy anyway. And Il Moro being what he was could not have behaved differently any more than the leopard can change his spots.

Guicciardini, who believed the worst about most of his contemporaries, believed the rumor that Lodovico poisoned Gian Galeazzo. His verdict on Il Moro follows:

"A prince, certainly most excellent for his eloquence and industry, and for many gifts of nature and spirit, a creature of very rare perfection; and lastly not unworthy of the name of mild and merciful, if the death of his nephew had not defiled him with bloody infamy. But on the other side, he carried a mind vain and full of thoughts busy and ambitious, and nourishing always intentions dissembled, he kept no reckoning of his promises and faith. He always presumed so much of himself, that seeming to be discontented, when praises were given the wisdom and counsels of others, he persuaded himself to be able by his art and industry to alter and turn the conceptions of everyone to what purpose he listed."

The Sforza dukes of Milan never won the loyal allegiance of their subjects. But their dynasty was nevertheless firmly rooted in Milanese soil. Lodovico and Beatrice's two sons, Maximilian and Francesco, ruled briefly and incompetently as dukes of Milan —as puppet dukes supported by the might of stronger powers.

THE GONZAGAS
OF MANTUA

On the night of August 16, 1328 a group of efficient conspirators murdered Passarino Bonaccolsi, the Lord of Mantua, massacred several hundred of his friends and relations and seized control of the city. The chief conspirator was a man of sixty, Luigi Gonzaga, who was Bonaccolsi's brother-in-law. Neither the family connection nor the Bonaccolsis' fifty-five years of successful rule in Mantua deterred Gonzaga. In the political anarchy of fourteenth-century Italy those who aspired to political power were never scrupulous about the means used to achieve their ends. The following year the people of the city elected Gonzaga hereditary captain-general and lord of Mantua, and the year after that he was recognized as imperial vicar of the city by the Holy Roman Emperor.

Thus was established one of the most distinguished of the ruling families of the Renaissance, a dynasty which endured into the eighteenth century and included four captains-general, four marquises and eleven dukes.

The ancient city of Mantua lies within a loop of the Mincio River just north of its confluence with the Po, within sight of the Alps. Before the Gonzagas it was famous for two reasons: Virgil was born near it, and since the ninth century the city had piously treasured the *Preziosissimo Sangue* (a phial of the most precious blood from Christ's wounded side).

The first four generations of Gonzagas, starting with Luigi, were medieval warriors. Stubborn defenders of their state and their power, eminently successful condottieri in the service of others, they quarreled, conspired and killed with unflagging enthusiasm. And they married into many of the other ruling families of Italy—Visconti, Este, Malatesta. Since their state was small and without substantial resources, they fought for others in order to earn the money which enabled them to live like lords. They were courageous, resourceful, dangerous men.

Gianfrancesco, the fifth-generation Gonzaga prince of Mantua, became the first marquis. He was the first true Renaissance prince in the Gonzaga family. A fine soldier like most of his ancestors and relatives, Gianfrancesco was a cultivated man, interested in art and scholarship. At his wedding to Paola Malatesta the festivities were prolonged and magnificent. A tournament held in celebration of the marriage was notable; forty-two of the knights who participated were members of the Gonzaga family.

In 1433 the Emperor Sigismund confirmed in person Gianfrancesco's title of marquis in a grand ceremony at Mantua. The Gonzagas had been important factors in the wars of northern Italy for a hundred years. But it was Gianfrancesco who increased the distinction and fame of the family by patronizing the new learning of the Renaissance. His own children became shining examples of the new humanist learning.

Gianfrancesco himself was interested in the revival of Latin and Greek. Although one historian has said that "his assassinations were not obtrusive," and although he possessed a violent and dangerous temper, Gianfrancesco was perfectly sincere in his desire to promote learning—no contradiction was involved here. In 1423 Gianfrancesco persuaded Vittorino da Feltre to come to Mantua to tutor his children and to establish a school. Few schools have played so important a role in the history of education.

Vittorino da Feltre was one of the great scholars of the Renaissance, a teacher of genius, a devout Christian and a good and lovable man. Learned in Latin, Greek and mathematics, an ardent believer in the importance of exercise, he had been a professor at the University of Padua and had conducted his own school at Venice.

F*

So anxious was Gianfrancesco to persuade Vittorino to come to Mantua that he allowed him to fix his own salary. When the famous teacher arrived at Mantua, he insisted on one condition: "I accept the post, on this understanding only, that you (the Marquis) require from me nothing which shall be in any way unworthy of either of us; and I will continue to serve you so long as your own life shall command respect."

Until his death twenty-three years later, Vittorino conducted his school at Mantua according to his own ideas. His most important pupils were the Marquis' children. But he also taught the children of other princely families, the children of other humanist scholars and a number of bright boys from poor families who did not pay tuition and were treated exactly like the others. The school was a boarding school. Master and pupils lived in a handsome villa near the Gonzaga palace formerly called "the Pleasure House." Vittorino changed the name to "the Pleasant House."

There Vittorino shared with some sixty or seventy boys the Spartan conditions he considered suitable for education. No heating was allowed in winter. Much stress was put upon exercise, more on classical literature and still more on Christian virtue. Vittorino resorted to corporal punishment only in the last extremity. His personality was so attractive that he won the lifelong affection of many of his students. Reading aloud was a regular practice and committing texts to memory was required. Two of the young Gonzagas excelled in memorizing.

The Marquis' third son, Gianlucudo, who became a priest and died young, was almost frighteningly precocious. At the age of twelve he composed a Latin poem in honor of the visit to Mantua of the Emperor Sigismund. At fourteen he added two new propositions to Euclid. Gianlucudo knew all of Virgil by heart and could recite the entire *Aeneid*, taking a day for each book.

His sister Cecilia was equally astonishing. At eight she had read the works of Chrysostom in Greek. We can presume that she had learned Latin even earlier. She, too, could recite masses of Latin poetry.

It was Cecilia's misfortune to be so beautiful that Oddantonio da Montefeltro, the notoriously depraved young count of Urbino, wanted to marry her. Marquis Gianfrancesco approved so useful a political marriage, but Cecilia indignantly refused to consider it. Gianfrancesco did not take kindly to having his daughter frustrate his diplomacy. He stormed at Cecilia, beat her and put her in prison. Cecilia pleaded with her father to let her become a nun. And her teacher, Vittorino, courageously supported her. Gianfrancesco gave up. Cecilia entered a convent, and died before she was twenty-five.

The affection Vittorino inspired in his most famous pupil, Federigo da Montefeltro, Duke of Urbino, is celebrated. In the great library of his palace at Urbino Federigo kept a bust of Vittorino with an inscription honoring the teacher's virtues.

Vittorino intervened in behalf of Gianfrancesco's eldest son, Lodovico, even more courageously than he did for Cecilia. The situation was delicate and dangerous. The Marquis preferred his second son, Carlo, to Lodovico. Carlo was ambitious, quarrelsome, treacherous—a professional condottiere. Gianfrancesco took Carlo with him on his campaigns, leaving Lodovico behind and feeling discriminated against. Full of youthful resentment, Lodovico in 1436, when he was only twenty-two, ran away and enlisted as a soldier serving Filippo-Maria Visconti, Duke of Milan, in his war against Venice. His offense was great because his father was commander of the Venetian forces.

Gianfrancesco raged. Lodovico insisted that he only wanted to study the art of war, which his father had prevented him from learning. The Marquis disinherited Lodovico and condemned him to death for treason. Carlo rejoiced; he might become heir. Scholars wrote letters of protest to the Marquis quoting copiously from the ancients, and his wife and other children pleaded for Lodovico. Urged by Vittorino, Lodovico contritely confessed his error—to no avail. Finally, Vittorino denounced Gianfrancesco's cruelty to his face. Risking his own position and perhaps his life, he argued so eloquently that Gianfrancesco consented to let Lodovico return to Mantua and to be reinstated as his son and successor.

After Gianfrancesco died at the age of forty-nine in 1444, the bad feeling between the two brothers continued. Carlo had hoped to be marquis. He had inherited a considerable part of Mantua's territory. It wasn't enough. He continued his career as a condot-

*LODOVICO GONZAGA, Marquis of Mantua,
among the members of his family and his court*

*". . . one of the most successful and admired of Renaissance princes
. . . a patron of artists and scholars and a man of learning himself."*
Mural by Andrea Mantegna.

tiere and became a professional traitor as well as a professional soldier. Carlo betrayed the short-lived Republic of Milan. He betrayed the great soldier Francesco Sforza. And he betrayed his brother by leading a Venetian army against Mantua. Lodovico, who by then had become a good soldier, too, defeated Carlo and preserved his state. Carlo fled to Ferrara, where he died an embittered exile, two years after his defeat.

Lodovico Gonzaga ruled in Mantua for thirty-four years as one of the most successful and admired of Renaissance princes and the most distinguished member of the House of Gonzaga. Continuing the military tradition of his family, he served Milan and Florence as a condottiere. Continuing the cultural tradition begun by his father, he became a patron of artists and scholars and a man of learning himself. A good disciple of his teacher, even after he became marquis, Lodovico refused to be seated in Vittorino's presence.

Lodovico collected manuscripts of Virgil and employed artists to illustrate the *Aeneid* and *The Divine Comedy*. He sponsored a printing press in Mantua which printed Boccaccio's *Decameron* in 1473. Lodovico's favorite authors were St. Augustine, Lucan and Pliny. It was Lodovico who rebuilt the Church of Sant' Andrea according to designs by the great architect Leon Battista Alberti. He asked for public contributions to help defray the expense because "its vast size and noble simplicity should be superior to any building of the kind in the leading cities of Italy, and worthy to stand beside the magnificence of Rome itself."

Lodovico was a builder. He built or improved four country villas. For two years he employed the great sculptor Donatello, who made a bust of Lodovico. And it was Lodovico who engaged Andrea Mantegna as court painter in 1460. Mantegna remained with the Gonzagas until his death forty-six years later in 1506. He served three Gonzaga marquises: Lodovico, his son Federigo, and his grandson, Giovanni Francesco.

Mantegna, a magnificent artist but a crusty, short-tempered, querulous man, was given a fine house of his own and a fixed salary, which, unfortunately, was sometimes in arrears. Lodovico was kind to Mantegna, supplying him with corn, wood and wine. Once when a long war had exhausted Lodovico's treasury and a plague raged in Mantua, Mantegna wrote Lodovico a bitter letter complaining that he had not been paid on time. Lodovico replied: "Andrea, we have received a letter from you which it really seems to us that you need not have written, since we perfectly remember the promises we made when you entered our service; neither, as it seems to us, have we failed to keep those promises or to do our utmost for you. But you cannot take from us what we have not got, and you yourself have seen that, when we have had the means, we have never failed to do all in our power for you and our other servants, and that gladly and with good will. It is true that, since we have not received our usual revenues during the last few months, we have been obliged to defer certain payments, such as this which is due to you, but we are seeking by every means in our power to raise money to meet our obligations, even if we are forced to mortgage our own property, since all our jewels are already pawned, and you need not fear but that before long, your debt will be paid gladly and readily."

The Gonzaga palaces in Mantua cover eight acres. In that huge complex of courtyards, palaces, long corridors, grand staircases and a church there is one room where Mantegna's art can be seen at its closest tie with the Gonzaga family. This is the *Camera degli Sposi*, or Bridal Chamber. In this elaborately decorated room with its vaulted ceiling Mantegna painted a series of frescoes which display typical scenes in the life of the Marquis and his family. They include two portraits of Lodovico, one not quite a full face, the other a profile.

In the first, Lodovico is seated in a fancy chair with a gray hound lying beneath it. He is dressed in a long robe and wears a round hat with a flat top. He holds a letter and is turning to speak to a secretary or court official. He is smooth-shaven, as were all his contemporaries. His face is neither good-looking nor homely. It is sharply intelligent and somehow intensely Italian. No one could mistake him for a Frenchman or a German. In the profile portrait, Lodovico is dressed in hunting clothes but seems to be wearing the same hat. His face is less individualized and is without expression.

It was during the reign of Marquis Lodovico that Aeneas Sylvius Piccolomini, Pope Pius II, presided over the Congress of

Mantua. Pius, who had been a humanist scholar and an ambitious and worldly diplomat before becoming a bishop, a cardinal and finally a pope, believed that he could organize a Crusade against the Turks who had recently conquered Constantinople. So he called the princes of Europe to meet him in Mantua in 1459. By this time, of course, no reigning prince took the idea of crusading seriously. Problems of war and peace at home were too demanding. Few important monarchs came to Mantua and some were not even represented. But Pius himself arrived in great state and in his *Commentaries* described his ceremonial entrance into the city with his usual pleasure in his own importance:

"He (Pius) entered the city in a procession arranged as follows: First came the servants of the Curia and the attendants of the cardinals; then the minor officials of the Curia; then twelve white horses, riderless and decked out with gold saddles and bridles; then three banners, on the first of which shone the sign of the Cross, on the second the keys of the Church, and on the third the five crescents which are the arms of the Piccolomini. These were carried by nobles in armor mounted on richly caparisoned horses. Next came a red and yellow canopy and after that the priests of the city in splendid robes carrying the sacred relics. They were followed by the ambassadors of kings and princes, the subdeacons, the auditors, scribes and advocates of the Apostolic palace under a golden cross. Then came a golden tabernacle borne on a white horse under a silk canopy and surrounded by many tapers, in which was the Eucharist, that is, the sacred Host of our Savior. Next rode Galeazzo of Milan and the Marquis Lodovico, then the venerable order of cardinals, and finally the Pope himself raised high on his throne, wearing the papal robes and the miter blazing with precious gems. He was carried on the shoulders of nobles and blessed the people as he proceeded. Behind him came the gentlemen of his bedchamber and his personal attendants, then the bishops, notaries, abbots, and a great throng of prelates. At the city gates Lodovico dismounted and presented the Pope with the keys of the city. This was done by all those whom the Pope visited on his journey except the Sienese and the Florentines, who, though under the heel of popular tyranny, wished to make a show of freedom by keeping the keys.

"From the gate all the way to the Church of San Pietro, which is the cathedral, not a foot of ground but was covered with carpets and the walls on both sides were covered with flowers and tapestries. Women, boys and girls crowded the windows and roofs, but still there was a great press and all the approaches were thronged with people. In many places were altars smoking with incense. No voice was heard except the shouts of the populace crying, 'Long live Pope Pius!' "

Pius brought with him twenty-six cardinals and each cardinal brought with him ninety to three hundred horsemen. It must have been a little like a circus coming to town. But this was not the end of public magnificence at the Congress of Mantua. Milan is less than a hundred miles from Mantua. But Francesco Sforza, its new duke, was four months late for the Congress. He certainly had no interest in a Crusade. Perhaps he waited until he could arrive in style. In any case, he came sailing up the Mincio River to Mantua with a fleet of forty-seven ships. Marquis Lodovico could assemble only twenty-two when he went out to meet Sforza.

The Congress was a failure. Only a few rulers promised to join Pius's Crusade, and none of these kept his promise.

Like his father before him, Marquis Lodovico had trouble over the marriage arrangements of one of his children. Lodovico was happily married to a German princess. He wanted his son, Federigo, to marry another. Federigo refused. Lodovico, who had his share of the Gonzaga temper, threatened to put him in prison. Aided by his mother and accompanied by six servants, Federigo fled from Mantua and went to Naples. On the way he was robbed by a band of outlaws. The chronicler Stefano Gionta made a fine tale of Federigo's flight from matrimony:

"Being unwilling, through fear of his father, to make himself known, he suffered great distress, through which cause the said Federigo fell sick of dysentery.

"Meanwhile his servants, having no means of livelihood, nor any trade or art, gave themselves to rough work such as is done by porters; and with their small earnings supported their lord, whom they kept secretly in the house of a poor woman, where they themselves too had lodging.

"The Marchioness had meantime sent messengers into different cities and countries to recover her son; nor could she ever obtain any news, so that she came to think he was dead, since she could hear nothing of him, nor even of his servants. Now it so happened that one of these messengers came to Naples, and presented himself there to the King, with letters from the aforesaid Marchioness, who prayed that he would search through all his territory if there were therein seven men of a company, and gave thereto an exact account of their names, stature and appearance.

"Then the King gave orders that search should be forthwith made by the heads of the quarters of the city and one of these said that in his quarter there were six men of Lombardy, since he knew nought of Federigo who lay sick in the woman's house, but that they were porters and men of low estate. Yet did the King will to see them; and when they came before him asked who they were, and what was their number. And they gave answer they were six men of Lombardy, since they wished not to make known their lord; and when their names were asked, they had changed them of purpose, so that the King, unable to discover anything, would have sent them away. But the messenger of the Marchioness had recognized them, and whispered to the King, 'My Lord, these be the servants of her who sent me to thee; but they have changed their names.'

"When the King having separated them one from another, took each apart, and questioned him of his lord; and they, finding themselves thus separate, told them all their story in every detail. Then the King sent for Federigo, whom he found upon a bed of straw, grievously sick, and had him carried to his palace and tended with every care; and sent the messenger back to his mother, to tell her how the men were found and in what misery they had been.

"Forthwith the Marchioness went to her husband, and throwing herself at his feet, sought of him a favor. The Marquis answered that he would grant her all and every favor, however great—save only that it concerned not Federigo. Then did the lady open to him that letter of the King of Naples, the which had such power that it softened the spirit of the Marquis when he heard in what wretchedness his son had been; and handing back the letter to the Marchioness he said to her, 'Do as you think fit.'

"Immediately the Marchioness sent money and good raiment, with strict orders that he should return to Mantua; and he arriving there, threw himself at his father's feet, begging pardon for himself and his servants. That pardon was granted, and to the servants withall was given such means as to enable them henceforth to live honorably as gentlemen—and they were called 'The Faithful Ones' of the House of Gonzaga, and from them the family of the Fideli of Mantua draws its origin.

"Then the Marquis, not to break his word given, willed that Federigo should take to wife Margherita, daughter of the Duke of Bavaria [apparently acceptable to the penitent son, even though she was German], and the wedding was duly celebrated; so that father and son remained henceforth on the best of terms."

Lodovico's second son, Francesco, became a cardinal, the first of many Gonzaga cardinals. An antiquarian and a dilettante of all the arts, he was a personal friend not only of Mantegna but also of Alberti, Poliziano and Pico della Mirandola.

Marquis Lodovico died at his country villa of Goito in 1478. He was sixty-five. He had been a successful and admirable prince, who had ruled for thirty-four years. Unlike many of his contemporaries, Lodovico was not accused of any major follies or of notable cruelties or crimes. He was a good ruler, a reasonably good father to his children and a discerning patron of art and learning.

Federigo was thirty-six when he succeeded his father. He, too, was a condottiere, serving as commander of the armies of Milan. Although he was never dismissed for gross incompetence, his role in several wars was inglorious to say the least. Federigo did not lack courage. He welcomed to his court Niccolo d'Este, nephew of Duke Ercole, rebel and pretender to the throne of Ferrara. Federigo thus boldly risked the enmity of Ercole and the risk of war with a state more powerful than his own.

Federigo's younger brother, Rodolfo, who, as we have seen, was killed at the Battle of Fornovo, continued an old Gonzaga custom of cutting off the heads of wives suspected, perhaps unjustly, of adultery. Rodolfo's unhappy wife was Antonia Malatesta.

Marquis Federigo was an affectionate father and an adequately capable ruler. He employed Mantegna to decorate a new villa he built at Marmirola. Federigo understood Mantegna's prickly temperament and wrote of him: "These excellent masters are often somewhat fantastic in humor, and we must be content to take what they choose to give us."

In 1484, only six years after he became marquis, Federigo died at the age of forty-four. He had three sons and three daughters. One son, his successor, Marquis Giovanni Francesco, and one daughter, Elisabetta, Duchess of Urbino, became two of the celebrated characters in the great drama of the Italian Renaissance.

❖❖❖❖❖❖❖❖❖ XI ❖❖❖❖❖❖❖❖❖

FRANCESCO AND ISABELLA

 FRANCESCO GONZAGA, fourth Marquis of Mantua, married Isabella d'Este, the most famous woman of the Renaissance. He himself was an interesting and flamboyant representative of the princes of his generation. Short, lithe, athletic, Francesco was a superb horseman, a brave but barely competent soldier, a crafty and successfully dishonest ruler and a great lover of wine and women. Flatterers called him the bravest man in Italy, but did not mention his appearance because he was one of the ugliest men in Italy. His face was flat, his eyes protuberant, his nose snub and wide, his hair and beard bushy. Born in 1466, Francesco belonged to the generation of princely Italians who sometime in the 1490s began to wear beards. He was eighteen when his father died and he became marquis, twenty-four when he married Isabella in 1490, and only twenty-nine when he commanded the Italian army at the Battle of Fornovo. His engagement to Isabella had been arranged by his father and the Duke of Ferrara when he was fourteen and Isabella was five.

In the spring of 1481 Marquis Federigo and Francesco made a state visit to Ferrara ostensibly to give Francesco the opportunity of meeting his future bride and her family (Isabella was only seven then), but actually to cement an alliance with Duke Ercole. Federigo and Francesco sailed down the Po in four state

FRANCESCO GONZAGA, *Marquis of Mantua*

"... *an interesting and flamboyant representative of the princes of his generation ... a crafty and successfully dishonest ruler and a great lover of wine and women.*"

bucentaurs, which were handsome but clumsy river barges. They were accompanied by a suite of six hundred persons.

Such a mass visitation would dismay modern presidents or dictators with the resources of great nations at their disposal. In the Renaissance they were the usual custom. The wealth and grandeur of the visitors required display, so hundreds of courtiers and servants dressed in expensive finery were essential. Similarly, the wealth and grandeur of the host required demonstration in extravagant hospitality. The Gonzagas and their more important friends and relations were put up in the various Este palaces. Humbler members of the Gonzaga entourage were scattered all over the city. Duke Ercole spared nothing in his preparations. Although notoriously parsimonious, he fed all six hundred Mantuans on lamb and veal for the four days of the visit. Horse races were held and the Gonzaga Barbary horses won the *palio*, a prize consisting of a cloth of gold. It is not recorded what the adolescent Francesco thought of the child Isabella.

Two years after he became marquis the young Francesco arranged suitable matches for his unmarried sisters. Elisabetta Gonzaga, whose culture and virtue were to inspire rapt devotion in the courtier-diplomat-writer, Baldassare Castiglione, married Guidobaldo da Montefeltro, Duke of Urbino. Maddalena married Giovanni Sforza, Lord of Pesaro, and died young. Since Giovanni was a cousin of the Duke of Milan, he was considered eligible, but because he was weak, stupid and vindictive, he was not really a desirable catch. Each sister was given a dowry of 27,000 ducats.

Francesco Gonzaga was vain, stubborn, brutal and selfish. Yet he was kind to women, fond of his sisters and in love with his wife during the first years of their marriage. His magnetism, gaiety and high spirits gave him a charm which appealed to men as well as to women. That charm plus his rank and power enabled him to seduce many girls and to father many bastards.

Francesco was always quick to take offense and slow to give up a grudge. His uncle, Bishop Lodovico, was anxious to become a cardinal; Francesco did everything he could to prevent the appointment. The situation became so tense that Bishop Lodovico and two more of Francesco's uncles, Rodolfo and Gianfrancesco, thought it prudent to leave Mantua. The Pope, Lorenzo de'

Medici and the Queen of Denmark all tried in vain to end the family feud. The Bishop finally recognized that he was checkmated and retired to his castle at Gazzulo. There he consoled himself by collecting antiques and books. The episode shows how essentially political the office of cardinal was. The ruler of a small state could, in effect, veto the appointment of a subject, even a member of his own family, to the College of Cardinals.

Another episode shows how stubbornly Francesco could cherish his resentment. Baldassare Castiglione was a Mantuan citizen and a remote connection of the Gonzagas. In 1505 Guidobaldo da Montefeltro wrote his brother-in-law, asking permission to invite Castiglione to enter his service. Francesco's reply was so curt it was barely polite:

> My Lord Duke, if Baldassare Castiglione chooses to enter your service, we are well content, and shall be ever ready to oblige you in anything that you may desire.
>
> > Francesco Gonzaga

Although he had consented, the Marquis regarded Castiglione as little better than a traitor. In May of 1506 Castiglione was sent on a diplomatic mission to England by Duke Guidobaldo. He wrote Gonzaga, asking permission to travel through Mantua and to pay his humble respects, assuring the Marquis of his loyalty and devotion as one of his subjects. "God grant that one day Your Excellency may at least allow me to know the cause of my disgrace, and bring me face-to-face with those who have persuaded you that I am not your true servant, for then I should count myself to be most fortunate." Francesco forbade Castiglione to enter Mantuan territory and continued to do so on several subsequent occasions when Castiglione requested permission to visit his mother.

Francesco Gonzaga and Isabella d'Este were married in Ferrara on February 11, 1940. The bride, who would not be sixteen for three months, was the eldest child of the oldest and most aristocratic ruling family in Italy. She had black eyes and rippling yellow hair which fell upon her shoulders. Two portraits of her, made some years later—a chalk sketch by Leonardo da Vinci and a painting by Titian—show a plumply pleasant face. Her contemporaries thought her beautiful. She was fiercely intelligent and formidably talented; she spoke Latin fluently, danced gracefully, played the lute and clavichord and sang in a lovely voice to her own accompaniment.

Duke Ercole gave Isabella a dowry of 25,000 ducats, a trousseau valued at 2,000 ducats and jewels valued at 3,000 ducats. But her mother, Eleonora of Aragon, daughter of the King of Naples, had had a dowry of 80,000 ducats. And when Anna Sforza married Isabella's brother, Alfonso, her dowry was 150,000 ducats. The difference was caused not only by Duke Ercole's firm grip on a ducat but also by the meager resources of Ferrara, as compared with those of the Kingdom of Naples and the Duchy of Milan.

Francesco was not as well educated or as intelligent as Isabella. He did not share her intense interest in art and was much less cultured than his father, grandfather and many contemporary princes. He loved hunting, kept hundreds of dogs and was passionately fond of horses. He imported horses from Spain, Barbary, and Arabia and produced a breed considered the best in Europe. Gonzaga horses won races all over Italy. A sporting man and a military man, Francesco admired his intellectual bride.

During the first years of their marriage Isabella sincerely loved her uncouth husband, forgave or ignored most of his infidelities (as was the duty of every Renaissance princess), and on one famous occasion pulled the hair of one of Francesco's mistresses in a shrilly undignified scene. When they no longer loved each other, Isabella would become impatient with her coarse and cynical husband. But because of her strong Italian sense of family and her pride as Marchioness of Mantua Isabella always did her best to promote Francesco's interests and those of Mantua, which were her own. Francesco always respected Isabella, but was sometimes exasperated by her.

At first all went well. In the same year as their wedding Isabella returned to Ferrara to visit her parents and wrote to Francesco: "I can have no pleasure when I am away from Your Highness, whom I love more than my life."

He replied: "Since you feel that you cannot be happy away from me any longer, which is only natural, considering the immense love we both feel for each other, it seems to me that now you have satisfied your illustrious father and mother's wishes, as well as your own affection for your family, you might return home for our own happiness, and so I shall look forward to your arrival with impatience."

Isabella was born not only a princess of the powerful and turbulent House of Este; she herself was born to rule and was ready and anxious to do so at seventeen. That was her age in November of 1491 when she wrote to a Mantuan artist who was slow about decorating one of her rooms at the palace at Mantua:

"Since we have learned by experience that you are as slow in finishing your work as you are in everything else, we send this to remind you that for once you must change your nature, and that if our *studiola* is not finished on our return, we intend to put you into the dungeon of the castello. And this, we assure you, is no jest on our part." The imperious tone came naturally to an Este princess accustomed to absolute power.

The young girl who could threaten an artist so fiercely grew up and became a woman of great poise and self-control. She was enormously charming, beloved by a host of friends, and blessed with immense energy. Even across the span of five centuries it is impossible not to admire her. Her intelligence, her force of character and her astute craft in achieving her ends were all superb. But it is difficult to like this coldly scheming woman with her vast ego and her immeasurable acquisitiveness.

Isabella liked many people. What she liked best was to be liked and admired. She was devoted to her eldest son, Federigo, particularly when he was a beautiful child. When he grew up and rejected her advice, she was understandably displeased. She did her best at great risk to herself to make her son Ercole a cardinal. She didn't care much about her daughters. When two of them became brides of Jesus and entered a convent, Isabella remarked almost blasphemously that she was content, "since this son-in-law would cause her no trouble."

Isabella was a prodigious writer of letters. She wrote weekly to her mother in Ferrara, to her sister Beatrice in Milan, and to her sister-in-law, Elisabetta Gonzaga, in Urbino. She wrote frequently to her half-sister Lucrezia Bentivoglio in Bologna, to her brothers and to her husband. And she wrote regularly and often to merchants, craftsmen, Mantuan agents, artists, scholars, writers, poets, cardinals, popes and princes. Some of her letters were personal and chatty. Some were business notes. Some were political, flattering efforts to keep herself in the good graces of powerful people. Isabella was interested in everything—in war, politics, personalities, art, poetry, family news, fashions and jewelry. She was as sincerely interested in beauty as she was in her own fame.

She took pleasure in setting fashions and in buying clothes and materials. She invented hats and new hairdos. Writing to an agent about to set out for France, Isabella said that she wanted "some gold chain, or anything else that is new and elegant. . . . These are the kind of things I wish to have—engraved amethysts, rosaries of black amber and gold, blue cloth for a *camora*, black cloth for a mantle, such as shall be without a rival in the world, even if it costs ten ducats a yard; as long as it is of real excellence, never mind! If it is only as good as those I see other people wear, I had rather be without it!"

Compared with her sister Beatrice at Milan, Isabella felt poor. While visiting at the Sforza court she wrote Marquis Francesco: "Would to God that we who spend money so gladly had half as much!"

Isabella often spent more than she could afford and went into debt to Venetian bankers. Sometimes she had to pawn her jewels and robes to help finance Francesco's campaigns or his efforts to make his brother Sigismundo a cardinal. But Isabella never stopped ordering things—paintings, sculpture, antiques, musical instruments, engraved medals, medieval romances, rare manuscripts of Greek and Latin authors, fine printed books from the press of Aldus Manutius in Venice, and illuminated volumes of poetry by contemporary poets dedicated to herself.

It wasn't that she was just greedy—Isabella was a true and insatiable collector of beautiful things. She did not just buy. She read the classic authors and the modern poets. She understood and admired works of art. Collecting was an obsession with her, part of her cultivated materialism. She could be unscrupulous and very tough in her scheming to acquire the treasures of her best friends.

In 1502 Cesare Borgia, in his campaign to conquer the independent states of the Romagna and central Italy, treacherously attacked Urbino. Duke Guidobaldo barely escaped and fled to Mantua. As soon as Isabella realized that the formidable Borgia's loot included two masterpieces of art which he had earlier presented to her beloved sister-in-law, Elisabetta, and to Guidobaldo, she wrote a letter to her brother, Cardinal Ippolito d'Este, who was well acquainted with Borgia:

"Most Reverend Father in God, my dear and honored Brother, The Lord Duke of Urbino, my brother-in-law, had in his house a small Venus of antique marble, and also a Cupid, which were given him some time ago by His Excellency the Duke of Romagna. I feel certain that these things must have fallen into the said Duke's hands, together with all the contents of the palace in Urbino, in the present revolution. And since I am very anxious to collect antiques for the decoration of my studio, I desire exceedingly to possess these statues, which does not seem to me impossible, since I hear that His Excellency has little taste for antiquities, and would accordingly be the more ready to oblige others. But as I am not sufficiently intimate with him to venture to ask this favor at his hands, I think it best to avail myself of your most revered Signoria's good offices, and pray you of your kindness to ask him for the said Venus and Cupid, both by messenger and letter, in so effectual a manner that both you and I may obtain satisfaction. I am quite willing, if it please Your Reverence, that you should mention my name and say that I have asked for them very urgently, and sent an express courier, as I do now, for, believe me, I could receive no greater pleasure or favor either from his Excellency or from your most dear and reverend Signoria, to whom I commend myself affectionately. Your sister, Isabella, Marchioness of Mantua (Mantua, June 30, 1502)"

Cardinal Ippolito easily arranged the gift and Cesare Borgia sent the statues to the art-loving Marchioness. The next year, when Duke Guidobaldo regained his state, Isabella refused to return to him the precious statue of a sleeping cupid. Since it was the celebrated first statue carved by Michelangelo and Isabella had the good taste to prize it, one can understand, if hardly approve, her determination to keep it.

Isabella displayed equally perfect taste when she pleaded with

Leonardo da Vinci to paint her a picture, even a little one. After the French conquest of Milan in 1499 Leonardo had left that city and settled in Florence. Isabella was the only Italian princess (or prince) who recognized Leonardo's genius, courted his friendship and invited him to visit her. Leonardo would not promise to paint a picture for her and never did so; but he did promise to paint her portrait, and while passing through Mantua he made the preliminary sketch in red chalk—which has survived. He never did paint the portrait in oil. Perhaps Leonardo was the exception among Isabella's contemporaries who did not find her interesting. After his death in France Isabella received a small picture, which has disappeared.

Isabella's taste in art was timeless. Her enthusiasm for the crude clowning of dwarfs was typical of her own time. Dwarfs had been jesters and fools at her father's court in Ferrara. At Mantua Isabella had a special suite of rooms built in the palace for a family of dwarfs. The ceilings were too low for normal people, but appropriate for dwarfs.

Her favorite dwarf, Matello, excelled in comical impersonations of drunkards and monks. When he lay dying, Isabella visited him and reported to the Marquis the jokes he had made on his deathbed. The whole Mantuan court mourned for the "foremost fool in the world," as Isabella called him. Matello's portrait was painted, and an epitaph and an elegy were written about him.

In 1489, a year before his marriage when he was only twenty-three, Francesco Gonzaga was appointed captain-general of the Venetian armies, a command he held for the next eight years. Why was so inexperienced a man given so high a rank? Probably because Mantua occupied a key position on the Venetian border and would make a useful ally. And also, perhaps, because so many Gonzagas had been notable soldiers in Venetian service.

In 1494, when Charles was preparing his invasion, he invited Francesco to serve as a condottiere in his army. Francesco declined, preferring to keep his Venetian command. It was a difficult year, full of uncertainties. Although Isabella liked her brother-in-law, Lodovico Sforza, Francesco did not. Neither prince could trust the other. And Isabella was annoyed when

Lodovico asked her to send him a regular supply of fish from Lake Garda. She wrote to the Marquis: "I am quite willing to see that fish should be sent to Milan occasionally, but not every week as he requests in his imperious fashion, as if we were his feudatories, lest it should appear as if we were compelled to send it, and it were a kind of tribute."

Although Francesco Gonzaga proved himself a mediocre general at Fornovo, he fought with great courage. After three horses had been killed under him, he fought on foot until his sword broke in his hand. A Mantuan official who risked his life to save the Marquis wrote to Isabella: "Since the days of Hector of Troy no one ever fought as he did. I believe he killed ten men with his own hands. And I think you must have said some psalms for him, for indeed it is a miracle that he is alive and unhurt."

Shortly after the battle, while he was in command of the siege of Novara, Francesco received a letter from Isabella which included a sentiment with which most wives of officers have always agreed: "I pray and entreat you to be very careful and not to expose yourself as I am sure you discharge your office best and most efficiently by giving orders to others rather than by fighting yourself."

When the Marquis returned to Mantua, he entered the city like a triumphant hero. Four days later he went on to Venice and was welcomed with great ceremony, the Doge and Senate coming out to meet him in the state bucentaur. All Italy seemed determined to regard Francesco as a hero, and Fornovo as a great victory.

Although the Marquis had realized the equivocal nature of the battle and had admitted as much in his letter to Isabella, he, too, began to think of himself as a victorious hero. He commanded Mantegna to paint a picture in celebration of his victory. Mantegna obliged with a masterpiece called *Our Lady Of Victory*, which shows the Virgin and Child with Francesco kneeling before them, clad in full armor except for his head, which is bare.

The following year Francesco commanded a Venetian force sent to the Kingdom of Naples to help drive out the French garrisons left there by Charles VIII. While in the city of Naples he fell sick, probably with malaria but perhaps with syphilis, and fled from the city because of a prophecy that he would die there. Francesco went home to Mantua to recuperate and reported to Venice in November. He was received grandly, but the Venetians were already suspicious of his fondness for the French. In June of 1497 the Marquis was summoned to Venice and abruptly dismissed.

The Venetians were convinced that Francesco was negotiating with the French. It was a great comedown—from the top condottiere post in Italy to unemployment. He accused Lodovico Sforza of intriguing against him. A Venetian ambassador wrote: "I hear he is very gloomy and goes clad in black, and wears an iron ring on his collar, which he has vowed not to lay aside until he has been on a pilgrimage to Loreto. And there is sorrow throughout the Montovano, and the people, who had been happy and smiling before, are now sad and out of heart."

Smarting with his disgrace, angry at the world, Franceso comforted himself by taking a semipermanent mistress named Teodora, who bore him two daughters. Probably he had not been a traitor to Venice, but had kept in touch with the French in case they made him a better offer later. According to Renaissance ideas about military honor, murky at best, it was wrong for a condottiere to switch sides during active hostilities, but perfectly all right to do so once peace had broken out.

It was not expected of a Renaissance prince that he be faithful to his wife. If he was, gossip might assume him impotent. But the young Marquis of Mantua was married to so charming and attractive a wife that his flagrant infidelities did seem somehow vulgar and unnecessary. After all, in the year of Fornovo Isabella was only twenty-one and a trifle young to have to cope with such problems. Floriano Dolfo, a humanist scholar in Bologna and an old friend of the Gonzagas, wrote to Francesco: "You are blessed beyond men in having a fair, wise and noble wife, who is altogether discreet and virtuous, and has shown herself a true mother of concord, ever anxious to gratify your wishes, while she prudently feigns neither to see nor to hear those actions of yours which must be hateful and injurious to her."

. . .

IN 1499 LOUIS XII prepared to attack Milan. Lodovico Sforza sought desperately for allies and naturally turned to his wife's brother-in-law, the Marquis of Mantua, the victor of Fornovo. With cold duplicity Francesco bargained with everyone, demanding high pay and high rank of Lodovico, of the Emperor Maximilian, who was ineffectually supporting Lodovico, of Venice and even of France! Finally he signed as a condottiere in Maximilian's service.

Nevertheless, the Marquis cynically took care not to fight anybody. After the French had defeated Milan and Lodovico had fled to Austria, Francesco proceeded to Pavia in the company of his father-in-law, Duke Ercole of Ferrara, who was also Lodovico's father-in-law, and there with suave diplomatic enthusiasm welcomed the King of France to Italy. Four days later Francesco and Ercole rode into Milan in Louis's triumphal entry into the captured city. (The two Italian princes were acting in exact conformity with the principle of expediency which ruled all Italian politics in their time. Wait and see which way the cat will jump. Join the winning side. Preserve one's own state and ignore the fate of friends and relatives.)

The next year, when Lodovico returned in triumph from Austria, he pleaded with Francesco for help against the French. The Marquis refused; but he hedged his bet just a little and sent a token troop of men-at-arms commanded by his brother Giovanni Gonzaga to Lodovico's assistance. Even that small gesture required a deal of explaining when the French reconquered Milan and took Lodovico prisoner.

The Marquis' judgment of France's preponderant power had proved sound. His skill as a diplomat and courtier also was useful; he charmed Louis XII. He sent the King presents, falcons, horses from the famous Gonzaga stud and paintings by Mantegna, and managed to become his good friend. Two years later he spent Christmas as the King's guest at his castle of Loches.

In 1502 Louis XII returned to Milan and Francesco met him there. So did several of the princes of Romagna whom Cesare Borgia had driven into exile. They hoped to enlist Louis's aid—an unlikely prospect because the King was backing Borgia with troops and money. Perhaps he resented the treachery with which

Borgia had attacked his brother-in-law Guidobaldo of Urbino, or perhaps he became imprudent at a moment when his tongue was loosened by wine—whatever the cause, Francesco recklessly denounced Cesare Borgia as a bastard. Since Francesco was the father of numerous bastards and every princely family had its quota of bastards, his choice of a term of abuse seems odd. He also called Borgia a priest's son, which seems to have been a much less socially desirable thing to be than a prince's bastard. A day or two later Cesare Borgia arrived unexpectedly in Milan, was cordially welcomed by Louis and openly challenged Francesco to a duel.

During Mass on the following day Francesco told the Venetian ambassador that he would fight Borgia with sword and dagger and rescue Italy from the Borgia menace. Francesco probably meant what he said at the time. But the French king reconciled the two men and they actually seemed to become friendly. Since the political friendship of neither could be trusted, it is not possible to know how they really felt about each other. One thing is certain. When Guidobaldo made an attempt to recover Urbino and Elisabetta pleaded with her brother for help, he refused to move against his dangerous ally Cesare Borgia.

In Mantua Isabella heard of Francesco's rash words and hastened to warn him to be more cautious. Borgia was not a man it was prudent to offend. Like most Italians, Isabella called Borgia Valentino after his French title, Duke of Valentinois. She wrote:

"I cannot conceal my fears for your person and State. It is generally believed that His Most Christian Majesty has some understanding with Valentino, so I beg of you to be careful not to use words which may be repeated to him, because in these days we do not know who is to be trusted. There is a report here— whether it has come from Milan by letter or word of mouth, I do not know—that Your Excellency has spoken angry words against Valentino before the Most Christian King and the Pope's servants, and whether this is true or not, they will doubtless reach the ears of Valentino, who, having already shown that he does not scruple to conspire against those of his own blood, will, I am certain, not hesitate to plot against your person. And being jealous for your life, which I count dearer than my own, and know-

G

ing how your natural goodness leads you to take no precautions for your safety, I have made inquiries of Antonio da Bologna and others, and hear from them that you allow all manner of persons to serve you at table, and that Alessandro da Baesso eats with you, leaving grooms and pages to do the offices of carvers and cupbearers. So that I see it would be perfectly easy to poison Your Excellency, since you have neither guards nor proper servants. I pray and implore you, therefore, if you will not take care for your own sake, to be more careful for my sake and that of our little son, and I hope that you will in future order Alessandro to discharge his office of carver with the greatest caution. If he cannot do this, I will send Antonio or some other trustworthy servant, because I had rather run the risk of making you angry than that both I and our little one should be left to weep for you."

In the winter of 1503 the French and the Spaniards were fighting each other for possession of the Kingdom of Naples. The Marquis of Mantua, who had won fame fighting the French in 1495, was second in command of the French army stationed on the banks of the River Garigliano. It was a miserable time—cold weather, constant rains, malaria and dysentery. Corrupt quartermasters failed to deliver supplies; the men were rebellious and hungry. The French commander fell sick, and Francesco Gonzaga took command. This made everything worse because the French soldiers bitterly resented serving under an Italian general.

Soon Francesco found himself confined to his tent with "the French boils," as the Italians called the new disease of syphilis. He grew worse, or pretended to, and had himself carried to Rome in a litter. Francesco's sickness was providential. The disastrous Battle of the Garigliano, in which the Spaniards won a great victory and drove the French permanently from Southern Italy, took place immediately after his departure. And he incurred no blame whatever.

In 1506 Pope Julius II summoned the Marquis of Mantua to come and help him in his campaign to drive the Baglioni out of Perugia and the Bentivoglio out of Bologna so that he could impose papal rule on both cities. Francesco arrived in Perugia after Gianpaolo Baglioni had discreetly surrendered the city and had himself enlisted as a reluctant condottiere in Julius' army. The Bentivoglio were even more cautious. They fled from Bologna before the papal troops came near the city. But before that, Francesco had written Isabella: "The faith which His Holiness places in us leaves us no choice in the matter, yet we cannot but feel compassion for that noble family of Bentivoglio, which has always been so friendly to us."

If the Marquis ever expressed similar sympathy for the misfortunes of the Sforza or Montefeltro families it is not recorded.

Fighting for Pope Julius in 1506 was hardly strenuous. But in 1509 it seriously inconvenienced Francesco. He was then a member of the League of Cambrai, an alliance instigated by Julius to dismember Venice's terra firma in Italy and divide it among the deserving allies. The other members were Louis XII, the Emperor Maximilian, Julius and Alfonso, Duke of Ferrara.

Before hostilities began, Francesco knew a moment of exquisite revenge. He had never forgiven Venice for the humiliation he experienced when the seigniory dismissed him. Now with so powerful an alliance threatening her, Venice sent an envoy to Mantua who pleaded with the Marquis to assume command of the Venetian forces. Francesco gloated while the envoy raised the offered payment from 60,000 to 100,000 scudi and even included the Duchy of Milan (to be won back from France). Finally he brusquely rejected all offers. He was certain he was on the winning side.

The French were triumphant at first and captured most of the cities in Venice's mainland empire. But the Venetians fought stubbornly, recaptured Padua and threatened Verona. Responding to a call for help from Verona, Francesco led a small force forward and camped for the night at the village of Isola della Scala. From there he sent an envoy to try to persuade a troop of Venetian stradiots, or light horsemen, to desert and come over to the League of Cambrai. So when a Venetian force rode into Francesco's camp just before dawn, they were welcomed by the guards who mistook them for deserters. The entire Mantuan detachment was captured.

Francesco himself nearly got away. He climbed out of the

window of the farmhouse in which he had slept and hid half-naked in a wheat field. A peasant found him, and the Marquis offered him many ducats to keep quiet. But the peasant, who was loyal to Venice, shouted loudly for help. Francesco was captured, and with him several of his finest horses, several suits of splendid armor, the tents, hangings, furniture and silver plate without which a marquis could not go to war in appropriate fashion.

When Francesco Gonzaga was paraded as a prisoner across the Piazza San Marco in Venice the crowds threatened to hang him on the spot. One onlooker shouted sarcastically, "Welcome, Marquis of Mantua."

Francesco stared at him coldly and replied, "I do not know who you are talking about. The man before you is Francesco Gonzaga and not the Marquis of Mantua, who is in Mantua." He meant that if he were killed his young son, Federigo, would reign in Mantua as another Gonzaga marquis.

The Marquis did not enjoy being imprisoned in the tower of the Doge's palace called the Torresella, which was fitted with new bolts and bars in his honor. At home in Mantua Isabella assumed control of the government at once and thoroughly enjoyed ruling. But she did her best to enlist influential help in obtaining her husband's release, sending envoys to Louis XII, Maximilian and even to the Sultan, who promised to use his influence with the Doge. Isabella also sent a tenor, a lute singer and several other Mantuan court singers to entertain her fretful husband in his Venetian prison. They were permitted to perform only a few times, and their upkeep was expensive. Isabella recalled them. Francesco rather surprisingly requested that Isabella send him a portrait of herself. She did, along with one of their daughter, Leonora, recently married to Francesco Maria della Rovere, the new duke of Urbino.

In 1510, after the great political turnabout which found Pope Julius allied with Venice against France, the Marquis' release became almost automatic. The Pope arranged it. But Venice insisted that Francesco's son, Federigo, be handed over as a hostage for his father's good behavior.

Even when it was agreed that the boy should be a hostage at the papal court instead of at Venice, Isabella kept postponing his departure, loudly proclaiming her maternal reluctance to part with her child. Francesco exploded with fury at the delay and wrote Isabella from prison that if she did not send ten-year-old Federigo to Rome at once he would strangle her with his bare hands.

Isabella, who was familiar with the Gonzaga temper, was not impressed. She dispatched Federigo when she was ready. With him she sent a major-domo, several tutors, a lutist and some sacred relics.

Shortly after his release the Marquis assumed command of the papal and Venetian armies against France. His enemy Venice had imprisoned him; France was his recent ally; his brother-in-law, Alfonso of Ferrara, was still a loyal ally of France. But Francesco was a professional condottiere and business was business.

Marquis Francesco was in Bologna with the army. Isabella was in Mantua with a foreign policy of her own. She favored France rather than the Pope and Venice, and she was determined to help her brother defend Ferrara. Isabella arranged matters so that French troops could freely cross Mantuan territory on their way to Ferrara, and she persuaded Francesco that he was too sick to attack Alfonso.

During Francesco's imprisonment Isabella had ruled Mantua with an astute head and a firm hand. Shortly after his release Marquis Francesco wrote to her: "*We are ashamed* that it is our fate to have as wife a woman who is always ruled by her head." He probably meant that he was ashamed to have a wife more coldly intelligent and less impulsively emotional than he was.

Isabella, bitterly aware of what she had put up with and of what she had done for him, replied: "Your Excellency is indebted to me as never husband was to wife; nor must Your Excellency think that, even did you love and honor me more than any person in the world, you could repay my good faith."

In 1511 Francesco's health became worse and, although still a member of the anti-French alliance, he gave up active service as a condottiere. His syphilis and his inactivity made him weak, depressed and miserable. He quarreled with friends, servants and Isabella and complained when she was absent. And in 1512 Francesco became involved in a situation which some of his contemporaries considered the crowning treachery of a slippery career.

The young French military genius, Gaston de Foix, learned that the Venetians had recaptured Brescia. To march to that city, where the citadel still held out for the French, would require four days longer if he had to circle around Mantuan territory. A direct passage might enable him to arrive in time to relieve the beleaguered citadel and reconquer the city. Francesco, the nominal ally of Venice and the papacy, allowed De Foix to cross his state.

Foreseeing that he might do so, Gianpaolo Baglioni, his fellow condottiere and comrade in arms, wrote the Marquis urging him not to allow the French to pass: "And this I say because it seems to me that the good name and fame of Italy suffer too much by constant compliance with the demands of these our deadly barbarian foes, especially when such weakness is shown by men of position and prowess, such as Your Highness. Bestir yourself, I beseech you, and with your wonted courage show a brave face to these French. Your obligation to the Church and to Venice so require, but much more so does your duty to Italy, whose fame, honor and safety are in your hands, and who now looks chiefly to you for help and comfort, that she may be free."

This letter from the cynical Baglioni is remarkable for its appeal to Italian national feeling at a time when such feeling was almost unknown among the ruling princes. But the former lord of Perugia had felt the same emotion eighteen years before, as we have seen, when he sallied forth to attack the troops of Charles VIII and was only stopped by the caution of his elders.

The last seven years of the Marquis of Mantua's life were dreary. His disease worsened. Finally, on the morning of March 29, 1519, after making his will and providing generously for the members of his family, Francesco received the last sacraments and called for his wife and children. Isabella, their children, his sister the dowager Duchess of Urbino and his daughter the current Duchess assembled around his bedside.

Turning to his son Federigo, then seventeen, he said: "My dearest son, I leave you a beautiful state and a large revenue. See that you act justly and keep the love of your subjects, and carry out my last orders if you wish to rest in peace." He praised

Isabella for her wisdom and resourcefulness and said that he trusted her completely. A contemporary chronicler who was present wrote: "Nothing was to be seen on the faces of all present but tears; nothing was to be heard but the sobbing of the women, while the children stood by, as it were, stunned and silent." The Marquis of Mantua died that evening.

GIOVANNI FRANCESCO GONZAGA, fourth marquis of Mantua, was not an admirable man. Few of his kind were. He was merely representative of his class. His failings were many, but his charm, energy and zest for life were appealing, and although he was hated, he was also loved. And he was admired. He successfully achieved the highest obligation of a prince as the Renaissance understood it: he had preserved his state in a time of turmoil. He died peacefully in his bed and left that state to his eldest son.

Isabella continued as before, ruling Mantua until Federigo grew old enough to take over, visiting Ferrara and Venice, maintaining her correspondence with a host of friends, buying pictures, jewels and antiques. She was only forty-four when Francesco died, but she was fat, and in spite of her energy, seemed far gone in middle age. More than twenty-five years earlier her cousin, the distinguished poet and courtier, Niccolò da Correggio, had called her "the first lady of the world." He had been sincere. In the opinion of her contemporaries Isabella was still the world's first lady, the most charming, cultivated and admired woman of her time.

In March of 1525 she went to Rome, ostensibly to try to negotiate a cardinal's hat for her second son, Ercole, but actually to get away from Mantua, where Marquis Federigo's brazen flaunting of his arrogant mistress deeply distressed his mother. Pope Clement VII gave her an interview, but he politely evaded granting her request that he make Ercole a cardinal. Cardinal Pompeo Colonna invited her to stay in the Colonna palace and there she stayed for two years.

She lived in state, admired by cardinals, courtiers, poets and scholars. When she heard of the death of her brother-in-law, Cardinal Sigismondo Gonzaga, Isabella rushed to the Vatican and

ISABELLA D'ESTE GONZAGA, Marchioness of Mantua

"... *the first lady of the world.*" Chalk drawing by Leonardo da Vinci.

again urged Pope Clement to make her son Ercole a cardinal. She was so insistent that Clement reluctantly agreed to do so in the event that he increased the number of the Sacred College.

In March of 1527 Ercole was still not a cardinal, Isabella was still in Rome and Federigo was urging his mother to come back to Mantua. Rome was in deadly danger. The half-starved, unpaid German *Landsknechte* and Spanish *tercios* of the Emperor Charles V's army were marching on Rome to appease their frustration and fury by sacking the Eternal City. But Isabella refused to flee. She did not yet have that red cardinal's hat for Ercole!

Pope Clement had antagonized everybody. He had dithered, allied the papacy with France, switched to the side of the Emperor Charles in the never-ending war which was devastating Italy, and even fought against Charles. Now no one was willing to help him. Clement had unwisely disbanded his army. In his terror he tried to raise some troops and to pay them he appointed five new cardinals, who each paid forty thousand ducats for his promotion. Ercole Gonzaga was one of them. On May 5, with the imperial soldiers just outside the walls of Rome, Ercole's red hat was solemnly handed over to Isabella. By then it was too late for her to leave the city.

But Isabella was not quite as reckless as she seemed. The commander of the imperial army attacking Rome was Charles de Bourbon, son of Isabella's sister-in-law, Chiara Gonzaga. A high officer in that turbulent army was Ferrante Gonzaga, Isabella's son. Isabella cleverly sent messages to them both, asking them to protect the Colonna palace if they captured the city. She also ordered the massive palace to be fortified, garrisoned and provisioned for a siege. Bourbon sent a message that he would protect the house as soon as he was able. A number of Roman nobles and ladies fled to Isabella for safety. As many as three thousand people are said to have been inside the Colonna palace.

The horrible atrocities of the sack of Rome rank among the great infamies of history. There had been other sacks and other horrors in the long wars, but nothing as ghastly as the pillage, destruction, torture, rape and murder which raged throughout the city while Pope Clement cowered in the Castel Sant' Angelo and Isabella waited inside her Roman palace. It is estimated that thirty thousand people died—tortured and murdered, or of plague and starvation. Another twenty thousand had fled the city.

As soon as some signs of order appeared, young Ferrante Gonzaga escorted his mother to the Tiber River, where several galleys were waiting to take her and some friends and servants on the first part of their journey to Mantua. Isabella had been in Rome only for a week of the sack.

The last important event in which Isabella played a part was the great conference held in Bologna during the autumn of 1529 and the winter of 1530 in which the triumphant Emperor Charles V settled the affairs of Italy to his own satisfaction. Clement VII, meekly submitting, was the second most important personage in Bologna. Although dukes, marquises and assorted princes were there, Isabella may well have been the third most important celebrity present. She arrived on October 31, accompanied by a bevy of pretty ladies-in-waiting, several courtiers and a crew of servants. A palace was turned over to her for her use, and she stayed in it for four months. Isabella was anxious not to miss any of the excitement or social pleasures of the conference. While Charles and Clement dictated the fate of Italy, and Charles was formally crowned Emperor in a glittering ceremony, Isabella enjoyed herself and cultivated influential people. She cultivated Charles so well that after the conference he came on to Mantua and stayed four weeks as a guest of the Mantuan court.

Expense was no objection to young Marquis Federigo and his mother. They rotated Charles and his entourage about their country villas. And they arranged a great hunt in which five thousand horsemen joined the Emperor! The spectacle must have been marvelous, but the hunt itself must have been a triumph of confusion. And on April 8, 1530 Emperor Charles V made Marquis Federigo a duke. The vast expense was justified, and Isabella had achieved her greatest triumph.

Not quite nine years later, on February 13, 1539, Isabella d'Este Gonzaga, Marchioness of Mantua and first lady of the world, died. She was sixty-four. There were other learned, talented and courageous women in Renaissance Italy, but none was so versatile, so dominating and so universally admired. Uninterested in religion, she accepted its forms and doctrines without thinking about them. Not notably moved by the violence and corruption of her era, she accepted the world as it was—and enjoyed living in it.

XII

THE ESTE
OF FERRARA

COMPARED with the ancient and noble house of Este, the Sforzas were vulgar upstarts and the Gonzagas were only raw recruits to the aristocracy of Italy. The Este were members of the medieval nobility in Carolingian times. For centuries they ruled the little town of Este in the Euganean Hills near Padua. But late in the twelfth century a Marquis Obizzo d'Este seized Ferrara and early in the thirteenth century his son, Marquis Azzolino, and his heirs were solemnly elected perpetual lords of the city by the people of Ferrara. This is the first recorded instance of an Italian city deliberately voting to exchange its liberty for the arbitrary rule of a despot. Later in the thirteenth century another Obizzo acquired the lordships of Modena and Reggio.

Ferrara lies in the flat and swampy Po valley some thirty-five miles from the Adriatic and about fifty-five miles southwest of Venice. The Este marquises always had to keep a watchful eye on their mighty neighbor. They were all such notable warriors and ruthless rulers, however, that they were admired and feared throughout the valley of the Po.

The twelfth medieval marquis of Ferrara, Niccolò III, was also the first Renaissance prince in the Este dynasty. A transitional figure, he combined a medieval enthusiasm for pilgrimages to holy sites with a Renaissance interest in classical learning. Niccolò became marquis in 1393, when he was only ten years old. In 1402, when he was nineteen, he took over the direct rule of his state and ruled with great success for thirty-nine years until his death on December 26, 1441.

Niccolò d'Este was an able and treacherous soldier in his younger days when he had to make good his claim to his state. But during most of his reign he was a prudent statesman who avoided war. All his life he was famous for his insatiable sexuality. "A fat man, jolly, given up to lust," said Pius II of the Marquis of Ferrara. His subjects sang a jingle about him: *"Di qua e di la del Po, tutti figli di Niccolò"*—On this and that side of the Po all are children of Niccolò.

In his history in verse of the House of Este, Ugo Caleffini wrote that Niccolò had eight hundred mistresses and would have had a thousand if he had lived a little longer. Pope Pius said that Niccolò kept whole troops of concubines, "plebeians and countrywomen as well as nobles." No estimate has ever been made of his bastards. But he is supposed to have acknowledged twenty-seven children, both legitimate and illegitimate.

He married three times. His first wife had no children. His second wife, Parisina Malatesta, had twin daughters. His third wife, Ricciarda da Saluzzo, had two sons, Ercole and Sigismondo. Three of Niccolò's bastard sons played major roles in the Este story—Ugo, Leonello and Borso.

In 1413, when he was thirty years old, Niccolò and several of his friends made a pilgrimage to Jerusalem, sailing on a Venetian galley. In Palestine, disguised as humble pilgrims, they rode on donkeys to the holy city. There Niccolò prayed fervently and knighted five of his companions. On their return voyage Niccolò and his friends were entertained by the King of Cyprus and the Marquis, like Odysseus, demonstrated his strength by drawing a bow which no one else could draw.

Within a year Niccolò was off on another pilgrimage, this time to the shrine of St. Anthony at Vienne in France. On his return journey Niccolò and his party were treacherously imprisoned by a Piedmontese nobleman, who offered to sell them to the Duke of Milan. Niccolò was rescued by the timely intercession of the Count of Savoy. The robber baron (a petty marquis) was promptly beheaded, and his castle razed to the ground. Niccolò had sportingly put in a good word for his captor—to no avail.

The Marquis of Ferrara was sincerely concerned for the welfare of his people, kept taxes reasonable and tried to economize on Este family expenses. Niccolò did not go so far as to limit his own pleasure in splendid costumes; nor did he restrict the expenditure of the Marchioness Parisina, who patronized painters, collected medieval romances and maintained a racing stable. It was on his children that the Marquis economized. The young Este princes sometimes had no change of clothes and had to sleep on straw mattresses concealed beneath fancy fabrics.

Niccolò was fat and jolly, but he was also was cruel, vengeful and absolutely convinced of his right to rule others despotically. He was equally convinced that it was his privilege to enjoy as many women as he wished but that his wife should be above reproach. His young wife, Parisina Malatesta, who had married Niccolò when she was fifteen and he thirty-six, did not agree with him.

In 1424 Parisina fell in love with a handsome young man her own age, her stepson Ugo d'Este. Ugo was Niccolò's favorite son and his heir. On a journey to some neighboring town the young couple became lovers. The following year in Ferrara one of Parisina's maids who had been beaten by her mistress betrayed the guilty couple to a courtier, who in turn informed Niccolò. A doubtful but imperishable legend has it that by means of an artfully arranged mirror Niccolò looked across the courtyard of the Este castle and into the chamber where the lovers were embracing.

Parisina and Ugo were arrested at once, to be confined in a dungeon for one day and beheaded the next. Niccolò refused to speak to them or look at them. All through the night before the executions Niccolò in a frenzy of grief and rage roamed through the corridors of the palace, gnawing on his sceptre, calling for his beloved son Ugo and crying out for his own death. In his great emotional turmoil the Marquis issued a decree that henceforth any woman in his domains who committed the same offense as Parisina's would be beheaded. As far as it is known, only one woman, the wife of a judge, was executed under the new law.

There were other aspects of Niccolò's complex character. He was one of the first princes in Italy to become interested in the new humanist learning of the Renaissance. He reopened the University of Ferrara, founded by his father, which had been closed during the wars. He invited Giovanni Aurispa, the first great collector of Greek manuscripts, to come to Ferrara. He also invited a famous doctor in Padua to come and be his court physician—this was Michele Savonarola, whose grandson, Girolamo, was to die a martyr's death in Florence.

The execution of Ugo d'Este made his younger brother Leonello the heir. At twenty-two Leonello wanted to learn Greek and Latin. He would have agreed with Pope Pius II if he could have read the scholar pope's famous letter on a liberal education in which Pius said: "Literature is our guide to the true meaning of the past, to a right estimate of the present, to a sound forecast of the future. Where Letters cease, darkness covers the land; and a Prince who cannot read the lessons of history is a helpless prey of flattery and intrigue."

Niccolò agreed with Leonello that he needed the instruction of a distinguished scholar, and at Leonello's suggestion invited Guarino da Verona to come to Ferrara. Guarino, who had studied at Constantinople, accepted. For seven years he taught Leonello, and then he settled down for the rest of his life as professor of eloquence and of Greek and Latin letters at the University of Ferrara. His appointment was nearly as important an event in the history of humanism and the culture of the Renaissance as that of Vittorino da Feltre to teach the children of Gianfrancesco Gonzaga, Marquis of Mantua.

Guarino became so famous as a scholar that students flocked to study under him from all over Italy and from many European countries. They crowded his lecture hall and stood in line to get in. Guarino wrote books and translated classics to supplement his income. He became an intimate friend of Leonello, whom he called "the flower of princes." Guarino's students, wrote Vespasiano da Bisticci, learned "not only literature, but also good manners and conduct, for he was scrupulously honest and most particular in his view of life. Guarino was the means of leading many into a good way of life, being himself an example of virtue."

The artist Pisanello also came to Niccolò's court and painted portraits of several of the Marquis' children, including two of Leonello. His bronze medallions of Niccolò show a tough, dissipated, aging face. The atmosphere of the court of Ferrara was considerably relaxed in Niccolò's last years. Guarino's influence was certainly beneficial. So must have been Leonello's, for he was to become one of the most enlightened and virtuous princes of his time. The scholar Aurispa wrote of Niccolò: "I love this Marquis of mine not otherwise than as a good son loves a sweet and gentle parent."

It is difficult to think of Niccolò III as lovable, sweet or gentle, but we know that he was many-sided and Aurispa presumably had personal knowledge of aspects of the formidable Marquis which have not been described for the benefit of posterity. In his will Niccolò named as his heirs first Leonello, then Leonello's brother Borso, and then after these two bastard princes his two much younger legitimate sons, Ercole and Sigismondo.

In December 1441, when Leonello succeeded his father as Marquis of Ferrara, he was thirty-four years old. His first wife, Margherita Gonzaga, sister of Marquis Lodovico of Mantua, had died the year before. They had one child, a boy called Niccolò for his grandfather, who was to continue the Este tradition of family violence. In addition, Leonello had an illegitimate son, born before the arrival of Niccolò.

The portrait paintings of Leonello d'Este by Oriolo and Pisanello and Pisanello's medallions are all profiles and show a thoughtful, intelligent-looking young man with a low forehead, a long, large nose, pale eyes and an expression of composed self-confidence. Does he look like the intellectual scholar and artistic dilettante we know that he was? It is hard to know.

At the age of fifteen Leonello had been sent by his father to learn the art of war under the great condottiere Braccio da Montone, Lord of Perugia. He stayed with Braccio for two years and presumably did not enjoy the experience. He never showed any interest in warfare, did not become a soldier, and as Marquis, kept Ferrara at peace and helped mediate peace for others.

Like most of his contemporary princes, Leonello was extravagant and loved magnificence; and also like most of them he was fond of hunting, horses and dogs. But he was one of the first to become a learned and cultivated man. He was fluent in Greek and Latin, wrote elegant Latin letters and wrote a book of sonnets in Italian. He is supposed to have written a Latin commentary upon his own actions which has not survived.

Leonello delighted in patronizing scholars, writers and artists. In addition to Guarino, who remained his intimate friend until the Marquis' death, he was a close friend of Leon Battista Alberti, the great architect and the most astoundingly versatile Renaissance man before Leonardo and Michelangelo. But it was as a writer that Leonello admired Alberti. He instigated Alberti to write his famous three-volume work on architecture; but he never employed Alberti to design, build or rebuild a church or other building, as did both Sigismondo Malatesta and Lodovico Gonzaga. Alberti was so fond of Leonello, or else such an adroit courtier, that he called him the "delight of the human race."

Among the painters at Leonello's court was Roger van der Weyden, who came from Flanders to teach the technique of painting in oils. Leonello collected pictures, antiquities, medals and jewels. His dogs had jewels on their collars, and his horses had them on their harnesses. Leonello also collected books, particularly the works of Greek and Latin authors then available. He was as interested in books of theology as he was in the classics and paid Poggio one hundred gold florins for two volumes of St. Jerome's letters. It was Leonello who was the first to doubt the authenticity of a collection of spurious letters supposedly written by St. Paul to Seneca.

With such an enthusiasm for scholarship it was only natural that Leonello should take an interest in the Ferrara university which was languishing in mediocrity or worse. He began by banishing all the incompetent teachers from Ferrara and recruiting capable scholars to replace them. In a decree announcing his campaign for educational reform Leonello wrote:

"It is an ancient opinion not only of Christians but of the Gentiles that the heavens, the sea, the earth must someday perish; in like manner as of many magnificent cities nothing but ruins leveled with the ground are seen, and Rome the conqueror herself lies in the dust and is beheld reduced to fragments; while only the understanding of things divine and human, which we call wisdom, is not extinguished by length of years, but retains its rights in perpetuity."

That wisdom could be taught may seem to us, more than five hundred years later, a naïvely optimistic notion. But Leonello's belief that it could tells us much about the excited enthusiasm for learning which was so vital a force in the making of the Renaissance.

This gentle, contemplative scholar who ruled for only nine years in Ferrara is not charged with any crime or any act of cruelty. Some scandalous gossip accused him of sexual excesses, but the gossip was not general and is not supported by other contemporary sources. In an age of general sexual laxity it is not surprising that a few people believed that Niccolò's son would behave like Niccolò.

When Leonello married for the second time in 1444, he spared no effort to make the occasion splendid according to the best Renaissance ideas about wedding festivities. The bride was Maria of Aragon, bastard daughter of Alfonso the Magnanimous. The balls, parties and pageants lasted for two weeks. The piazza of Ferrara was used for a tournament and for a pageant in which St. George, patron saint of Ferrara, slew the dragon. And, most spectacular of all, a forest was set up in the piazza, complete with real oak trees and with real underbrush. The forest was stocked with bullocks, steers, wild boars and goats. These were methodically slaughtered to the plaudits of the crowd, a repulsive form of entertainment which, however, offended no one.

The prolonged wedding festivities, with hundreds of guests and probably thousands of their servants, provided Leonello with an opportunity to display a munificent hospitality. Some 2,000 oxen were consumed, as well as 40,000 pairs of fowl, thousands of pheasants and pigeons, 20,000 jugs of wine, 10,000 bushels of grain and 15,000 pounds of sweets. Are such impressive figures accurate? We do not know. They may have been exaggerated to glorify the wealth of Ferrara. They may even have been padded so that stewards and merchants could make a dishonest profit.

Leonello completed the Este palace of Belfiore just outside the city walls and there he kept his collection of antiques, books and art. He imported a choir of singers from France to sing in his private chapel. He had a special hero worship for Julius Caesar, and his private apartments were decorated with pictures of other ancient heroes. In 1449 Maria of Aragon died. She had no children. The following year, Leonello d'Este, the gentlest, most attractive and most admirable member of his turbulent family, died at the age of only forty-three. Guarino delivered the oration at his funeral. And an anonymous Ferrarese diarist summed up the opinion of Leonello's grieving subjects:

"He was a lover of justice, of most honest life, a lover of piety, most devoted to the divine religion, a lover of the poor, liberal to the needy, a studious hearer of Holy Scriptures, patient in adversity, moderate in prosperity. He ruled his people in peace with great wisdom."

Leonello's younger brother and successor, Borso d'Este, was the most popular and successful ruler Ferrara ever had. Thirty-seven when Leonello died, Borso ruled for twenty-one years in a nonstop performance of unmatched splendor and ostentatious magnificence. Handsome, affable and jovial, Borso habitually concealed his considerable political acumen beneath a mask of hearty geniality. The mask was not hypocritical. The geniality was sincere. But it was useful, too, to a ruler who charmed his subjects when he could and intimidated them only as much as he thought necessary for sound political expediency.

When Leonello fell ill, Niccolò's two legitimate sons, Ercole and Sigismondo, were away at the court of Naples where Ercole was making a reputation as a gallant young soldier. Borso was careful not to let them know of Leonello's illness and death until he had firmly seized the reins of power as marquis of Ferrara. A small faction in the city supported Leonello's fourteen-year-old son, Niccolò; another supported Ercole. But neither caused Borso any trouble in establishing his rule.

Borso's good looks did not last long. High living made him fat, jowly and double-chinned. But he always retained his ease of manner and his benign expression. Except for a few malcontents who dabbled in conspiracies, the Ferrarese adored him, called him "the divine Borso" and basked in the reflected glory of his magnificence. So great was Borso's reputation for wealth and grandeur that Moslem princes sent him presents under the misapprehension that he was king of all Italy.

Although Borso was a member of the oldest aristocratic family in Italy, his passion for displaying his wealth was as childishly vulgar as that proverbially attributed to the newly rich. But that, after all, was what most Renaissance ruling families were—vulgar and newly rich, even the older families. Borso always wore cloth of gold, and the gold chain he wore around his neck was supposed to be worth seventy thousand ducats. In the fifteenth century the Venetian ducat and the Florentine florin were the standard currencies of Italy and circulated in much of Europe. Their purchasing power is impossible to reckon accurately, but authorities have estimated that they were worth at least as much as ten dollars today and perhaps as much as twenty dollars.

Borso's generosity to his fellow princes, courtiers, favorites and even to his servants and messengers was so lavishly spectacular that it provoked a folk saying: "He who would find the heavens open should experience the liberality of Duke Borso."

Such splendor could be maintained only by an efficient tyranny. Borso rigidly enforced his laws and was never known to show mercy to a thief. He was ruthless about taxes, urging his tax collectors to "squeeze all the juice possible" from his subjects. He imposed fines for swearing and gambling; informers were paid one third of the fines collected from those they betrayed. Anyone who spoke ill of Borso, or who was suspected of opposing him, was fined or had his property confiscated. Borso made the sale of salt, meat, fish, fruit and vegetables his personal monopolies.

Such practices offended only a few. They were the customs of the time, a normal part of life in the princely states. The word liberty did not apply to ordinary citizens. It only meant freedom from the rule of another state, or from the injustices of a usurper. So Borso walked in the piazza every morning, beamed on his subjects, listened to their grievances and dispensed justice. He was dearly beloved, so dearly that in later years anyone who wanted to refer to the good old days spoke of "the time of Duke Borso."

Borso was not a cultivated intellectual like his brother Leonello. He did not read or speak Latin; he was not interested in art save as an expression of Este magnificence. He did support the university and paid the expenses of poor students, but hunting was more in his line than books. "Fortune, the enemy of every virtuous man, has not willed to add to thy other rare ornaments the ornament of letters," wrote one of Borso's courtiers.

Like most Renaissance princes, Borso regarded his states as his personal property. Like the proprietor of a large business, he tried to run his properties well. Borso reformed laws, built dikes to control floods, fostered local industries, gave grain to the hungry during famines and saw to it that taxes, if heavy, were fair. And throughout his reign Borso kept Ferrara out of war, that is, except for one gingerly and half-hearted participation in an anti-Medici war of no great consequence.

Why Borso opposed Piero de' Medici, the son of the great Cosimo and the father of the great Lorenzo, is not entirely clear. Could the bastard son of an ancient house be offended that a family of middle-class bankers was ruling a powerful neighboring state? Or was Borso's desire to ingratiate himself with Pope Paul II sufficient explanation? Paul was a Venetian and Venice was then supporting an anti-Medici faction. And Paul could make Borso duke of Ferrara, which he dearly wished to be.

In any case, Borso's only resort to military force came in 1466 and 1467. In the first year he dispatched a contingent of cavalry and infantry to the Florentine border to support a small and mismanaged conspiracy against Piero de' Medici. The next year Borso sent his brother Ercole to fight in the only battle of the little war. Ercole had two horses killed from under him and was wounded in the foot, which made him limp for the rest of his life.

Two years later, in 1469, a conspiracy against Borso was organized by a faction of the Pio family, rulers of Carpi, with backing from Galeazzo Maria Sforza, Duke of Milan, and the probable connivance of King Ferrante of Naples and of Piero de' Medici, who presumably had not forgiven Borso for his part in the recent anti-Medici war. Agents approached Ercole and promised him the lordship of Ferrara, several towns in the Romagna and an annual salary of fifty thousand ducats if he would lead the putsch against Borso. Ercole, with astute craft, revealed all to Borso, who promptly executed three of the ringleaders and imprisoned others, who may even have been innocent.

In the same year a Ferrarese diplomat warned Borso that Piero de' Medici was conspiring to poison him. We need not believe this charge against the decent and generally inactive Piero, but Borso probably did. So it is all the more surprising and amusing to read the letter of condolence Borso sent Lorenzo de' Medici on Piero's death:

"It would be a difficult thing to express with letters the great grief, the great anguish and sorrow of soul that we have conceived by the death of the magnificent and most renowned Piero, your father; for, seeing that we were united continually by singular love, benevolence and close friendship with him (and first with the magnificent Cosimo, your grandfather, and with all the House of Medici, which bond of mutual charity had sweet and gracious beginning from our most illustrious predecessors, and has been preserved, and is preserved still better by us, their successors), not only through the great love we bear you, do we share with your Worship in the grief for the loss of so worthy and excellent a father, whose nobleness, marvelous intellect and admirable virtues certainly merited a longer life; but also for our own sake we grieve greatly, it seeming to us that we have suffered a grievous loss of a true and excellent friend, as was your father to us, and as we were equally to him."

As an example of Renaissance hypocrisy and diplomacy this flow of crocodile tears can hardly be matched.

On ceremonial occasions it was Borso's custom to be escorted by the seven leading bastards of the House of Este. Borso, a bastard himself who never married, had no bastards of his own, as far as is known. When Borso rode out to welcome an important guest, he was always accompanied by three of his half brothers, sons of Niccolò, named Alberto, Gurone and Rinaldo; by Leonello's bastard son, Francesco; and by the three bastard sons of Meliaduse (deceased), Borso's bastard half-brother—Niccolò, Scipione and Polidoro.

It was grand to be a rich and famous marquis, but it would be grander to be a rich and famous duke. Borso contrived to become duke of Modena and Reggio, which were imperial fiefs, in 1452,

when the feckless Hapsburg emperor Frederick III came to Italy
to be crowned by the Pope and enriched his exchequer by selling
knighthoods and noble titles all up and down the peninsula.
The most ineffectual and incompetent ruler of the celebrated
Hapsburg dynasty rode into Italy at the head of a train of twelve
hundred horsemen. Borso entertained the whole party as his
guests for ten days in munificent fashion, all the time trying to
charm and bribe Frederick into making him a duke. Frederick
hesitated, wondering whether a bastard, even so rich and hospita-
ble a bastard, was really eligible to become an imperial duke.
Frederick arrived in Ferrara in the winter, went off to Rome and
Naples without making up his mind and returned to Ferrara in
May finally persuaded.

The ceremony in which Borso was made duke of Modena and
Reggio was one of the two great peaks of Borso's life and a
typical expression of the Renaissance love of pageantry and magnificence. Ella Noyes described it in *The Story Of Ferrara:*

"Every window and loggia was hung with brilliant cloths.
Early in the morning the Emperor issued from the palace, leaning
upon two pages and clad in the Imperial mantle of gold tissue,
sewn with precious stones. Before him went heralds and trumpeters, ambassadors, princes, dukes, beneath the glorious façade
of the Duomo, which is the same today as it was then. At the
angle where the whole marketplace lies before you stood a high
tribune covered with painted hangings and supporting a throne
arrayed in cloth of gold. As the Emperor ascended and seated
himself, another procession wound into the upper end of the
Piazza from behind the Cathedral, and approached in slow and
stately march, four hundred knights on horseback, two by two,
each one bearing a pennon of white taffeta, in signs, says the
chronicler, of joy, save the two last, who carried green standards
representing Borso's Imperial fiefs, and were followed by a single
knight, who held aloft a great red banner symbolizing· Imperial
justice. A noble of the house of Bevilacqua came next, carrying
the naked sword of the prince in front of Borso himself, who was
dressed in cloth of gold and wore jewels of inestimable splendor
and worth. The horsemen, parting as they neared the throne,
ranged themselves in a semi-circle, through which the marquis
passed, and mounting the steps, knelt before the Emperor, with

his sword-bearer and the three standard-bearers behind him. Frederick raising him, seated him beside himself and caused him to be vested in a garment of red wool and a long rose-colored mantle lined with ermine; a ducal beretta was set upon his head. Borso then rose, and the Emperor committed to him the three standards, the naked sword and a golden sceptre, and kissing him declared him Duke of Modena and Reggio."

It took Borso nineteen more years before he achieved his other ambition and became duke of Ferrara through the gracious co-operation of Pope Paul II. But before that, Borso experienced a somewhat trying time with another pope, Pius II, an old friend from whom Borso optimistically expected to obtain anything he wanted. "Nor would he have been wrong if he had asked for things more fit for us to grant," wrote Pius waspishly. Borso asked to be made duke of Ferrara, which Pius was willing to arrange. But Borso also asked to have the taxes Ferrara paid the papacy abolished, which Pius refused because to do so would be to admit officially that Ferrara was no longer a fief of the Holy See. The papal claims to ultimate sovereignty over papal states may have been remote and sometimes ineffective, but no Renaissance pope could conceive of abandoning them.

In 1459 Pope Pius journeyed to Mantua for the congress at which he hoped to enlist the rulers of Europe for his Crusade against the Turks and stopped off in Ferrara for eight days. Borso spared nothing to please the humanist pope. "The Duke promised on no account to absent himself from the congress at Mantua, alleging that it was his dearest wish to establish Christianity among all mankind."

But Borso had no intention of wasting money, time or effort on a Crusade. He kept postponing his arrival at Mantua. Pius was furious. "When summoned yet again he had changed his mind and refused, giving as an excuse the evidence of the astrologers, who said that the stars foretold his death if he went to Mantua. The Pope rebuked him for heeding pagan nonsense. . . . Finally he said he was sick of a fever and needed rest. But he left Ferrara for Emilia, where in the midst of the summer heat he went hawking."

To appease the angry pope, Borso had his envoy at the congress promise three hundred thousand gold ducats toward the expenses of the Crusade. The sum was enormous and Borso never paid a single ducat of it. So Pius's sketch of Borso is eminently fair:

"Borso was a man of fine physique and more than average height, with beautiful hair and a pleasing countenance. He was eloquent and garrulous and listened to himself talking as if he pleased himself more than his hearers. His talk was full of blandishments mingled with lies. He desired to seem rather than to be magnificent and generous. . . . During his lifetime the people erected in the piazza a statue representing him seated administering justice. It bore an inscription composed in flattery and adulation, for Borso loved nothing so much as praise. He bought as many precious stones as he could and never appeared in public without jewels. He collected rich household furnishings. Even in the country he used gold and silver dishes."

A revealing glimpse of the Renaissance attitude toward religion can be seen in Borso's arrangements to welcome Pius in Ferrara on his return journey from Mantua to Rome in 1460. When the supreme head of the Christian religion stepped ashore from the barge which had brought him down the Po, he found himself confronted by an array of statues of pagan gods and goddesses assembled in his honor. Borso had not thought them inappropriate, and it is possible that Pius, who was a humanist scholar before he was a churchman, did not find them inappropriate either.

In the winter of 1471 Pope Paul II notified Borso d'Este that he would be pleased to make him duke of Ferrara on Easter Day, April 14. Now at last Borso would no longer be duke merely of his two lesser cities, Modena and Reggio, and only marquis of Ferrara, the principal city of the Este. His somewhat simple-minded, almost childish, delight in his own grandeur required that he make his journey to Rome in proper style. On March 13 he left Ferrara, accompanied by more than five hundred gentlemen whose valets wore cloth of gold, and whose grooms wore silver brocade. A train of a hundred and fifty mules caparisoned in white, red and green carried the baggage. Eighty pages each led four greyhounds on leashes. There were trumpeters, pipers, falconers in charge of four different kinds of hawks, and a band

of Orientals leading several tame leopards (undoubtedly chee-
tahs). Different sources give different figures for Borso's retinue,
but they all agree that the procession was spectacular.

Twenty-four days after his departure Borso entered Rome.
Francesco Aristi wrote: "Our divine, loving and lofty Lord rode
on, all joyous and jocund and lordly, resplendent with that
Caesarian aspect of his, adorned with gold and gems, upon that
great charger that flashed back the light, gleaming in those won-
drously worked and precious trappings. The Prince seemed
rather another triumphing Caesar than like his own Borsian
serenity." Fawning flattery could be no more profuse; but beneath the rhetoric may have been geunine respect and affection.

Borso's investiture as duke of Ferrara was performed in St.
Peter's (in the ancient building which was torn down and replaced by the present structure). The ceremony was grand
enough to satisfy even Borso, who wrote back to his secretary in
Ferrara: "We have been treated as if we were a king or emperor."

In May, Borso left Rome and reached Ferrara on the eighteenth, worn out with feasting and travel, and stricken with
malaria. He was forced to cancel preparations for a magnificent
welcome home and slipped quietly into his capital. At fifty-eight
he was old. Most men of the Renaissance were old when past
fifty. Titian, Michelangelo and Pope Julius II, who performed
prodigies of energy in old age, were among the exceptions.

Borso lay ill in his palace, obviously dying. Pius had written of
him: "He never took a wife with the right excellent intention of
leaving to the rightful heirs the sovereignty, which he had
occupied in their stead while they were children."

But who were the rightful heirs? Pius obviously meant Ercole
and after him his brother Sigismondo, legitimate sons of old
Marquis Niccolò. But a strong faction in Ferrara supported
young Niccolò, legitimate son of Leonello. Ercole had secured
the official support of Venice. Niccolò was backed by Milan and
Mantua. A fleet of Venetian galleys came up the Po to aid
Ercole if he needed help. While Borso lay helpless on his deathbed Ercole fought Niccolò in the streets of Ferrara, beat him and

drove him out of the city. Borso died on August 19. Ercole assumed power, proclaimed himself duke, and in a letter to Lorenzo de' Medici announcing his assumption of the dukedom referred to Borso's "blessed and innocent soul." That was the key to Borso's remarkable popularity. He was an astute politician and an efficient tyrant. But there was something lovable about him which struck his contemporaries as a quality of innocence.

XIII

THE CRAFT AND PIETY OF DUKE ERCOLE

 No ONE EVER THOUGHT of Borso's successor as innocent. Ercole was the most complex, subtle and paradoxical of all the rulers of the House of Este.

Born in 1431, Ercole was two months short of his fortieth birthday when he became duke in 1471. He ruled for more than thirty-three years and died peacefully in his bed at the age of seventy-three. He was not as gentle, virtuous or cultivated as his elder half-brother Leonello. He was not affable and popular like his other elder half-brother, Borso. But he was a great patron of the arts and a highly successful sovereign.

Tall, handsome, swarthy, with an expression of calm self-command, Ercole had such a chilly personality that he was called the North Wind and the Diamond. Only his son-in-law, Lodovico Sforza, equaled him in his combination of contradictory qualities and psychological mysteries. As a youth growing up at the Neapolitan court Ercole won a reputation as a valiant and gallant soldier, but in his maturity he was a timid and incompetent general. No ruler of his time was as sincerely religious as Ercole. But he could be as cruel, treacherous and cynically opportunistic as a

ERCOLE D'ESTE, Duke of Ferrara

"*Tall, handsome, swarthy, with an expression of calm self-command, Ercole had such a chilly personality that he was called the North Wind and the Diamond. Only his son-in-law, Lodovico Sforza, equaled him in his combination of contradictory qualities and psychological mysteries.*"

Borgia. Intelligent, crafty, cautious, unscrupulous, Ercole could be blind to political disasters within his own duchy and shortsighted about foreign politics. He was a good husband and a reasonably good father to his six legitimate and two illegitimate children. During his reign Ferrara was nearly destroyed in a disastrous war, but it also reached its peak as a center of Renaissance culture.

No sooner had Ercole become duke than he took steps to insure that he would remain duke. He executed the supporters of his nephew and rival, Niccolò, the son of Leonello. An exile at the court of his uncle Lodovico, Marquis of Mantua, Niccolò was convinced that he was the rightful duke of Ferrara. He wrote letters soliciting support in his campaign against Ercole to princes and prelates all over Italy—he lamented, promised and conspired. Did Niccolò plan an armed assault on Ferrara, or perhaps an assassination? Ercole didn't know, but he was determined to prevent such unpleasant possibilities.

Early in December of 1471 Ercole dispatched one of his nobles, Count Niccolò di Rinaldo Ariosti, father of the great poet Lodovico Ariosto, to Mantua to take a present to the Marchioness. But the present was only a cover for Ariosti's real mission, to arrange the poisoning of Niccolò d'Este. The Count bribed one of Niccolò's servants, promising him in Ercole's name a palace in Ferrara, two castles and an annuity. He was given a poisoned dagger, and in case he shrank from using it, poison to put in Niccolò's food.

But the servant lacked the craft and confidence of which true Renaissance poisoners were made. He fell ill, feared that he had accidentally poisoned himself and confessed. Marquis Lodovico promptly had him executed. The Count escaped back to Ferrara, and Ercole, who did not hold his failure against him, made him governor of the citadel of Reggio. After all, Ariosti had done his best!

Ercole d'Este was a ruthless tyrant. Poison was part of the political world of his time. Nevertheless, there is something horrible in the spectacle of a man as devoutly and ostentatiously religious as Ercole trying to poison his own nephew. But the customs of his time were peculiar in this respect; no one seemed to hold against Ercole his attempt to murder Niccolò by poison, and his reputation did not suffer.

When Ercole was away in Naples, he had heartily disliked King Ferrante—which was certainly understandable—and had even fought briefly against him with the Angevins. But as duke of Ferrara Ercole found it expedient to conciliate the powerful king of Naples. A marriage was arranged between the new duke and Ferrante's beautiful daughter, Eleonora. In 1472 Ercole had the Este court painter, Cosimo Tura, paint his portrait together with that of his illegitimate daughter, Lucrezia, the child of his only known mistress before his marriage. He sent the picture off as a present to his bride-to-be at her father's court in Naples—a thoughtful gesture.

In June of 1473 Ercole dispatched a noble company of Ferrarese lords and servants to escort Eleonora back to Ferrara. On their return journey they were joined by so many Neapolitan lords and their servants that one contemporary estimate of the cavalcade was that it contained fifteen hundred people. This seems wildly unlikely. But it is possible—the Renaissance passion for magnificence being what it was. The bride was lavishly entertained in Rome and Florence on her way to Ferrara, where the wedding festivities lasted for a week. Ercole was notoriously stingy, but he spared no expense on his own wedding.

The marriage was happy. Eleonora was beautiful (she wore her long black hair loose over her shoulders in the Neapolitan fashion), pious, virtuous, courageous and capable of ruling the duchy in Ercole's absences. Ercole loved her, trusted her and admired her. He was even faithful to her—except for one lapse when Eleonora was away visiting her family in Naples and Ercole consoled himself with one of her ladies-in-waiting who bore him his only other bastard, a boy called Giulio.

The ducal couple had six children: Isabella and Beatrice, whom we have already met; Alfonso, "the hereditary prince of Ferrara"; Ferrante, Ippolito and Sigismondo.

While Ercole was enjoying the first fruits of power and the pleasures of domesticity, Niccolò continued to conspire against him. Learning through a spy in Ferrara that Ercole would be away from the city visiting his country villa of Belriguardo on

Sunday, September 1, 1476, Niccolò chose that day for his grand attempt to seize the city and make himself duke. With seven hundred mercenary soldiers he had hired in Padua and Verona he came sailing down the Po in five barges. The soldiers were hidden beneath piles of hay and straw. How Niccolò paid the soldiers, if he did, and who may have been his financial backers are interesting but unanswered questions.

Niccolò and his men marched into Ferrara without difficulty early in the afternoon. The church bells rang wild alarms, but the people stayed in their houses and no one joined the invaders. Niccolò rode around the piazza, shouting promises to the people and then seated himself in front of the Palazzo della Ragione, hoping to be acknowledged as the rightful duke. Instead, someone shot an arrow at him which killed one of his supporters.

When a messenger brought the news to Ercole, he rode back toward the city but was met by Eleonora's secretary, who told him that Niccolò had fourteen thousand men. Instead of scoffing at such an improbable figure, Ercole seems to have believed it. At any rate, he fled to recruit an army of his own. His flight was unnecessary. In the meantime Ercole's brother Sigismondo and his half-brother Rinaldo had rallied loyal soldiers and soundly defeated Niccolò's troops.

Niccolò managed to escape to his barges, but these, too, were captured after they had retreated only a little way. Once again Niccolò escaped, and this time he hid in a swamp. But his pursuers found him and brought him back a prisoner to Ferrara. The following day Ercole returned to his city. The streets were littered with dead men killed by his brothers and their soldiers. An eyewitness wrote:

"Messer Sigismondo and Messer Rinaldo d'Este, his brothers, went to meet him with all the nobles of the city; and, when he arrived in the piazza, and heard all the people crying '*Diamante, diamante*, Ercole, Ercole,' and saw his wife weeping with gladness, he could not contain himself, but began to weep, too, for joy at the fidelity of the people. And straightway he dismounted and entered into the Duomo, and went to the high altar to thank God, who hath liberated him from very great peril of his life and of his State."

Soon the principal leaders among the prisoners were hanging from the battlements and windows of the Castello Vecchio and the Palazzo della Ragione. And Niccolò himself was beheaded. But Niccolò was an Este, and although Ercole may have ordered his murder, he buried him with all the formal respect due a member of the ruling family. Ercole ordered all the leading citizens of Ferrara to march in Niccolò's funeral procession. Someone had carefully sewn Niccolò's severed head back onto his neck! His body was dressed in a long robe of gold brocade. On his head was placed a crimson cap, and his hands were covered by new gloves. As the funeral cortege proceeded to the Church of San Francisco, the body was carried in turn by delegations representing the knights of Ferrara, the lawyers and the physicians. It was buried in the Este family tomb. Niccolò had never married, but true to the Este tradition he had three bastard children. Ercole provided for them.

Throughout the autumn other suspects were executed until the toll of dead killed either in the fighting or in the reprisals was estimated at five hundred. Ercole thought that was enough and ordered that no more investigations be made of possible accomplices and sympathizers. Edmund Gardner in his *Dukes and Poets in Ferrara* told how Ercole ended the terror with an unexpectedly generous gesture:

"On Christmas Eve one of the judges presented him with a paper upon which was written a long list of nobles and gentlemen of the duchy, with a valuation of their estates, whom he accused of having been privy to Niccolò's conspiracy, urging the Duke to put them to death and to confiscate their goods. Ercole was standing by the side of a large fire. He took the paper from the hand of the officious judge and, without reading a single name, threw it into the flames. 'Thus, with their names and their possessions which are written here, let the memory perish of all that they have thought, tried and done against me.' "

Ercole destroyed Niccolò's faction with a cruel efficiency he was never to display again. In subsequent political crises he was crafty, devious and coldly expedient. But he really disliked action, preferring peace to war, and liked best to play the role of a splendid Renaissance prince, building and rebuilding, collecting

H

books, producing plays, patronizing the arts and at all times being magnificent. Although Ercole spent huge sums on making his court a great center of culture, he nevertheless acquired a reputation for avarice. Probably his policy of taxing as heavily as Borso had done was partly responsible for this. Borso had softened his taxation by affability, charm and accessibility to his subjects. Ercole remained aloof from the Ferrarese and was too reserved and inscrutable to charm anybody.

Ercole was negligent also about his administration. He sold high offices to corrupt scoundrels who demanded bribes and acted as unjust, petty tyrants. Blind to their crimes or indifferent to them, Ercole ignored the excesses of his own government for as long as he could. The people blamed the officials rather than their duke, and since no Ferrarese could imagine not being ruled by an Este, they remained loyal to Ercole even if they were not fond of him. One of them wrote: "He just takes all the pleasures that he likes and fills up his time with astrology and necromancy, giving very small audience to his people." Another said: "The Duke desires nothing else save every day to decorate and magnify this his city of Ferrara with new edifices and palaces."

The following were some of the ways Ercole spent money to improve or beautify Ferrara, to encourage the arts and to glorify the House of Este.

He supported the university, which employed forty-five professors and enrolled nearly five hundred students.

He erected a campanile near the old cathedral, a statue of his father, Niccolò III, and another of Borso.

He built a great park around the villa of Belfiore just outside the city walls and stocked it with goats, stags, antelopes, gazelles, wild boar and even with giraffes.

He collected gems, cameos, antique marbles and ivories while Duchess Eleonora collected gold and silver metalwork.

He maintained a fine choir for his chapel and imported violinists and lute players from Naples and tenors from France and Spain.

Ercole built a theater inside the old Gothic Palazzo della Ragione and produced Latin and Italian comedies. He particularly enjoyed the ribald comedies of Plautus and Terence which

were performed sometimes in Latin, more often in Italian translation. Ercole was said to have made the translation of Plautus'
Menaechmi himself, but this is doubtful. He did demand accurate versions from his translators. A performance of a Latin
classic in Ferrara was always accompanied by interludes of dancing, music and allegorical pageants, which were more popular
than the plays.

In 1491 Beatrice, writing to her sister Isabella, who had been
visiting in Ferrara, said: "I am quite sure that all those pageants
and spectacles were distinguished by the utmost beauty and gal-
lantry, as you say, since they were all planned by our dear father,
who orders these things with consummate wisdom and perfection."

Ercole bought for the ducal library a thousand books by classic
authors and employed a librarian. He employed seventy painters
who were used chiefly to decorate palaces. Ercole himself was
not much interested in painting.

Ercole was a great patron of poets and scholars. During his
reign his court was distinguished by the presence of Tito Strozzi,
considered the best of the many writers of Latin verse, and by
Matteo Maria Boiardo, Count of Scandino, author of the *Orlando
Innamorato*, considered the finest poem written in Italian in his
time.

Ercole rebuilt or redecorated nearly every church and convent
in Ferrara. And he maintained the three Este country villas of
Schifanoia, Belfiore and Belriguardo in a fashion worthy of the
Este standards of magnificence. Belriguardo, some dozen miles
away on the banks of the Po, was the largest. It was said to have
three hundred and fifty-four rooms. It had a huge gate, an immense courtyard, Gothic windows, a long avenue, a grand foun-
tain, halls, loggias, a chapel, terraces and elaborate gardens. It
could be reached by water.

In 1493 Lodovico Sforza visited his father-in-law and was so
impressed by Belriguardo that he wrote his wife, Beatrice, about
his impressions: "I would not for all the world have missed seeing
this place. Really, I do not think that I have ever seen so large and
fine a house, or one which is so well laid out and adorned with
such excellent pictures. I do not believe that there is another to

rival it in the whole world, and did not think it possible to find a villa at once so spacious and so thoroughly comfortable and well arranged. To say the truth, if I were asked whether Vigevano [the Sforza summer palace] or the Castello of Pavia, or this place was the finest palace in the world—the Castello must forgive me, for I would certainly choose Belriguardo!"

Ercole's lordly life was not quite as luxurious as it sounds. Famines, floods and outbreaks of plague beset Ferrara. In 1474 even the court lacked bread and the poor ate acorns and bark. And in 1478 Ercole, a peace-loving man, made a dreadful mistake. The Pazzi war, in which the papacy and Naples fought against Florence and Milan, had broken out, and Ercole accepted an offer to be the commander of the Florentine troops. Since he had no great reputation as a general, the Florentines probably hired him in order to bring Ferrara into the war on their side. Perhaps Ercole took the command out of simple vanity. A Renaissance prince was expected to be a soldier as well as a ruler, and Ercole may have fancied himself as an important condottiere.

In any case, his timid, incompetent and lethargic performance as a general won him no glory and the fact that he personally led soldiers against papal troops infuriated Pope Sixtus IV. The Pope's anger made him responsive to a suggestion from his infamous nephew (or son) Girolamo Riario that a new war should be waged when convenient against King Ferrante of Naples, who had betrayed Sixtus by making a separate peace with Florence, and against Ercole, who as the vicar of a papal fief was a rank rebel, in addition to his sin of never paying his tribute on time. To make sure that the war would be successful Riario and Sixtus made an alliance with Venice.

The Ferrara war lasted from 1482 to 1484 and brought terrible disasters to the duchy. Although Ferrara was an ally of Florence, Milan and Naples, Ercole received very little help. Venice was much too strong for him. The Venetians overran and kept all the Ferrarese land north of the Po and reached the very walls of Ferrara. The nervous strain proved too much for Ercole, who collapsed in his bed. The hungry and frightened citizens of the city demanded proof that he was alive.

Duchess Eleonora bravely exhorted them to do their duty and

help defend the city, but she had to permit hundreds of Ferrarese to file through the bedchamber where the prostrate duke lay. The city was full of starving refugees from the conquered districts, and the will to fight on was fast disappearing. It looked very much as if defeat would be total and that the duchy would be divided between the Venetians and Count Girolamo.

And then Pope Sixtus changed his mind and his side. He realized that the papacy was gaining little from the war and that if Venice was triumphant it might gain nothing at all. Could Venetian loyalty be counted on any more than the Neapolitan or his own? So in December of 1482 Sixtus denounced the wicked aggression of his former ally against the city of Ferrara, joined the League fighting Venice and broadcast his noble intentions far and wide. The Ferrarese and their allies were relieved and delighted. Venice was outraged. But the war dragged on. Men on both sides died of malaria. And the Venetians stubbornly held their own. Finally, by the autumn of 1484, everyone had had enough fighting and peace was made. But Venice kept the land she had conquered between the Adige and Po rivers.

Ferrara had suffered terribly. She had lost an important part of her territory. In defeat and humiliation Ercole learned a bitter lesson and never went to war again. Henceforth he put his trust in devious diplomacy and not in arms.

Ten years later when Charles VIII marched into Italy on the road to Naples, Ercole d'Este, Duke of Ferrara, welcomed the French king at Asti side by side with his son-in-law, Lodovico Sforza. Ercole bet on Charles to win and sent his son Ferrante to join Charles's campaign. When Charles retreated north and the League of Venice was formed against him, Ercole refused to join the League, tried to be neutral, offended Venice and Lodovico and at the last moment reluctantly sent a token force to fight under his other son-in-law, Francesco Gonzaga, at Fornovo.

Four years later, when Louis XII in alliance with Venice threatened Milan, Ercole refused Lodovico Sforza's anguished appeals for help. Since the death of his daughter Beatrice in January 1497 Ercole's friendship for Lodovico had rapidly cooled. Ferrara was too near the Venetian frontier, Ercole said, and he must guard his own house. With heavy odds against Milan, Ercole had no intention of risking his own state by joining an already lost cause. He had not forgotten the Ferrara war. Besides, the art of politics as understood in Renaissance Italy did not include hazardous gambles in behalf of underdogs.

So Ercole joined Francesco Gonzaga and ceremoniously welcomed the King of France at Pavia and rode beside him in his triumphal entry into Milan. Ercole believed that the preservation of his duchy required humble subservience to the conqueror, who had driven his son-in-law and his grandsons into exile. He continued to shun Lodovico's cause when the Sforza duke recaptured Milan and afterward when Lodovico languished in a French dungeon.

For many years before the coming of the French, Ercole had displayed increasing signs of a highly emotional religious piety. In fact, Ercole's scrupulous fasting, his unfailing attendance at all church services and ceremonies and his conviction that he was specially favored by the Virgin Mary seem like medieval anachronisms. Other princes conformed and accepted; Ercole most fervently believed. The paradoxical duke of Ferrara, who could be cruel and treacherous, who had a passion for ribald pagan plays, was anxious to make his city holy. To do so he became a disciple of his most famous subject, Savonarola (who had moved to Florence in 1481), and he spared no effort to secure for Ferrara a resident, private saint.

Savonarola's sublime assurance of his own role as a prophet of God, his torrential eloquence and his importance as the actual ruler of the theocratic state of Florence, of which Christ himself was supposed to be king, profoundly impressed Ercole. He corresponded with the fiery Dominican monk, pleaded for his advice during the crisis of Charles's retreat, and piously studied Savonarola's letters and tracts. In 1496 Ercole decided that the time had come to reform Ferrara and make it holy according to the ideas of Savonarola. Ercole did not go so far as to recruit children into reform squads or to destroy works of art, jewelry and books in bonfires of "vanities." But he did publish a ducal edict forbidding blasphemy, gambling, sodomy, the keeping of concubines in public or private by married men and the renting of houses to harlots or their panders. Shops were to be shut on feast days, and nothing was to be sold in the piazza save necessities.

There is no record that the worldly, sophisticated and pleasure-loving city of Ferrara was noticeably changed by Ercole's efforts. And just as his subjects ignored Savonarola's rules of conduct so Ercole himself ignored the one piece of extremely good and practical advice Savonarola sent him:

"Let your Lordship especially set diligent watch, supervision and restraint upon your ministers and officials, which matters more than all the rest. These are often wont to counter the clemency, goodness and reputation of the Sovereign by perverse suggestions, and by wicked and impious exactions, and by fraudulent adulation; wherefore such men should be abhorred as enemies by your Excellence."

In 1497 Ercole began to waver and slip away from the influence of Savonarola. He was disappointed that so many of the prophet's prophecies did not come true. He was perplexed by Pope Alexander's excommunication of Savonarola. Everyone in Italy knew that the Pope was a cheerful old reprobate, lustful, promiscuous, avaricious, treacherous and totally unscrupulous. But he was the vicar of Christ on earth and his sins could not diminish his authority as pope. At least, that was sound doctrine and Ercole probably accepted it. Ercole was careful not to antagonize Alexander by making any public statements in defense of Savonarola. He was privately sorry for the prophet's martyrdom, but that was as far as he thought it prudent to go.

In the same year, 1497, Ercole found just the saint he wanted for Ferrara. She was a twenty-year-old Dominican nun named Lucia Brocadelli then living in a convent in Viterbo. Lucia was born in Narni. As a child she danced with angels; St. Caterina of Siena came down from Heaven and taught Lucia to read and write. Married against her will, she remained a virgin, joined the Dominican nuns, became the abbess of the convent in Viterbo and received the wounds of the stigmata. She frequently talked with Christ.

Ercole sent an invitation to the young nun in Viterbo to come to Ferrara, where he would build her a convent of her own and entrust it to her sole charge. Lucia promptly accepted. Ferrara was a far more important place than Viterbo and the awed devotion of its sovereign must have been flattering. But the town of Viterbo and the nuns in the convent refused to let her go. To part with their holy woman who brought fame to the town was unthinkable.

The Duke of Ferrara was not the man to take no for an answer when his religious passions were aroused. He promptly organized a kidnapping attempt. Any means were obviously justified in so pious an enterprise as obtaining a genuine saint for Ferrara. But the attempt failed. Throughout the year 1498 Ercole and the town fathers of Viterbo fought each other in the papal court over possession of the nun from Narni. But in 1499 Ercole lost patience, and his agents got to work again organizing another conspiracy to bring Lucia to Ferrara. This time, with the conniv- ance of Lucia's mother and uncle, they were able to smuggle the girl, hidden in a basket, out of Viterbo—her story's only resem- blance to Sir John Falstaff's.

On May 7 Lucia arrived in Ferrara and soon afterward Ercole himself laid the first stone of her convent. While the convent was built Lucia watched the workers carefully and continued her regular spiritual intercourse with St. Caterina. One evening St. Caterina joined Lucia in a tour through the unfinished building, blessing each room. The two saints, the dead one and the living one, sang together Savonarola's favorite hymn, "*Ave Maria Stella*," and when St. Caterina left she gave Lucia a rod as token of her rule over the convent.

Such special favor from Heaven was more than enough to make anyone self-satisfied. It made Lucia arrogant and harsh. Some of the nuns recruited to staff her convent refused to stay there. But Ercole continued to revere her and often went to see her for spiritual comfort and holy conversation.

In 1499, just at the moment when Ercole was making it clear to everybody that he would not lift a finger to help Lodovico resist the joint attack of France and Venice, he heard that his fierce and imperious son, Ippolito, an archbishop since he was eight and a cardinal since he was fourteen, was preparing enthusiastically to fight for his brother-in-law. Ippolito was archbishop of Milan. He had ordered from one of the famous Milanese armorers a suit of pure white armor. Ercole was scandalized and wrote his bellicose son:

"If we still have any paternal authority over Your Lordship

[Ippolito was just twenty], we command you to desist from these warlike ways, and to strive to live like a good archbishop and a most reverend cardinal. If, perchance, anyone has persuaded you that, by arming, you give the victory to the most illustrious Lord Duke of Milan or benefit him, hold for certain that he who gave such advice loves not His Excellence, and Your Lordship less. For your taking up arms would offend Our Lord God and provoke Him to anger, and would make Him contrary to the side for which you bore arms. But if you wish to help the said most excellent Lord Duke (as we all should wish), let Your Lordship do your proper office. Pray to Our Lord God for the safety and victory of His Excellence and of his armies, and make all the religious and secular clergy throughout your province pray; be present yourself at these prayers, as is your duty, without intermission. These will be good white arms, without danger of irregularity and with great merit. If you armed, you would commit a mortal sin and be worthy of excommunication."

In vain. Ippolito fought for Lodovico and fled with him into exile in Austria. It was not easy to be a devout prince in the Renaissance. It was more difficult still to persuade others to act devoutly; hardest of all was to influence his own son to act like a proper Churchman and he a cardinal! Of course, many other cardinals did not act properly either.

If it wasn't one problem it was another. In February of 1501 Pope Alexander horrified Ercole by officially proposing that his bastard daughter Lucrezia marry Ercole's oldest son, Alfonso, "Hereditary Prince of Ferrara." Nothing could have been more upsetting. Alfonso was incensed. His sister Isabella in Mantua was shocked. The daughter of a priest marry the heir of the noble House of Este! And such a daughter!

Lucrezia was beautiful, blond, cultured. But she was the most notorious woman in Italy. She had been divorced from her first husband, Giovanni Sforza, Lord of Pesaro, and the humiliated prince had spread scandalous stories about his wife and her family. Lucrezia's second husband, Alfonso, Duke of Bisceglie, had been murdered—in all probability by her own brother, the terrible Cesare Borgia. In 1498 Lucrezia had given birth to a child whose paternity was a mystery. Later in 1501, in November, before Lucrezia left Rome to marry Alfonso in Ferrara, horrendous tales were to circulate all over Italy that Lucrezia had been present at the Vatican at appallingly depraved entertainments.

At this time both Ercole and Alfonso were widowers. Eleonora, the beautiful bride from Naples, had grown fat in middle age. But she retained Ercole's devoted admiration and that of her daughters and subjects. She died in 1493. Alfonso was twenty-four; when he was only fifteen, he had married Anna Sforza, youngest sister of the unhappy Duke Gian Galeazzo, who was then eighteen. Anna died in childbirth in 1497.

Alfonso d'Este was not an attractive or likable person. Handsome in a coarse, virilely masculine fashion, he was brutal, brave, cruel, arrogant and licentious. Ignoring the cultural opportunities of the court of Ferrara, Alfonso preferred to hunt in the marshes of the Po until he exhausted his companions; or to work in his own foundry, casting cannon. He was famous for the enthusiasm and frequency with which he patronized prostitutes. Like all the Estes, he was musical and could play the violin; but he never acquired the good manners and conversational grace which were the ideal of the Renaissance ruling class. Duke Ercole is said to have regarded Alfonso as a sort of uncivilized monster. Three years before, Alfonso and his brothers, Ferrante and Sigismondo, had all suffered from syphilis at the same time.

In a private letter, not to Alexander, Ercole protested: "We shall never yield nor consent to give Madonna Lucrezia to Don Alfonso; nor could Don Alfonso ever be induced to take her." But Pope Alexander insisted and threatened. Ercole pleaded with King Louis of France for help but received none. Instead, Louis strongly urged the marriage. And always present was the threat of Cesare Borgia, who had begun his conquest of the Romagna, backed by France as well as by the Pope.

Ercole was desperate. "We are resolved never to contract this relationship with the Pope. It does not appear to us advisable to tell him absolutely that we will not; because such a repulse would make him an even bitterer enemy to us than he is now." Ercole was whistling past the graveyard—Alexander was openly threatening to deprive him of his duchy if he did not consent to the marriage.

So Ercole bowed to superior force and consented. But Alfonso did not. Ercole, who could recognize a political necessity when it hung over his head like a sword, fumed with rage. He swore that he would marry Lucrezia himself if Alfonso would not. That was the final argument. Alfonso had more than enough brothers already. The possibility of acquiring more brothers young enough to be his own children—all legitimate Estes with just claims to palaces and lavish allowances—was not pleasing. They might even conspire against him. So Alfonso surrendered, too.

But the wily Ercole was determined to make the best of a poor bargain. His terms were high, but not so high they would drive the Pope into furious action. Ercole demanded 200,000 ducats as Lucrezia's dowry; that Lucrezia should bring with her jewels, clothes, brocades, tapestries, etc., worth 75,000 ducats; that Ferrara's annual tribute to the papacy be reduced to a token 100 ducats; that two Bolognese castles, worth about 100,000 ducats, be turned over to him; and that he be granted the right to appoint the bishops of Ferrara.

Pope Alexander was disgusted. The noblest prince in Italy haggled "like a merchant." Still, Lucrezia urged him on. She longed to get away from the fetid papal court. She didn't care what kind of man Alfonso might be. She had been married to two weaklings. The tough, bull-necked Alfonso might be a pleasant change. Marriage alliances weren't supposed to provide happiness; they were supposed to confirm political alliances, although they often did not. Alexander, who loved his children, wanted his daughter to be duchess of Ferrara. So the Pope accepted Ercole's terms, and plans for the marriage proceeded.

Ercole, who rightly feared Cesare Borgia, wrote him that he had been pleased by the marriage "because of the reverence which we bear to the holiness of our lord, and the excellent qualities of the most illustrious Madonna Lucrezia; but much more because of the love and affection which we bear to Your Excellence." On September 1, 1501 the marriage contract was signed. The same day Ercole wrote his future daughter-in-law: "To us this thing has been a supreme satisfaction and very great consolation to us in our old age. We rejoice thereat with Your Ladyship, whom we first loved in no ordinary wise because of your own singular virtues, our reverence for the Holiness of our lord, and because you are the sister of the most illustrious duke of Romagna [Cesare's new title], whom we hold as our honored brother."

In spite of such tactful courtesy Ercole refused to send an escort to Rome to fetch the bride until the dowry was paid in hard cash. So it wasn't until December 23, 1501 that the Ferrarese cavalcade of more than five hundred persons, arrayed in gorgeous finery and led by young Cardinal Ippolito d'Este, arrived in Rome. There was much ceremonial hospitality and much diplomatic cordiality. Ferrante d'Este gave Lucrezia a ring in Alfonso's name. Ippolito gave her a casket of Este family jewels from Duke Ercole said to be worth 70,000 ducats.

On January 6, 1502 Lucrezia left Rome, riding on a white mule covered with gold and silver trappings. In addition to all the Ferrarese lords and servants, she was accompanied by twenty ladies-in-waiting, a squad of women servants, a major-domo, a secretary, two chaplains, a maître d'hôtel, a keeper of the wardrobe, tailors, cooks, a smith, a saddle maker, an intendant, a reader, ten grooms, ten pages, fifty muleteers, lords from a half dozen noble Roman families, three bishops, one cardinal, two hundred of Cesare's men, twenty trumpeters and four Spanish clowns. Her trousseau included two hundred blouses, some sewn with gold and pearls, a dress which cost 20,000 ducats and a hat which cost 10,000.

But before the departure of this costly and curious company Ercole had received reassuring words from Rome. With the Ferrarese delegation he had sent his most intimate and trusted councillor, Gian Luca Castellini da Pontremoli, secretly charged to make a thorough inspection of Lucrezia Borgia and report his findings. If Castellini's verdict was too damning, maybe Ercole could yet wriggle out of the monstrous marriage. The confidential agent wrote:

"She is an incontestable beauty and her manners add to her charm. In a word, she seems so gifted that we cannot and should not suspect her of unseemly behavior, but presume, believe and hope that she will always behave well. . . . Your Highness and Lord Alfonso will be well satisfied, quite apart from her perfect grace in all things, her modesty, her affability and propriety; she is a Catholic and shows that she fears God." What more could any prospective and apprehensive father-in-law ask? Lucrezia Borgia was obviously an ideal bride for his disconcerting son.

The enormous cavalcade marched north at a leisurely pace, stopping at Gubbio, Urbino, Pesaro (where Lucrezia had lived during her first marriage), Imola and Bologna. Sometimes the journey was held over an extra day while Lucrezia washed and dried her beautiful golden hair. The arrival in Ferrara was as grand a state ceremony as anyone could wish, with Lucrezia displaying her courage by being thrown from her horse and getting up with great cheerfulness and immediately mounting another.

Alfonso proved to be no better as a husband than could reasonably be expected. He never loved Lucrezia, but he learned to respect her. Ercole was exasperated by his daughter-in-law. Lucrezia, who was used to the imperial extravagance of the Borgia court in Rome, spent far too much money for Ercole's thrifty nature to bear. He even refused to give Lucrezia as much money as he had promised for the expenses of her household. But otherwise, the notorious wife of the "Hereditary Prince" did not begin her life at the Este court too badly.

Not long after the marriage the Ferrarese ambassador at the papal court assured Pope Alexander that all was well with the young couple, that Alfonso regularly made love to Lucrezia at night. The ambassador added that Alfonso also regularly made love to other women by day, but that was a matter of no consequence. "As he is young, that is as it should be," said Pope Alexander, expressing his own lifetime philosophy on these matters, if not the official teachings of the Church on adultery.

The death of the dreaded Borgia pope in August of 1503 was a relief to most of the princes of Italy, including the elderly Duke of Ferrara. Ercole wrote to his ambassador in Milan:

"To make thee clear about that which thou art asked by many whether we are sorry for the death of the Pope, we assure thee that it does not displease us in any respect; on the contrary. . . . Never was there a Pope from whom we had not more favor and satisfaction than from this, even after the affinity contracted with him; we have had only and hardly had what he was bound to do, for which we did not depend upon his faith; in nothing else, great or small, have we been gratified by him."

A year and a half later, in January of 1505, Ercole d'Este, Duke of Ferrara, died peacefully in his bed. He had been listening to music and beating time to it. He was seventy-three years old and had reigned for thirty-three and a half years. Ercole lacked the political sagacity of Lorenzo de' Medici. He lacked the military ability of his son Alfonso. He lacked the flamboyant courage which was one of the few virtues possessed in rich abundance by most princes of the Renaissance—except, of course, by such notable exceptions as Alfonso II of Aragon, Lodovico Sforza and Filippo Maria Visconti.

But Ercole d'Este was no petty lordling. His interests were many, his talents considerable, his personality impressive. In his younger days he confronted crises with decisive action and cruel efficiency. In his later years he successfully preserved his state in a time of troubles by crafty diplomacy. He created a brilliant and cultivated court and generously patronized poets, scholars and musicians. He personally sponsored the revival of Latin comedy. Amoral in the fashion of his era, he was moderate in his sins and uniquely sincere (among princes) in his devotion to his religion. He was loved by only a few, but he was respected by everyone.

✦✦✦✦✦✦✦✦ XIV ✦✦✦✦✦✦✦✦

THE ENEMY
OF THREE POPES

 ALFONSO D'ESTE, the new duke of Ferrara, was born on July 21, 1476, the third child and first son of Ercole and Eleonora. He was twenty-five when he succeeded his father. A crude, slow-thinking, insensitive creature, Alfonso was physically strong and more intelligent than was at first suspected. His energy was prodigious. His arrogance, courage and stubborn will were all exceptional. He lacked the charm of his uncles Leonello and Borso and lacked his father's patient guile. But Alfonso was a warrior who fought heroically to keep Ferrara safe for the Este dynasty and a diplomat who could, when he had to, turn on a charm, which, although not natural to him, was immensely useful.

As a boy and adolescent, Alfonso grew up with little contact with his father. Aloof, proud, he ignored the society of his social equals and spent as much time as possible mastering the art of casting bronze cannon, or working in a shop where he made majolica vases—Alfonso liked to use his hands. He not only made cannon; he trained gunners to use them. In the wars to come Alfonso's artillery was to play a major part.

Like all his contemporaries, Alfonso loved crude practical jokes. Once, in the summer of 1491 when he was just fifteen, Alfonso was visiting his sister Beatrice at the court of Milan.

ALFONSO D'ESTE, Duke of Ferrara

"... a warrior who fought heroically to keep Ferrara safe for the Este dynasty and a diplomat who could, when he had to, turn on a charm, which, although not natural to him, was immensely useful." Portrait by Titian.

After midnight Alfonso and the gallant Galeazzo Sanseverino disguised themselves as robbers, broke into the house of one of Lodovico Sforza's ministers, tied him up, blindfolded him and led him through the streets of Milan on a donkey and into the great hall of the Castello Sforza. There the crude trick was greeted with much mirth, and the unfortunate victim was released.

The day after Ercole's death Alfonso rode through the streets of Ferrara to be hailed as the new duke according to the custom of the time. A heavy snow was falling. Alfonso was dressed in white. Those who looked for omens might have considered the snow symbolical of troubles to come: the numerous wars which brought immense suffering to Ferrara. But before the horrors of general war swept across Lombardy and the Romagna, Alfonso found himself confronted with personal, domestic problems. One was caused by his beautiful Borgia wife, who yearned for the admiration and affection of men; Alfonso only gave her grudging respect. The other was caused by the ferocity and vindictiveness of Alfonso's violent brothers.

While Duke Ercole was still alive, Lucrezia had been charmed by the poetic talents and courtly grace of a young Venetian visiting in Ferrara. Pietro Bembo was a courtier, poet, scholar and prolific letter writer who lived to become the literary arbitrator of Renaissance Italy and an important and influential cardinal. But when he and Lucrezia toyed with each other's affections, he was only a brightly promising young writer. How much of their feeling for each other was only a rhetorical and courtly convention and how much was sincere emotion it is impossible to tell. But the probability is that they were genuinely attracted to each other, that they were tempted to enjoy a love affair, but drew back. After all, the grim young heir of Ferrara was not a man to be trifled with. Bembo was cautious, and Lucrezia had seen more than enough intrigue and violence in Rome. Their amorous friendship continued after Alfonso became duke, but it ended when Bembo decided it would be prudent to stay away from Ferrara.

Alfonso, suspicious by nature, was always dangerous. He built a private passageway between his rooms and Lucrezia's, which must have been disconcerting to Lucrezia. She knew that Alfonso had not built it only so that he could easily visit her. Alfonso wanted to be able to drop in on his beautiful wife when he was not expected. Nevertheless, Lucrezia was foolish enough, or susceptible enough, or unhappy enough to fall in love once more. She chose for the object of her dangerous affections her husband's brother-in-law, Francesco Gonzaga, the irresistibly fascinating (to women) Marquis of Mantua.

As we have seen earlier, Francesco Gonzaga was continually depressed by the superior intellect and shrewder political judgment of his wife, Isabella. Numerous other women solaced him. But in Lucrezia he found a beautiful, cultured woman who made no claim to intellectual or political eminence. Lucrezia just wanted the affection of a charming and considerate man, and Gonzaga knew how to provide it.

In the autumn of 1505 Lucrezia was staying in Reggio, mourning the death of a baby which had lived for only twenty-five days. Gonzaga invited her to come and visit him at his nearby fortress of Borgoforto on the banks of the Po. Without waiting to consult Alfonso, Lucrezia accepted. She spent two days there and was delighted by the Marquis' promise to use his influence to effect the release of her brother Cesare from his Spanish prison. Gonzaga did try, but nothing came of his efforts. Then Lucrezia received another invitation, to proceed to Mantua and visit Isabella. This time Lucrezia wrote, asking Alfonso's permission, which was politely granted.

The visit was not entirely successful. Isabella, who never liked Lucrezia, now liked her less. Alfonso was silently suspicious. But Alfonso soon had more important worries than his wife's affection for his brother-in-law. On November 1 the first act in the great Este melodrama of fraternal hatred took place.

It was begun by the flippant insolence of a pretty young slut, Angela Borgia, Lucrezia's eighteen-year-old cousin and lady-in-waiting. Angela was pregnant, probably by Giulio d'Este, Ercole's only illegitimate son. And Cardinal Ippolito was infatuated with Angela.

Ippolito d'Este was a conspicuous example of that breed of noble prelates who disgraced the Church during the Renaissance. Arrogant, brutal, lustful, vain, hot-tempered and unscrupulous,

Ippolito was born to fight and to rule. Except for the revenues he drew from his numerous Church sinecures he had no interest in religion. When they were boys, Alfonso and Ippolito had glowered at each other like fighting cocks. Even their servants sometimes fought each other in the streets. But the two Este princes were united by a bond of brotherhood, and because Alfonso recognized that Ippolito was his equal in craft and courage, he depended upon him for advice and support.

Both brothers were treacherous and violent; both were promiscuous. (When Ippolito led the Ferrarese delegation to Rome to fetch Lucrezia, he made friends with his future brother-in-law, Cesare Borgia, and was introduced by the Pope's son to the most famous prostitutes of the city.) Both were vengeful: Alfonso was methodical and secretive, Ippolito sudden and explosive.

So when pretty, provocative Angela Borgia mocked Ippolito's advances and said that Giulio's beautiful eyes were worth more to her than Ippolito's whole body, she dropped a lighted torch into a powder keg. On November 1, 1505 Cardinal Ippolito was riding outside the walls of Ferrara accompanied by members of his own court and by several grooms. Coming back to the city from the villa of Belriguardo was Giulio. When he drew near, Ippolito shouted, "Kill that man, gouge out his eyes!"

Whether the meeting was accidental, or whether Ippolito lay in wait for his half-brother, we do not know. At any rate, his grooms flung themselves on Giulio, dragged him from his horse and stabbed him in both eyes with their daggers. Ippolito fled into exile beyond the borders of the duchy. Giulio was left bleeding on the ground.

The crime was committed nearer the villa of Belriguardo than Ferrara. When Giulio was found he was taken there, and doctors were summoned from Ferrara. Both his eyes were horribly damaged, but the doctors managed to save the partial sight of one. Five days later he was brought back to Ferrara.

Alfonso was confronted with a frightful dilemma. Justice cried out for Ippolito to be severely punished. But Ippolito was an Este, Alfonso's loyal brother and an able and helpful supporter of the new Duke who had been duke for barely a month. And Ippolito was a cardinal of the Holy Catholic Church. Justice probably demanded that Alfonso banish Ippolito forever on threat of imprisonment if he returned to Ferrara. But he did no such thing. He allowed Ippolito to return and tried to patch things up with formal apologies and reconciliations.

The hollow ceremony in which Ippolito and Giulio made their nominal peace in Alfonso's presence meant nothing. Ippolito still hated Giulio, and Giulio still dreamed of revenge, but now he felt that he should revenge himself on Alfonso also, on Alfonso who had denied him justice, who preferred Ippolito to himself. And Giulio found a sympathizer in his brother Ferrante. Together they denounced Alfonso and Ippolito and soon found themselves planning a conspiracy which would dispose of them both and leave the duchy to be ruled by themselves.

It was a badly botched conspiracy. The brothers enlisted several others, including a priest from Gascony. They tried out poisons and once lay in wait to assassinate Alfonso, who took another road. Someone had talked too much; Ippolito had discovered the plot and warned Alfonso. Ferrante and Giulio were arrested together with two of their principal accomplices. All four confessed, were tried and condemned to death.

The two lesser, non-Este conspirators were beheaded and quartered in the great piazza of Ferrara. Ferrante and Giulio, condemned to the same end, watched the executions. Then at the last moment it was announced that Duke Alfonso would generously spare their lives and commit them to perpetual imprisonment. The two unfortunate Este brothers were shut up in two rooms, one above the other, in one of the towers of the castle. The doors were walled up and food was lowered to them from a small hole near the ceiling. Later Ferrante and Guilio were permitted to visit each other and were given a larger, pleasanter room, from which they could watch the people on the piazza.

And there they remained—Ferrante until his death forty-three years later, Guilio until his release fifty-three years later. During his own lifetime Duke Alfonso was never known to feel any sympathy for his imprisoned brothers, or to feel any remorse for his severity to them. After all, had he not been merciful according to the standards of princes in his time?

The priest among the conspirators fled to Rome. But Pope

Julius II turned him over to Alfonso. Since no secular prince could lawfully execute a priest, Alfonso hung his prisoner in an iron cage fastened to one of the castle towers. By then it was January and the poor wretch was only lightly dressed; he seemed destined to die of pneumonia before he starved. But someone gave the prisoner a napkin. He hanged himself with it.

Alfonso had shown that he was as coldly determined to rule as any of his ancestors. Lucrezia was equally determined to indulge her craving for affection. She knew the fierce nature of her husband and was intimately acquainted with the Renaissance passion for revenge. Nevertheless, by 1507 she was in regular, secret correspondence with the engaging Marquis of Mantua. Messengers went back and forth across the Po bearing letters written in a partial code. These passed through several intermediaries. Lucrezia's were written for her by Ercole Strozzi, the man she liked best at the court of Ferrara.

Son of the poet Tito Strozzi and a distinguished poet himself, Ercole Strozzi was handsome, rich, vain and arrogantly clever. He was also crippled and walked with the aid of a crutch. While Strozzi risked his life writing Lucrezia's love letters, he was involved in a dangerous love affair of his own. He was the lover of Barbara Torelli who had fled from the abominable cruelties of her husband, Ercole Bentivoglio. This Ercole was one of the brutal sons of Giovanni Bentivoglio, who the year before had been driven from his city of Bologna by Pope Julius II.

Duke Alfonso was known to dislike Francesco Gonzaga and to despise Ercole Strozzi. So why the lame poet risked mortally offending the Duke is puzzling. Moreover, Strozzi already had his quota of deadly enemies in the Bentivoglio family. But some men, driven by inner furies, court danger and self-destruction. Some men nourish their own egoism by secret mockery of others. Perhaps Strozzi took malicious amusement in helping to deceive Alfonso and would have been more amused still if his intervention could contribute to making a cuckold of the mighty duke of Ferrara. Whether matters ever went that far is not known.

Lucrezia finally gave birth to a healthy infant on April 3, 1508. The boy was named Ercole after his grandfather and lived to succeed his father as the fourth duke of Ferrara.

Two months later, on the morning of June 6, 1508, early risers found the body of Ercole Strozzi lying on the ground at a street corner near the Casa Romei. Like Caesar's, it had been pierced by many dagger wounds—twenty-two of them. Strozzi's crutch lay at his side. Some of his long hair had been pulled out and then left beside his head.

The murder was never solved. And, in fact, no visible effort to solve it was made by the ducal authorities. Rumors spread and gossip seethed. Who would dare kill the rich and famous poet, a favorite of the Duchess? Perhaps some member of the Bentivoglio family? Possible, but unlikely. They were in exile and more concerned about regaining Bologna than about bothering with the murder of so prominent a citizen of Ferrara. Who else then? Obviously Duke Alfonso himself, who was well served by spies, who might easily have discovered Lucrezia's flirtation with Gonzaga and Strozzi's part in it. To punish Lucrezia would only cause a scandal. To eliminate Strozzi would be gratifying and would serve as a highly effective warning.

It is all speculation. But it fits with the circumstances and with the violent character of Duke Alfonso. He need not have been personally involved. There were plenty of bravoes who took care of such matters for a reasonable fee.

Ercole Strozzi had been dead only a few days when Lucrezia imprudently wrote Gonzaga again, this time using the murdered man's brother as her letter writer and intermediary. Gonzaga replied; but the correspondence withered. Even so, in 1511 when Pope Julius was attacking Ferrara, the Marquis of Mantua concluded that he would soon take the city. So Gonzaga wrote Pope Julius asking (of all things!) for full power over Duke Alfonso's wife! Julius must have encouraged him because Gonzaga ordered that an apartment for Lucrezia be prepared in a Mantuan palace and personally superintended its redecoration. What Isabella thought of this enterprise is not on record, and since Alfonso successfully defended Ferrara, nothing came of it.

From then on, the affection between Lucrezia and Francesco rapidly cooled. The Marquis' syphilis depressed him, and his increased religious interests may have contributed to his indifference. Nevertheless, when the Marquis of Mantua died in 1519, the Duchess of Ferrara wrote a touching letter of condolence to the Marchioness of Mantua:

"This bitter loss has affected me so deeply that, instead of being able to comfort others, I am in sore need of comfort myself. I grieve from my heart for Your Excellency in this great sorrow, and can never express how much grief it has caused me. But since it has thus pleased God, we must bow to His will, and I know Your Highness will bear this grief with your well-known courage and wisdom."

There is no reason to doubt the sincerity of this letter. Lucrezia had loved Gonzaga and the memory of her love was dear to her. Perhaps she was wise enough in matters of the heart to realize that Isabella, who had loved him too, might also cherish her youthful love and the man who had inspired it.

ALFONSO MAY HAVE HAD certain suspicions about his wife, but he trusted her political good sense. When he was away from Ferrara, he appointed her regent of the duchy. It wasn't long before he had more pressing matters to worry him than his domestic troubles.

Pope Julius II had begun his campaign in 1506 to impose papal authority on all the nominal feudatories of the Church. It was then that he drove the Baglioni out of Perugia (temporarily) and the Bentivoglio out of Bologna (temporarily). That promising move was only the beginning. Venice was next on the warrior pope's agenda. The serene republic had, by shrewd politics and crude force, expanded into the Romagna, which was theoretically papal territory. Venice had obtained control of Ravenna, Faenza, Rimini and Cervia. Pope Julius was determined to regain those towns for the papacy.

So in 1508 he instigated a new anti-Venetian alliance composed entirely of states in friendly alliance with Venice. It was called the League of Cambrai and was cynically and crudely aimed at the dismemberment of Venetian territory and the destruction of the only strong state left in Italy. France, Spain, the Empire, Ferrara and Mantua all joined. But Julius, whose idea it was, did not join until March of 1509. He waited before committing himself until it looked like a sure thing. Then he appointed Alfonso commander of the papal troops.

Duke Alfonso had what seemed to him a good reason for joining—the opportunity to regain the lands between the Adige and Po rivers taken from Ferrara by Venice in the Ferrara war, when the Duke was a small boy. But Alfonso with typical princely deceitfulness concealed his plans until the last moment. Even after Alfonso had conferred with King Louis XII about the part he would play in the coming war, the Ferrarese ambassador in Venice was assuring the Venetians that the Duke of Ferrara was "a good son of the republic" and had only talked to the French king because he could not avoid doing so. The Venetians were deceived by this duplicity and offered to make Alfonso commander of their army!

In the early days of the War of the League of Cambrai the French soundly defeated the Venetians and annexed much territory to their duchy of Milan. Alfonso captured the Rovigo district north of the Po, and the papal forces easily seized the Romagna towns held by Venice.

This was enough to make Julius think. For the time being he had what he wanted. Of course, he wanted much more. He wanted to increase the temporal power of the papacy and win military glory for himself and the Church. But it was not part of his plan to see Venice utterly destroyed. And he desperately wanted to drive the French, his allies for many years, out of Italy.

In a later chapter we will consider the treacherous politics and contradictory character of the greatest of the Renaissance popes. Here it must be enough to record that in the midst of a major war, which he had started himself, Julius suddenly switched sides. His uncle, Sixtus IV, had set him a useful example in treachery. Sixtus had switched from being an ally of Venice to being an enemy; Julius did the reverse. In 1510, with much pontifical righteousness he declared that the war against Venice was over and that he was now an ally of Venice.

King Louis of France did not think that the war was over. So the Pope and Venice would have to fight the French and "drive the barbarians" out of Italy. Neither did Alfonso think the war was over, and he was an ally of France. So he was confronted with a nice dilemma because he certainly did owe allegiance to his feudal suzerain the Pope. But it did not take him long to decide that it would be expedient to remain loyal to the French, whose military might in northern Italy seemed irresistible. Julius raged.

Previously Julius had excommunicated the Venetians with all the terrible threats and theological horrors at his command. This was customary whenever a pope went to war. Now Julius turned on Alfonso with even more eloquent invective. Speaking to his recent enemy and present ally, the Venetian ambassador in Rome, Julius said of his bull of excommunication against Alfonso d'Este: "It will be more terrible than the bull against you; for you were not our subjects, but he is a rebel." The excommunication, which impressed one contemporary diplomat so much that he said it made his hair stand on end, was not confined to Alfonso. It included all who supported him, which meant all his subjects, the King of France and all who fought against the papacy in the French armies.

Henceforth the Pope was Alfonso's personal enemy. He was determined to drive the Este out of Ferrara and to make the duchy just another papal state under his own rule. In the first part of the war which followed, Venice, Spain and the papacy opposed France and Ferrara. There were other belligerents, but they played less important roles. The war's complexities need not be sorted out here in detail.

Alfonso proved himself a valiant and resourceful soldier. He could be wildly reckless. On one occasion there was a sudden emergency, and Alfonso, who had no weapon with him, picked up a stick and led an attack upon a detachment of the enemy. He did so well with it that he was compared to Hercules and his famous club.

He could be merciless. On one occasion he recaptured a fort taken by Spanish and papal troops who had massacred all hundred and fifty members of Alfonso's garrison. In revenge for the massacre of his own men Alfonso executed everybody in the Spanish garrison of two hundred, including the commander.

He could be resourceful. When the Venetians sent a large fleet of galleys up the Po to attack Ferrara, Alfonso and his brother Cardinal Ippolito used shore-based cannon to fire on the enemy fleet with such skill that they almost completely destroyed it. Between two thousand and three thousand Venetians perished. Only two galleys escaped. The rest were captured, burned or sunk, and immense booty was taken. It was a great triumph for Alfonso.

Alfonso's defense of Ferrara was aided by a French force of several hundred mounted knights and some three thousand infantry. Second in command was the famous Chevalier Bayard, the knight *sans peur et sans reproche*. The French knights were country gentlemen and heroic soldiers—simple, relatively unsophisticated and still medieval in their outlook, compared with the elegant, worldly and polished members of the Renaissance court of Ferrara. One of them, the anonymous biographer of Bayard, who called himself the Loyal Servant, wrote about Lucrezia Borgia:

"Above all, the good Duchess, who was a pearl on this earth, gave them special welcome and prepared for them every day banquets and festivals in the Italian manner marvelously splendid. Nay, I venture to state that in her time and long before there has not lived a more triumphant princess. For she was beautiful, good, gentle, and courteous to all. She spoke Spanish, Greek, Italian, French, and to a certain extent excellent Latin, and she could write in all these tongues. And there is nothing more certain than that, although her husband was a bold, wise prince, this said lady by her charm has been the reason that he performed good and great exploits."

Here speaks a medieval man still bemused by the chivalric legend. If Lucrezia and Alfonso had known a French officer was going to write a book about Bayard in which he would give the Duchess credit for the military achievements of the Duke, they would have been both astounded and amused.

Alfonso's most important contribution to the war against Pope Julius, Venice and Spain came on April 11, 1512, the day before Easter in the bloody battle of Ravenna. This was the first battle in history won by artillery—used by the French and Alfonso.

The French army of about twenty-three thousand men included five thousand German *Landsknechte* and numerous Italians, among them three hundred mounted arquebusiers of Alfonso's. It was commanded by twenty-three-year-old Gaston de Foix, Duke of Nemours, a hero to the French and a remarkably capable general.

The Spanish-papal army was commanded by Ramon de Cardona, Viceroy of Naples. Its high officers included Pedro Navarro, one of the first soldiers in history to win fame as an engineer, and three of the most famous condottieri: Fabrizio Colonna, Gianpaolo Baglioni and the Marquis of Pescara.

Alfonso maneuvered his twenty-four large cannon, including his largest and finest called "the Great Devil," around and behind the French army until he could take up a position on the extreme left. There his guns worked terrible havoc on the enemy. Colonna, whose cavalry was under fire by the French cannon, said afterward that he saw one ball knock over thirty-three men at arms!

After the battle a story circulated that at one point Frenchmen and Spaniards were all mixed together in one confused mass into which Alfonso's guns fired with terrible effect. Alfonso is said to have shouted with great enthusiasm: "You cannot make a mistake, they are all our enemies." The story was so widely spread that the Duke formally denied he had ever said anything of the kind.

The battle was bravely fought with terrible losses on both sides, but finally the Spanish and papal troops were driven from the field. Many of their officers were captured, among them the papal legate, Cardinal Giovanni de' Medici. Casualty statistics are unreliable, but Sir Charles Oman, author of *A History of the Art of War in the Sixteenth Century*, estimated that the French lost some four thousand and their enemies some nine thousand. Among the French dead was Gaston de Foix, who had recklessly pursued the fleeing foe and was killed in a futile skirmish after the victory was won.

The triumph of the French was complete. The enemy was routed, and panic spread in the Vatican. But war's unpredictability soon reversed the result. Gaston's death brought confusion and demoralization to the French. Their German mercenaries quit; the Swiss attacked them. Then the Venetians attacked them with renewed vigor. The French had to retreat to save Milan, and soon after that retreated farther—right out of Italy. Alfonso might have been held partly responsible for this disastrous reversal of fortune because, after Ravenna, he had been offered the command in Gaston de Foix's place. He had had the wisdom, or caution, to refuse it.

But the crisis for Ferrara was only just begun. Pope Julius was riding high again and yearning, if not for Alfonso's blood, at least for his duchy. Alone in Italy, the only Italian ally of France who had fought for her, Alfonso knew his fate was sealed if he could not placate the terrible pope. A pardon for his rebellion and contumacy was essential. So, aided by the intervention of his sister Isabella and the Marquis of Mantua, he obtained a safe-conduct from Julius and went to Rome. Julius told the Venetian ambassador: "I intend to take Ferrara from him and to deprive him of his dominions. I have given him a safe-conduct for his person but not for his state."

The Duke of Ferrara arrived in Rome on July 4 and was welcomed by his little nephew, Federigo, Isabella's and Francesco Gonzaga's son, who was a hostage at the papal court for his father's good conduct. Alfonso stayed in the palace of Cardinal Sigismondo Gonzaga and was kept there in what amounted to house arrest.

Five days later in a formal consistory in the Vatican Alfonso d'Este was absolved from his excommunication by Pope Julius. He had to make an abject confession and apology:

"Holy Father, I confess that I have sinned grievously against the Divine Majesty and Your Holiness and this Holy Apostolic See, and that I have committed a very great sin of ingratitude for so many benefits received from your Holiness. But, relying upon your clemency, I have come to your feet, supplicating you humbly, by the mercy of the Omnipotent God and your own benignity, that you be pleased not to consider my demerits, but pardon me and restore me to the Holy Mother Church, as I offer myself to be ever obedient to Your Holiness and to this Holy Apostolic See."

The ceremony, of course, was meaningless. Alfonso did not mean a word of his official apology. Pope Julius did not mean a word of his forgiveness. Alfonso was determined to remain duke of Ferrara and Julius was determined to seize his state.

A few days later the boy Federigo Gonzaga entertained his uncle Alfonso in the Vatican and showed him Pinturicchio's frescoes in the Borgia apartments, which Pope Julius had vacated because he did not like being reminded of his hated enemy Pope Alexander VI. Alfonso expressed a desire to go to the Sistine Chapel to see the frescoes of Michelangelo on the ceiling. The crusty, arrogant little genius was summoned to introduce his work to the crusty, arrogant prince. The artist and the Duke climbed to the top of the scaffold together and remained there long in intimate conversation. Michelangelo promised Alfonso a picture. Asked if he wished to see Raphael's murals in the Vatican Alfonso refused on the grounds that he ought not to see the room where the Pope slept. Perhaps it was during this hazardous visit to Rome that Alfonso's interest in painting, which was strong in his later years, was awakened.

Negotiations between Duke and Pope dragged on. Julius demanded the prompt surrender of Ferrara to himself and also the release from prison of the two captive Este brothers, Ferrante and Giulio. Alfonso refused. The treacherous pope moved into the fortress of Sant' Angelo and summoned Alfonso to a conference there, intending to arrest him as soon as he entered the grim old building. Warned by friends, Alfonso did not go and fled from Rome instead.

He was aided by two Colonna princes, Fabrizio and Marcantonio, who were grateful to Alfonso for his kind treatment of Fabrizio after his capture at the battle of Ravenna. This is one of the few examples of gratitude and something like chivalrous behavior to be found in the history of the Italian princes of the Renaissance. The two Colonna princes escorted Alfonso with a troop of horsemen and galloped through the Porta San Giovanni, scattering the guards out of their way in a brisk charge. The party reached the Colonna fortress of Marina safely, and there Alfonso disappeared.

The furious pope sent out patrols and secret agents to arrest the Duke and even established a blockade of armed ships to intercept him in case he tried to sail north from Neapolitan territory. Some three months later the Duke of Ferrara arrived safely in his native city. Where he had been, what routes he took or what disguises he may have used are still mysteries.

The following spring Pope Julius died, much to Alfonso's relief. He thought that his troubles with popes were over, and cheerfully went to Rome to take part in the coronation of Giovanni de' Medici, Pope Leo X. In the coronation procession Alfonso personally carried the banner of the Church. He wore a magnificent cloak of white and gold brocade and a black velvet cap, which had a single diamond supposedly worth ten thousand ducats. Whenever Alfonso rode across the piazza in front of the Vatican, the people cheered him and shouted *"Duca, Duca"*—the same Roman citizens who had wept and extravagantly mourned the death of Pope Julius, Alfonso's great enemy. The new Pope, Leo X, had removed all of Julius' ecclesiastical censures of Alfonso and had restored to him all his various dignities.

During the next few years the Duke of Ferrara enjoyed a short respite from war's excursions and alarms and papal plans to destroy him. He became a patron of painters, particularly of Dosso Dossi. He frequently employed Titian and Giovanni Bellini. Raphael promised Alfonso to paint for him "the best picture he ever did, a *Triumph of Bacchus in India*." But Raphael had so many commissions in Rome he never even began the Duke's picture. After three years and no signs that Raphael meant to keep his promise, Alfonso lost his temper and wrote the Ferrarese ambassador in Rome:

"We wish you to find him and tell him that you have letters from us by which we write you that it is now three years since he has given us only words; and that this is not the way to treat men of our rank; and that, if he does not fulfill his promise toward us, we shall make him know that he has not done well to deceive us. And then, as though from yourself, you can tell him that he had better take care not to provoke our hatred, instead of the love we bear him; for as, if he keeps his promise, he can hope for our support, so on the contrary, if he does not, he can expect one day to get what he will not like. Let all this conversation be between you and him alone."

Today, when fine artists are held in far greater esteem than dukes, such a letter, threatening one of the greatest artists of the entire Renaissance period, seems outrageous. And since the Strozzi murder case was celebrated, Raphael might have had good cause to be apprehensive. Nevertheless, in the social climate of the early sixteenth century when dukes were infinitely more important than painters, no matter how talented, one can understand the impatience of a purchaser who had been put off for three years by a painter who may never have intended to paint him a picture at all.

An artist Alfonso treated more respectfully was Lodovico Ariosto, author of the *Orlando Furioso*, generally regarded as the finest poem of the entire Italian Renaissance. Ariosto had been a gentleman of Cardinal Ippolito's court, a post he disliked because the Cardinal sent him on so many journeys that Ariosto complained he was little better than a messenger. Complaints did the poet no good, and finally he was dismissed. Alfonso at once hired Ariosto as a gentleman of his own household, thinking that the House of Este should not disgrace itself by discharging so great a poet. Alfonso paid Ariosto seven gold scudi a month and paid the expenses of the poet, two other persons and two horses.

Like his father, Alfonso was a builder. Evidently thinking that the three enormous Este country villas were not enough, Alfonso built a fourth, Belvedere, on an island in the Po. It was as magnificent as Este taste demanded, with vast halls, a chapel decorated by Dossi, marble loggias, fountains, gardens with orange groves and box hedges, and terraces and staircases leading down to the river.

In June of 1519 Lucrezia Borgia, after a difficult pregnancy during which she was ill and weak, gave birth to a stillborn child. A week later, knowing that she probably would not live much longer, Lucrezia wrote a touching letter to Leo X, the prodigal Medici pope who was already scheming to deprive Alfonso of his duchy:

"Most Holy Father and Honored Master:

With all respect I kiss Your Holiness's feet and commend myself in all humility to your holy mercy. Having suffered for more than two months, early in the morning of the 14th of the present, as it pleased God, I gave birth to a daughter, and hoped then to find relief from my sufferings, but I did not, and shall be compelled to pay my debt to nature. So great is the favor which our merciful Creator has shown me, that I approach the end of my life with pleasure, knowing that in a few hours, after receiving for the last time all the holy sacraments of the Church, I shall be released. Having arrived at this moment, I desire as a Christian, although I am a sinner, to ask Your Holiness, in your mercy, to give me all possible spiritual consolation and Your Holiness's blessing for my soul. Therefore I offer myself to you in all humility and commend my husband and my children, all of whom are your servants, to Your Holiness's mercy. In Ferrara, June 22, 1519, at the fourteenth hour. Your Holiness's humble servant, Lucrezia d'Este."

Lucrezia, who knew so much about the corruption of the Renaissance papacy, never lost her faith in the spiritual powers of the pope. Two days after writing her last letter she died. She was thirty-nine years old. She had borne Alfonso at least seven children, of whom five lived. She had seen much and endured much and remained a brave and likable woman.

On the night of Lucrezia's death the Duke wrote to his nephew Federigo Gonzaga, the young Marquis of Mantua:

"Illustrious Sir and Honored Brother and Nephew: It has just pleased our Lord to summon unto Himself the soul of the illustrious lady, the duchess, my dearest wife. I hasten to inform you of the fact as our mutual love leads me to believe that the happiness or unhappiness of one is likewise the happiness or unhappiness of the other. I cannot write this without tears, knowing myself to be deprived of such a dear and sweet companion. For such her exemplary conduct and the tender love which existed between us made her to me. On this sad occasion I would indeed seek consolation from Your Excellency, but I know that you will participate in my grief, and I prefer to have someone mingle his tears with mine rather than endeavor to console me. I commend myself to Your Majesty. Ferrara, June 24, 1519, at the fifth hour of the night. Alfonso, Duke of Ferrara."

What are we to make of this letter? Was it merely a correct letter suitable to the circumstances? Or was the brutal, promiscuous duke really moved by the death of the wife he had never loved?

Soon Alfonso consoled himself by taking a mistress of humble birth. Laura Dianti was called by one contemporary "a wench of most lofty spirit." She bore Alfonso two sons. Two children didn't seem to justify the pet name Alfonso bestowed upon her, Eustachia, which means "good-conceiver." Alfonso built her a little palace and employed Titian to paint her portrait as well as his own.

Late in the same year as Lucrezia's death Pope Leo decided that the time had come to seize Ferrara, as Julius had tried and failed to do. Alfonso was ill and could hardly believe the news when Marquis Federigo Gonzaga sent him a warning that a papal force was on the march. Alfonso prepared once again to defend his city. But he wrote a crafty letter to the Pope, pretending that he thought the troops were not authorized by the Pope and were not being sent against him. Alfonso told the Pope to be sure and warn his local governors in the papal states against this sudden emergency! Leo did just that and called off the attack.

Two years later in 1521 Leo concocted a scheme to kidnap both Alfonso and Cardinal Ippolito. Nothing came of this either. But in the same year Leo, in alliance with Emperor Charles V, was at war with France, and Alfonso remained loyal to France as he had before. Leo excommunicated the Duke of Ferrara—the second time Alfonso suffered this dread penalty. The powers arrayed against him seemed irresistible, but once again the death of a hostile pope saved Alfonso. Leo died on Dec. 1, 1521. Alfonso was so pleased he gave fifty gold scudi to the messenger who brought the good news. And he had medals struck with the motto *Ex ore Leonis*, "Out of the Lion's Mouth," a pun which summed up his situation exactly.

War and political treachery continued to beset Italy in the next few years and Alfonso was kept busy in one crisis after another. He tried in vain to recapture his city of Modena, taken from him by Julius, and thus incurred the wrath of the new pope Clement VII, who had been Cardinal Giulio de' Medici. Once again Alfonso had a pope for his personal enemy.

In 1525 Alfonso, still loyal to France, sent money and arms to help Francis I, the gallant young king of France, in his invasion of Italy and found he had backed the wrong horse. At the battle of Pavia Francis was disastrously defeated and captured by the

I

armies of Emperor Charles V. French fortunes seemed so low that Alfonso thought it expedient to switch sides. He became an ally of the Emperor.

Two years later when the mutinous, half-starved German *Landsknechte* and Spanish *tercios* of the imperial army commanded by the Charles de Bourbon, Constable of France, marched south to the sack of Rome, Alfonso supplied them with money, food and ammunition. He has been bitterly criticized for this betrayal of the Holy City.

But according to the political ideas of his time the circumstances were certainly extenuating. If Alfonso had refused help or had opposed the imperial forces, his own state might have been destroyed, and he would have failed in the one supreme obligation of a Renaissance prince—to preserve one's own state. Moreover, Rome was not just the religious capital of Europe; it was the capital of the temporal power of the papacy, which for several hundred years had fought, betrayed and conspired on the same low level as the other Italian states. Popes Julius, Leo and Clement had all been Alfonso's implacable enemies. So when Alfonso helped Constable Bourbon's troops on their way to Rome, he was only taking revenge on Pope Clement and the papacy according to the traditional customs of princes.

Others felt the same way. Duke Francesco Maria della Rovere of Urbino, Julius's nephew, had been attacked by Leo X and driven out of his state temporarily. In 1527 he commanded a Venetian army which could have cut off the invaders and saved Rome. Rather than help a Medici pope, Della Rovere carefully did nothing. Second in command to the Duke of Urbino was Malatesta Baglioni, Lord of Perugia, whose father, Gianpaolo Baglioni, had been treacherously murdered by Pope Leo. Baglioni did not love the Medici either and gladly cooperated in Della Rovere's policy of vindictive inaction.

Having failed to recapture his city of Modena from the papal forces before, Alfonso judged it a good time to try again, shortly after the sack of Rome. Corrupt and cruel papal governors, feuds and an outbreak of the plague had reduced Modena to a state where the return of Este rule seemed almost desirable.

Alfonso instructed his herald: "Tell them I want Modena because it is mine, and because the majesty of the Emperor has invested me with it. If they will not give it me for love, I shall take it for myself by force; and let them look to it, lest a worse thing befall them than the *Landsknechte* have done in Rome." The city surrendered meekly, and Alfonso entered in triumph of June 6, 1527, riding through the streets in the rain.

But five months later the Duke of Ferrara rashly decided it would be wise to switch his allies again. He left Emperor Charles V and returned to Francis I—a mistake which caused him much diplomatic effort to rectify a few years later when Charles was settling the fate of all Italy.

The following year, 1528, Ferrara was stricken with the plague from March until November. Although many people fled from the city, Alfonso never left it except for a few days' absence at a time. He shared the danger with his poorer subjects with the unfailing courage which was his only notable virtue. During the same year Pope Clement kept instigating conspiracies against Alfonso, to murder or kidnap him. Few princes ever had more trouble with popes than Alfonso.

In the summer of 1529 Emperor Charles V came to Italy, landing at Genoa, to be crowned by Pope Clement and to arrange Italian affairs to suit himself and to a lesser extent to suit the Pope. Clement wanted to restore Medici rule over Florence, which had been ruled by the Medici popes from 1512 to 1527. But after the sack of Rome Florence had revolted and once again was a republic. So an imperial-papal army besieged Florence. Alfonso, fearing the worst from an emperor he had deserted and a pope who wanted to murder him, tried to appease them by sending a small force and some cannon to help the besiegers.

Charles planned to meet Clement at Bologna, where he would be crowned and where he would settle all outstanding political issues. Alfonso knew that if Clement had his way he and all the Este would be exiled from Ferrara and his state would be absorbed into the Papal States. His only hope lay in winning Charles's friendship and in convincing him of the righteousness of the Este cause before Clement poisoned his mind.

Charles and his grand escort were proceeding leisurely toward Bologna. Alfonso intercepted the Emperor and entertained him magnificently in his cities of Modena and Reggio. The young Hapsburg emperor was only twenty-nine. He had the protruding jaw and lower lip of his family. Far more intelligent than any Hapsburg ruler before or after him, Charles was earnest, self-confident and comfortably aware of his overpowering military strength.

Alfonso was fifty-three, big, burly, bearded, enormously experienced in war, politics and the wicked ways of the world. He set himself to charm the Emperor and to make sure that he understood why the Este family were the rightful lords of Ferrara no matter how many popes said they were not. Charm wasn't usually Alfonso's strong point. But this time necessity mothered invention and Alfonso converted Charles to his point of view.

Charles went on to Bologna, and Alfonso waited until March before going there himself in lordly state. After some negotiating Clement and Alfonso agreed to let Charles arbitrate their dispute. But not until April of 1531 did Charles announce his verdict: Alfonso would retain his cities; he would pay the papacy an annual tribute of seven thousand ducats; and for his repeated defiance of popes he would pay a penalty of a hundred thousand ducats. The decision was generally considered just.

Three years later, in 1534, Pope Clement VII died, and for the third time the Duke of Ferrara rejoiced in the death of a hostile pope. Unfortunately for him, he did not long outlive his enemy. On October 31, 1534 Alfonso d'Este, Duke of Ferrara, Modena and Reggio, died, according to a popular story, from eating too many melons.

ALFONSO WAS the last true Renaissance Este to rule in Ferrara. Unscrupulous, tyrannical, treacherous and arrogant, he was a fine soldier and a surprisingly adroit diplomat. By his military skill he saved the Este state from Pope Julius and by his diplomatic skill he saved it from Popes Leo and Clement. A less enthusiastic patron of the arts than his father Ercole, he still had the good judgment to maintain Ariosto as an ornament of his court and to employ Dossi, Bellini and Titian, and to try to employ Raphael.

As a prince he was entirely successful. He handed down his state to his eldest son, Ercole II, who reigned until 1558. But Ercole's reign, in which his duchess, a French princess, was convicted of Protestant heresy and briefly imprisoned, belongs more to the Reformation and Counter Reformation than to the Renaissance. His son, Alfonso II, died in 1597, the last of the Este lords of Ferrara. There was no male heir of the direct line to carry on the Este dynasty, which had been founded so many years before by Obizzo d'Este in the twelfth century. Ferrara at last fell under the control of the papacy.

XV

THE GOOD DUKES
OF URBINO

FEDERIGO

"ON THE SLOPES of the Apennines, almost in the center of Italy, toward the Adriatic Sea, there lies, as everyone knows, the little city of Urbino. Although situated in a mountainous region, less pleasant than some we may have seen, it is favored by Heaven in that the country is exceedingly fertile and rich in fruits of the earth. And besides the pure and health-giving air of the region, all things necessary for human life are to be found here in great abundance. But among the greatest blessings which it enjoys, this I count to be the chief, that from remote times it has always been governed by the best of princes, although, in the universal calamities of Italy in the recent wars, it was deprived of them for a time."

So wrote Baldassare Castiglione in the opening pages of *The Courtier*, his work on the ideal Renaissance gentleman, inspired by his long and happy residence at the court of Urbino. But Castiglione's nostalgia for better days misled him into an egregious exaggeration. The counts of Montefeltro, who became counts of Urbino in the thirteenth century, were an undistinguished lot. Until the middle of the fifteenth century they were no better and not much different from their neighbors. But then one remarkable man, Count Federigo, transformed the reputation of his dynasty and won fame and influence for himself and his state. He was an outstanding soldier, an able scholar, and a great patron of learning and the arts. His son, Guidobaldo, was a soldier, too, but a mediocre one. He was, however, also a man of culture.

Federigo, who was made a duke late in his life, and Guidobaldo, who succeeded him as ruler of the state of Urbino, were exceptional among the princes of their time. Judged by the standards of any age, they were both good men. They were not perfect, or without faults and flaws, as, of course, no man is. But in direct contradiction to the customs of their age and the opportunities of their princely position, they lived decently. They were not cruel. They kept their word. They behaved honorably. And their contribution to Renaissance culture was enormous. Most of their contemporary princes admired them. If they had imitated the conduct of the Montefeltro dukes, the whole history of the Italian Renaissance might have been different.

The duchy of Urbino was small, isolated and poor. Its greatest extent after Federigo expanded it with some useful conquests was approximately sixty miles from north to south and the same distance from west to east. Its principal cities were Urbino and Gubbio. There were several hundred mountain villages, guarded by forts and castles. To the north was the tiny republic of San Marino. To the east, separating Urbino from the Adriatic, was the state of the Malatesta, lords of Rimini, Cesena, Pesaro and Fossombrone, hereditary enemies of the Montefeltro. On the west, in the valley of the Tiber, were Assisi and Perugia. And north of those towns and also on the west was the Tuscan territory ruled by Florence.

Federigo, the bastard son of Count Guidantonio, was born in Gubbio in 1422. His mother is unknown. But since, as Commines remarked, illegitimacy counted for little in Italy, Federigo was brought up as a prince, though naturally in a position subordinate to that of his younger legitimate brother Oddantonio. When he was five years old, Federigo was engaged to Gentile Brancaleone, the daughter of a petty lord who ruled a small mountain district. He spent two years at the Gonzaga court in Mantua, where he attended the school of Vittorino da Feltre and absorbed his master's love of Latin, history and mathematics which lasted all his life. He also seems to have taken to heart many of Vittorino's ideas about virtuous conduct.

At fifteen Federigo left boarding school and assumed a man's estate. He married and immediately began to rule his wife's domain. And while still only fifteen he went off to war as a condottiere. War was his profession, and he continued to practice it with great success until his death forty-five years later.

While Federigo was learning the condottiere's craft, his promising younger brother inherited the state of Urbino in 1442. Oddantonio ruled so badly, indulged himself in so many depravities and raped so many women that he ruled for only fourteen months—a committee of outraged citizens assassinated him. At the time Federigo was away on business, fighting in defense of the nearby city of Pesaro. Upon hearing the news he hurried back to Urbino. After all, he was the only surviving male member of the Montefeltro family. But when he reached Urbino, he could not enter the city. The gates were shut against him.

The people who had eliminated a wicked prince wanted a few points settled before submitting to the rule of his half-brother. There were twenty points and Federigo agreed to all of them. The most interesting were: a general amnesty for all those who had taken part in the liquidation of Oddantonio; the imposition of no new taxes except in emergencies; the employment of two doctors to take care of all taxpayers, their salaries to be paid by the state; and the employment of a schoolteacher and an assistant, also to be paid by the state. These enlightened measures were agreed to by a young soldier of twenty-two.

Only two years later Federigo seized an opportunity to add an important town to his territory and to diminish the strength of his enemy, Sigismondo Malatesta, the bellicose lord of Rimini. The opportunity arose because of the Malatesta family custom of dividing their state among the important members of their clan. The towns of Fossombrone and Pesaro had been inherited by

Galeazzo Malatesta, a weak and peaceable man who had no desire to defend his cities by engaging in constant warfare with his cousin Sigismondo. Galeazzo offered to sell the two cities to Federigo so that he could retire from the stormy politics of the Romagna and live quietly in Florence.

The Count of Urbino realized that he could not afford to buy both cities and that he might antagonize too many powerful people if he did. So he proposed to Francesco Sforza that he buy Pesaro and present it to his brother Alessandro, while Federigo would buy Fossombrone. The deal went through. Alessandro became lord of Pesaro at a cost of twenty thousand ducats. And Federigo became lord of Fossombrone at a cost of thirteen thousand ducats. Sigismondo, of course, raged. His timid relative, who ought to have surrendered to him, had sold away two of the most important towns of the Malatesta state and had strengthened his enemies. Henceforth Sigismondo never ceased trying to reconquer the two towns. The feud between Sigismondo and Federigo was permanent.

To detail the numerous events of the Count's military career for forty-five years would only induce tedium. Most of his campaigns were minor affairs, fought for mean and petty purposes, but Federigo conducted them with unusual skill. He was celebrated for his ability to capture forts and castles, and he was also known for his prudence, judgment and successes. When victory eluded him, which was seldom, he still avoided defeat. At various times he served as a commander for two kings of Naples, Alfonso and Ferrante; for two dukes of Milan, Francesco Sforza and Galeazzo Maria Sforza; for three popes, Pius II, Paul II and Sixtus IV; for Florence under the leadership of three Medici, Cosimo, Piero and Lorenzo; and for several leagues of Italian states.

It wasn't only skill that distinguished Federigo as a condottiere. He was always faithful to his *condotta*, or contract. As long as his contract was in force, he remained loyal to his employer, never taking money from the enemy, never treacherously changing sides. Such reliable behavior was so unusual in an age of treason and cold expediency that the Count was as famous for his honor as for his military prowess.

When the Venetians were preparing to attack Ercole d'Este in

I *

FEDERIGO DA MONTEFELTRO, Duke of Urbino

"*. . . in an age of treason and cold expediency . . . as famous for his honor as he was for his military prowess.*" Portrait by Piero della Francesca.

the Ferrara war they sent an envoy to Federigo, by then Duke of Urbino. Vespasiano da Bisticci, who as Federigo's book collector knew him personally, wrote: "The Venetians knew that none but the Duke of Urbino could hinder their attempt on Ferrara, wherefore they sent word to him offering 80,000 ducats per annum if he would stay at home. It would be enough if he would recognize that he was in their pay. While the Venetian messenger was in Urbino on this business, it chanced that one of the Duke's chief officers was in his closet, and after the Venetian had left, he turned to the Duke and said, 'eighty thousand ducats is a good price for simply staying at home.' Whereupon, the Duke replied wisely, 'To keep faith is still better, and is worth more than all the gold in the world.' "

Federigo could be exceedingly gallant and generous in war. When he captured the city of Fano, which had been stubbornly defended for Sigismondo Malatesta by his son Roberto, Federigo captured Roberto himself and Roberto's mother and sisters. According to the customs of the time Federigo could have shut them all up in a dungeon as a reprisal against his enemy; or he could have demanded high ransoms. He did neither. He set them free.

Federigo could be crafty. After the town of Verucchio surrendered to him, its citadel held out for Sigismondo. Federigo forged Sigismondo's signature to a letter telling the commander that reinforcements would arrive at a certain time. When the time came the gate was opened, not to friends, but to Federigo's own soldiers, who promptly took the citadel.

And once, the only occasion recorded, Federigo acted in a manner unworthy of his high standards of honor. Giovanni Santi, in a long poem celebrating Federigo's achievements, wrote that when the Pazzi conspirators planned the assassinations of Lorenzo and Giuliano de' Medici they asked Federigo to join their plot. Federigo refused with indignation, denouncing the conspiracy as revolting and infamous. But he did not warn Lorenzo. Later, when Lorenzo wrote and demanded to know why Federigo had kept silent, he equivocated. He said it was not necessary to offend a good friend (meaning either Pope Sixtus or Girolamo Riario) by warning an enemy. But Lorenzo was not a personal enemy, only a nominal one because Federigo was commander of the papal armies. Previously Lorenzo had been a good friend, and, in fact, after Federigo as a condottiere serving Florence had subdued the rebellious city of Voltera, he had been showered with honors by the grateful republic. The sorry episode shows that even a man as notably honorable as the Duke of Urbino could be infected by the prevailing morality of his day.

In his forty-five years of professional soldiering Federigo da Montefeltro fought many battles, but not one within the boundaries of his own state. He was paid high salaries. In active service his pay was sometimes higher than the retainer he received to keep him from serving another employer. As a young man fighting for Alfonso of Naples he was paid 8,000 ducats a month. As a battle-scarred veteran of sixty fighting for the League which defended Ferrara his annual pay was 165,000 ducats—45,000 being his own share, and the rest payment for supplies and wages for his soldiers. When we consider that the purchasing power of a Venetian ducat or a Florentine florin was at least as great and maybe much greater than ten dollars today, we can understand how Federigo was able to maintain his court in a style worthy of the highest standards of Renaissance magnificence.

The appearance of few princes of the Italian Renaissance is as familiar as that of Federigo because of the celebrated portrait by Piero della Francesca which hangs in the Uffizi Palace in Florence. From a distance we are struck by Federigo's scarlet hat and robe. On closer inspection we notice the solid strength of his profile with its powerfully jutting chin and the large, curiously shaped nose without a bridge. The portrait is a profile, as are several others which show Federigo listening to a scholarly lecture and reading a manuscript book while dressed in full armor.

There is a good reason why these portraits are all profiles. Federigo lost his right eye and the bridge of his nose in a jousting accident. It occurred in a tournament which he held in 1450 in Urbino to celebrate the accession of his friend Francesco Sforza to the dukedom of Milan. Guidangelo de' Ranieri, a knight of Urbino, had returned from Florence, where he had won first prize in another tournament, just in time to take part. Federigo insisted that the champion joust with him, much against Guidangelo's will. They galloped toward each other, and the knight's lance pierced the Count's visor, smashing the top part of Federigo's nose and completely destroying his right eye. Federigo remained in his saddle and cheerfully told his shocked friends that his wound wasn't serious and that he would see better than most with his left eye alone. Pope Pius II, who employed Federigo regularly, agreed. He remarked: "This captain of ours with his single eye sees everything."

ALL THAT IS KNOWN of Federigo's first wife, Gentile, is that she was fat and barren. Federigo needed heirs to carry on the Montefeltro dynasty—which was not a difficult problem. He fathered four bastards; three sons and a daughter. Two of the sons died of the plague. Antonio grew up, and, as we have seen, fought under the Marquis of Mantua at the Battle of Fornovo. Gentile died in 1457.

Three years later Federigo married Battista Sforza, daughter of Alessandro Sforza, the Lord of Pesaro. Because her father was a widower, Battista had been brought up at her Uncle Francesco's court in Milan. As precocious as her cousin Ippolita, she was famous for her skill in delivering Latin orations. Federigo was then thirty-eight, Battista only thirteen!

Nevertheless, the marriage was happy. The tiny, learned girl ruled Urbino competently during her husband's many absences. And she bore him eight children—seven daughters and a son. Six months after the birth of her son, Battista died. She was only twenty-five.

Federigo, writing to Pope Sixtus, said: "She was the beloved consort of my fortunes and domestic cares, the delight equally of my public and private hours, so that no greater misfortune could have befallen me."

It was Pope Sixtus who made the Count of Urbino a duke in 1474 in a great ceremony in Rome. The Pope's motive was unquestionably to strengthen the commitment of the foremost condottiere of the time to the Church. To cement their alliance even more, on the day after Federigo became a duke his daughter Giovanna was married to Sixtus' nephew, Giovanni della Rovere,

brother of Cardinal Giuliano della Rovere (the future Pope Julius II). Sixtus bestowed the town of Sinigaglia on his nephew, which Federigo had conquered from Sigismondo Malatesta for the Church. Federigo's grandson by this marriage, Francesco Maria della Rovere, succeeded his son Guidobaldo as duke of Urbino.

FEDERIGO DA MONTEFELTRO was the last of the great Italian condottieri. There were many after him; but they all played lesser roles. The great wars which followed the invasion of Charles VIII made it impossible for the mercenary captains to continue to dominate the stage. Larger armies fought bloodier battles and often were commanded by major sovereigns—a king of France, an emperor of Germany and even the pope himself. But if Federigo had been only a condottiere he would interest us little today.

His benevolent rule in his duchy, his humanist learning, his passion for books and beauty and his patronage of the arts all made him by the standards of his own time the ideal ruler. Lorenzo de' Medici was more brilliant. But he was not a soldier, and he was not as close to his people or as beloved by them. In Urbino, Federigo was always accessible to his subjects. Even at his meals they could speak to him between courses. When he rode about his duchy or walked the streets of Urbino he chatted regularly with his humblest subjects and was never escorted by an armed guard.

"One of the best and wisest of rulers," Vespasiano called him. "Such another character, virtuous in every respect, the age could

---

BATTISTA SFORZA DA MONTEFELTRO,
Duchess of Urbino

"The tiny, learned girl ruled Urbino competently during her husband's many absences. And she bore him eight children—seven daughters and a son."

not produce." Vespasiano wrote with admiration about Federigo's learning, his great library and his mercy and kindness. But
most of all he emphasized Federigo's popularity. "His subjects
loved him so greatly for the kindness he showed them that when
he went through Urbino they would kneel and say, 'God keep
you, my lord.' So kind was he that they all loved him as children
love their parents."

Federigo spent fourteen years rebuilding the palace of Urbino,
transforming a medieval castle into one of the most beautiful of
Renaissance palaces. His architect was Luciano da Laurana, a native of Istria. The palace, which perches on the edge of a steep
slope, commands a wonderful view of the plain below and the
surrounding mountains. Its proportions are graceful and its architectural details are intricate and elaborate. Unfortunately, the
façade of the side which faces the piazza of Urbino was never
finished and seems raw and crude. Inside are two hundred and
fifty rooms, six hundred and sixty windows, two bathrooms with
marble baths, a theater, a greenhouse, a riding school, a place for
storing snow (presumably for cooling fruit and white wine) and
the famous ducal library. A nearby stable had stalls for three
hundred horses. Daily Federigo fed some five hundred persons,
members of his family and his court, visitors, officials and servants.

The servants included an astrologer, a librarian, five men who
took turns reading aloud during meals, architects, engineers, singing boys, dancing masters, twenty-two pages, thirty-one cooks,
nineteen table waiters, fifty grooms, one keeper of hounds and
one keeper of the "camel-leopard" (a giraffe).

Federigo's hospitality was lavish, but guests were carefully
graded with a fine sense of hierarchy. The master of the household had the duty of checking up on the quality of strangers
arriving at the court and privately classifying them for the Duke.
There were three classifications: people of political, ecclesiastical
and family importance, who were welcomed and lodged inside
the palace; people of lesser distinction, who were put up in another building but were waited on by the Duke's servants; and
humbler people, who were lodged in an inn at the Duke's expense.

Every day Federigo attended Mass. He was sincerely devout, read many of the Church fathers and particularly admired St. Thomas Aquinas. He drank no wine, believing it bad for his gout. Instead, he drank the juice of cherries, pomegranates and apples. He ate no sweetmeats.

Federigo was a master of Latin and was interested in Greek. He excelled in mathematics and delighted in reading history and theology. He was the greatest book collector of the Italian Renaissance; all the books he purchased were manuscript copies, which he had bound in scarlet and silver. He employed between thirty and forty copyists, some in Urbino, more in Florence and some elsewhere. Vespasiano, who was Federigo's agent in these matters, wrote that his library was far more complete than that of the Vatican, Oxford University or of the Medici. "In this library all the books are superlatively good, and written with the pen, and had there been one printed volume it would have been ashamed in such company." So much for that new invention of Gutenberg's.

The library, which was eventually merged with the Vatican library, cost Federigo thirty thousand ducats. The rules for the guidance of the librarian in Guidobaldo's reign, which were probably the same as in Federigo's, are interesting:

"The librarian should be learned, of good presence, temper and manners; correct and ready of speech. He must get from the guardrobe an inventory of the books, and keep them arranged and easily accessible, whether Latin, Greek, Hebrew, or others, maintaining also the rooms in good condition. He must preserve the books from damp and vermin, as well as from the hands of trifling, ignorant, dirty and tasteless persons. To those of authority and learning, he ought himself to exhibit them with all facility, courteously explaining their beauty and remarkable characteristics, the handwriting and miniatures, but observant that such visitors abstract no leaves. When ignorant or merely curious persons wish to see them, a glance is sufficient, if it be not someone of considerable influence. When any lock or other requisite is needed, he must take care that it be promptly provided. He must let no book be taken away but by the Duke's orders, and if lent must get a written receipt, and see to its being returned. When a number of visitors come in, he must be specially watchful that none be stolen. All which is duly seen to by the present courteous and attentive librarian, Messer Agabito."

Life at Federigo's court was always decorous and seemly. There was music, but the Duke did not care for "loud instruments" like the trombone. The books read aloud at meals were solid works of history and theology. It all sounds a trifle stiff and overly sedate, but Duke Federigo was consciously setting an example of sobriety in an age of violent passions.

When Federigo took command of the armies of the league formed to defend Ferrara against Venice and the papacy, he opposed his former friend and employer, Sixtus, who had made him a duke. Federigo won no great victories, but remained bravely in the malarial swamps near the Po and finally came down with malaria himself. He was brought into Ferrara and died there in Duke Ercole's palace. His body, dressed in crimson velvet with his sword by his side and the English Order of the Garter on his breast, was brought back to Urbino and buried beside his wife in the Church of St. Bernardino. The year was 1462. The Duke was sixty years old.

By a strange coincidence, on the same day that the Duke of Urbino died in Ferrara, Roberto Malatesta, the son of Sigismondo and the son-in-law of Federigo, died in Rome. Some years earlier, after Sigismondo's death, Federigo had helped Roberto defend Rimini against a papal army. He had no further quarrel with the Malatesta and subsequently arranged a marriage between his daughter Elisabetta and Roberto. Federigo had been fighting to defend Ferrara against Venice and the papacy. Roberto had just won a famous victory over the Neapolitans in defense of Rome.

The two men were thus nominal enemies—a circumstance which during the Renaissance did not necessarily generate hard feelings. Formerly Federigo had fought even against his own father-in-law, Alessandro Sforza.

THE UNFORTUNATE Elisabetta heard the news of the deaths of her father and husband on the same day. She had no children and chose to spend the rest of her life in a convent. When the wills of the Duke of Urbino and the Lord of Rimini were examined, it was discovered that they had appointed each other their executors and guardians of their children.

Marcilio Ficino, the philosopher courtier, said that Federigo was the ideal of a perfect man and a wise prince. Castiglione wrote: "In his days Duke Federigo of glorious memory was the light of Italy. Nor is there any lack of truthful witnesses still living, who can bear testimony to his prudence, humanity, justice, liberality, unconquered courage and military skill."

King Ferrante, whose own faithlessness perhaps made him appreciate fidelity in others, said at an earlier date of Federigo: "Who in this age has more fairly taken arms? Who has led armies under happier auspices? Whose conduct in pitched battles or in sieges has been more exemplary? . . . He is not less eminent at home than abroad, not less excellent in council than in arms. And, what is still more remarkable, all this superiority is the fruit of his genius, not less than his prowess, and especially of his good faith, which, although the basis of every virtue, is the rarest of them all, and which, almost banished from earth, has taken refuge in heaven."

Such tributes demonstrate the admiration and affection the Duke of Urbino inspired. His contemporaries recognized that Federigo da Montefeltro was not only the best soldier of his generation, but also the best ruler, superior in character to all other Italian princes.

GUIDOBALDO

THE NEW DUKE of Urbino, Guidobaldo da Montefeltro, was ten years old when his father died in 1482 and he became the ruler of an important state. Since his mother had died a few months after his birth, Guidobaldo grew up in the care of servants and was instructed by tutors. A tall, handsome boy with fair hair, a long body and short legs, Guidobaldo was fond of hunting and good at all sports and military exercises. On his deathbed Federigo had appointed his nephew and intimate friend,

Ottaviano Ubaldini, to be a guardian and sort of informal regent to rule Urbino and advise Guidobaldo.

His first important advice must have been concerned with a strange offer that came to the boy duke from the League of Naples, Florence and Milan which was defending Ferrara against Venice and the papacy. The league offered Guidobaldo the same command his father had held. This seeming absurdity can only be explained as a tribute to Federigo and as a means of continuing the service of Federigo's tough and well-trained troops. Guidobaldo accepted, and at the age of ten began *in absentia* his career as a condottiere.

Two more times Guidobaldo accepted mercenary contracts while still too young to leave his home and earn his pay. King Ferrante of Naples hired him for three years at a total wage of fifteen thousand ducats, and Pope Innocent hired him to fight Ferrante. But it wasn't until 1487 that Guidobaldo saw action in the Pope's service against a rebellious baron. He was fifteen, the age at which his father had first borne arms.

No prince of the Renaissance, not even his father, was as steeped in the new learning and as devoted to books and study as Guidobaldo. He wrote and spoke both Latin and Greek fluently. His knowledge of classical literature was immense. Like Federigo, he was especially interested in history and theology, and his favorite authors were Xenophon and St. John Chrysostom. His memory was phenomenal. He could recite whole books by Homer and Virgil and was said to be able to remember anything he wished to. He enjoyed studying philosophy, ethics, geography and poetry.

That this brilliant intellectual, who would have preferred to spend his life in his own fine library, served regularly as a condottiere, even after he was partially crippled by gout (or arthritis or whatever it was), is an illuminating comment on his position as the great Federigo's son and on the economic necessities of princely magnificence. The tradition was so strong, the need to earn money to defray the expenses of a brilliant court so great, that Guidobaldo never considered not following in his father's footsteps.

When the boy duke went riding through his duchy, he was

GUIDOBALDO DA MONTEFELTRO, Duke of Urbino

"... this brilliant intellectual, who would have preferred to spend
his life in his own fine library, served regularly as a condottiere,
even after he was partially crippled by gout ..." Portrait by Piero
della Francesca.

sometimes accompanied by a band of musicians, which included four trumpeters, three drummers, a sackbut player and a company of bagpipers. Such a combination of instruments may not sound attractive to modern taste, but presumably Guidobaldo and the people of Urbino enjoyed it. A guard slept in Guidobaldo's bedroom, where in cold weather there was a fire and all the year a bell and a night light.

In October of 1489 Duke Guidobaldo, then seventeen, was married to Elisabetta, daughter of Marquis Federigo Gonzaga of Mantua and youngest sister of the future marquis Francesco. The bride was eighteen. Her beauty, virtue, culture, kindness, courage in adversity and loyalty to her husband were all to become famous.

The marriage of Elisabetta and Guidobaldo was happy. It was also remarkable. The couple were devoted to each other, and this in spite of the unhappy fact that the Duke was impotent. The doctors who tried to help could not, and so Guidobaldo's misfortune was blamed on sorcery or poison. Elisabetta patiently and faithfully remained a loyal wife. She was much admired for her chastity, and Guidobaldo himself does not seem (as far as is recorded) to have suffered any ridicule. In the bluntly outspoken and sexually enthusiastic age in which he lived, this is eloquent evidence of the nobility of his character which inspired general liking and respect.

The Duke's achievements as a condottiere were negligible. He was checked, defeated or captured by abler commanders. Never lacking in courage, he lacked ability and luck. Serving King Alfonso II of Naples against the French, Guidobaldo took part in a skirmish and was defeated. At the Battle of Fornovo he was represented by his half-brother, Antonio, perhaps because he was incapacitated by gout. He fought for Florence against Pisa and for Pope Alexander against the French garrisons in Naples and won no laurels. And in 1497, fighting for Alexander against the rebellious Orsini barons, Guidobaldo was defeated and captured. The Orsini shut him up in their castle of Soriano and demanded a ransom of forty thousand ducats. Alexander, in whose service Guidobaldo had been captured, was utterly indifferent to his plight and refused to pay a ducat toward his ransom. The Duke raised the sum himself (perhaps reduced to only thirty thousand ducats) by selling Duchess Elisabetta's jewels and by soliciting contributions from his most prosperous subjects.

A year later, in the autumn of 1498 Guidobaldo, in the service of Venice, participated in an attack upon Florence and ineptly allowed himself to be cut off and surrounded in the mountain town of Bibbiena. Supplies ran low. Men deserted. The weather was cold and wet, and Guidobaldo's gout prostrated him. He sent a request to his enemies to be allowed a doctor. The request was refused. Finally in February of 1459 Paolo Vitelli, the Florentine commander, mercifully permitted Guidobaldo to go home to Urbino. It was all highly depressing and demonstrated once and for all that the Duke of Urbino had no gift for war. For Guidobaldo's sake we can hope that he did not brood long over the question of what Duke Federigo would have thought of such a performance.

About this time the fiery cardinal of San' Pietro in Vincoli, Giuliano della Rovere, suggested to the Duke that he make their mutual nephew, Francesco Maria della Rovere, then aged eight, his heir. The boy was the son of Giovanni della Rovere, the Cardinal's brother who had been made lord of Sinigaglia by Pope Sixtus IV, and of Guidobaldo's elder sister, Giovanna da Montefeltro. It was sadly clear to Guidobaldo that he could have no children of his own and he wanted to maintain his family dynasty. In want of a son a nephew would have to do. Since Urbino was a papal fief, this required the approval of Pope Alexander, an implacable enemy of Cardinal Giuliano. Nevertheless, the pope gave his approval. Probably at that time he did not foresee the Borgia conquest of Urbino by treachery.

In 1501 Giovanni della Rovere died, and Francesco Maria, now twelve, was sent to Urbino to grow up at the court of the state he was destined to inherit.

During the next few years the story of the Duke of Urbino, like those of many other Italian princes, was part of the story of Cesare Borgia. Pope Alexander's brilliant son was a hero, a villain and a legend in his own time. His short and glittering career cast a baleful spell over Italy. He had been a cardinal and had left the Church to become a soldier, a conqueror and a despot—all sup-

posedly in the service of the Church, to impose its direct rule on Papal States misruled by petty tyrants. It was widely believed that Cesare really intended to create for himself a state, which would include much of Italy, under his personal authority.

Strikingly handsome, a splendid athlete, magnetically and sometimes sinisterly charming, Cesare combined many abilities. He was a suave and subtle diplomat, a master of dissimulation, a capable soldier, an able administrator and a popular leader. He campaigned in the name of the Church and was financed by it. The King of France was his ally and supported him with men and money. Cesare defeated some of his enemies in ordinary warfare, but when he could, he preferred to defeat them by treachery—it was quicker and cheaper. He deceived and betrayed, attacked without warning and killed without cause or excuse. He murdered and raped.

Numerous historians have pointed out that Cesare Borgia was morally not much worse than many of his contemporaries. This is true. Perhaps what made him seem worse was his swaggering theatricality, his self-dramatization and his pretense that he was acting for the benefit of the Holy Church and its success.

We have seen how he began his conquests with the capture of Imola and Forli. Next on his schedule was Faenza, whose popular young lord, Astorre Manfredi, he murdered. Now in the late spring of 1502 he announced that he would drive the villainous Varani family out of Camerino, a tiny state lost in the mountains of the March of Ancona. Pope Alexander sent Guidobaldo a

---

CESARE BORGIA, Captain-General of the Church and Duke of Romagna

"Numerous historians have pointed out that Cesare Borgia was morally not much worse than many of his contemporaries. This is true. Perhaps what made him seem worse was his swaggering theatricality, his self-dramatization and his pretense that he was acting for the benefit of the Holy Church and its success."

request to lend Cesare his cannon, which was then considered the best in Italy, for the Camerino campaign. As a loyal vassal of the Church the Duke complied and sent with the cannon a contribution of supplies and draft oxen.

Cesare marched out of Rome in June. When he reached Spoleto, he sent a messenger to Guidobaldo asking for the use of a thousand infantrymen to be sent to help the city of Arezzo in Tuscany which had revolted against Florentine rule. Two of Cesare's chief condottieri, Vitelozzo Vitelli and Gianpaolo Baglioni, were helping the Aretines, perhaps with the intention of seizing the city for themselves—undoubtedly with Cesare's connivance, if not at his express orders.

What was Guidobaldo to do? He did not wish to offend his affectionate friend Cesare who was also captain-general of the Holy Church. Nor could he afford to offend Florence, a state much more powerful than his own and in close alliance with France, which was much more powerful still. So Guidobaldo wrote Cesare a diplomatic letter courteously declining and explaining all the reasons why he could not collect a thousand men and dispatch them to Arezzo. With the letter to sweeten his refusal the Duke sent Cesare a present, a fine war horse.

On the evening of June 20, 1502, the Duke of Urbino had dinner with his friend the prior of the Franciscan monastery of San Bernardino, which was a half-hour's ride east of the city. After dinner the two men sat in the garden discussing religion and philosophy, as they frequently did. Guidobaldo was relaxed. He was not concerned with Borgia's attack on Camerino, which was ruled by the brutal Varani. His wife, Elisabetta, was away in Mantua, visiting her brother and sister-in-law, Francesco and Isabella d'Este. Only six months before, Guidobaldo and Elisabetta had vacated the palace of Urbino and turned it over for a week to Lucrezia Borgia on her journey to Ferrara.

Although he was a fine scholar, a benevolent ruler and a highly intelligent man, the Duke of Urbino was entirely too trusting and innocent for his own good. He did not seem to understand the treachery and violence of his own time. So he was utterly confounded when at about eight in the evening an exhausted messenger burst into the peaceful monastery garden with the news that

Cesare Borgia and his army had invaded Urbino, had passed through Gubbio and were already at Cagli. After a shocked pause Guidobaldo struck the table and exclaimed, "I am betrayed!"

Two other contingents of Borgia's army were invading the duchy from other directions. The Duke's few troops were scattered in many places. Moreover, his own artillery could be used against him. No resistance was possible. Guidobaldo rode at once to the palace and there prepared to flee.

At eleven-thirty that night the Duke of Urbino left his city, accompanied by his young nephew, Francesco Maria, an equerry, three chamberlains (officers of his domestic staff) and several archers. He hoped to reach the mountain fortress of San Leo. Avoiding roads, the party filed through the forests on the mountainside—forests which have long since disappeared. They climbed steep ridges, crossed deep gulleys. At dawn some shepherds warned them that a detachment of Cesare's troops had cut them off from San Leo.

The Duke made a wide detour and went to the fortress of San Agata instead. There he divided the party, sending the exhausted Francesco Maria across Tuscany to a safe refuge with his other uncle, Cardinal Giuliano, in Savona near Genoa. Guidobaldo hoped to find political asylum in Venice. To avoid attracting notice he dismissed the archers and rode northward with the three chamberlains. Suddenly a band of peasant robbers rushed out of ambush and attacked the fugitives with clubs and pitchforks, shouting, "Death! Death!"

As they galloped off, the horse of one of the chamberlains stumbled and threw its rider to the ground. He was a particularly trusted servant carrying a satchel stuffed with gold coins which Guidobaldo had scraped together to support the Duchess and himself in exile. The robbers fell upon this unexpected treasure and murdered the unfortunate chamberlain. Guidobaldo and the other two chamberlains escaped, and nearly a week later they arrived in Mantua—filthy, exhausted and Guidobaldo desperately sick with gout. Writing to Cardinal Giuliano from Mantua the Duke said: "I have saved nothing but my life, a doublet and a shirt."

Borgia's threats made it necessary for Guidobaldo to leave

Mantua. He went to Venice where he was welcomed with considerable pomp and given an allowance to support him during his exile.

In Urbino, Cesare established his own dominion with his usual thorough efficiency and stripped the ducal palace of its art treasures, removing four cartloads of silver, pictures, tapestries and books to the castle at Forli. We have seen how he presented two of the choicest pieces, which he himself had previously given to the Duke and Duchess, to Isabella d'Este at Mantua. He also gave away a magnificent set of tapestries depicting the Trojan war to Georges d'Amboise, the Cardinal of Rouen, and King Louis XII's most influential adviser.

In his biography of Cesare, Carlo Beuf says that at this time an unverifiable story circulated from city to city that "Cesare had offered Guidobaldo a red hat in exchange for his definite renunciation of any claim to the dukedom. The offer included annulment of his marriage and a new, suitable husband for Elisabetta." This insulting and humiliating proposal seems entirely possible. Cesare was mentally as well as physically cruel.

During the rest of the summer, while the Duke and Duchess remained safely in Venice, trouble was brewing for Cesare. King Louis XII stood by his ally Florence and ordered Cesare to see that his captains retired at once from Arezzo. To make sure they would do so, Cesare had to threaten to attack Baglioni and Vitelli in their own cities of Perugia and Città di Castello. The two condottieri were incensed. They were also frightened, as were many other princes who feared that Cesare would attack them without warning as he had Guidobaldo.

So, late in September, an anti-Borgia confederation was formed. It included the Duke of Urbino, the lords of Siena and Bologna, Baglioni, Vitelli and the Orsini family. While they were arguing about what steps to take, news arrived that revolt had broken out in the duchy of Urbino. On October 2 a band of peasants organized by one of Guidobaldo's squires broke into the castle of San Leo by a ruse and massacred the Borgia garrison with axes and pitchforks. Soon, other loyal subjects of the Duke recaptured the other towns in the Duchy and the city of Urbino itself.

The confederates then attacked and defeated several units of Cesare's troops, and Guidobaldo was able to return to Urbino. He was greeted with joy. The entire population thronged the streets, so that he could ride only with difficulty through the crowd to the cathedral, where he gave thanks for his safe return. Then Guidobaldo retired to his sacked palace and collapsed on his bed, physically and emotionally exhausted. But he received all who wished to see him in his bedchamber. An anonymous diarist wrote: "I was plundered at Montecalvo by the soldiery of goods to the value of twenty-five ducats, which prevented me from sowing this year. But my losses seemed as nothing when I saw my Prince, and especially when I touched his hand. Such were the caresses bestowed upon me by my lord, whom God preserve."

When Cesare Borgia heard of the revolt of Urbino and the restoration of Guidobaldo, he said to Machiavelli, "Let them go. I have taken the duchy once and I have not forgotten how I did it."

Guidobaldo did not enjoy his restoration long. Cesare received reinforcements from King Louis and with consummate diplomacy broke up the alliance against him. "I will eat the artichoke, leaf by leaf," said Cesare. He did. The lords of Siena and Bologna decided that discretion was the better part of valor, resigned from the alliance and made new pacts of friendship with Cesare. Four of the leading rebels were persuaded to attend a meeting of peace and reconciliation with Cesare in the town of Sinigaglia.

So, abandoned by his friends and once more threatened by the overpowering might of Cesare, the Duke of Urbino fled from his city for the second time.

Before he left, Guidobaldo made a speech to the people of Urbino, explaining that he lacked the resources to resist Cesare alone and that it would be best for his subjects if he fled and spared them the horrors of a hopeless resistance. Some of the men urged him to fight anyway and pledged themselves to die with him. Women offered jewels to pay for arms and ammunition. But Guidobaldo refused, knowing that brave gestures were not enough. Tired, tormented by his chronic illness and deeply depressed, he rode out of the Montefeltro palace and cried out, "My God, my God, why hast Thou thus punished me?"

Once again the Duke of Urbino was an exile in Venice. And after Cesare had treacherously murdered the condottieri who had attended his peace meeting, he was once again ruler of Urbino. Soon afterward he easily conquered Assisi, Perugia and Siena and seemed to threaten all Italy.

But in September of the following year Cesare's father, the wicked, old Alexander VI, died; Cesare fell desperately ill himself, and the Borgia power collapsed. The exiled Princes returned in triumph to their various states and for a second time, Guidobaldo was welcomed home to Urbino with fervent enthusiasm.

Baldassare Castiglione, in a letter to King Henry VII of England described the Duke of Urbino's second return to his city: "Guidobaldo came back to his own and recovered the State of which he had been so unjustly deprived, amid the rejoicing of all Italy. Troops of children flocked to meet him with olive branches in their hands, singing for gladness at the sight of their beloved Prince. Old men, tottering under the weight of years, hurried out to meet him with tears of joy streaming down their cheeks, mothers with babies in their arms, and persons of every age and sex joined the crowds that thronged the streets. The very stones seemed to dance and exult in his coming."

The election of Cardinal Giuliano della Rovere as Pope Julius II was a great relief to Guidobaldo. Julius was his personal friend, the brother-in-law of his sister and the uncle of his heir. In May of 1504 Julius summoned Guidobaldo to Rome to be made Captain-General of the Church in place of Cesare Borgia. This honor must have been a gesture of friendship and family alliance because no one knew better than Julius that Guidobaldo was a mediocre commander. Guidobaldo tried to decline, but the Pope insisted.

So poor, ailing Guidobaldo traveled to Rome, carried in a litter and modestly tried to enter the city unobtrusively. But Julius, who did everything in as grand a manner as possible, sent a delegation to welcome the Duke officially. Guidobaldo was required to don a cloth-of-gold doublet and to mount a handsome mule caparisoned in purple velvet and to ride across Rome while guns roared and soldiers saluted. Guidobaldo had planned to spend the night as the guest of a friend in a private house. But

Julius commanded him to come to the Vatican. When Guido-baldo arrived, he found the Pope and the entire College of Cardinals assembled at the foot of the principal staircase to greet him.

The fierce old pope was genuinely fond of the gentle duke. Soon word went around Rome that "anyone who wants to enter the good graces of His Holiness perforce has to pay court to the Duke of Urbino." Knowing this, Cesare Borgia, who was powerless, humiliated, and no longer the dominating figure of two years before, asked twice for an interview with Guidobaldo. Twice Guidobaldo refused. Why should he wish to meet the man who had betrayed him, twice driven him out of his duchy and robbed him of his most valuable possessions? But Cesare contrived to find Guidobaldo in the Pope's waiting room. One of Guidobaldo's courtiers described the following scene in a letter.

Guidobaldo was seated on a couch when Cesare entered the room, cap in hand, and fell upon his knees before his former victim. The astonished duke rose and stepped back. Then with his unfailing courtesy he raised Cesare to his feet and listened patiently while Cesare fervently apologized for the wrongs he had done him and with fawning hypocrisy tried to excuse himself on the grounds of his youth and the evil counsel of his father, Pope Alexander, whom he cursed. Cesare promised to restore Guidobaldo's library and other treasures, which were stored in the citadel of Forli still controlled by one of Cesare's officers.

To all this, Guidobaldo listened politely. If he felt any gratification at the humble manner of his enemy, he did not show it. But neither did he try to help the fallen Cesare. That would have been too much to expect even from the good duke of Urbino.

In June of 1504 Guidobaldo returned to Urbino and as commander of the papal army marched against the citadel of Forli, whose castellan still held out for Borgia. But as soon as the Duke and his army appeared outside the walls, the citadel was surrendered. Guidobaldo recovered almost all of the loot taken from his own palace, including most of the famous library.

From then until his death Guidobaldo da Montefeltro lived peacefully, although nominally supporting some of Pope Julius' campaigns. Urbino prospered, and under the joint influence of Guidobaldo and Elisabetta the court circle developed there which Castiglione made famous in *The Courtier.*

Pope Julius continued to be fond of Guidobaldo and kept him in Rome for more than a year. On his march to Bologna to drive out the Bentivoglio family and impose papal rule (a program not very different from Cesare's), Julius arrived in Urbino on September 25, 1506. It appears that most of the papal army stayed outside the city. But the Pope, twenty-two cardinals, numerous servants and a guard of four hundred men entered in state. The Duke did his best to welcome them in proper style. Roads were repaired. Triumphal arches were erected. Flowers and evergreen branches were strewn across the way, and the walls were hung with bright cloths.

Outside the walls the Pope was met by forty-five young nobles, dressed in white silk. When the Pope dismounted from his mule, the young men seized it and held it for a ransom of sixty ducats according to the curious custom of the time. At the gate Julius was met by Guidobaldo, who did not dismount because of his illness, and by the court, the clergy and municipal officers of the city. As a gesture of good will toward the Pope's enterprise Guidobaldo presented him with a hundred sacks of flour, a hundred sacks of barley and wheat and an unrecorded number of sheep and chickens.

How much Castiglione's account of life at the cultivated court of Urbino is an idealization and how much is accurate reporting we do not know. Presumably the long conversations on the qualifications of the perfect courtier are Castiglione's inventions; but parts of them could have been inspired by some actual discussion. Castiglione modestly set the scene in a time when he was away on a diplomatic mission to England, but his modesty failed of its purpose. The worldwide popularity of his book made Castiglione more famous than any other member of the court, even more famous than the Duke himself.

Guidobaldo engaged Castiglione as a courtier and soldier in the winter of 1504, when they were both in Rome. Castiglione remained in Urbino for the next twelve years, serving Francesco Maria after Guidobaldo's death. A poet, a soldier, and an accomplished diplomat, Castiglione came nearer to living up to his own ideal of a courtier than anyone else. He much admired Guido-

BALDASSARE CASTIGLIONE, *poet, courtier and diplomat*

"The worldwide popularity of his book made Castiglione more famous than any other member of the court, even more famous than the Duke himself." Portrait by Raphael.

K

baldo, and his feeling for Duchess Elisabetta seems to have been a mixture of love and reverence.

Another prominent member of the Urbino court circle was Giuliano de' Medici, youngest of the three exiled Medici brothers, a handsome, highly cultivated gentleman with a taste for the arts and fine living and no noticeable drive or ambition. Everyone liked Giuliano, and one young lady, whose identity is uncertain, liked him so much that she bore him a bastard son who grew up to be Cardinal Ippolito de' Medici.

Also of the court circle was Cesare Gonzaga, a member of a younger branch of the reigning family of Mantua, a cousin and intimate friend of Castiglione and a soldier and poet. Here, too, were the Fregoso brothers, sons of Federigo's bastard daughter, Gentile, and of an important Genoese nobleman; they were nephews of Guidobaldo. Ottaviano was a soldier and lived to become doge of Genoa. Federigo was a soldier, a diplomat and a priest who became bishop of Gubbio and a cardinal.

A guest who prolonged his visit to Guidobaldo's court was Pietro Bembo, a Venetian poet, scholar, prolific letter writer and dictator of Latin prose. Worldly and self-indulgent, Bembo was clever and able. He became secretary to Pope Leo X and later a cardinal. The amorous friend of Lucrezia Borgia arrived in Urbino in 1506, when he judged it prudent to leave Ferrara. He remained for the next six years, using his leisure to write poetry, taking an active part in the social and intellectual life of the court and correcting the proofs of *The Courtier*.

In 1507 Bembo wrote to a friend in Rome: "There is little to say about our doings here; but we laugh, we jest, we play games, we invent new tricks and practical jokes, we feast and study, and now and then we write poetry. If I had more time, which I have not today, I would send you a proof of this in a beautiful canzone which my dear M. Baldassare Castiglione has composed during the last few days."

Many years later Bembo wrote to a young protégé who was lamenting his poverty: "Be of good cheer, and do not allow melancholy to depress you, remembering that I went to Urbino with only forty ducats in my pocket, and remained there six years, and without ever receiving more than fourteen ducats from my family."

Another prominent courtier was Bernardo Dovizi, a witty and likable man. He was the friend and secretary of Cardinal Giovanni de' Medici who, when he became Pope Leo X, made Dovizi a cardinal. Dovizi, usually known as Bibbiena for his birthplace, repaid the hospitality of the Montefeltro court by actively helping Leo in his campaign to drive out Duke Francesco Maria and install Lorenzo de' Medici, the Younger. Also a notable member of the court was Bernardo Accolti, who was called the *Unico Aretino*. A man of sublime egoism, he recited his own improvised verses to general acclaim.

Many evenings when the ailing duke had retired, these men and the court gathered to converse and play intellectual games in the Duchess' quarters. Elisabetta sometimes sang verses from the *Aeneid* and accompanied herself on the lute. Her great friend, Emilia Pia, widow of Antonio da Montefeltro, often was delegated to play the part of hostess and to guide the conversation.

The conversation must have been good. Judging by *The Courtier* it was florid, pedantic and stiff; but this is a modern reaction. It was also sometimes ribald.

In addition to these prominent courtiers, Urbino was full of second-rate poets and scholars whose names are not worth recording. And it was the birthplace of two of the great geniuses of the Renaissance: Bramante, the architect, and Raphael, the painter. Unfortunately for Urbino, both of them won their fame in other cities.

The Urbino court under the benign influence of the Duke and Duchess ought to have been an exception to the general rule that bloody violence was an integral element in the princely courts of Renaissance Italy. Unfortunately, it wasn't. In 1507 a murder was committed within the ducal palace which might have caused an enormous scandal. It didn't only because it was efficiently hushed up.

In September Francesco Maria della Rovere, now seventeen years old, returned from Rome and discovered that his widowed sister, Maria Varana, whose husband Cesare Borgia had murdered, was enjoying a love affair. The lover was Giovanni Andrea who, when he was only a squire, had accompanied Guidobaldo on his night flight from Urbino to escape capture by Cesare. Since then he had been knighted and was a favorite of Guidobaldo.

Francesco Maria had inherited the terrible temper of the Della Rovere family. As lord of Sinigaglia and heir of Urbino he believed passionately in the double standard; no matter how their men behaved, the women of princely families should be virtuous. To him it seemed even more shocking that Andrea was of humble origin. So Francesco Maria, with malice aforethought and cold premeditation, arranged a sensationally treacherous murder.

While Duke Guidobaldo and Castiglione were out of town he invited Andrea to his rooms to have dinner and a fencing match. The unsuspecting lover came and ate a good dinner as the guest of his would-be murderer. Then, when they prepared to fence, two servants seized Andrea's arms, Francesco Maria stabbed him with a knife and the servants finished him off. Francesco Maria left the body lying in its own blood and a servant posted outside the door to prevent anyone from entering. Then he fled to his own city of Sinigaglia.

To speculate about the teen-age murderer's thoughts as he sat across the dinner table from his victim would be interesting, but futile. One thing only is certain. Francesco Maria was not usually a scheming villain. Even though four years later he committed another murder (also with ample provocation), he led a normal life, won the loyalty of his subjects as duke of Urbino, won the friendship of many of his contemporaries and served as a competent condottiere.

Shortly after Francesco Maria's flight the Duchess knocked on the door of the murder chamber. The servant said: "Madonna, it is of no use. I have the lord's order to keep the door fast; and if you could open it you would see a sight that would be very displeasing to your eyes." But Elisabetta insisted. The door was opened, and she burst into tears. "That same evening," wrote the Venetian ambassador, "he sent some of his servants to kill his sister's carver, who had been employed to bear letters to her lover."

Duke Guidobaldo returned to Urbino and arranged an elaborate funeral for the murdered man. But he did nothing to punish Francesco Maria. How could he? The young lord was his nephew and his heir, the only person who could continue his dynasty and the beloved nephew of the powerful pope. Little more was heard about the crime.

Baldassare Castiglione wrote to his mother: "There has been some disturbance here about an unfortunate event in the ducal family. However, things are settling down now, and the Lord Prefect is here again, so I hope there will be no further trouble in the matter." His mother wanted to know more.

Castiglione was curt: "You need not distress yourself about the death of Gio. Andrea—may God pardon him!—because these things, when they are once done, cannot be undone. Everything has been arranged, thanks to the wisdom and dexterity of the Lord Duke, and the Lord Prefect is here again, and is restored to His Excellency's favor, and he who no longer lives is already forgotten."

It sounds callous. But in the Renaissance, people had to be able to take murders calmly. If they couldn't they would have been upset much of the time.

Bembo dismissed the case with the chilling brevity: "He who might remain standing, and falls by his own fault, deserves to lie there against his will."

Soon after the murder, life at the Urbino court seemed normal again. But a shadow lay over everyone because Duke Guidobaldo grew worse. At intervals when he felt better he was carried about in a chair. When his attacks of gout returned, he was confined to his bed in great pain. To distract himself from his sufferings he would recite long passages from his favorite authors. He grew emaciated and prematurely old. But always he remained calm, patient and courageous.

In February of 1508 Guidobaldo had himself carried in a litter to Fossombrone where the altitude was lower and the climate milder. The court went with him. But early in April it snowed at Fossombrone, and the temperature fell below freezing. And the duke was obviously dying.

The Duchess and Francesco Maria were constantly at his bedside. "Why, my friends, would you deprive me of what I most desire?" asked Guidobaldo. "Is not death, that delivers us from such cruel pains, the best and mildest of friends?" He then urged the Duchess and Francesco Maria to trust and love each other and commanded Francesco Maria to obey his uncle the Pope in all respects. He died on the night of April 9, 1508. He was only thirty-six.

Duchess Elisabetta flung herself upon his body and then fainted. For two days she alternated between apathy and hysteria. And, in the manner of Renaissance princes, she cultivated her grief. Isabella d'Este sent the Mantuan ambassador to convey her condolences. He was admitted to the widow at night and found her, wearing a veil, and seated on a mattress, in a room draped in black with only a single candle on the floor. "I was led in by my cloak like a blind man. She offered me her hand, and I stood for a time like a mute, unable to speak for we were both sobbing."

The night after his death the body of the Duke was carried from Fossombrone to Urbino on the shoulders of mourners, surrounded by a crowd of torch bearers which grew with new recruits as it progressed. The body was placed in the great hall of the palace of Urbino where it lay in state for two days on a catafalque draped with black velvet and gold damask. The body was dressed in a black silk doublet and crimson hose, with a black velvet hat and black velvet slippers. It was partly covered by the mantle of the Order of the Garter with a hood of crimson velvet lined with white silk.

After attending a solemn Mass in the cathedral young Francesco Maria made public his uncle's will naming him heir to the duchy and making the Duchess regent until he was twenty-five.

Guidobaldo was buried in the Church of San Bernardino beside his father. The inscription over his tomb reads:

"To Guidobaldo, son of Federigo, third Duke of Urbino, who, emulating even in minority his father's fame, maintained his authority with manly energy and success. In youth he triumphed over adverse fortune. Vigorous in mind, although enfeebled by disease, he cultivated letters instead of arms; he protected men of general eminence instead of mere military adventurers; and he ameliorated the commonwealth by the arts of peace, until his court became a model to all others. He died in the year of God MDVIII, of his age XXXVI."

Duchess Elisabetta was thirty-seven, still considered beautiful, elegant and attractive. She soon recovered from her excessive grief and resumed her duties. She did her best to help her nephew and lived with quiet courage until her death in 1526. When Bembo heard that she had died, he wrote: "I have seen many excellent and noble women and have heard of some who were more illustrious for certain virtues, but in her alone among women all virtues were united and brought together. I have never seen or heard of anyone who was her equal, and know of very few who have even come near her."

XVI

THE EVILHEADS
OF RIMINI

ON THE ADRIATIC SEA, some twenty miles north of Urbino, lies the popular summer resort of Rimini. A city of nearly eighty thousand people, its population soars in the summer when its many big hotels are packed with Italian and German vacationers and its beaches swarm with sun-worshipers. Signs of past glories are there, but they must be looked for. A handsome Roman bridge with five tall arches begun by Augustus and finished by Tiberius and a triumphal arch erected in honor of Augustus are evidence of Rimini's antiquity. Two buildings still proclaim Rimini's importance in the Renaissance: the Church of San Francisco, always called the Tempio Malatestiano, and a huge fortress-palace. Both of these were built by Sigismondo Pandolfo Malatesta, the ablest and most celebrated member of a fierce and turbulent family which ruled Rimini and many other towns for generations.

In the twelfth century the Malatesta were aristocratic and powerful landowners in the small towns of the Apennines. By the middle of the thirteenth century they were the most powerful family in Rimini. The true founder of the family greatness was Malatesta da Verucchio, a thirteenth-century adventurer who successfully combined murderous treachery with religious devotion. This energetic and resourceful tyrant lived to be a hundred and one, dying in 1312 with exemplary piety. He had many children. Two of his sons were actors in a tragic love story which Dante made immortal in his *Inferno*.

About the year 1275 Giovanni Malatesta, called *il Sciancato*, "the Lame," married Francesca da Polenta, whose father the Malatesta had helped when he seized power and made himself lord of Ravenna. According to the old story, Giovanni was brutal and ugly as well as lame. His brother, Paolo, called *il Bello*, went to Ravenna to bring the bride to Rimini; Francesca looked out of the window, mistook the beautiful Paolo for her husband and fell in love with him. Some eight or nine years later Giovanni discovered the adultery of Francesca and Paolo and killed them both.

Obscure sinners of a most conventional sort, Francesca and Paolo would never have become world-famous and the subjects of many poems and plays if Dante had not relegated them to the second circle of Hell. There he let Francesca describe with sad eloquence the occasion when reading aloud about the love of Lancelot and Guinevere her eyes met Paolo's and then they kissed—and on that day they read no more. (Boccaccio wrote: "It is possible that it happened like that. But I hold it to be a possible fiction rather than based on anything known to the author.")

Long before Malatesta da Verucchio made himself lord of Rimini his ancestors had acquired the sobriquet Malatesta, which replaced any name they may have had before. It has been translated as both evilheads and wrongheads. In the fourteenth century a respectful historian traced the family pedigree back to Noah through Tarquin and Croesus. In the next century another historian, no less respectful, traced it back to Scipio Africanus. Genealogy has always been an art as well as a science.

In his will Malatesta da Verucchio included a plea for perpetual peace among his sons and grandchildren. This did not prevent a series of feuds, betrayals and reconciliations which ended in massacres. Dinner parties from which murdered cousins were carried out in sacks were a Malatesta specialty. Finally two of the grandsons, brothers named Malatesta and Galeotto, became joint lords and cooperated with each other. Malatesta's nickname, *il Guastafamiglia*, is interesting; it means family destroyer. Galeotto's

K*

two sons, Carlo and Pandolfo, succeeded to power and also cooperated with each other.

Both became famous condottieri. Carlo was not always successful. Twice he was taken prisoner. But as a statesman and diplomat he was widely respected, even though he was as crafty and untrustworthy as most of his contemporary princes. After the death of Giangaleazzo Visconti, the great duke of Milan, Pandolfo seized the city of Brescia in Lombardy and held it as its lord for seventeen years. There his three bastard sons were born. Pandolfo was married three times but had no legitimate children. When Duke Filippo Maria Visconti reassembled his father's state, Pandolfo was forced to surrender Brescia and return to Fano in the Malatesta domains.

The brothers belonged to a generation which was born in the Middle Ages and died in the Renaissance. Both wrote Latin and spoke French as well as Italian. Carlo, grave and austere, was learned in theology, and was called by his subjects Marcus Cato. He is best known for an incident in Mantua where he was serving as a sort of unofficial regent for his young nephew, Gianfrancesco Gonzaga.

In 1407 or thereabouts Carlo was profoundly shocked by the impious reverence shown by the Mantuans for a statue of their city's most famous citizen, Virgil. In righteous, puritanical fury Carlo had the statue taken down and thrown into the Mincio River. Such vandalism was much condemned by the humanist scholars, who considered Carlo little better than a barbarian. Yet it was this same Carlo who approved a suggestion of Pandolfo's that a room in the Malatesta fortress at Rimini be decorated by a then unknown Florentine artist named Lorenzo Ghiberti, the same Ghiberti who not long after was to win undying fame as the sculptor of the bronze doors of the Florentine baptistery. When Carlo died in 1429, he was sixty-five years old. He had no sons of his own, and Pandolfo's three bastards were to carry on the Malatesta dynasty.

In 1429 the Malatesta state had passed the peak of its power and wealth. From Cervia in the north to Sinigaglia in the south the state stretched for some sixty miles along the Adriatic coast in Romagna and the March of Ancona. Rimini was much the most important town, but Cesena, Fano and Fossombrone were all important. Pesaro was held by a rival branch of the family.

The Malatesta family was not as rich as it had been. The fifteenth century was economically not as prosperous as the fourteenth; constant wars were a drain on the family exchequer in spite of salaries earned as condottieri. The need to earn the money involved the Malatesta in wars which seriously damaged the economy of their state. It was a vicious circle.

In the fourteenth century Rimini was a prosperous city. Its size is unknown, but one of its suburbs had a population of ten thousand. By 1511, however, the population of Rimini itself had shrunk to five thousand. In Carlo's time sixty locally owned ships rode in the harbor of Rimini. In 1524 there were none. Perpetual war, heavy taxation, economic decline and pestilences had ruined the city. For much of this decline and fall several Malatesta lords were largely responsible.

In their good years the Malatesta owned many castles, farms, vineyards, gardens and mills. They owned property in Bologna, Florence, Ferrara and Venice. They obtained money from rents, from the sale of produce and from a salt monopoly, as well as from taxes. No member of the Malatesta family paid taxes. Neither did anyone they especially favored. They paid cash to their soldiers. Their subjects paid taxes on real estate, bread, wine and legal transactions. In special emergencies they paid extra taxes to pay the hire of mercenary soldiers.

The constant wars and the regular devastation of the state would not have harried the Malatesta domain had the Malatesta lords been wise and peaceably inclined. But if they had cherished peace and abhorred war, they would not have been Renaissance princes—least of all, members of one of the most fanatically warlike families in all history.

CARLO MALATESTA was succeeded by Pandolfo's eldest bastard, Galeotto Roberto. He was eighteen, and so impressed by Uncle Carlo's piety that he had no interest in being a lord or a soldier. Being a saint was what Galeotto yearned for. He had visions and talked to God. He wore a Franciscan monk's robe and under it a hair shirt. He flogged himself. He spent as much time as possible with the sick and especially liked being with patients suffering from horrible ulcers. He ate so little that he seemed to be starving himself to death.

Such behavior profoundly impressed the people of Rimini, who credited Galeotto with miracles and called him Galeotto the Blessed. In the ordinary course of diplomatic relations Galeotto had married Margherita, a bastard daughter of Niccolò d'Este, that insatiably promiscuous marquis of Ferrara. When Niccolò heard that his son-in-law was piously determined to remain chaste, even though married, he snorted that he had not intended to give his daughter to a hermit.

Galeotto died at the age of twenty-one. His young wife survived him by more than forty years. She never married again and wanted to be buried by his side.

Galeotto Roberto was hardly a typical Malatesta. Neither was his successor, his younger brother Sigismondo Pandolfo, who was one of the most extraordinary characters of the entire fifteenth century.

XVII

THE PRINCE OF
ALL WICKEDNESS

SIGISMONDO PANDOLFO MALATESTA was born in Brescia in 1417. In 1432, when he was fifteen years old, he succeeded his brother Galeotto Roberto as lord of Rimini and reigned for the next thirty-six years. He died in 1468 an exhausted old man of fifty-one. Pope Pius II, who hated Sigismondo with rancorous personal malice, described him:

"Sigismondo, of the noble family of the Malatesta but illegitimate, was very vigorous in body and mind, eloquent, and gifted with great military ability. He had a thorough knowledge of history and no slight acquaintance with philosophy. Whatever he attempted he seemed born for, but the evil part of his character had the upper hand. He was such a slave to avarice that he was ready not only to plunder but to steal. His lust was so unbridled that he violated his daughters and his sons-in-law. He outdid all barbarians in cruelty. His bloody hand inflicted terrible punishments on innocent and guilty alike. He oppressed the poor, plundered the rich, spared neither widows nor orphans. No one felt safe under his rule. Wealth or a beautiful wife or handsome children were enough to cause a man to be accused of crime. He hated priests and despised religion. He had no belief in another world and thought the soul died with the body. Nevertheless he built at Rimini a splendid church dedicated to St. Francis, though he filled it so full of pagan works of art that it seemed less a Christian sanctuary than a temple of heathen devil-worshippers. In it he erected for his mistress a tomb of magnificent marble and exquisite workmanship with an inscription in the pagan style as follows: 'Sacred to the deified Isotta.' The two wives he married before he took Isotta for his mistress he killed one after the other with the sword or poison."

These lines have damned forever the reputation of Sigismondo Malatesta. Pius's habit of calling Sigismondo "the prince of all wickedness," "the poison of all Italy" and other opprobrious epithets has also influenced posterity's opinion. During his reign the Pope excommunicated Sigismondo no less than three times. He burned him in effigy on the piazza in front of St. Peter's in Rome. And in a ceremony unique in Church history Pius "canonized to Hell" Sigismondo while he was still alive. Has any other mortal sinner been so hated by a pope?

Pius hated Sigismondo so intensely that the lines quoted above contain nearly as much scurrilous defamation as they do truth. Beyond doubt, the lord of Rimini was a mighty sinner; but the verdict of history is that he was innocent of several of Pius's most damning accusations.

Pius II was a humanist scholar, a career diplomat and bureaucrat who entered the Church late in life for ambition's sake. He was intelligent, and usually he was honest. In his *Commentaries* he wrote a fascinating autobiography (the only autobiography by a pope), which is full of information about his contemporaries and the life of his time.

Why did the Pope hate Sigismondo? Because Pius was a passionate Sienese patriot and he believed, perhaps correctly, that while serving Siena as a condottiere Sigismondo had treacherously communicated with the enemy. Because Pius was a passionate believer in the temporal power of the Church which Sigismondo stubbornly defied. Because Pius imposed peace terms on Sigismondo requiring him not to wage war for ten years, and Sigismondo with brazen impudence had gone to war against the Church within a few weeks. Because Pius was the supreme official representative of Christian orthodoxy, and Sigismondo was a flamboyant individualist who mixed elements of Christianity, paganism, Neo-Platonism and skepticism into a private religion of his own. And because Sigismondo was as proud as Lucifer, with no proper respect for His Holiness, Pope Pius II. Sigismondo Malatesta was a master of the art of making enemies. But he also made friends. He held the loyal admiration of his soldiers and subjects. Italian ruling princes were expected to wage war, patronize artists and father bastards. Sigismondo excelled at all these. He was one of the finest soldiers of his time; a poet and a scholar; insatiable in his love of women. The keys to his character were energy, arrogance and irresponsibility—all in excess.

The notorious lord of Rimini was tall, strong, tireless. He had red-gold hair, a hooked nose, small blue eyes with oddly flat lids. He was handsome in a sinister way. At thirteen, while his saintly brother Galeotto prayed, Sigismondo led a sally out from the gate of Rimini and drove off an attacking force. At fifteen, Sigismondo escaped from besieged Rimini in disguise, raised an army in Cesena and defeated Carlo Malatesta of the rival Pesaro branch of the family. And at fifteen he broke his engagement to the daughter of the great condottiere, Carmagnola, who was beheaded by the Venetians in the Piazza San Marco for treachery. There was no point in marrying the daughter of a dead traitor and perhaps incurring the distrust and suspicion of the most powerful state in Italy. Sigismondo had been paid the greater part of a large dowry, which included a particularly handsome suit of armor. He refused to return any of the money when he repudiated the engagement. So at the age of fifteen he began the habit of keeping money not properly his which in later years was to blacken his reputation and earn him several powerful enemies.

In February of 1434 Sigismondo married Ginevra, a daughter of Marquis Niccolò d'Este of Ferrara and sister of Margherita d'Este, widow of his brother Galeotto Roberto. Sigismondo was seventeen, Ginevra sixteen. They had a son who died in infancy, and Ginevra herself died at the age of twenty-two—she had been ill and neglected. Her father, Niccolò, and her brothers, Leonello and Borso, remained good friends with Sigismondo which they certainly would not have continued to be if they had believed him guilty of her murder. Nor is it likely that Sigismondo, rash

and impetuous as he was, would have killed her and risked the enmity of the powerful House of Este. The accusation of murder was not made until many years later.

Sigismondo's second wife was Polissena Sforza, bastard daughter of the great Francesco, whom he married when she was only fourteen. In 1449 Polissena fled from Rimini to a refuge in the Apennines to escape the plague. There she died, presumably of the plague. But there were conflicting stories, some of them reporting that she was murdered. At the time Sigismondo was away in Lombardy, fighting his father-in-law in the ordinary way of professional soldiering. Although he was obsessed by his beloved mistress, Isotta degli Atti, it seems unlikely that he would have murdered his wife. And, in fact, he did not marry Isotta until seven years later. Francesco Sforza did not accuse Sigismondo at the time; but later he wrote Pope Pius II a letter in which he raised the charge of murder.

He wrote, "The said Signor Don Sigismondo had my daughter, his wife, strangled by Count Antonio with a napkin through no fault of hers." Sforza claimed that Sigismondo sent for Polissena's confessor and ordered him to swear that she had confessed the guilt of adultery. When the friar refused, according to Sforza, he was thrown into a dungeon. Sforza said that a reliable eyewitness had informed him, "for she was our daughter and our own flesh and blood."

But this was in 1462, more than twelve years after the alleged murder. If the new duke of Milan had felt strongly about it, he might have denounced Sigismondo before. In 1462 he and Pius were opposed to Sigismondo; it looks very much as if the wily Sforza were indulging in a bit of unscrupulous political propa-

---

SIGISMONDO MALATESTA, Lord of Rimini

"A man of perpetual violence . . . But there is something suspicious about the horrendous accusations. Could one man have been that wicked?" Mural by Piero della Francesca.

ganda. Even so, we cannot be sure. Sigismondo had no objection in principle to murder. And he was a man of perpetual violence.

The Pope's other charges of incest and rape are equally doubtful. Sigismondo certainly had no sexual morals. But there is something suspicious about the horrendous accusations. Could one man have been that wicked? Pius's successor, Pope Paul II, did not think so. He awarded Sigismondo the Golden Rose, gave him a house in Rome and made him Captain-General of the Church—all this for the man his predecessor had excommunicated three times.

The third important woman in Sigismondo's life (there were countless unimportant ones) was Isotta degli Atti, daughter of one of the leading nobles of Rimini. Sigismondo fell in love with her when she was twelve years old and he was a tough, licentious soldier of twenty-eight. In spite of her father's disapproval Isotta became Sigismondo's mistress. By the time she was fourteen Sigismondo had begun work on her tomb.

Although Sigismondo was never faithful to Isotta, his love for her was genuine and lasting. He wrote her love songs, which were sung in the streets of Rimini. He wrote her fifteen Petrarchan sonnets, ten of them lamenting her death although she lived longer than he did. To placate her offended family Sigismondo gave them his banking business and knighted her brother in a grand ceremony. In 1453 Isotta wrote Sigismondo an emotional letter demanding that he make an honest woman of her by marriage. He refused.

But three years later, after Isotta had been his mistress for eleven years, they were married. As said before, this was seven years after the death of Polissena Sforza, a persuasive argument that Sigismondo did not have her murdered in order to be able to marry Isotta. The tomb which Sigismondo built for Isotta was part of an ambitious project: the rebuilding of the old brick Church of San Francisco into an example of the finest Renaissance classical architecture which would also be a monument to Isotta and Sigismondo Malatesta.

The old Gothic church was transformed without being torn down. The designs were drawn by Leon Battista Alberti, the first great architect of the Italian Renaissance. The old walls were encased in marble. Round arches, classical columns and pediments and many statues and bas reliefs carved in the Renaissance manner inspired a general admiration which still endures. But the presence of pagan deities and of much personal glorification of Isotta and Sigismondo has shocked some, amused others and struck nearly all as odd.

The church is profusely decorated with monograms in which S for Sigismondo and I for Isotta are entwined, with roses and elephants (the symbols of the Malatesta family), and with dancing Cupids and bas reliefs of Venus, Diana, Mars, Mercury, Apollo, Jove and Saturn. There are tombs for the Malatesta family, empty sarcophagi intended for poets, artists and scholars of Sigismondo's court and a tomb containing the bones of a Byzantine scholar, Gemistus Pletho, who was known for his desire to replace Christianity with a revised form of Neo-Platonism. Sigismondo brought Pletho's bones back from Greece, where he had served as a condottiere for Venice against the Turks. Sigismondo regarded them as holy relics and buried them with reverent ceremony.

There are other surprising things in the church. A statue of the Archangel Michael, which Sigismondo had set up over the altar, has the face of Isotta. Her tomb is curious. It is supported by two Malatesta elephants, and an armorial shield bears their entwined initials. A crowned helmet is topped by two elephants' heads, trunks rampant. Hidden beneath an ornamental plaque is a secret expression of Sigismondo's devotion: "Isotta of Rimini—For Beauty and Virtue the Ornament of Italy." A fresco painted by Piero della Francesca shows Sigismondo kneeling in prayer before his patron saint.

Across the handsome façade of the never-completed building Sigismondo had the following inscription carved in Greek letters:

TO GOD IMMORTAL · SIGISMONDO PANDOLFO SON OF PANDOLFO · SAVED FROM MOST SERIOUS AND GRAVE DANGERS DURING THE WARS OF ITALY · VICTOR IN HIS UNDERTAKINGS SUCCESSFULLY CONCLUDED FOR GOD AND FOR HIS CITY · DEDICATED THIS TEMPLE—A MONUMENT AS FAMOUS AS SACRED.

It is no wonder that the church of San Francisco at Rimini is always called the Tempio Malatestiano. Surely no other church is so blatantly personal a momument to the vainglory of its builder.

The other famous building Sigismondo constructed in Rimini was a new castle, of which he himself was the principal architect. It had six towers eighty feet tall, walls fifty feet high, three central courts and a moat a hundred feet wide and thirty-five feet deep. This fortress-palace took nine years to build. Above its main gate are Sigismondo's name and the Malatesta arms.

Most of the artists, poets and scholars who thronged the court of Rimini were a second-rate lot. Only Della Francesca and Pisanello, whose sojourns were brief, are remembered today. Pisanello made two beautiful medallions for Sigismondo. On one is an excellent portrait in profile of Sigismondo. Its resemblance to Della Francesca's painting in the Tempio Malatestiano is remarkable.

Considering how much of his time Sigismondo spent fighting wars—his own and other people's—it is surprising that he was able to find the time to discuss philosophy, write poetry, build castles and temples and make love to women. His military career is a more confusing tangle than that of any other Italian condottiere. Even Francesco Sforza's seems simple in comparison. We shall not try to sort it out.

As a professional condottiere Sigismondo Malatesta fought for the papacy, the Kingdom of Naples, Venice, Florence and Siena. As the ruler of a considerable state he fought as an ally and friend of Francesco Sforza and for three causes which obsessed him throughout his life. The two kinds of campaigning alternated or took place almost simultaneously. A quick look at each kind must suffice.

As a condottiere, Sigismondo ranked with Federigo of Urbino, his favorite enemy. He was a crafty tactician, an effective leader of men, whose hardships he always shared, tireless and enormously brave in battle. But Sigismondo changed sides too often and earned a reputation for unreliability, if not for treachery. Part of the trouble was that the interests of the Malatesta state were not the same as those of his employers, and they often demanded instant action.

Fighting to help his father-in-law Francesco Sforza defend his dominion in the March of Ancona, Sigismondo chafed at the devastation of his own state, the expense and the lack of any tangible gain for him. So when Sforza sent him to Venice to collect money owed him Sigismondo kept it all. He had spent that much on Sforza's war, Sigismondo said. This was the second time Sigismondo kept money he should have handed over to its rightful owner. It did not endear him to his comrade-in-arms and father-in-law, but the official friendship of the two condottieri survived a while longer. It ended when Sforza bought Pesaro from Galeotto Malatesta and presented the city to his brother, Alessandro Sforza. This dismemberment of Malatesta territory was a betrayal Sigismondo could not forgive.

He had suffered much because of his alliance with Sforza. He had even been excommunicated by Pope Eugenius for fighting the Church in defense of Sforza's state. So Sigismondo in a rage switched sides, became a commander for papal troops and was forgiven by the Pope. In alliance with Alfonso of Naples and Filippo Maria of Milan he drove Sforza out of the March. Many years later Sforza denounced Sigismondo as the murderer of his daughter. Was he making his own delayed payment for the misappropriated money and the change of sides?

Sigismondo's third theft was singularly ill advised. He was always hard up, but it was not prudent to make an enemy of King Alfonso of Aragon. The King of Naples, then at war with Florence, engaged Sigismondo as a condottiere and sent him a fancy retainer of twenty-five thousand florins. To prevent Sigismondo from fighting against them the Florentines outbid Alfonso. In addition, they astutely sent as ambassador to Sigismondo their chancellor, Gianozzo Manetti, a learned and charming man. Manetti fascinated Sigismondo with his erudite conversation and delighted him with a present of newly translated ancient manuscripts.

It was diplomacy of a rarefied subtlety. Sigismondo resigned from Alfonso's service, kept the money and after a short delay signed a contract as a condottiere with Florence. By his energetic and brilliant tactics Sigismondo prevented Alfonso from capturing the city of Piombino. The powerful King of Naples never forgave the double offense.

In his private wars as lord of Rimini Sigismondo had three major goals. The first was to reincorporate Pesaro in the Malatesta state. He probably could have taken it from his feckless relative alone, but Alessandro Sforza in alliance with Federigo of

Urbino was another matter. In his frustration Sigismondo threatened to murder Alessandro.

Sigismondo's second personal commitment was to his feud with Federigo. The two men were both professional soldiers, both cultivated patrons of the arts, both rulers of small neighboring states. Urbino and Rimini were only about twenty miles apart. But Federigo and Sigismondo were hereditary as well as personal enemies. Roughly equal in ability and power, they differed so much in personality that they hated each other. Federigo was tactful and prudent; Sigismondo was arrogant and reckless. Federigo made no other enemies. Sigismondo made many.

It was Federigo's part in obtaining Pesaro for Alessandro Sforza and Fossombrone for himself which drove Sigismondo to challenge him to a duel. His formal letter has survived:

Magnificent Lord:

Your Lordship knows the differences which for a long time have existed between us, and if you judge rightly you will see that the fault is yours and not mine. Patience is not one of my virtues, and it seems that you are not disposed to make amends. On the contrary, every day you increase your offenses. Recently you have written calumnies about me to the court at Rome and have spoken evil of me. I am determined not to put up with this and to show you that I am a better man than you are. You are, in addition, a traitor and have outrageously treated me. I therefore send to you Giovanni da Sassoferrato, my chancellor, with full powers to challenge you to a duel. By your former letter you have already accepted; but, although Giovanni has authority to make the challenge public, I wished to write this private letter as more secure, requesting you not to change. If you are the brave man you claim to be, I demand that you send me one of your confidants, a man completely informed of your intentions, so that the conditions, time and place for the combat may be agreed upon. The man you send to me I wish to come in security with four horses and this letter will serve as a safe-conduct for his coming, his stay and his return in complete liberty. In case you should not accept my challenge, which I do not believe you will,

I warn you that I shall proceed against you according to custom
in these affairs and according to my own pleasure.

Sigismundus Pandulphus de Malatestis

Rimini, xxi February 1445

Nothing came of this challenge. Each prince accused the other
of backing out. Several years later it was Federigo's turn to challenge Sigismondo. Nothing came of that either. They continued
to raid each other's lands, to attack each other's castles and to
sack each other's towns. Their private war was small. It was also
wasteful, cruel and totally unnecessary.

In 1457 Borso d'Este, a peaceable man for the most part, arranged a truce between the warring princes and invited them to
come to Ferrara to attend a meeting of peace and reconciliation.
Borso was an old friend of Sigismondo's. They were brothers-in-
law and seem to have been fond of each other. Borso would
send Sigismondo presents of eels from his private reservoir, and
in return Sigismondo would send Borso ripe figs.

Sigismondo arrived in Ferrara first. In the Este palace he stayed
in his room, nursing an injured leg. Federigo arrived later and
was escorted by Borso to meet Sigismondo the following morning. Sigismondo, limping and leaning heavily on a cane, shook
hands with his enemy. But the two men spoke not a word, did
not bow and remained coldly expressionless.

Borso pretended not to notice the Arctic climate, put himself
between them and led them up and down for several turns in the
loggia before taking his difficult guests in to dinner. The next
day, in an effort to break the ice Borso took them to his villa of
Belfiore for the actual peacemaking. In vain. Complaints, recrim-
inations, denunciations and unprintable insults broke up the peace
conference. Federigo and Sigismondo reached for their swords
and would have fought in Borso's presence if they had not been
restrained. Borso did his best, but the war continued.

The third goal for which Sigismondo fought was to preserve
the independence of his state against the claims of the Church.
Nominally a vassal of the Church whose "vicarate" had to be
renewed by each pope, Sigismondo considered himself a totally
independent ruler and with persistent intransigence tried to act
like one. Some popes, particularly Nicholas V, did not seem to

object. But even Paul II, who had gone out of his way to honor Sigismondo at a time when the Lord of Rimini was at the nadir of his fortunes, tried to get him to give up Rimini and accept Spoleto instead.

Surrender the town of his ancestors? The town where he had erected buildings intended to make his name immortal? Sigismondo was so enraged that he considered assassinating the Pope.

But it was Pius II who defeated Sigismondo and stripped him of most of his territory. Pius could not have done it alone. Sigismondo's reckless policies had made enemies anxious to help the Pope defeat him. King Alfonso of Aragon was one. So was his son King Ferrante. Sigismondo had compounded his offense against the Kingdom of Naples by fighting for the Angevin cause. Federigo, of course, was always happy to merge his private war with Sigismondo with Pope Pius's larger war against him.

In spite of spectacular victories and stubborn resistance Sigismondo Malatesta was overpowered by the coalition against him. His lands were devastated and his towns captured. Finally he admitted defeat and was stripped of all his possessions save Rimini itself and the land around it extending to a perimeter five miles from the city walls.

Pope Pius imposed humiliating peace terms. They required Sigismondo to promise to repeat the credo once a day for the rest of his life, to fast every Friday, to visit the seven pilgrimage churches of Rome and to make a pilgrimage to the Holy Sepulcher in Jerusalem.

Defeated, impoverished and humiliated, Sigismondo Malatesta was still a mighty warrior and still lord of Rimini. The Venetians offered him a command in Greece fighting the Turks. Sigismondo accepted, fought ably but was not supported by supplies, reinforcements and fresh horses. The campaign was a failure. The mortality was frightful. Sigismondo came home to Rimini with only one consolation, those precious bones of Gemisthus Pletho.

It was then that Pope Paul II first honored him and soon afterward enraged him by demanding that he give up Rimini. Sigismondo spent the last two years of his life in a state of political impotence and spiritual frustration. He died on October 9, 1468.

XVIII

ROBERTO THE MAGNIFICENT

 ACCORDING TO THE TREATY imposed by Pope Pius, if Sigismondo died without a legitimate heir, Rimini would revert to the Church's direct rule. Although Sigismondo was the father of at least a dozen bastard children, he had no living legitimate child. So Rimini "rightly" belonged to the church. But Isotta, the grieving widow, assumed power in her own name and in that of the elder of her two bastard sons, Sallustio. She had another son by Sigismondo named Valerio.

Pius's successor, Pope Paul II, was justly incensed. Such conduct was no better than theft from the Church. In Rome at the time was another of Sigismondo's bastard sons, Roberto, then aged twenty-six and already famous as a talented soldier. In recent wars Roberto had fought bravely and capably at his father's side. Roberto promised Pope Paul in writing that if supported with adequate funds he would capture Rimini for the Church.

Roberto had no trouble in doing so. There was sentiment in Rimini for another warrior Malatesta. But no sooner had he seized the city than Roberto informed Pope Paul that he no longer intended to turn Rimini over to the Church. After all, it had been ruled by a Malatesta for many generations. So Paul did the only possible thing. He declared war on Roberto. Once again the little exhausted city was at war with a pope.

Venice joined the Pope. But Milan, Florence, Naples and Federigo of Urbino (of all people!) sided with Roberto because they all objected to an increase in papal power in the Romagna. Federigo had no objections to Malatestas in general—only to Sigismondo. Roberto was his friend. The papal army was decisively defeated; so Roberto continued to be lord of Rimini and also recaptured the Malatesta town of Fano.

In many ways Roberto resembled Sigismondo. He was a greatly admired condottiere and earned the name Roberto the Magnificent. He was treacherous, lecherous and cruel. In the summer of 1470 three convenient deaths made Roberto's position as lord of Rimini more secure. The bodies of his two-half brothers, Sallustio and Valerio, were found in the streets. And in the great fortress-palace built by Sigismondo, Isotta degli Atti pined away and died of a wasting disease which looked remarkably like a poisoning. Roberto was widely given credit for three murders.

The next year Roberto became engaged to Elisabetta da Montefeltro, one of Federigo's daughters, and four years later the wedding took place. Federigo, who was so much more virtuous than most of his contemporary princes, did not object to having a son-in-law who was a brutal and treacherous soldier suspected of murdering his step-mother and half-brothers.

In 1478, fighting for Florence in the Pazzi war, Roberto Malatesta won an important victory over the troops of Pope Sixtus IV. Four years later, in 1482, fighting for Sixtus in the War of Ferrara he won a much more important victory over the Neapolitan army commanded by Alfonso, Duke of Calabria. Only a month after this triumph the magnificent Roberto died in Rome, probably of malaria or dysentery. Sixtus gave him a splendid funeral and erected a monument to him in St. Peter's.

Roberto's son, Pandolfo, only seven when his father died, was as wicked as his ancestors, but not nearly as brave and able. Feeble, petulent, lecherous and vindictive, Pandolfo was the last Malatesta to rule in Rimini and a disgrace to the family name. He is believed to have fought at Fornovo. In the year of that battle Pandolfo and some playful friends murdered an envoy of the King of Hungary and robbed the body. A contemporary chronicler wrote that Pandolfo wanted to exercise "such a tyranny that he could have any woman he pleased and for any purpose." According to Caterina Sforza, who was certainly not overscrupulous about tyrannical government, Pandolfo offended his subjects in "their property, their persons and their honor."

Pandolfo Malatesta was driven out of Rimini by Cesare Borgia. He returned, but felt so insecure he sold out to Venice for a small pension. Two more times Pandolfo and a son of his named Sigismondo managed to return to power in Rimini, but each time after a display of incompetence and cruelty, they were driven out. They died in obscurity. And so ended the story of the Malatesta in Rimini, fizzling out in petty malice after more than two centuries of power and splendor as well as of cruelty and corruption.

✦✦✦✦✦✦✦✦ XIX ✦✦✦✦✦✦✦✦

THE HIGH AND MIGHTY BAGLIONI

DURING THE RENAISSANCE when the young warriors of the House of Baglioni rode or walked through the streets and piazzas of Perugia the people would stop whatever they were doing and stare at them with awe and admiration, fear and hatred. Tall, blond, beautiful in their brutal fashion, they moved with the controlled grace of panthers and looked at all around them with the fierce arrogance of falcons. The Baglioni, brave as the Knights of the Round Table, were able condottieri for six generations and the aristocratic de facto rulers of the most important town in Umbria and of many lesser towns and villages. But they never achieved official recognition from the Perugians as their lords. They never acquired any hereditary title. And they never learned to govern others or themselves. Cruel, treacherous, vindictive, the Baglioni were as famous for their family feuds and intramural murders as they were for their eminence in arms. Their extraordinary story combines heroic courage with moral blindness. Probably no family contributed more to the political anarchy of Renaissance Italy than "the High and Mighty Baglioni."

High in the hills of Umbria, commanding a superb view of the valley of the Tiber below, Perugia was an important city in Etruscan times. In the Middle Ages it was a free commune which dominated a large area around it, including the cities of Orvieto, Spoleto, Todi, Assisi, Gubbio and Cagli. Throughout the thirteenth and fourteenth centuries Perugia was almost constantly at war with neighboring states; and for much of the time it was convulsed by civil strife between social classes and rival families. The grim medieval city with its mighty walls and its hundreds of towers was ruled by a faction of prosperous city merchants who had driven out the aristocratic noble families. But late in the fourteenth century Pandolfo Baglioni, identified by one chronicler as "the Perugian Satan," drove out the communal government and established himself as tyrant of Perugia. Little is known about Pandolfo except that in 1393 the city rose against him. Pandolfo was murdered in the principal piazza, and in the general massacre which followed, some sixty other members of the Baglioni family were said to have been killed.

So fierce was the Perugians' hatred for Pandolfo that they tore down his palace and the houses of the other Baglioni and used the bricks to pave streets. The surviving Baglioni and other noble exiles from Perugia retired to their country castles and continued the war for the next twenty-three years, raiding up to Perugia's walls, harrying the countryside until packs of wolves overran the peasants' farmsteads and even stalked through the streets of Perugia.

In 1416 Braccio Fortebracci da Montone, a Perugian nobleman who nearly succeeded in making himself lord of all central Italy, conquered Perugia and established himself as its sole ruler. With him came Pandolfo's son, Malatesta Baglioni. After Braccio's death Malatesta shrewdly made an agreement with Pope Martin V recognizing the Pope's nominal suzerainty over Perugia in return for his support of the noble families as rulers of the city.

Malatesta and his relations were only the most important and powerful of the half-dozen noble families which dominated Perugia. Nearly as strong and just as ruthless and violent were the Degli Oddi. For some two hundred years the Baglioni and the Oddi feuded with each other. Any fancied slight or insult, any dispute or rivalry was sufficient cause for a murder, an ambush or a pitched battle. Compared with these ferocious Perugian nobles the Montagues and Capulets of Verona were affectionate friends.

In Perugia the general Renaissance cult of revenge was carried to such an excess that it became an infectious madness and a curse.

Malatesta Baglioni died in 1437 leaving four redoubtable sons, of whom the eldest, Braccio, was considered the real founder of the family greatness. In 1456 and again in 1482 the Baglioni and the Oddi fought bloody battles in the streets of Perugia. In 1488 the Baglioni finally triumphed and drove the Oddi from the city. From then on, the Oddi lived as exiles, always scheming to return and to avenge themselves upon their enemies. And from then on, the Baglioni ruled the city.

They preserved Perugia's republican forms in imitation of the Medici in Florence. But they lacked the Medici tact, popularity and political skill. The Baglioni packed the city council of ten with their own members and with their loyal supporters. But often they would forget republican pretenses and rule like the lords they really were. After Braccio's death, his brothers Guido and Rodolfo ruled jointly.

They ruled with great magnificence, sent and received diplomatic embassies, munificently entertained princes and prelates, and sent their bellicose sons off to serve as condottieri all over Italy. They lived in a cluster of palaces built upon the Colle Landone, where the Hotel Brufani e Palace now stands. And they were aided by the moral encouragement and financial subsidies of Lorenzo de' Medici. The magnificent Lorenzo preferred Perugia to be a virtually independent and friendly state rather than to have it fall under the direct control of the papacy and so increase the power of potentially unfriendly popes.

The Baglioni brothers ruled; but they did not rule well. The tradition of irresponsible violence and vendetta in their family was too strong. Secure in the patronage of the Baglioni, their friends and supporters and followers could defy the laws and kill their enemies with impunity. Francesco Matarazzo, a poet, humanist scholar and chancellor of Perugia, who was a Perugian patriot and a loyal admirer of the men he called "the High and Mighty Baglioni," wrote:

"Very true it is that there were many famous men and worshipful in every walk of life in out city; but not to depart from exact truth since the day when the Oddi with their followers were banished from our city, matters went from bad to worse. Martial exercises were neglected; and all the young men turned them to the trade of soldiery, yet submitted not to drill or discipline, and were men of evil life. Every day there was seen lawlessness of every sort, and the city was brought to such a pass that there was in it neither right rule nor justice, but every man rendered judgment in his own cause on his own authority, and by his own strong hand. And the Pope sent many legates if so be that he could bring back the city to obey his rule; but all as many as came departed again fearing to be cut to pieces; for many they threatened to throw out of the windows of the Palace of the Priori."

During the last decade of the fifteenth century there were few dull or peaceful moments in Perugia. Twice, once in 1491 and again in 1495, the exiled Oddi and their numerous supporters tried to regain power in the city by major attacks. Twice they were defeated. The Baglioni slew a nephew of Pope Innocent VIII. They threw a legate of Pope Alexander VI out of the window. And when Alexander himself came to Perugia, fleeing from Charles VIII of France, old Guido Baglioni replied to his covert threats by mustering the formidable forces of Perugia and parading them before the Pope.

A surprising episode unknown to most histories of aviation occurred when Rodolfo Baglioni's daughter, Pentesilea, was married to a famous condottiere, Bartolomeo d'Alviano. As a special entertainment for the wedding guests a mathematician called Giovanni Battista Danti demonstrated a flying machine he had constructed. The inventor himself sat in the middle of a clumsy contraption shaped like a bird and launched himself from the tower of the Church of Santa Maria Vergine. Like a glider, the machine hovered for a moment and then began to sink. One of its wings caught on some stonework and its wooden rods broke. The crowd shouted in excitement. But the flying machine fell only onto the roof of the church, and its pilot escaped with a broken leg.

Our knowledge of Perugia and the Baglioni in this period comes chiefly from the pages of Francesco Matarazzo's *Chronicles of the City of Perugia 1492–1503*. This remarkable book was admirably translated some sixty-five years ago by Edward Strachan Morgan. It is a personal, close-up, emotional history written by a witness of many of the events recorded. Matarazzo deplored the crimes of the Baglioni and the violent anarchy of their rule. But he was enormously attracted by the beauty and courage of the Baglioni, and by the almost epochal glamour of their deeds.

His divided opinion shows throughout his chronicle. "Though the city suffered terrible things at the hands of these nobles—strange and unheard-of oppression—yet because of the High and Mighty House of the Baglioni she was held in honor throughout the whole of Italy in respect of the great dignity and splendor of that house, the pomp it maintained and its great name."

The attack of the Oddi in the summer of 1495 came after several months of skirmishing and raiding during which the Oddi were reinforced by numerous other exiles and by men from Assisi and Foligno. The Baglioni were forced to withdraw behind the walls of Perugia. And one night two of the gates were opened to the enemy by traitors. The surprise was complete. The Oddi would have triumphed had it not been for the heroic courage and extraordinary skill at arms of two of the Baglioni: Simonetto, youngest son of Rodolfo, and Astorre, oldest son of Guido. Matarazzo's narrative continues:

"Now the man of whom I told you, the servant from the house of the Baglioni who ran to see the truth of that which the watch at the gate had told, came and found the enemy at San Luca, and he escaped away and ran and came to the house of his masters and found His Highness Simonetto Baglioni, son of Rodolfo, and spake and said to him, 'Go not forth, my Lord, for the enemy are all in the town and have nearly reached the Piazza.' To this he answered and said, 'Rather will I die in this fierce strife than let my enemy drive me out of my house to beg my bread.' And when he had said this, alone as he was, having with him no companion, with his shirt on his back and stockings on his feet, with a buckler on his arm and a sword in his hand, he went forth against the enemy; and under the archway of the Court House of their Highnesses the Priori he met the enemy who was just then coming into the Piazza. Forthwith he set upon the foe and did battle with him bareheaded as I have told you and in his shirt; and no man born of woman was ever seen of so high a temper and so brave, and full sure am I that never again in Perugia will be seen a man of such dreadful daring.

"He was at the present eighteen or nineteen years old, he had not as yet shaved his beard, yet so strong he was and so courageous, so fitted for the deeds of arms that he was the world's wonder; and he tilted so gracefully and bravely as to pass the belief of every man on earth. From morning till night he could have aimed at the bottom of a goblet with his spearpoint and never missed. Peerless was he in all ways, though indeed every man of that house was more worshipful than the other, and they had no equals for deeds of arms."

Simonetto fought alone without armor in the narrow archway like Horatius at the bridge. Matarazzo says that he was surrounded by three or four hundred men—which sounds absurd. At any rate, Simonetto held up the enemy long enough for his older cousin Astorre to hear the alarm, put on his armor, mount his horse and charge to the rescue. When he arrived, Simonetto was prostrate on the pavement with twenty-two wounds.

Astorre in his turn fought alone. While he did so Simonetto recovered consciousness and staggered away. Astorre's singlehanded battle inspired Matarazzo to equal raptures of enthusiasm. Before Astorre could be knocked off his horse, help arrived and soon the streets were full of the warrior Baglioni and their followers. The victory of the defenders was complete. The exiles fled, leaving behind them hundreds of dead and some two hundred prisoners, who were promptly hanged as traitors. "And the dogs lapped the blood of many Christians, and a tame bear also ate of the flesh of the dead, a thing grievous to tell of."

Now it happened that on that exciting night of September 5, 1495 a young painter from Urbino was staying in Perugia, a twelve-year-old apprentice in the studio of the great Perugino. His name was Raphael and the clangor of arms, the shouts of the soldiers and the general unholy din must certainly have awakened him. We can be sure that from some safe vantage point he looked out to see what was going on.

A few years later Raphael painted a picture of St. George

L

slaying the dragon and in his stanze mural in the Vatican a picture of an angelic mounted warrior driving Heliodorus out of the
temple. St. George and the avenging angel look remarkably alike.
Both wear on their helmets the Baglioni crest of a falcon. It was
the belief of John Addington Symonds that these two pictures
preserve forever Raphael's memories of Astorre Baglioni when he
charged forth to rescue his wounded cousin and to save Perugia
from the hereditary enemies of his family.

THE
GREAT BETRAYAL

For five years after the Oddi attack of 1495 the Baglioni prospered. Guido, "subtle and wise beyond all men of his time," was the recognized leader of the family. Rodolfo suffered miserably from the French disease and took a less active part in the family affairs. The young men went off to fight in the small wars which diverted the Italians in the interval between the departure of Charles VIII in 1495 and the arrival of Louis XII in 1499. Astorre and Gianpaolo, Rodolfo's second son, defeated the men of Assisi and served the Florentine republic in its wars against rebellious Pisa and against Siena. Astorre won a victory over the Sienese and his reputation as a condottiere rose. Gianpaolo defeated the Pisans in a small engagement and his reputation rose; in fact, the Florentines were so pleased with Gianpaolo that they sent him a present of two live lions.

In 1500 seventy-five-year-old Guido had five living sons: Astorre; Gentile, former bishop of Orvieto, who had left the Church to marry and lead the life of a country nobleman outside of Perugia; Morgante, a fine soldier, who lived in the Baglioni town of Spello; Gismondo; and Marcantonio, a semi-invalid, who spent most of his time at the court of Naples.

Rodolfo, seventy years old, had three sons: Troilo, a priest; Gianpaolo, who lived to become one of the foremost condottieri of his time; and Simonetto, "that noble youth."

There were three more members of the younger generation. Youngest of these was Grifonetto, grandson of Braccio, already the father of three infant sons. Grifonetto had inherited his father's and grandfather's property and was much the richest of all the Baglioni. His house was the finest. In its court he kept an enormous lion. Grifonetto, says Matarazzo, "for beauty was a second Ganymede." But he was vain and vicious, stupid and ambitious. He envied the fame and power of his relatives and considered himself their superior, the rightful head of the house because of his descent from the great Braccio. He kept bad company.

Two of his worst associates were also members of the family—poor relations and bitter young wastrels denied positions of responsibility by Guido. Filippo was the bastard son of Braccio and so Grifonetto's uncle. Carlo was the grandson of a long dead brother of Guido and Rodolfo. Carlo was brave and a good soldier like all the Baglioni, but born to be a villain.

Chief accomplice in folly and conspiracy of these three young Baglioni criminals was a dissolute and deadly young aristocrat named Girolamo della Penna. Della Penna nursed a private hatred for Gismondo Baglioni, who returned it, and was notoriously treacherous and dangerous. Simonetto shrewdly saw through Della Penna, and realizing the menace he might be, asked his uncle Guido for permission to kill him. Guido refused. Then Simonetto asked his "wise and prudent" elder brother Gianpaolo for permission. Gianpaolo refused. According to the customary Baglioni practice Della Penna certainly ought to have been killed; but his death would not have made much difference because Filippo was already successfully playing the part of Iago.

Filippo persuaded the jealous, resentful Grifonetto that his wife was sleeping with his cousin Gianpaolo. The charge was mere slander. But it was believed, and that was enough to change the course of history in Perugia. Soon Grifonetto was deeply involved in a conspiracy to murder Guido, Rodolfo and all their sons, and then to rule Perugia jointly with Carlo. Filippo would be high in their councils, and Della Penna would rule one of the five wards into which the city was divided.

But it was necessary to find a suitable time when as many of the Baglioni as possible would be assembled together. So the four traitors planned their mass murder for the festivities which would be held in celebration of the marriage of Astorre to Lavinia Colonna Orsini.

Astorre and his bride returned to Perugia on June 28, 1495 and settled down as temporary guests of Grifonetto in his grand house because Astorre's rooms in his father's house were being refurbished. For more than a week, banquets, pageants and tournaments filled Perugia with merrymaking with each ward striving to outdo the others in hospitality to the bridal couple. Why the conspirators failed to strike is inexplicable. But they waited, and while they waited Gianpaolo left Perugia with a mounted force to suppress an outbreak of arson and cattle rustling by the men of Todi. So the murderers had to wait longer for Gianpaolo to return and be killed.

Their preparations were thorough. Numerous other noblemen who resented the Baglioni domination joined them. Squads of soldiers were assigned to attack each individual marked for death. Equipped with battering rams to break down doors, they were to rush into action at a signal: the dropping of a great stone from the balcony of Guido's house into the courtyard. The sound of the crash would start the killing. "The great betrayal," as it came to be called all over Italy, finally took place during the night of July 14.

"The evening came [wrote Matarazzo]; and that same night the great calamity was to fall on us, the great betrayal was to be wrought. And the traitors dined together as young men are wont to do, and then went to San Luca, where on that evening of the year pardons and indulgences are given. And they kissed one another, speaking no word of the great betrayal, and they remained together till bedtime. Then, when they thought that their victims were fallen asleep, they brought together, each one of them, a number of men whom they could trust. Then all assembled in the house of Carlo Baglioni, and all were sore afraid, and their spirit failed them, and they all stood as dead men, fearing to set hand to so great an enterprise. But Carlo Baglione at this decisive moment showed more spirit than them all, and gave courage to all of them."

The stone was heaved over the balcony, and the bloody work

began. Filippo Baglioni broke into Astorre's room in Grifonetto's palace and in the presence of Astorre's terrifed bride killed the unarmed soldier. As he fell, Astorre cried out, "Oh miserable Astorre, dying like a coward!"

"And when he was dead the traitor Filippo thrust his hand into the breast of the noble lord through a wound he had in his breast, and, as men say, dragged out the heart of him and bit it with his teeth."

While Filippo was murdering Astorre, Della Penna broke into the room where Gismondo, his personal enemy, was sleeping and cut his throat. Old Guido died bravely, hacked down by a dozen men, crying out in accordance with his fatalistic convictions, "My time has come to me."

Simonetto heard the crash of the stone and then the noise when Carlo Baglioni burst in the door of Rodolfo's palace. For the second time in his young life he jumped from his bed, picked up a shield and sword and without armor rushed out to do battle with his enemies. His squire was slain at the doorway of his room, but Simonetto managed to fight his way out, down the staircase, through the courtyard and into the street before he died beneath the blows of a score of men.

In another room of Rodolfo's palace Gianpaolo awoke and seized a shield and sword to defend himself. With him was a squire whose only weapon was a great spit. Grifonetto and his men attacked them, soon joined by Carlo and his. For a short interval Gianpaolo and his squire held the top of the stairs, and then while the gallant squire still wielded his spit Gianpaolo climbed through a window onto the roof of the house. Thence he fled across the roofs of several houses, finally finding refuge among some law students at the university. These gave him an academic robe in which he escaped from the city.

Gentile Baglioni heard the tumult, mounted a horse and rode out to see what was the cause. He found out when he was attacked; but he was able to wheel his horse about and gallop out of the city. Sick, old Rodolfo, who was often carried about in a chair, escaped through his garden disguised in a woman's dress. He went to a church, where he waited until loyal servants brought him a horse on which he, too, escaped. Since Morgante

Baglioni was in Spello and Marcantonio in Naples, only four of the adult male Baglioni were killed. The murderers were not nearly as efficient and thorough as they had hoped to be.

Grifonetto's mother, Atalanta, a Baglioni by birth as well as by marriage and a widow for more than twenty years, fled from her son's house, where she had been living, and went to live in her own house inherited from her father. Grifonetto's wife went with her mother-in-law. And to save Gianpaolo's two sons, Malatesta aged nine and Orazio aged six, from being murdered, too, Atalanta took them with her to her house. With furious contempt Atalanta denounced her son for his cowardice and treachery and she swore that never again would she cross the threshhold of his house.

Appalled by what he had done, lacking entirely the Renaissance acceptance of murder as an ordinary and useful political means, Grifonetto broke down. "Not once, nor twice, but again and again he returned to speak to his sweet mother, and she, for the wrath and scorn that were in her, would not listen to her son; nay, rather cursed him and the place where she bare him and the hour of his birth."

Grifonetto repented volubly. "He bewailed his great mistake, but as he had called for the music so must he finish the dance."

All day long on the following day Gianpaolo recruited an army among the towns and villages still loyal to the Baglioni, and on the afternoon of the sixteenth he marched up to the gates of Perugia with eight hundred horsemen and a large number of infantry. It was a remarkable feat of military organization.

With Gianpaolo came his cousin Gentile and his friend Vitelozzo Vitelli, Lord of Città di Castello—both at the head of their troops. "And so it was that to the sound of the trumpet about two hours before sundown the army, all dazzling to see, squadron by squadron in battle array marched toward the disordered city of Perugia." Within the walls Carlo Baglioni ruled as the newly installed lord. But the "legitimate" Baglioni had sympathizers in the city. Some of them opened two of the gates, and Gianpaolo led his army in, riding "on his black horse, in his hand a sword, like to Saint George."

The battle was not long contested. Gianpaolo's men slaughtered some two hundred of Carlo's supporters and then sacked one of the wards known to oppose the Baglioni. All the accomplices and collaborators of the traitors that Gianpaolo's soldiers could catch were massacred in the piazza, and some who fled into the cathedral for sanctuary were killed there.

Carlo Baglioni and Girolamo della Penna were not among those killed. They had jumped down from the city walls and disappeared. Grifonetto deliberately sacrificed himself. He walked up to Gianpaolo, who held the point of his sword against his cousin's throat. "Farewell, Grifonetto, you traitor," he said. "God be with you, for I will not slay you. I am not the man to soil my hands with the blood of my own house, as you have done in the blood of yours." Gianpaolo turned away, and others slashed at Grifonetto until he fell upon the pavement.

Atalanta and Grifonetto's wife came through the turmoil and slaughter and reached the handsome youth before he died. They knelt beside him, wept and forgave him. Atalanta, some time later, took an unusual step to preserve the memory of the family tragedy and her own grief. She commissioned Raphael to paint a picture of the entombment of Christ.

To cleanse the desecrated cathedral Gianpaolo had its floor and walls washed down with wine.

Grifonetto's death raised to five the number of Baglioni dead. Carlo and Filippo Baglioni and Girolamo della Penna and their supporters were now fugitives and bitter enemies of the men they had failed to murder, and were always called the "new exiles" to distinguish them from the Oddi and their supporters, henceforth called the "old exiles."

In solemn recognition of the great betrayal Gianpaolo, Morgante and Gentile went into theatrically dramatic and ostentatious mourning: "Their Highnesses and all their household and all their soldiers were dressed in black. The trappings of their horses, the lances of their horsemen and footmen were likewise hung with black, every pennon and banneret black, black even the cords of their trumpets. Everything showed the same dark color. In the city was no one any more who played or sang, there was little laughter, no gay colored cap was seen, but every man was dressed in black, and all of the Great House went about like men of royal blood, with swordsmen before them night and day, who kept guard over their high and mighty persons."

From the day of his return in bloody triumph Gianpaolo Baglioni was indisputably the head of his violent family and the first citizen of Perugia. He was twenty-nine years old and only at the beginning of a spectacular career.

✦✦✦✦✦✦✦✦✦ XXI ✦✦✦✦✦✦✦✦✦

DRIVEN
BY DESTINY

IN HIS FAMOUS HISTORY of the wars of Italy Francesco Guicciardini wrote that Gianpaolo Baglioni was "more driven by destiny than by reason." The remark could apply almost equally well to all of the other princes of the Renaissance who were involved, whether they wished to be or not, in all the terrible wars which ravaged Italy from Lake Como to the Bay of Naples. Yet, in some respects Guicciardini seems mistaken. No professional soldier and minor lord tried harder than Gianpaolo Baglioni to conduct his affairs by the cold light of reason.

An enigmatic character who inspired contradictory opinions among his contemporaries, he left no revealing letters; he never played a starring role upon the national stage and received little attention from diplomats and chroniclers as compared with the interest shown in marquises, dukes and popes. Gianpaolo Baglioni is remembered by historians chiefly because Machiavelli in his *Discourses* denounced him for not rising to new heights of villainy.

Machiavelli knew Gianpaolo personally and, as a good Florentine patriot, disliked and distrusted him as an enemy of Florence. Guicciardini, another Florentine, referred to Gianpaolo's "infamous disloyalty." One widely circulated story told how Gianpaolo publicly boasted that his illegitimate son, Constantino, was twice a Baglioni since his mother was Gianpaolo's sister. There is small doubt that Gianpaolo's reputation was bad. How much it was deserved it is impossible to know.

But Matarazzo, who presumably knew Gianpaolo much better than Machiavelli did, wrote of him, "his nature ever led him to be tender-hearted." And according to the chronicler Girolamo di Frolliere: "This Gianpaolo was ever a gallant and valiant knight of marvelous, almost heaven-inspired sagacity. . . . He was handsome and of a gracious aspect, pleasant and benign; eloquent in his conversation, and of great prudence; and every gesture harmonized with his words and manner. In his desire to please all, even strangers, if perchance he was unable or unwilling to serve them, he showed himself so gracious and so willing, that they left him satisfied and pleased. He was much given to the love of women and he was greatly loved by them by reason of his delicate and lordly bearing."

Tender-hearted? Benign? Probably he was when nothing was to be lost by kindness. At other times Gianpaolo hanged prisoners in mass lots for the psychological effect the hangings would have on others. It was all a matter of expediency. And so with perhaps equally good cause Gianpaolo's enemies denounced his cruelty and treachery and his friends praised his mercy.

What is certain about him is that he was not a monster like his psychopathic friend, the condottiere Vitelozzo Vitelli, who encouraged his soldiers to commit abominable atrocities on helpless peasants. And it seems equally certain from the record of his life that Gianpaolo was able, intelligent, cautious, suspicious and cynical. He was a good and brave soldier, but not a distinguished one. He always tried to measure the odds and to avoid fighting foes with larger battalions.

Gianpaolo Baglioni was a professional soldier not only because it was the tradition of his family but also because he enjoyed the trade of fighting. He had only two goals in life: to practice his profession and to maintain his domination over Perugia. After the great betrayal and his expulsion of Carlo Baglioni and the other traitors, Gianpaolo no longer made much pretense of maintaining the republican forms of government. He ruled as lord of the city in partnership with his able cousin Morgante. While Gianpaolo was absent earning his pay as a condottiere, Morgante reorganized the administration of affairs in Perugia, eliminated as much of the city's traditional violence and injustice as he could and personally protected the weak from the strong. "His Highness Morgante was full of justice and equity," wrote Matarazzo.

Unfortunately, Morgante died in 1502, probably of malaria. Old Rodolfo had died in 1501. Gentile lived much of the time in Spello and always played a subordinate part to that of his more forceful cousin. Gianpaolo was left in sole command.

Giapaolo served as a condottiere for Siena and for Cesare Borgia. He defeated several of Carlo's efforts to establish himself near Perugia, and he and Morgante together defeated a considerable force assembled by the "old exiles."

When Cesare Borgia made his treacherous attack on Urbino, Gianpaolo was not present because he had been assigned to help capture Camerino from Giulio Cesare Varano, an old enemy of the Baglioni. The fall of Urbino and the consequent great increase of Borgia power alarmed Gianpaolo so much that he was one of the chief organizers of the confederacy against Cesare, insisting that the members must stand together "in order not to be devoured by the dragon."

We have seen how Cesare's artful diplomacy broke up the alliance against him and lured four of the too trusting leaders to the trap he had set for them at Sinigaglia. Gianpaolo was far too astute and suspicious to accompany them. He protested violently and warned his allies not to believe the blandishments of the treacherous Cesare. Gianpaolo's accurate knowledge of Cesare's character saved his life, but it could not save his state.

Cesare crossed the Apennines with a powerful force and marched on Perugia. As the last survivor of the anti-Borgia alliance Gianpaolo lacked the resources to oppose the conqueror of much of central Italy. He fled. Cesare annexed Perugia to the Papal States and installed Carlo Baglioni to rule the city in his name. It was Gianpaolo's turn to be an exile. He remained one, serving as a captain in the Florentine army, until the death of Pope Alexander in the summer of 1503.

As soon as Gianpaolo heard of Alexander's death, he left Florence to march on Perugia. He had only a few men with him, but when he entered Perugian territory his fame as a soldier and perhaps his position as the "rightful" lord of Perugia attracted many men to his banners. Aided by his cousin Gentile, no mean soldier himself, Gianpaolo soon had an army large enough to attack the city.

Carlo Baglioni led the defense and fought bravely. But in a battle that lasted four hours Gianpaolo and Gentile triumphed. Carlo fled once more, and once again Gianpaolo was the acknowledged lord of Perugia. He remained so for only three years.

In 1506 Pope Julius II began his program of imposing papal rule on as much of Italy as possible. He announced that he would drive the Baglioni out of Perugia and the Bentivoglio family out of Bologna. With all the pomp and panoply of glorious war, and accompanied by most of the cardinals then in Rome, Julius proceeded to Orvieto and there Gianpaolo Baglioni came to meet him. Gianpaolo was accompanied by Guidobaldo of Urbino and by fifty men-at-arms.

Guidobaldo was not a friend of the Baglioni. He had welcomed the "new exiles" and allowed them to live within his state. But Guidobaldo was a friend of Pope Julius and a highly intelligent man. He undoubtedly tried to persuade Gianpaolo of the folly of resisting the warrior pope. Gianpaolo, always a realist, probably did not need to have anyone point out the odds against him. At any rate, Gianpaolo submitted to Pope Julius and on the following day returned to Perugia.

Machiavelli had been assigned by the Florentines to accompany the Pope as a diplomatic observer. He reported in a dispatch sent from Orvieto that Gianpaolo had agreed to the following terms:

He would surrender to the Pope all fortresses in the Perugian state.

He would surrender his sons to be hostages for his good behavior and to live at the court of the Duke of Urbino.

He would acknowledge the authority of the Pope and relinquish his claim to be lord of an independent state.

He would serve as a captain in Julius' army.

And the Pope would put his own garrison of five hundred men in Perugia.

It must have been a terrible humiliation to the proud, fierce Gianpaolo. Particularly galling was Julius' intention to allow both the "old exiles" and the "new exiles" to return to Perugia. Gianpaolo warned that if Carlo Baglioni and his followers did return to Perugia they would run the risk of being cut to pieces in the streets. Perhaps his warning was just wishful thinking.

Pope Julius approached Perugia in leisurely fashion and entered the city in state on September 13. Huge crowds filled the streets and squares to see the Pope and most of Julius' troops could not keep up with the Pope. There was considerable tension. Could the humiliated Gianpaolo be trusted?

Machiavelli wrote in a dispatch: "The Pope and the Sacred College are more at the discretion of Gianpaolo than he is at theirs. And if Gianpaolo does no harm to him who comes to deprive him of his state, it must be attributed to his good nature and humanity. Once Gianpaolo said that there had been two ways for him to save his state; the one by force and the other by humility; that he had not been willing to employ the first, but had adopted the second, and for that reason had put everything into the hands of the Duke of Urbino."

Many years later, in his forced retirement to the little village of Sant' Andrea, seven miles out of Florence, Niccolò Machiavelli tried to sum up the lessons of history as he knew them in his *Discourses*. By then Gianpaolo's submission to Pope Julius appeared to him in another light. He wrote:

"Sagacious men who were with the Pope observed his temerity and the cowardice of Baglioni, and could not understand why the latter had not by a single blow rid himself of his enemy, whereby he would have secured for himself eternal fame and rich booty, for the Pope was accompanied by all the cardinals with their valuables. Nor could they believe that he had refrained from doing this either from goodness or conscientious scruples; for no sentiment of piety or respect could enter the heart of a man of such vile character as Gianpaolo. . . . He dared not attempt an act (although having a justifiable opportunity) for which everyone would have admired his courage, and which would have secured him eternal fame, as being the first to show these prelates how little esteem those merit who live and govern as they do."

There is savage irony in the fact that such little fame as Gianpaolo Baglioni has today rests on the curious sentences just quoted. They were written by a bitter man, deeply resentful of the worldly behavior of Renaissance popes; by an intellectual and writer who delighted in provocative ideas. If Gianpaolo had murdered the Pope and all the cardinals, one can easily imagine Machiavelli writing an eloquent denunciation of such a monstrous crime. If Gianpaolo had committed such an enormity, he would, of course, have insured his own destruction. Every power in Italy would have fallen upon him in righteous wrath.

For the next seven years Perugia was ruled by legates appointed by Julius II, and Gianpaolo spent his time fighting as a condottiere for Julius and his allies. He was absent from Perugia, but he remained its principal and most influential citizen. And when the grim old pope died in 1513, Gianpaolo returned to resume his direct, personal lordship. He was welcomed by rejoicing crowds which seemed deliriously happy to have the foremost living Baglioni back to rule them once again. It was the third time Gianpaolo returned to Perugia after being forced to leave the city—once after the great betrayal, once after the Borgia conquest and once after the domination of Pope Julius II.

To describe Gianpaolo's long and complicated career as a condottiere is unnecessary. He was present when Julius drove the Bentivoglio out of Bologna, and several years later he was with the Pope at his celebrated winter siege of the city of Mirandola. In 1512 Gianpaolo, commanding a Venetian force against the French, was defeated in a fierce fight at the village of Isola della Scala by Bayard and Gaston de Foix, whose troops far outnumbered his; he had to swim across the Adige River to escape. He was also present with the papal troops at the great battle of Ravenna.

In 1516, when Pope Leo X began a war to drive Duke Francesco Maria della Rovere out of Urbino in order to give the duchy to his worthless nephew Lorenzo de' Medici the younger, Gianpaolo fought for the Pope and captured the city of Gubbio.

The following year Della Rovere marched against Perugia, and Gianpaolo received no help from Leo. Hard pressed by superior forces, he raised a sum of ten thousand ducats and paid it to Della Rovere to stop ravaging the Perugian countryside and go away.

Leo was furious. He regarded Gianpaolo as little better than a traitor and suspected him of secret agreements with Della Rovere. For the next three years Gianpaolo continued to rule in Perugia, but the omens were bad. He and his cousin Gentile quarreled, and Gianpaolo forbade Gentile to enter Perugia. Gentile began to cultivate Pope Leo. In 1520 came the alarming news that Pope Leo had organized troops in Siena, Florence, Camerino and other towns with the intention of driving Gianpaolo out of Perugia. Like his greater contemporary Alfonso d'Este, Duke of Ferrara, Gianpaolo could never long remain safe from the enmity of popes.

Gianpaolo's situation looked bleak. It became more ominous when Leo sent him an official summons to come to Rome and defend himself against various charges. Cautious as usual, Gianpaolo sent his son Malatesta, twenty-nine years old and a famous warrior, to sound out the pope. Malatesta returned and said that Leo seemed affable and well-intentioned. Other friends also urged Gianpaolo to go to Rome. After all, the Baglioni were old friends of the Medici and Gianpaolo himself had fought for two popes, Julius and Leo. But Gianpaolo forgot that on several occasions he had betrayed Florence. Leo had not forgotten. Finally Leo sent Gianpaolo a safe-conduct, and the harassed lord of Perugia went to Rome. He did not have the caution and foresight now which had kept him from going to Sinigaglia.

On March 16, 1520, Gianpaolo arrived in Rome. The next day he went to see Pope Leo, who was waiting for him in the Castel Sant' Angelo—just as Julius II had treacherously waited for Alfonso d'Este who, having been warned, did not come. As soon as Gianpaolo entered the castle, he was arrested and thrown into a prison cell.

For three months he was kept there with no formal charges against him. It is known that he was interrogated and tortured. It is known that Gentile had much to do with Gianpaolo's arrest—still another example of betrayal within the Baglioni family. On

June 11 Gianpaolo Baglioni, who had survived the dangerous reigns of Popes Alexander and Julius, who had survived family treasons and countless battles, was beheaded by the orders of fat, bland, epicene Leo X. Gianpaolo had executed many persons himself. He had lived by the sword and he perished by it.

Pope Leo defended himself, saying that the safe-conduct he had given Gianpaolo was to *come* to Rome and said nothing about *leaving* Rome.

XXII

THE SONS
OF GIANPAOLO

WHEN GIANPAOLO'S SONS, Malatesta and Orazio, learned of their father's execution, they fled from Perugia. Both young men were already tough and experienced soldiers; but they realized, as had Gianpaolo, that they lacked the strength to defy the armies Pope Leo had assembled to send against Perugia. Their departure left the city undefended against Gentile Baglioni, who returned under the special favor of the Pope and ruled Perugia according to the instructions of a papal legate.

After Pope Leo's death in 1521 the two brothers returned in triumph to Perugia, just as their father had done after the deaths of Pope Alexander and Pope Julius. They drove out Gentile, betrayer of their father and collaborator of their enemy. And they also expelled three of Gentile's most important supporters, the three young sons of Grifonetto.

In the autumn of 1522, under the pressure of the new Medici pope, Clement VII, a peace was patched up between Gianpaolo's sons and Gentile, and Gentile returned to Perugia. Malatesta was away, serving as a condottiere for Venice. Orazio remained in Perugia, and he and Gentile snarled at each other. It seemed as if another family murder would occur at any moment.

In March of 1523 Pope Clement summoned Gentile and Orazio

to Rome and they both went. Why Orazio went is a total mystery; it was only a little more than three years after his father's fatal journey to Rome.

Clement arrested both Gentile and Orazio and shut them both up in the Castel Sant' Angelo. He soon released Gentile, but Orazio was kept in prison for nearly four years. In January 1527 Clement released him because he desperately needed a good soldier to help defend Rome against the imperial army. Orazio did little to defend the city, but he did take charge of the defense of the Castel Sant' Angelo. There he became acquainted with Benvenuto Cellini, who boasted of Orazio's friendship in his autobiography. The two young men were much alike, both high-spirited, reckless, violent and murderous.

While Orazio had languished in jail, Gentile was back in Perugia as a willing tool of Pope Clement. Malatesta was away earning fame as a condottiere. When the horrors of the sack of Rome were over, Orazio resumed his trade as a soldier and in June met Gentile in Perugia. They formally made peace with each other and sealed it with a ceremonial kiss. Together with Malatesta they would rule in family amity. Naturally then, the time had come for another demonstration of the Baglioni passion for revenge.

One month later Gentile Baglioni, sometime bishop of Orvieto, brave soldier and traitor, was murdered by Orazio's orders. And Orazio personally murdered Grifonetto's son, Galeotto. Having thus lived up to the family tradition, Orazio went off to the wars again. He had succeeded Giovanni de' Medici as commander of the troop known as the Black Bands. The next year Orazio died in battle during the siege of Naples.

Orazio's death left his elder brother Malatesta sole lord of Perugia. He did not live to enjoy his power long. The Florentines had revolted against the rule of Medici popes. A combined papal and imperial army threatened Florence. So Malatesta Baglioni was hired to defend their city against the armies of Pope Clement and Emperor Charles V. The fact that Gianpaolo had betrayed Florence did not prevent the Florentines from hiring his son. Malatesta signed a contract for one year at a salary of two thousand gold florins. He brought with him ten subordinate officers and more than a thousand Perugian soldiers. But the Florentine cause was hopeless.

Almost as if in recognition of their need for more than human aid, the Florentines, as they had done in Savonarola's time, proclaimed Jesus Christ king of their radical republic. With no military tradition behind them, with inadequate mercenary forces, the Florentines faced a much larger army of seasoned veterans. The siege began on Oct. 12, 1529. All the buildings within a mile of the walls of the city had been torn down, including many beautiful villas and palaces of the rich.

The hardships of the siege were terrible. There were many sorties and skirmishes. Food became scarce, and the people ate cats and rats. Malatesta was a sound professional general. He did what he could, but he recognized the futility of prolonged defense. It would increase suffering. Also, he was fighting against Pope Clement, his nominal suzerain, and he did not wish to lose his lordship of Perugia.

So, sound military judgment plus his desire to win the pope's favor prompted Malatesta to negotiate with the enemy and arrange a surrender. It was treason, but practical treason. If he had continued the defense to the last possible moment, Florence might have been sacked as cruelly as Rome had been.

Before Malatesta enforced the surrender, he discovered a Florentine plot to poison the pope. It was a perfect opportunity to win Clement's gratitude. Malatesta sent a warning to the enemy general, saying that "he was serving Florence as a soldier, not as an executioner, and could not tolerate such practices."

Florence surrendered on August 12, 1530, forced to do so by Malatesta who trained guns on the city. The siege had lasted almost ten months. The total number of deaths within the beleaguered city was estimated at 36,000, or a third of the inhabitants. In the defending army 8,000 died; in the besieging army 14,000.

Clement was pleased with Malatesta. He confirmed Malatesta's rule in Perugia, and according to a plausible rumor, rewarded him with fifty thousand ducats. The new Medici government in Florence gave Malatesta a present of six cannon and two lion cubs. Malatesta returned to Perugia in triumph. But the Doge of Venice expressed the opinion of many of Malatesta's contemporaries: "He has sold that city and the blood of those poor citizens ounce by ounce, and has assumed the cap of the greatest traitor in the world."

Only a year later Malatesta Baglioni died of syphilis in the village of Bettona near Perugia. On his deathbed he foresaw the papal tyranny which would soon crush his native city: "Help me if you can, for after my death you will be made to draw the cart like oxen."

And Frolliere commented: "This has been fulfilled to the last letter, for all have borne not only the yoke but the goad."

The new Farnese pope, Paul III, ruled Perugia with a cruelty and corruption greater than anything the city had known under the splendid and barbarous Baglioni. Pope Paul demolished the Baglioni palaces and built on their site a huge fortress-prison which was not torn down in its turn until the middle of the nineteenth century.

 XXIII

THE RENAISSANCE PAPACY

WHEN LORENZO DE' MEDICI'S SECOND SON, Giovanni, was about to depart for Rome to take up his position as a cardinal at the papal court, his father wrote him some words of caution and advice: "You are going to a sink of vice and you will find it hard to conduct yourself decently." This was written during the pontificate of Innocent VIII when the brazen corruption of the papacy, the cardinals and the Roman clergy had not yet sunk as low as they were soon to do in the reign of Alexander VI.

The reasons for the moral decline of the Church in the Renaissance were many and dated back well into the Middle Ages. During the absence of the popes in Avignon and during the Great Schism much of Italy suffered a political state of near anarchy. The distant popes seemed far more intent on collecting funds and on imposing their rule by military conquest than on exercising the spiritual leadership of their exalted office. The cardinals and legates they sent to Italy did much to debase the reputation of the Church.

A horrible example was Robert of Geneva, a cardinal and a

legate representing the Pope in a war to impose papal authority on the Romagna. In 1377 he led a company of Breton mercenaries to suppress a riot in conquered Cervia and encouraged them to massacre most of the population. "I will have more blood—kill all—blood, blood!" he shouted. So more than four thousand corpses were soon strewn about the streets and ditches of the little city. Robert became the schismatic Pope Clement VII (not to be confused with the Medici Pope Clement VII).

When the popes returned to Rome from Avignon early in the fifteenth century, conditions in Italy were only a little better. It was plain to all the popes that the papacy as an institution and even their own lives were not safe unless the temporal power of the church was secure. That meant not only that the popes must be absolute rulers of the city of Rome but that wherever possible they should rule the states of the Church directly and not just through nominal vicars. The larger the area the popes actually ruled the safer the Church would be. So all the popes waged wars and some of them—notably Sixtus, Innocent, Alexander and Leo —waged them to make their relatives princes under papal supremacy.

This involvement in power politics was fatal to the spiritual leadership of the Church. The popes were princes of a secular state. Most of them were as treacherous, dishonest, unscrupulous and avaricious as the despots who ruled in Lombardy or the Romagna. Inevitably, then, they were regarded with suspicion and dislike by other rulers. And the prevailing disillusion was aggravated by the papal custom of invoking religious sanctions for immoral political behavior, behavior as cynical as that of the secular princes. The immoral personal behavior of many of the popes only increased the disillusion of thoughtful observers. Putting his outrage as violently as possible, Guicciardini, the Florentine statesman and historian, wrote: "In our corrupt times the goodness of a pontiff is commended when it does not surpass the wickedness of other men."

All the Renaissance popes, save two, from Martin V to Clement VII were politically minded men obsessed by the temporal power of the Church and little interested in the Kingdom which is not of this world. The exceptions were Nicholas V

(1447–1455), whose chief interests were scholarship and book collecting; and Adrian VI (1522–1523), a good, devout and unworldly Dutchman, who in his twenty-month reign failed to bring about any significant reforms.

The popes varied in character and abilities. We can respect Nicholas as a patron of learning; Pius II because he honestly did his best for the Church according to his exceedingly limited vision of what that best was; Julius II (with reservations) because of his powerful personality and his patronage of great artists; and Adrian for his sincerity and ineffectual good intentions. Little good can be said of the rest. Many of them took and offered bribes, sold Church offices and bestowed Church and secular positions upon their unworthy relatives. Popes and cardinals alike flaunted their mistresses, wallowed in ostentatious luxury, and waged wars against their fellow Christians to secure control of a few castles or of some district of small importance. Their worldly example was imitated by less exalted members of the clergy. No wonder that virulent anticlericalism flourished in Renaissance Italy.

Nevertheless, there were also many virtuous and sincere priests, monks and nuns and a few saints. In a time of poor communications the illiterate peasants remained ignorant of the scandals in Rome and elsewhere. The better informed felt contempt for the flagrant abuses of the papacy but still revered the sacred powers of the pope, distinguishing between the office and the man.

It was annoying to rulers and their subjects to be excommunicated whenever they found themselves opposed to the papacy in war; but that dread punishment was invoked so often that it lost some of its terrors. Everybody knew that after the war was over the excommunication would be revoked. Papal interference in local politics and papal enthusiasm for waging wars disgusted the best judges of politics. Lorenzo de' Medici said: "This ecclesiastical state has always been the ruin of Italy, for its rulers are ignorant and do not understand statecraft, and so they run the whole world into danger."

Membership in the College of Cardinals was regularly a political reward. Many of the cardinals behaved like secular politicians and were so regarded. Machiavelli considered the Cardinal of Volterra a representative of the Florentine state and referred to him as "our Cardinal." The honor of becoming a cardinal went as a matter of course to relations of royalty, to royal favorites and to members of the ruling families of Italy. And, of course, to the relations of popes. Boys became cardinals at a ludicrous and disgracefully early age.

Alfonso, son of the King of Portugal, was a cardinal at seven (with the restriction that he should not assume his office until he was fourteen!). Giovanni de' Medici was a cardinal at thirteen (to assume office at sixteen), Ippolito d'Este at fourteen, Francesco Piccolomini at seventeen, and Cesare Borgia at eighteen.

These boys did not all buy their red hats, but many cardinals did. We have seen how Clement VII sold five at once. It was a common practice.

Since several popes committed murders it is not surprising that four cardinals conspired to murder a pope, Leo X. Papal officials could be equally murderous. In Bologna in 1435 the papal governor arranged the murder of Antongaleazzo Bentivoglio. The popular lord of the city, Sante Bentivoglio, commented: "The blood of my own kin has taught me a bitter lesson as to the little faith that can be placed in priests."

Only the year before in Florence, Rinaldo degli Albizzi had remarked of Pope Eugenius IV: "He who trusts a priest's word is like a blind man without a guide."

Many of the best-informed observers in Renaissance Italy recorded bitter opinions about the Church in their time.

Machiavelli wrote: "Owing to the evil example of the papal court, Italy has lost all piety and all religion: whence follows infinite troubles and disorders; for as religion implies all good, so its absence implies the contrary."

Guicciardini wrote: "My position under several popes has compelled me to desire their aggrandizement for the sake of my own profit. Otherwise, I should have loved Martin Luther like myself—not that I might break loose from the laws which Christianity, as it is usually interpreted and comprehended, imposes on us, but that I might see that horde of villains reduced within due limits, and forced to live either without vices or without power."

The Roman diarist Infessura wrote that in the reign of Innocent VIII the vicar of the Pope published an edict forbidding the clergy to keep mistresses, either openly or in secret. "When the Pope heard of this he summoned the vicar and commanded him to annul the edict, saying that the practice was not forbidden."

Pope Pius II, who published an edict forbidding the clergy to keep bawdy houses, wrote: "All prelates of the Church are slaves to money."

Nearly fifty years after the death of Pius II a memorial was submitted to the newly elected Pope Leo X which listed evils in the Church which ought to be eliminated. Among them were the deplorable facts that worship of God was neglected; churches were held by pimps and catamites; nunneries were dens of prostitution; justice was a matter of hatred or favor; piety was lost in superstition; the priesthood was bought and sold; revenues of the Church ministered only to the vilest excesses; and the people were repelled from religion by the example of their pastors.

This sorry state of affairs continued until the shock of the Protestant Reformation inspired the Counter Reformation. But Leo was not the kind of man to bother himself about such trifles as those listed in the memorial. The Counter Reformation had to wait.

✤✤✤✤✤✤ XXIV ✤✤✤✤✤✤

THE FOUNDING
UNCLE

 MACHIAVELLI HELD a low opinion of Francesco della Rovere, Pope Sixtus IV—as he did of numerous Renaissance personages. "He was the first who began to show how far a pope might go, and how much which was previously regarded as sinful lost its iniquity when committed by a pontiff."

The Pope thus curtly dismissed began life as the son of a poor fisherman near Savona on the Genoese Riviera and ended it as one of the most spectacular popes of the Renaissance. He did much to lower the already low standards of the papacy and much to raise the cultural standards of Rome. Although he had no acknowledged children (he was a Franciscan monk before he became a cardinal and a pope), he was the founder of the famous Della Rovere family. Counting himself, it included two popes, several cardinals, a lord of Sinigaglia, a lord of Imola and Forli, and three dukes of Urbino.

Many of the traits and attitudes which distinguished his great nephew, Julius II, were conspicuous in Sixtus. He was a lover of power, glory and magnificence. He was interested in art. He waged wars enthusiastically. His temper was notorious and his caprices incalculable. But Julius had some moral scruples—not many, but a few. Sixtus had none. Julius possessed a spark of genuine greatness and a grandeur of spirit which impressed

FRANCESCO DELLA ROVERE, Pope Sixtus IV

"... *one of the most spectacular popes of the Renaissance. He did much to lower the already low standards of the papacy and much to raise the cultural standards of Rome.*" From the brass tomb by Antonio Pollaiuolo in St. Peter's.

everyone who encountered his magnetic and domineering personality. Sixtus could only frighten people. He could not inspire admiration or liking. His sins were too glaring.

Francesco was born in 1414. At the age of nine he was sent to be educated at a Franciscan monastery. Later he studied at the universities of Padua, Bologna, Pavia, Siena, Florence and Perugia. He became known as a scholar and theologian and rose to become general of the Franciscans. He was made a cardinal in 1467 and was elected pope in August of 1471. At the time of his election he was respected as a man of blameless life.

Almost at once he destroyed his good reputation. To win the election he bribed several accommodating cardinals, the arrangements being entrusted to his favorite nephew, Pietro Riario. Immediately after the election Pope Sixtus declared that he had found only five thousand florins in the papal treasury. This must have been a barefaced lie because his predecessor, Pope Paul II, had been famous for his parsimony and because Sixtus began at once to squander huge sums on his greedy relatives.

Power's famous tendency to corrupt has seldom been more conspicuously demonstrated. The learned Franciscan monk became a venal, treacherous and violent pope. Perhaps it was the golden opportunity which seduced him, the opportunity for the poor peasant boy to wield immense power, to live in great magnificence and to raise his family to the seats of the mighty.

Four months after his election Pope Sixtus made two of his nephews cardinals: Pietro Riario and Giuliano della Rovere, who would become Julius II. Soon, he showered other honors on his relatives. Nepotism was a way of life with Sixtus. In all, he bestowed riches or titles on two brothers, four sisters, eleven nephews and two nieces.

Such generosity was expensive. To raise money Sixtus adopted two thoroughly deplorable methods. He sold offices—everything from election to the College of Cardinals to the smallest favor—at the papal court to the highest bidder. And he speculated in grain, after acquiring a monopoly, selling the best grain outside the Roman region and the worst to his own subjects at high prices. Infessura, the diarist who hated popes on principle, said that the bread made from the bad grain was "black, stinking and abominable."

Infessura is not a reliable witness. He accused Sixtus of sodomy; whether this was pure malice or a charge with some substance we have no way of knowing. But Sixtus did make his valet, a young man of twenty, cardinal and bishop of Parma. The youth was uneducated, of obscure origin and very handsome. Though stupid, he was considered harmless.

In St. Peter's Cathedral in Rome there is a brass tomb and statue of Pope Sixtus IV made by Antonio Pollaiuolo. The massive head wears a jeweled miter. The eyebrows are bushy, the nose long, the mouth looks as if it were toothless, the jutting chin projects so far that it is in no way softened by the double chin beneath it. The face is strong, intelligent, brutal.

When Pietro Riario, the Pope's nephew, was made a cardinal in December of 1471, he was twenty-five. A gay, witty, likable young man, he was much beloved by the Pope and extremely influential with him. Without interest in religion, suspected of being an unbeliever, he dedicated himself to the joys of conspicuous display and of perpetual debauchery. When he rode through the streets of Rome, he was attended by a hundred horsemen. He decked his mistresses in jewels; even their slippers were decorated with pearls. Pietro seemed totally frivolous. But this cheerful young wastrel was the prime mover in a grandiose political scheme which would have done irreparable damage to the Church if it had been successfully accomplished. On a triumphant peregrination among the states of Italy Pietro made an agreement with Duke Galeazzo Maria Sforza of Milan to crown him king of Lombardy in return for his support of Pietro's plan to become pope. It was said that Sixtus was prepared to abdicate in his favor. So outrageous a scheme to make the papacy the personal property of one family to be handed around among its members never came to anything. Pietro died too soon, in Rome in January of 1474, exhausted by his unceasing dissipations.

In his twenty-five months as a cardinal Pietro Riario had squandered two hundred thousand gold florins and amassed a debt of sixty thousand more. When we remember that a florin was worth at least ten dollars, and perhaps twenty, his achievement can be appreciated at its true worth. Commenting on Sixtus' prodigality with money, the distinguished nineteenth-century historian Ludwig von Pastor wrote: "Sixtus did not know the value of money, and, having grown up in a mendicant order, gave with full hands as long as he had anything to give."

Pope Sixtus mourned extravagantly, in his grief calling Pietro his son and only hope. He repented the extravagances he had allowed the young cardinal and promulgated a set of rules for cardinals restricting their food and the number of their attendants, and regulating their dress. The rules, of course, were ignored.

Pietro's place as Sixtus' most influential favorite was soon taken by his brother, Girolamo Riario, whose unsavory career and violent death we have already described.

Pope Sixtus IV waged four wars in his thirteen-year pontificate. He suppressed the revolts of the Umbrian cities of Spoleto and Todi against papal rule. Spoleto was brutally sacked, according to one rumor, with the encouragement of the Pope.

He fought against the intransigent Colonna family, as indeed a number of popes felt it necessary to do.

He launched the Pazzi war against Florence which was caused by Girolamo's conspiracy to murder the Medici brothers. Sixtus knew about the assassination plans, but he was evasive and careful not to give them his explicit approval. The verdict of history is that he was guilty as an accessory before the fact.

And he was responsible for starting the war of Ferrara.

By waging the two larger wars, the Pazzi and that of Ferrara, Sixtus alarmed much of Italy. No one knew when or where he might fight another. But in neither of these wars did Sixtus acquire any useful gain for the papacy. The war of Ferrara ended in 1484 with a peace treaty about which Sixtus was not even consulted. When he heard its terms, he exploded with rage and denounced the "shameful and ignominious" treaty. His anger was so great that when the seventy-year old pope died a few days later it was widely believed that he died of sheer fury and frustration.

The tough, arrogant peasant from Savona was brutal, dishonest, violent and untrustworthy. His temper was notorious and his wild energy astonishing. He was certainly a bad pope. But he was not an entirely bad man. His efforts to increase the temporal power of the papacy were reasonable and even conventional according to the customs of his time. His labors to rebuild and beautify the city of Rome and his patronage of outstanding artists have done much to soften his reputation with posterity.

Sixtus had the major streets of Rome widened, straightened and repaved. He improved the city's water supply; repaired bridges, walls, gates and towers; built a new bridge, the Ponte Sisto, named after himself, across the Tiber; built a new structure to house the Vatican library and the Sistine Chapel above it; rebuilt the ruined hospital of Santo Spirito, whose main ward was 365 feet long; built new churches and repaired others.

He employed the best painters in Italy to decorate the Sistine Chapel: Perugino, Signorelli, Pinturicchio, Botticelli and Piero di Cosimo.

In 1475 the Vatican library contained 2,527 volumes in Latin and Greek. Sixtus added 1,100 more volumes to the library and opened it to the public.

In his own fierce way Sixtus was concerned for religion. He authorized the creation of the Inquisition in Spain and appointed the fanatical Torquemada to head it. And he empowered the inquisitors in Rome to forbid the publication of any book they wished.

Although interested in art, Sixtus had no belief in artistic freedom. He ordered that one painter be hanged because in a battle scene he painted a defeat of papal troops. The unfortunate man's life was saved when his sentence was changed to banishment from Rome, only after a plea that he was mentally irresponsible!

There is an irony in the pontificate of Sixtus IV in the fact that probably his most important and influential decision was to make his nephew Giuliano della Rovere a cardinal, thus laying a firm base for the extraordinary career of Julius II.

❖❖❖❖❖❖❖ XXV ❖❖❖❖❖❖❖

THE

TERRIBLE POPE

IN THE UFFIZI GALLERY in Florence hangs Raphael's great portrait of Giuliano della Rovere, Pope Julius II. An old man sits in an ornate chair gazing downward in a mood of melancholy abstraction. His head is covered by a velvet cap. His fingers are decorated by five or six large rings. The white beard, furrowed cheeks and firm mouth, turned down at the corners, suggest age and spent passions. But nothing suggests the monstrous egomania—the furious will to dominate and the ruthless determination which made Julius II the greatest of Renaissance popes and the wonder of his time—which made men call him with a mixture of fear and admiration the Terrible Pope.

Giuliano della Rovere was born near Savona on December 5, 1443. He was the ablest of the three brothers Della Rovere and the two brothers Riario whom Pope Sixtus IV raised from obscurity with avuncular benevolence. Little is known about Giuliano's childhood and youth. When he was made a cardinal by his uncle in December of 1471, he was twenty-eight years old.

As a cardinal, Giuliano was immensely rich because of the benifices showered upon him by Sixtus. Tall, powerful, handsome in a blunt and rugged fashion, he was arrogant, reckless and imperious. He had several mistresses, but his indulgence in this respect was modest, compared with that of other cardinals. His reputa-

GIULIANO DELLA ROVERE, Pope Julius II

"... the greatest of Renaissance popes and the wonder of his time
... the Terrible Pope."

tion for intelligence was low, but for honesty high. This is interesting because as pope he was to display a mastery of intrigue and dissimulation equal to that of his enemies the Borgias. Guicciardini believed that Giuliano deliberately cultivated his reputation as a bluff, honest man in order to help his eventual election as pope.

In the election of 1484, which made the amiable, foolish and ineffectual Gianbattista Cibo Pope Innocent VIII, Giuliano acted as Cibo's political manager, making large promises and the necessary bribes. His candidate was corrupt and avaricious. He was also lazy and stupid. So Giuliano dominated Pope Innocent; he lived in the Vatican, countermanded the Pope's instructions when he disapproved of them and acted as if he were pope himself.

When the Neapolitan barons revolted against King Ferrante in 1485, Giuliano, who liked nothing so much as a good rousing war, saw to it that Pope Innocent entered the war in alliance with the rebellious barons. Virginio Orsini and several other barons of the Roman region allied themselves with King Ferrante and fought their feudal lord, the Pope. Virginio besieged Rome, and Cardinal Giuliano conducted the defense. Orsini, who could teach modern propagandists something about their craft, had pamphlets distributed in Rome denouncing Pope Innocent and accusing Giuliano of unnatural vice. He said that when he captured Rome he would carry Giuliano's head on a lance throughout the city. Fortunately for the warlike cardinal, Rome was relieved by the condottiere Roberto Sanseverino, father of Galeazzo.

Later in Innocent's pontificate, Giuliano was sent on a diplomatic mission to France and conducted it so ably that his reputation was much enhanced. But when he returned he found that his influence over the Pope had been largely replaced by that of Lorenzo de' Medici.

The election of Rodrigo Borgia as Pope Alexander VI was a terrible blow to Cardinal Giuliano because he had wanted to be elected pope himself. The two robust, energetic, unscrupulous men hated each other. We have seen how Giuliano hated Pope Alexander so much that he went to Lyons and vehemently urged

Charles VIII to get on with his march on Naples in the hope that Charles could be persuaded to call a Church council to depose Alexander. Giuliano accompanied Charles throughout the entire expedition. Naturally, then, he thought it wise to spend most of his time in the next few years in exile in France. In 1499 Giuliano went to Lyons again and urged King Louis XII to get on with his conquest of Milan. What he had against Lodovico Sforza is not clear. In any case, when Louis entered Milan in triumph, there was the Cardinal riding in his triumphant procession.

Alexander's death in 1503 was a relief and a pleasure to Giuliano. He hastened to Rome to take part in the conclave which would elect a new pope. When he arrived in Rome, Guiliano made a public announcement much in the manner of candidates at presidential conventions. "I have come here to take care of my own interests and no one else's. I will not vote for D'Amboise [the Cardinal of Rouen]. I am a good Italian. If I myself cannot attain the supreme dignity, I will see to it that a man shall have it who is able to assure the welfare of religion and the peace of Italy."

This political statement is interesting for two reasons. The man who had twice urged French invasions of Italy called himself a good Italian at a time when such a concept was almost unknown. And the man who was soon to do more than any man of his generation to destroy the peace of Italy spoke of peace as something he desired. Giuliano was a good politician. Nevertheless, he failed to be elected.

The conclave chose a compromise candidate, Francesco Piccolomini, a nephew of Pope Pius II, the father of twelve bastard children, a man eighty-four years old who suffered from gout and an open sore on his right leg. In memory of his uncle he chose the name Pius III. Two months later he was dead, after a reign so short that he does not really count as one of the Renaissance popes.

Before the conclave which was to elect the next pope began, Rome seethed with excitement. Giuliano della Rovere was easily the most likely candidate. His wealth, his commanding presence and his vast promises all were useful allies. But his furious temper had made him many enemies. It was rumored that the Cardinal had letters in his support from both the King of Spain and the King of France. Machiavelli, in Rome to report on the conclave to the Florentine government, wrote: "It was said that the reason for this general support was that he had promised to each whatever he asked, and consequently it is thought that the difficulty will be in the fulfilling of these promises."

Among Giuliano's promises was one to Cesare Borgia, who, though no longer powerful, was thought to have control of the Spanish cardinals' votes. In return for those votes Giuliano promised Cesare that he would reinstate him as Captain-General of the Church and confirm him as duke of the Romagna. Why Cesare believed his old enemy is a mystery. But he had little choice. No one else was as likely to be the next pope. Machiavelli had something to say about this, too: "The Duke lets himself be carried away by sanguine confidence; he believes that the word of others is more to be trusted than his own, and that the bond of the bargain will hold."

On November 1, 1503 after a conclave of only one hour Giuliano della Rovere, Cardinal of San Pietro in Vincoli, was elected pope. He chose the name Julius in deliberate rivalry with his dead enemy, Pope Alexander VI. Both Christian priests were thinking of military conquerors when they chose their new names. Pope Julius II was fifty-nine years old. His coronation was postponed until November 26 because astrologers promised that it would be an auspicious day.

A few weeks later the Venetian ambassador, Antonio Giustinian, wrote: "No one has any influence over him, and he consults few or none. One cannot count upon him, for he changes his mind from hour to hour. Anything that he has been thinking overnight has to be carried out immediately the next morning, and he insists on doing everything himself. Everything about him is on a magnificent scale, both his undertakings and his passions. His impetuosity and his temper annoy those who live with him, but he inspires fear rather than hatred, for there is nothing in him that is small or meanly selfish."

The new pope was rude in his language, crude in his manners, changeable in his ideas and deceitful. He had three bastard daughters and suffered from syphilis. He regularly drank too much wine. People could tell if he had dined and how well by the flush in his complexion. Julius promptly appointed twenty-seven new cardinals, one of them a nephew. When the nephew died five years later, Julius replaced him with another. His nepotism was not as flagrant as that of several popes and his simony was not so brazen. But he was conspicuously guilty of both these fashionable offenses.

Pope Julius II began his reign with uncharacteristic restraint. He felt his way cautiously among political pitfalls and financial shortages. His plans were expensive. He planned to impose papal rule on as much of Italy as possible, and that meant war. And he planned to make the Church more magnificent than ever before and in the process make its pope more magnificent than any of his predecessors. So Julius economized and bided his time. In January of 1505 the Venetian ambassador wrote: "The Pope has given up all his old liberality and only cares to save money. He sells every office, and will not even pay his bills, if he can discharge them in any other way. And I hear that he has already accumulated 100,000 ducats since he took possession of the papal throne."

Julius was a good fiscal manager. In spite of all the money he spent on waging wars, in spite of all the money it cost to build a new St. Peter's, at his death there was more money in the papal treasury than there had been since the death of Pope John XXII in 1335.

The first real problem Julius had to solve was that of Cesare Borgia to whom he had promised so much in order to become pope. Commenting on that promise, Julius said with typical Renaissance cynicism: "Necessity forces men to do what they dislike while they depend on others, but once they are free they act otherwise." Once Julius felt himself free enough he had Cesare arrested.

Julius had already broken one promise to Cesare when he made his old friend Guidobaldo of Urbino captain-general of the Church. Now he broke another by preventing Cesare's return to the Romagna and his resumption of his rule there. The former terror of Italy was now powerless, shorn of the sinister charm and the cold confidence which had once sent shivers through the courts of Italy. But Cesare Borgia still dreamed of a comeback and was a useful pawn in the game of Italian politics.

Several castles garrisoned by his men in the Romagna held out for him and would not surrender without his express command. Julius wanted those castles. So Cesare languished in prison and Julius waited. Finally Cesare gave up. Julius permitted him to retire to less strict confinement in the port of Ostia, and there a local official let him escape to Naples.

Julius, who cherished his enemies with vindicitive zeal, but who did not murder them as was the custom of many of his contemporaries, learned that Cesare was planning to return to the Romagna from Naples. His wrath boiled over, and he wrote furiously to Ferdinand and Isabella denouncing the Spanish government in Naples for harboring a dangerous enemy of the Holy See. It was easy to placate the importunate pope; Cesare Borgia was shipped across the Mediterranean to a Spanish prison.

He escaped, but only to be killed in a petty skirmish in the Kingdom of Navarre. His sister, Lucrezia, mourned when she heard the news, but most Italians were delighted—none more so than Pope Julius, who rejoiced in the death of an enemy.

Julius' unchristian behavior could be counted on. He was an ardent hater, and particularly hated King Ferrante of Naples, Pope Alexander VI, Cardinal Ascanio Sforza, Duke Alfonso of Ferrara, King Louis XII of France, Venice and Florence. Ferrante and Louis were Julius' former friends and allies. Venice was a former enemy which he stopped hating when he decided that he hated France more.

Once firmly settled on the papal throne Pope Julius II began his plans to make Rome, the Church and himself magnificent. He widened and improved streets. One of them, the Via Giulia, is still notable because of its Renaissance buildings. He reformed the coinage. He organized a Swiss Guard and had Michelangelo design the uniform which its members still wear. He issued a papal bull denouncing the practice of simony. Perhaps this was an attempt to atone for his own guilt in using bribes to secure his election. He was scrupulous about performing his ceremonial duties; but it was noticed that when he was supposed to kiss the feet of the poor he was careful to kiss his own thumbs.

And almost at once Julius demonstrated his interest in art. It has been argued that he wasn't really interested in art—that he saw art only as a symbol of greatness and magnificence. The truth of the matter is that Julius' love of art and of self were so inextricably mingled that they became one.

Julius in effect founded the Vatican museum when he collected and installed in the Belvedere Garden numerous newly discovered examples of ancient sculpture. At the time of his election he already owned the Apollo Belvedere. He had it placed on a pedestal to the left of the entrance to the garden. When the Laocoön was found, Julius sent the architect Sangallo to inspect it. Sangallo met Michelangelo at the excavation site. The pope bought the arresting group of a father and his two sons struggling in the coils of snakes and had it also installed in the Belvedere Garden. His other purchases included a recumbent Ariadne, a torso of Hercules and a Venus.

Three of Julius' artistic projects made Rome a world center of art as well as of religion. They were the construction of St. Peter's Cathedral, the mural paintings by Raphael in the Vatican palace and the painting of the ceiling of the Sistine Chapel by Michelangelo. The cathedral came first on the Pope's agenda. He decided to tear down the ancient cathedral of St. Peter's and replace it with a much larger and grander one. Many of the cardinals were shocked by this desecration of a sacred building which dated from the fourth century. But Julius was determined. He always was.

Sangallo and the great Bramante were ordered to design competitive plans. Julius chose Bramante's. The great church which we see today was begun in 1506 and not finished for twenty years. Bramante was succeeded as its architect by Raphael, Sangallo, Michelangelo and Della Porta. The cost was so enormous that Julius instituted the sale of indulgences in order to raise funds. These were sold in so aggressively mercenary a fashion, especially in Germany, that their sale outraged Martin Luther and many others and helped bring on the Protestant Reformation.

On the 18th of April 1506, Pope Julius II performed the ceremony of laying the cornerstone for the new St. Peter's. A procession of cardinals and other dignitaries accompanied him to the

site where a deep hole had been dug. The elderly pope climbed
down into the pit and then shouted to the crowd to back away so
that loose dirt would not be kicked down upon him. A vase
containing medals and coins was placed in a small hole and then a
block of marble was lowered into position above it. This Julius
sprinkled with holy water. Later in the same day the Pope wrote
a letter to King Henry VII of England (perhaps he wrote to
other monarchs but it is his letter to Henry which has survived)
in which he said that "by the guidance of our Lord and Savior
Jesus Christ he had undertaken to restore the old basilica which
was perishing through age."

Early in 1505 Pope Julius summoned the Florentine sculptor
Michelangelo Buonarroti to Rome. The ugly, sensitive, proud
young artist was not quite thirty years old. He had already completed his great statues, the "Pietà" and the "David." But what
Julius had in mind for him to do is unknown, and at first he
could not even tell Michelangelo. Finally Julius decided that what
he wanted was a gigantic marble tomb which would be a memorial to his own greatness.

Michelangelo, whose dynamic genius always responded to
grand conceptions, was enthusiastic. He established himself in a
studio near the Vatican and began to sketch grandiose plans.
Julius frequently dropped in on him to chat. The two men were
alike in their pride, their short tempers and their dedication to
their goals. But their goals differed. Michelangelo's was art; Julius' was self-glorification.

The first plan of the tomb was enormous; it involved a huge
structure ornamented with more than forty colossal statues. A
revised plan drawn up later still included thirty-eight of these
huge, allegorical figures. The only one ever completed was that
of Moses, considered by many to be Michelangelo's finest work.
Some have even speculated that in its fierce dignity and power it
was intended to resemble the man who commissioned it, Julius
himself.

The story of how the unfinished tomb of Julius II haunted
Michelangelo and burdened his mind belongs in a biography of
the great artist and not in this sketch of his difficult employer.

The remarks of John Addington Symonds about the tomb of

M *

Julius II to be found in his biography of Michelangelo are interesting not only for the description of a pope's tomb but also for the Victorian rhetoric: "Whatever may have been the artistic merits of Michelangelo's original conception for the tomb, the spirit was in no sense Christian. Those rows of captive Arts and Sciences, those Victories exulting over prostrate cities, those allegorical colossi symbolizing the mundane virtues of a mighty ruler's character, crowned by the portrait of the Pope, over whom Heaven rejoiced while Cybele deplored his loss—all this pomp of power and parade of ingenuity harmonized but little with the humility of a contrite soul returning to its Maker and its Judge."

But Julius, who so often changed his politics and his alliances, changed his mind about the tomb. He ordered Michelangelo to stop work on it. Perhaps he was superstitious about erecting his own tomb while he lived. Perhaps it cost too much, particularly when he was committed to the building of St. Peter's and was soon to go to war.

Nearly forty years later, Michelangelo, who was always suspicious of other artists, wrote: "All the dissensions between Pope Julius and me arose from the envy of Bramante and Raphael of Urbino, and this was the cause of my not finishing the tomb in his lifetime. They wanted to ruin me. Raphael had good reason; for all he had of art he owed to me."

Michelangelo was quite naturally incensed to have his work on the great tomb stopped. He was also personally offended because when he went to the Vatican to protest he was refused admission. And he was frightened. He fled back to Florence in the spring of 1506 and wrote in a letter: "There was something else which I do not wish to communicate; enough that it made me think that, if I stayed in Rome, that city would be my tomb before it was the Pope's. And this was the cause of my sudden departure."

What frightened Michelangelo we do not know. All we do know is that he was timid by nature and on several occasions fled when no man pursued.

Before he left Rome, Michelangelo wrote curtly to the Pope: "Most blessed Father, I have been turned out of the palace today by your orders; wherefore I give you notice that from this time forward, if you want me, you must look for me elsewhere than at Rome."

Julius sent messengers after the fleeing artist who caught up with him before he reached Florence. But Michelangelo refused to return to Rome. In Florence Michelangelo found himself the center of a cause célèbre. Julius sent three briefs to the Florentine seigniory about the truant sculptor. In the last he wrote: "Michelangelo, the sculptor, who left us without reason, and in mere caprice, is afraid, as we are informed, of returning, though we for our part are not angry with him, knowing the humors of such men of genius. In order, then, that he may lay aside all anxiety we rely on your loyalty to convince him in our name that if he returns to us he shall be uninjured and unhurt, retaining our apostolic favor in the same measure as he formerly enjoyed it."

Michelangelo in his own account of this episode wrote: "The seigniory sent for me and said: 'We do not want to go to war with Pope Julius because of you. You must return; and if you do so, we will write you letters of such authority that, should he do you harm, he will be doing it to the seigniory.' Accordingly, I took the letters and went back to the Pope."

This is an oversimplification. Throughout the summer of 1506 Michelangelo refused to budge out of Florence. It wasn't until November 21 that Michelangelo returned to Pope Julius and then he joined the Pope in Bologna. Julius was there majestically laying down the law and preening himself on his bloodless conquests of Perugia and Bologna. When the apprehensive artist entered the city, he attended Mass at the Church of San Petronio and was there recognized by several of Julius' grooms, who took him to the Pope who was seated at dinner. Julius stormed at Michelangelo for not coming back to Rome when summoned. Michelangelo knelt before him and prayed loudly for pardon. Julius only scowled fiercely. Cardinal Francesco Soderini, a brother of the head of the Florentine republican government, tried to put in a helpful word for a fellow Florentine: "Your Holiness might overlook his fault; he did wrong through ignorance. These painters, outside their art, are all like this."

Such impudence made Julius angrier than before. "It is you,

not I, who are insulting him. It is you, not he, who are the ignoramus and the rascal. Get hence out of my sight, and bad luck to you!" The Cardinal gaped in astonishment and then was hustled out of the room by servants, who, if we can believe Michelangelo's account, kicked and beat him.

Shortly thereafter Pope Julius ordered Michelangelo to make his statue in bronze to be placed on the façade of the Church of San Petronio. Michelangelo made a clay model of the Pope seated in state upon his throne. The right hand was raised in a commanding gesture. But Michelangelo was undecided about what the left hand should be doing. When Julius came to inspect the model, Michelangelo asked him if he would like the left hand to hold a book. "What, a book?" asked Julius. "A sword! I know nothing about letters, not I."

He then inquired what the raised right hand was doing—blessing or cursing? Michelangelo replied: "Holy Father, it is threatening this people of Bologna if they are not prudent."

Pope Julius left Bologna to return to Rome on February 22, 1507. Michelangelo remained in Bologna to work on the statue. A year later, in February 1508, the huge statue was hoisted to its position above the great central door of the church. It was three times life-size and fourteen feet high. It remained in place less than four years. When the French drove the papal forces out of Bologna and restored the Bentivoglio family to rule the city, a mob pulled the statue down and sent it to Alfonso d'Este, Duke of Ferrara, who used the bronze to make a new cannon which he mockingly named *La Giulia*. Alfonso is supposed to have saved the head, which weighed six hundred pounds.

Thus perished a work which in all probability was one of the world's great masterpieces. It showed Julius seated on his throne, wearing the triple tiara on his head, his right hand lifted to bless and his left hand holding neither a book nor a sword but the keys of St. Peter.

Shortly after Michelangelo had returned to Florence, Pope Julius again summoned him to Rome, this time to decorate the ceiling and vaulting of the Sistine Chapel. Michelangelo wrote: "The Pope was still unwilling that I should complete the tomb and ordered me to paint the vault of the Sistine. We agreed for

3,000 ducats." Michelangelo yearned to work on the tomb and did not enjoy his difficult task. "I am still in great distress of mind, because it is now a year since I had a penny from the Pope. And I do not ask, because my work is not going forward in a way that seems to me to deserve it. That comes from its difficulty, and also from *this not being my trade*. And so I waste my time without results. God help me."

Julius frequently came to visit Michelangelo to check on his progress. The fretful sculptor would help the aged pope climb up the scaffold to examine the paintings which Michelangelo found unsatisfactory. Once Julius demanded to know when the whole project would be finished. Michelangelo answered bluntly: When he was able to finish it.

Julius lost his temper. "Do you want to make me hurl you from this scaffold?"

Michelangelo was angry in his turn. "That you shall not do," he said, and then had the scaffold taken down. He toiled in the Sistine for four and a half years in all, finishing his great work in October of 1512.

The other great artist associated with Pope Julius II is Raphael, who probably came to Rome late in 1508 and was working for Pope Julius in the Vatican in January of 1509. The handsome, brilliantly talented young artist from Urbino was twenty-five years old. His remarkable gifts were complemented by a sunny disposition and an engaging personality. Everybody liked Raphael. Only a few liked Michelangelo and Julius. At that time several well-known painters were busy decorating the rooms into which the Pope had moved because he could not abide remaining in his former private quarters where Pinturicchio's paintings perpetually reminded him of his enemy Pope Alexander VI, "that circumcised Jew."

Raphael had only begun painting when the Pope decided that he wanted him to do the whole job himself. So without a qualm he dismissed such well-known painters as Perugino, Signorelli, Sodoma and Lotto, and their pictures were scraped off or painted over. The Pope's rooms, called the *stanze*, were one floor above those used by Alexander. Raphael's mural paintings, which make the stanze one of the great tourist attractions of Rome, include his celebrated "School of Athens" and "The Expulsion of Helio-dorus from the Temple." Raphael's reputation fluctuates with critical fashions. Nevertheless, his stanze paintings rank among the masterpieces of the Italian Renaissance.

They would not have been painted if an impetuous old man suffering from gout and the "French disease" had not had the perception to recognize Raphael's talent and also the habitual arrogance necessary to dismiss the other painters and to junk their work.

Pope Julius' employment of Michelangelo and Raphael left the world in his debt. But the difference in the payments made to the two artists will always disgrace Julius' name. He was a great patron of artists. But this did not mean he was interested in finan-cial justice to artists. Michelangelo received three thousand ducats for his four and a half years' work in the Sistine Chapel; Raphael was paid twelve thousand ducats for each of the three stanze he painted in the Vatican!

Early in the morning of August 27, 1506 Pope Julius II marched out of Rome and took the road to Orvieto. The su-preme head of the Christian Church was going forth to war in personal command of the troops he had assembled for the con-quest of the important cities of Perugia and Bologna and the expulsion of their ruling despots.

Both cities owed a nominal allegiance to the papacy. Both had long exercised virtual independence and could invoke numerous agreements and precedents confirming their nearly independent status. But Julius was determined to impose the rule of the Church on every city to which it had even the frailest claim and on some to which it had no legal claim at all. This was his con-ception of his duty—to magnify and glorify the Church. The Church, as Julius thought of it, of course, was much more a secular state than a brotherhood of all Christian believers. Besides, Julius enjoyed waging war and had pleasurably anticipated wag-ing this one for years.

We have seen how Gianpaolo Baglioni prudently submitted to the martial pope, surrendered Perugia without resistance and dis-creetly enlisted in the papal army as one of Julius' condottieri. Giovanni Bentivoglio, Lord of Bologna, was not so astute. He tried to dicker with the man least open to arguments and diplomatic bargaining in all Italy.

After he had settled affairs in Perugia to his satisfaction, Julius led his enlarged army (Francesco Gonzaga had joined him, as well as Gianpaolo Baglioni) through the Apennine passes to Urbino. He now had twenty-four cardinals with him, many of them enduring the rigors of campaigning in bad weather much against their will. From Urbino the papal army marched to the little city of Cesena in the Romagna. There envoys from Giovanni Bentivoglio eloquently protested to the Pope against his plans to expel their lord and to rule their city himself. They cited treaties made with several popes which acknowledged the rule of the Bentivoglio family, treaties which had been confirmed by Julius himself.

Machiavelli, who found the Pope nearly as interesting as he did Cesare Borgia, sent a dispatch from Cesena reporting that Julius insisted that he was going to liberate Bologna from a tyrant "and that as to the treaties, he cared neither for those made by other popes, nor for that made by himself, for neither his predecessors nor himself could have done otherwise; and that it was necessity and not his free will that had made him confirm the treaty; but that the time had now arrived for correcting these things, and that it seemed to him if he did not do so he would have no excuse to offer to the Almighty. If Bologna's government pleased him, he would confirm it; if not, then he would change it; and to be able to do so by force of arms he had provided himself with an army that would make all Italy tremble, let alone Bologna."

On October 7 Julius published a bull excommunicating Giovanni Bentivoglio and all his supporters, deposing him and denouncing him as a rebel against the Church. Anyone who would slay Bentivoglio was offered an indulgence.

As the Pope's army approached Bologna from the southeast, a French force, dispatched by King Louis XII from Milan to Julius' aid, marched on the city from the northwest. During the night of November 1 the French fired three rounds of cannon just to encourage Bentivoglio. The following morning Giovanni, his sons and grandsons, friends and loyal followers rode out of the city in a cavalcade of about five hundred horsemen. Sensibly recognizing the overpowering force of the troops arrayed against them, they abandoned the city without striking a blow in its defense.

Giovanni Bentivoglio's wife, Ginevra, remained behind in the palace, hoping that by her presence she could prevent its being looted. But Pope Julius refused to enter Bologna while she was there. So Ginevra, too, fled and on the following morning the Pope made his entry into the city.

The day after his entry, November 11, Pope Julius proceeded to the cathedral of Bologna in all the might and majesty of a conqueror who has subdued a powerful enemy in a brilliant campaign. He was carried in an ornate sedan chair through thirteen triumphal arches. He wore a purple cape, shot with gold thread and fastened with a buckle set with emeralds and sapphires. On his head he wore an exceptionally large miter decorated with pearls and other jewels. Alexander, as he rode in triumph through Persepolis, was not much grander.

Standing in the crowd was one observer who was not impressed. Erasmus, a Dutch priest and humanist scholar who was to become one of the great writers and one of the great men of the sixteenth century, was shocked. "I could not but groan when I compared this triumph, which many a secular prince would have thought too pompous, with the majestic tranquillity of the Apostles, who conquered the world by the word of Christ."

Not long afterward an anonymous satire called *Julius Exclusus* was published. It was widely and probably correctly attributed to Erasmus. In form it was a dialogue between St. Peter and Pope Julius II. The majestic pope, fully expecting to be welcomed with trumpets to the courts of Heaven, boasts to the saint who had been a humble fisherman.

"Ah, would to God you had seen me borne aloft in Bologna! The horses and chariots, the marching battalions, the galloping generals, the flaming torches, the pretty page boys, the steaming platters, the pomp of bishops and glory of cardinals, the spoils and trophies, the heaven-splitting cheers and the blare of trumpets and the thunder of cannon and the largesse flung to the crowd, and I borne aloft, head and author of all. Caesar and Scipio were nothing to me."

Such savage irony emphasized the difference between Julius' pursuit of power, glory and the things of this world and the noble and spiritual teachings of Jesus. The symbolical keys, which Julius thought would unlock the gate of Heaven, were only keys to riches and to power. St. Peter, staring at the lordly prelate before him with his jeweled tiara and his gorgeous robes, did not even recognize him as one of his successors in the apostolic succession.

Julius remained in Bologna for more than four months. His return to Rome was timed so that he entered the city in another ostentatious display of military glory on Palm Sunday. Without fighting a single battle Julius had conquered two cities and substantially increased the size of the area ruled by the Church. The crowds which thronged the streets of Rome to welcome him shouted: "Blessed is he that cometh in the name of the Lord."

✣✣✣✣✣✣ XXVI ✣✣✣✣✣✣

LET THE WORLD PERISH PROVIDED I OBTAIN MY WISH

THROUGHOUT THE YEAR 1507 and all of 1508 Julius schemed and negotiated. He brooded over the Romagna which ought, of course, to be entirely subservient to the Church. But the Venetians had snatched Rimini and Faenza and showed no signs of letting them go. Furthermore, if Julius should decide to drive Alfonso d'Este out of Ferrara and to incorporate his state into papal territory he couldn't count on Venice to help him or to remain neutral. Venice, the only strong state left in Italy, was too strong for Julius to attack unaided. When it was pointed out to him how dangerous an attack on Venice might be, Pope Julius summed up his religious, political and military philosophy in a few words: "Let the world perish provided I obtain my wish."

On one occasion Julius, while talking with the Venetian ambassador, lost his temper and shouted, "I will make Venice a little fishing village again."

The Venetian was not intimidated. He replied, "And unless you are reasonable, Holy Father, we will make you a little parish priest."

If allies were necessary for a war with Venice, Julius knew how to find them. At his instigation in December of 1508 the celebrated League of Cambrai was organized for the holy and edifying purpose of chastising Venice (then the chief European bulwark against the Turks) and after the defeat of Venice of crusading against the Turks. Never was a brutal aggression more hypocritically or sanctimoniously disguised. The principal allies, the kings of France and Spain and the emperor of Germany, had no intention of crusading. All three were Venice's allies. All three planned to dismember Venice's mainland empire and divide the spoils among themselves. Mantua and Ferrara, which joined later, also had territorial ambitions. Careful not to commit himself until he saw that the League was well established, Julius did not publicly join it until March of 1509.

The League of Cambrai has been called a crime. However that may be, it was a dreadful blunder on Julius' part. We have already seen how Julius, while still a cardinal, twice urged kings of France to conquer Italian states, Naples and Milan. Now for the third time he was largely responsible for a French attack designed to ruin an Italian state. To satisfy his petty ambitions Pope Julius personally instigated a general war which continued long after his death and brought terrible devastation and suffering to Italy.

When the French began their attack on Venice, Julius excommunicated the Venetians. Two members of the Orsini family, Giulio and Renzo, were engaged by Venice to fight the French as condottieri. They were paid fifteen thousand ducats to bring five hundred men at arms and three thousand infantry to the war. Julius ordered the Orsini not to fight for Venice and not to return the money. He absolved them of the sin of keeping it because it was the money of excommunicated persons.

"Holy Father," said one of the Orsini, "we do not wish to blacken our reputation for good faith."

"Do not by any means return the money," thundered the Pope.

But the Orsini, who were certainly dishonorable, were more honorable than the Pope. They returned three thousand out of the fifteen thousand ducats to Venice.

The French swept over the Venetian terra firma, captured Bergamo, Brescia and Cremona for themselves, and turned over to their passive ally Emperor Maximilian the cities of Verona, Vicenza and Padua. Thus overpowered, Venice could not defend the Romagna cities, and so they surrendered them to Julius. Now that he had what he wanted, Julius began to feel sorry for his enemy, Venice, and to resent his long-time ally, France. Venice, though crippled, was displaying admirable courage and had re-captured Verona from Maximilian. But the French were a menace.

Julius worked himself into a lather of hatred for the French. "Those Frenchmen have taken away my appetite and I cannot sleep. Last night I spent in pacing my room, for I could not rest. My heart tells me all is well; I have hopes all will be well after my past troubles. It is God's will to chastise the Duke of Ferrara and free Italy from the French."

A French cardinal tried to flee from the anti-French climate of Rome, but was brought back and imprisoned in the Castel Sant' Angelo. When he pleaded that no cardinal should be imprisoned without a trial, Julius answered: "By God's body, if he makes me angry I will have his head cut off in the Campo de' Fiori."

So in February of 1510 Pope Julius II made a separate peace with Venice, declared the war over and prepared to go to war against Ferrara and France with Venice as his ally. It was not his first treacherous deal or his first sudden switch of sides. But it was the greatest political betrayal of his life—callously deserting his allies and then attacking them. If his creation of the League of Cambrai was a crime, so was his repudiation of it.

Gloating over his spectacular treachery against King Louis XII, his former friend, Julius said: "I have struck a dagger into the heart of the King of France."

The Venetians were relieved of the excommunication and in a humiliating ceremony in Rome were welcomed back into the Pope's good graces. Julius smugly said to the Venetian envoys; "We grieve over the censures we were driven to use. Be mindful to stand well with popes. Then it will be well with you and you will not lack favors."

From then on the Pope could concentrate on his twin projects of capturing Ferrara and of driving out the barbarous French. His army based in Bologna was not doing well against Ferrara. In Rome Julius ignored diplomatic protocol and lashed out at ambasssadors. When an envoy from Duke Alfonso d'Este brought him a displeasing letter, Julius ordered the man hanged. Fortunately, he changed his mind in time and by way of apology gave the poor fellow two ducats instead.

Soon after, Cardinal Ippolito d'Este sent the poet Ariosto as an ambassador to Julius. Ippolito wrote: "This gentleman of mine not only could not obtain any grace or concession, but His Holiness threatened to have him thrown into the river if he did not leave his presence, and to do the like to any other of my people who should come before him."

Even worse, when the Duke of Savoy sent an envoy with an offer to mediate between the Pope and the King of France, Julius had the envoy thrown into prison and tortured.

In September of 1510 Pope Julius marched north in terrible weather to take personal command of the war against Ferrara and the French. He established himself in Bologna, scolded, stormed and denounced. His nephew, twenty-one-year-old Francesco Maria della Rovere, "that ninny," was not conducting the siege of Mirandola vigorously enough. Julius was determined to capture the town because he considered it the strategic key to Ferrara and because he hated its ruler, Francesca, widow of Lodovico Pico, who had cooperated with the French. Besides, she was the daughter of Trivulzio, the great mercenary soldier long in French service.

In October Julius suddenly became very ill. While he lay prostrated in his bed with a high fever the French approached Bologna, and the delirious old man succumbed to panic and shouted, "I shall be taken by the French. Let me die. I will take poison and end all."

But the French withdrew. Julius recovered and was his normal imperious self again. He excommunicated the French general, Chaumont d'Amboise, and all who served with him. And he grew a beard (he was the first Renaissance pope to wear a beard), swearing not to shave it off until he had driven the French barbarians out of Italy.

In January of 1511 in an exceptionally severe winter, Pope Julius II, recently recovered from a serious illness and sixty-seven years old, proceeded to Mirandola to take charge of the siege himself. "His singular passion was invincible against all reason," wrote Guicciardini. The snow was said to be five feet deep. The warrior pope wearing armor beneath a white cloak, with snow on his whiskers, personally superintended the placing of cannon, riding through the lines in the snow. He lived in a small cottage "no further from the walls of Mirandola than a common crossbow will shoot twice." A cannonball fired from the beleaguered town entered the kitchen of the cottage and killed two of Julius' cooks. Julius moved into a little church even nearer to the city walls than the cottage and encouraged his soldiers by promising them the privilege of sacking the city—a strange promise indeed from the representative on earth of the Prince of Peace.

Guicciardini expressed the reaction of many contemporaries (in Fenton's Elizabethan translation): "Truely it was a thing notable, and in the eyes of men strange and new, that a French King, a Prince secular, in an age and disposition flourishing, trained from his first years in warres, should take his rest in his Court and Chamber at home, and administer by Captaines a warre that was made against him abroad; and on the other side to see a souveraigne Bishop, a supreme Pastour, a Vicar of Christ on earth, being a body diseased, aged and dejected, and nourished in a calling contrary to armes and warre, to go in person to a warre stirred up by himself against Christian Princes, and to lie in camp before a place of little name, where submitting himself as a leader of soldiers to paines and daungers, he retained no other thing of the Pope than the habit and the name."

Finally a breach was made in the walls. Mirandola surrendered on terms, and Julius demanded money from the town to give to his soldiers to compensate them for being denied the pleasure of sacking the town as he had promised them. And so impatient was the Pope to enter the captured city that he had himself carried through the breach in a litter before the gate was opened!

In spite of his crudely secular behavior, much of the ancient, sacred prestige of the papacy still belonged to Julius. When D'Amboise, the French general, knew that he was dying, he sent a message to Julius saying how devoutly he repented the deeds he had done against the Church and requesting a public declaration of absolution and pardon. Julius sent it to him, but it arrived only after D'Amboise's death.

Trivulzio assumed command of the French army and with his customary skill and vigor soon was threatening Bologna. Julius retired from Bologna to Ravenna. He left the defense of Bologna to his nephew Francesco Maria della Rovere and to the papal legate, Francesco Alidosi, who cordially hated each other. The Pope was unaccountably fond of the handsome, corrupt and depraved Cardinal Alidosi whose cruelties had won the Church government the hatred of everyone in Bologna. It is almost certain that Alidosi was a traitor in treasonous correspondence with the French.

Pietro Bembo, Paride de Grassi, the papal master of ceremonies, and Guicciardini all despised Alidosi and considered him a vile scoundrel. Why, then, did Julius love him? We do not know, but scandalous rumors accused the two men of a homosexual relationship.

The defense of Bologna was badly botched. A fifth column revolted in favor of the Bentivoglio family, and the French captured the city. Alidosi and Della Rovere both blamed the other's incompetence and accused each other of treason. But the young duke of Urbino was the first to reach Julius in Ravenna. The Pope was sick again, bitterly disappointed by the loss of Bologna and furiously angry. He is said to have shouted before Della Rovere arrived: "If the Duke should fall into my hands I will have him drawn and quartered!"

Needless to say, Francesco Maria's interview with his uncle was unpleasant. When he left the Pope's audience chamber in Ravenna, bitterly humiliated and blackly angry, convinced that his enemy was a traitor and also convinced that the Pope suspected himself of treason, Francesco Maria had the misfortune to meet in the street the cause of all his woes.

The Cardinal-legate was riding on a mule accompanied by a troop of a hundred horsemen. Francesco Maria's Della Rovere temper exploded at the sight of the smiling villain. He dismounted and rushed upon his enemy. Conflicting accounts have

him piercing the Cardinal with his sword or plunging his dagger through Alidosi's belly into his saddle. The mortally wounded man fell to the ground and was stabbed several more times by the Duke's servants. It all happened so quickly that no one intervened. The Duke, a murderer for the second time at the age of twenty-one, sprang back on his horse and fled to Urbino.

So universally hated was Alidosi that many members of Julius' entourage rejoiced. Paride de Grassi exclaimed: "Blessed be the Lord, blessed be the Duke, blessed be this murder."

Julius' sorrow was as great as his anger. He wept and refused to eat. He had loved both men, his old friend and his nephew. And now with Mirandola and Bologna lost to the French, his army defeated, his shame and sorrow prostrated him. The aged pope got into a litter and had himself carried to Rimini and then to Rome.

Two problems demanded Julius' prompt attention. What was he to do about King Louis XII's attack upon him as an unworthy pope, and what was he to do about his beloved nephew who had murdered his most intimate friend?

Louis had not taken the Pope's betrayal and attack meekly. He raged at "this priest-king, who for years had been the guest at his court and the confidant of his policy, who had first enticed him into war with Venice, and now, faithless to his alliance, stirred up all the powers against him."

So Louis ordered the French Church to refuse to recognize Julius as a lawful pope, and he organized a Church council in the medieval tradition to condemn and depose him. In preparation for the council to be held at Pisa, Louis instigated a slander campaign and had a search made throughout Italy for women who

---

FRANCESCO MARIA DELLA ROVERE,
Duke of Urbino

"... a murderer for the second time at the age of twenty-one ..."
Portrait by Titian.

would claim that they had had sexual relations with the Pope. Only three were found—not nearly enough to cause any substantial scandal.

The Council at Pisa held in September of 1511 was a fiasco. Only five cardinals attended. They accused Pope Julius of being "an inveterate simoniac, of infamous and abandoned manners, not fit to discharge the office of a pontiff, as being the author of many wars, and notoriously incorrigible, to the univeral scandal of Christianity." There was much truth in these charges, but little attention was paid to them. Why should anyone be shocked by conduct which had been customary for many years?

But Julius was profoundly shocked. He pronounced the cardinals who attended the Council schismatic, excommunicated them and proclaimed a rival and official Church council to be held at the Lateran the following year. He excommunicated King Louis XII and anyone who supported him, which meant most of the population of France. He excommunicated the Florentines for allowing the schismatic council to be held on their territory at Pisa and for being passive allies of France. And he summoned Francesco Maria della Rovere, Duke of Urbino, to come to Rome to be tried for the murder of Cardinal Alidosi.

Francesco Maria arrived in Rome, accompanied by his friend, courtier and diplomatic adviser Baldassare Castiglione. He gave himself up to the justice of the College of Cardinals and announced: "I cannot convince myself that so just an act should bring me to grief, even though the Holy Father speaks of proceeding against me."

He was arrested, forced to pay bail amounting to a hundred thousand silver scudi and then made to await the findings of a commission of six cardinals. In an age which took murders lightly and those committed by dukes more lightly still, this is interesting evidence of the serious nature of the crime when a duke murdered a cardinal who was also the Pope's intimate friend. Francesco Maria's defense was a justification of his crime. His lawyer did not try to excuse him because of extenuating circumstances, his youth and hereditary Della Rovere temper; he insisted instead that the murder was a just punishment for horrible treasons.

While the commission deliberated, Pope Julius fell sick again of a quartan ague (malaria) and collapsed into a coma which lasted a full day. Rome seethed with rumors that the Pope was dead. Palace officials sacked his private apartments. But the tough old Pope recovered and demanded wine. His doctors refused such a request from a man near death. Julius, who never accepted a refusal from anybody, sent for the captain of his guard and said: "If you do not give me wine I will have you shut up in a dungeon in the Castel Sant' Angelo." Soon he was himself again.

His affection for his nephew, who was the most important member of the Della Rovere family after himself, returned. He was convinced of Alidosi's treason. So Julius granted Francesco Maria absolution for his crime, allowed him to go back to Urbino and returned to him twelve thousand out of the hundred thousand silver scudi. Francesco Maria, however, was not content with an absolution on a personal basis from his uncle. He demanded and received an official consistorial bull which fully absolved him of the charge of murder.

Even after this the Pope continued to have suspicions about his nephew. Castiglione wrote: "Since the beginning of these wars the Pope has always thought and said that the Duke not only failed to do his utmost against the Duke of Ferrara and the French, but was in secret communication with them, and has often declared that he was a traitor and should be drawn and quartered, and many similar words, which he has repeated a thousand times and now maintains more strongly than ever."

Julius mistakenly believed that Castiglione himself was the middleman through whom Francesco Maria maintained his correspondence with the French.

In the spring of the next year, 1512, Julius even issued a bull declaring Della Rovere a rebel. So Francesco Maria was not present at the great battle of Ravenna. But as soon as he knew about that disastrous defeat of the papal and Spanish armies, he hurried to Rome again and offered his services to his suspicious and changeable uncle. And Julius, who loved his nephew, forgave him and reappointed him to the command of the papal troops.

Francesco Maria della Rovere continued to serve as a distinguished commander in the Italian wars, although often accused of excessive caution and delay. His temper continued to be a menace. When he lost it he would punch in the face people with whom he was arguing. On one famous occasion he knocked Guicciardini, then a high official in the papal service, to the ground. On another he had three Venetian guards beaten to death because they had dared challenge his right to bear arms on Venetian territory.

Francesco Maria was generally liked by his equals. He retained the respect and affection of his subjects, even when Pope Leo X waged war against him to deprive him of his duchy and present it to his own nephew, Lorenzo de' Medici the younger. He died in 1538, supposedly of poison poured into his ear by his barber. It sounds wildly unlikely. But could the story be the source for an important part of the plot in the most famous play in the English language?

In October of 1511 Pope Julius formed a new alliance which he called the Holy League, which he hoped would drive the French out of Italy. Venice and the papacy were joined by Spain. When the League of Cambrai fought Venice, the only part taken by Spain was to capture several Neapolitan ports held by the Venetians. Now Julius was bringing Spanish power into northern Italy. It was another terrible blunder. Spain and France fought each other across much of Italy for many years. And in the end Spain ruled the duchy of Milan, the Kingdom of Naples and dominated Tuscany.

We have seen, while considering the career of Alfonso d'Este, how the papal and Spanish armies were defeated at the battle of Ravenna in April of 1512 and how panic spread to Rome. Galleys were even prepared for the flight of the Pope and cardinals. But soon news came of dissension among the French commanders, of the desertion of their German mercenaries, of attacks by the Swiss and Venetians and of the total collapse of French power in Italy. Julius boasted, "I will stake a hundred thousand ducats and my crown that I will drive the French out of Italy."

Soon Francesco Maria della Rovere, once more in command of the papal troops, recaptured Ravenna and Bologna without fighting. He then occupied Modena and Reggio for the Church, thus amputating a major part of Alfonso d'Este's domain. In October,

Pope Julius even had the effrontery to annex the Lombard cities of Parma and Piacenza, claiming that they were lawful parts of the Church states. This was blatant humbug because the two cities had never owed allegiance to the Church; for many years they had been integral parts of the duchy of Milan.

But such technical trifles did not bother Pope Julius. He had now achieved a spectacular triumph far greater than he could in any reasonable moment have expected. But Julius was rarely reasonable. He was emotional, volatile, stubborn, arrogant and terrible. His whims he constantly confused with obvious justice and divine right. And now he could gloat. The French were, temporarily, back in their own country beyond the Alps. And the temporal power of the Church was vastly increased. Julius, who never looked beyond today, did not foresee the continuing wars he had made certain. He could not conceive how his passion for worldly power had damaged the spiritual power of the Church. Indeed he was proud to have served the Church well. According to his own peculiar philosophy he had.

One of the results of the French defeat and the emergence of Spanish power in northern Italy was the end of the Florentine Republic. Pope Julius and the Spaniards believed that Florence should be punished and that the republic could not be trusted. It was too old in its erring ways of supporting France. So the Medici must be restored, which they were—after one of the most brutal sacks in Italian history, that of Prato, a small city less than ten miles from Florence. The Florentine militia so hopefully organized by Machiavelli did not dare stand up to the Spanish professional soldiers. The end of the republic, save for a brief revival later, was also one of the results of Julius' invitation to the Spaniards to help him fight the French.

Throughout the autumn of 1512 the tireless old pope boiled with plans for further wars and conquests. He was still determined to drive Alfonso d'Este out of Ferrara, and he also had a new project—now he was going to drive his most recent allies, the Spaniards, out of Italy. He announced that he hated the Spaniards as much as he did the French.

On Christmas Eve Paride de Grassi came to tell Pope Julius that it was time for Vespers. The Pope said, "You had better tell the Sacred College and the Sacristan to bring me the Holy Oils, for I feel very ill. I shall not live much longer." From then on he did not leave his bed. Eight doctors, considered the best in Rome, could not tell what his sickness was. He ate only two eggs a day.

Throughout January of 1513 his phenomenal strength kept the Pope alive. "If God grants me life," he said, "I will free the Neapolitans from the Spanish yoke which is now on their necks."

On February 4, Pope Julius admitted that he was dying. Shortly thereafter he summoned all the cardinals in Rome to his bedside. Speaking in Latin he confessed that he had been a great sinner and humbly deplored his faults and errors without mentioning any particular sins. He asked for the cardinals' prayers and gave them some good advice. Then he switched to Italian and asked that his beloved nephew, Francesco Maria della Rovere, Duke of Urbino, be confirmed in his lordship of the city of Pesaro which Julius had just given him. So on his deathbed the Pope indulged in a final sin of nepotism, making sure that his nephew, who already ruled Urbino and Sinigaglia, should rule another important town.

The family feeling which distinguished so many of the princes of the Renaissance was too strong in Giuliano della Rovere to be controlled by any deathbed qualms of conscience. On February 20, Julius received the last sacraments. He died in the night on February 21. He was sixty-nine years old.

His funeral was the occasion of extravagant mourning by the Roman population. Paride de Grassi wrote: "They thronged to kiss his feet and gaze on his dead face, for all recognized in him a true Roman Pontiff and Vicar of Christ, a defender and protector of the weak against tyrants, and the deliverer of Italy from the barbarians."

This opinion coincided with Julius' own. Guicciardini, who understood the significance of Julius' pontificate far better, summed it up (again in Fenton's Elizabethan translation):

"He was a prince of incredible constancie and courage, but so full of furie and unruled conceptions, that the reverence that was borne to the Church, the condition of Princes, and the condition of times, did more to stay him from his ruine, than either his moderation or his discretion: worthy no doubt of great glory, if either he had been a Prince secular, or if that care and intention he had to raise the Church into temporal greatness by the means of warre, had bin employed to exalt it by the mediation of peace, in matters spiritual; Nevertheless, he was lamented above all his predecessors. & no less esteemed of those, who having lost the true consideration of things, or at least ignorant how to distinguish & praise them rightly, judge it an office more duely appertaining to Popes, to increase the jurisdiction of the See Apostolic by armes and bloud of Christians, than by good example of life and due curing and correction of corrupt manners, to travel for the saving of those soules, for whom they glory so much that Jesus Christ hath named them his Vicars on earth."

The judgment is just. But such sententious self-righteousness was incongruous in a man who made of cynicism a philosophy.

A GUIDE TO THE PEOPLE IN THIS BOOK

All family trees are abridged to omit unimportant members not mentioned. Names capitalized are of persons discussed at some length. Broken lines indicate illegitimate offspring.

THE HOUSE OF ARAGON IN NAPLES

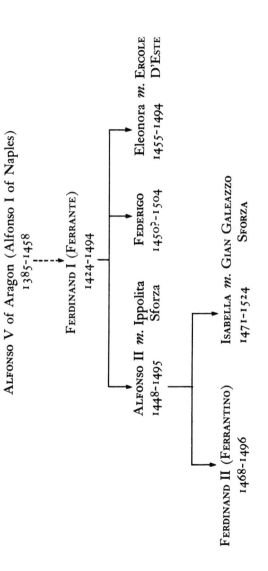

ALFONSO V of Aragon (Alfonso I of Naples)
1385-1458

FERDINAND I (FERRANTE)
1424-1494

ALFONSO II *m.* Ippolita Sforza
1448-1495

FEDERIGO
1450?-1504

Eleonora *m.* ERCOLE D'ESTE
1455-1494

FERDINAND II (FERRANTINO)
1468-1496

ISABELLA *m.* GIAN GALEAZZO SFORZA
1471-1524

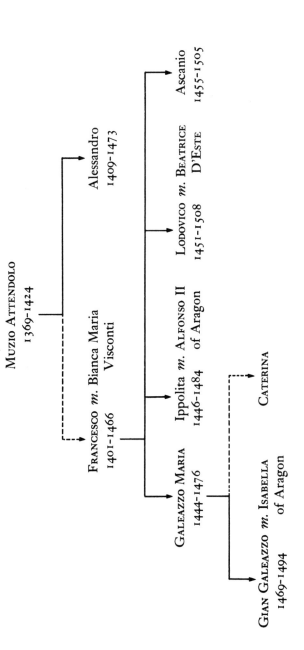

THE SFORZA IN MILAN

Muzio Attendolo
1369-1424

Francesco *m.* Bianca Maria
1401-1466   Visconti

Alessandro
1409-1473

Galeazzo Maria
1444-1476

Ippolita *m.* Alfonso II
1446-1484   of Aragon

Lodovico *m.* Beatrice
1451-1508   D'Este

Ascanio
1455-1505

Caterina

Gian Galeazzo *m.* Isabella
1469-1494   of Aragon

THE GONZAGA IN MANTUA

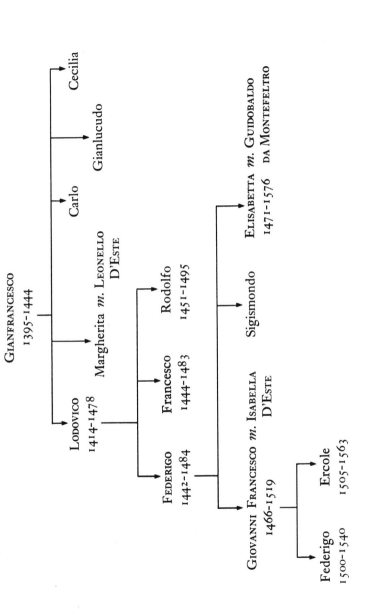

GIANFRANCESCO
1395-1444

Carlo

Gianlucudo

Cecilia

LODOVICO
1414-1478

Margherita *m.* LEONELLO
D'ESTE

FEDERIGO
1442-1484

Francesco
1444-1483

Rodolfo
1451-1495

GIOVANNI FRANCESCO *m.* ISABELLA
1466-1519   D'ESTE

Sigismondo

ELISABETTA *m.* GUIDOBALDO
1471-1576   DA MONTEFELTRO

Federigo
1500-1540

Ercole
1505-1563

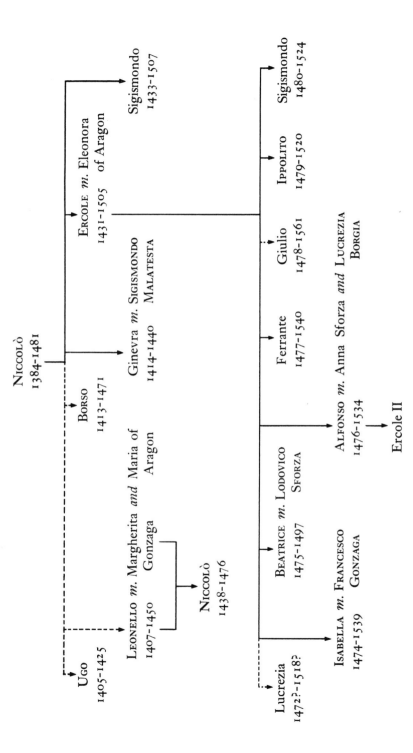

THE ESTE IN FERRARA

Niccolò 1384-1481

Ugo 1405-1425

Leonello *m.* Margherita *and* Maria of Gonzaga Aragon
1407-1450

Niccolò 1438-1476

Borso 1413-1471

Ginevra *m.* Sigismondo Malatesta
1414-1440

Ercole *m.* Eleonora of Aragon
1431-1505

Sigismondo 1433-1507

Lucrezia 1472?-1518?

Isabella *m.* Francesco Gonzaga
1474-1539

Beatrice *m.* Lodovico Sforza
1475-1497

Alfonso *m.* Anna Sforza *and* Lucrezia Borgia
1476-1534

Ferrante 1477-1540

Giulio 1478-1561

Ippolito 1479-1520

Sigismondo 1480-1524

Ercole II

THE MONTEFELTRO IN URBINO

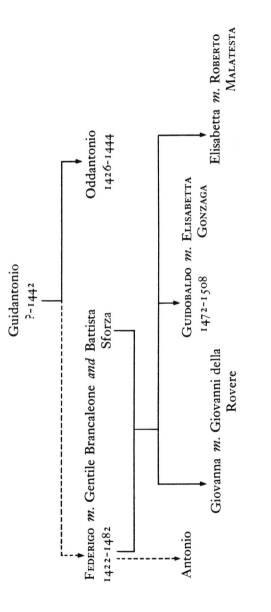

Guidantonio
?-1442

Oddantonio
1426-1444

FEDERIGO *m.* Gentile Brancaleone *and* Battista
Sforza
1422-1482

Antonio

GUIDOBALDO *m.* ELISABETTA
GONZAGA
1472-1508

Giovanna *m.* Giovanni della
Rovere

Elisabetta *m.* ROBERTO
MALATESTA

THE MALATESTA IN RIMINI

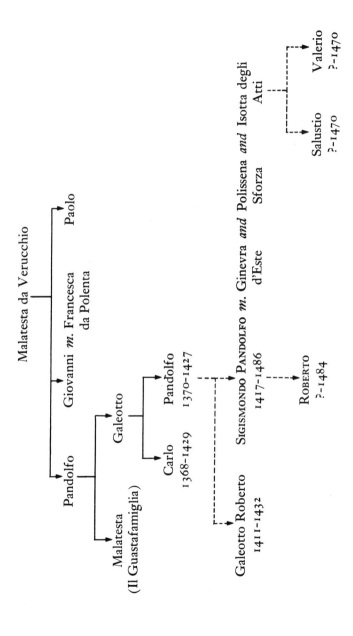

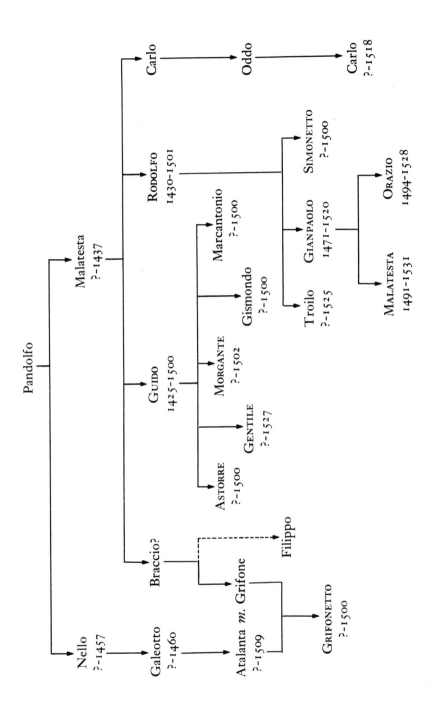

THE DELLA ROVERE IN ROME AND URBINO

FRANCESCO DELLA ROVERE (POPE SIXTUS IV)
1414-1484

His nephews:

GIULIANO DELLA ROVERE (POPE JULIUS II)
1443-1513

Giovanni *m.* Giovanna da Montefeltro
1458-1501

FRANCESCO MARIA DELLA ROVERE
1490-1538

His other nephews:

PIETRO RIARIO
1446-1474

GIROLAMO RIARIO *m.* CATERINA SFORZA
1448-1488

THE MEDICI IN FLORENCE

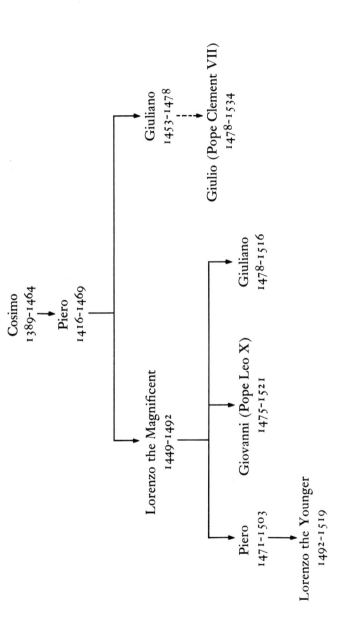

Cosimo
1389-1464

Piero
1416-1469

Lorenzo the Magnificent
1449-1492

Giuliano
1453-1478

Giulio (Pope Clement VII)
1478-1534

Piero
1471-1503

Giovanni (Pope Leo X)
1475-1521

Giuliano
1478-1516

Lorenzo the Younger
1492-1519

N*

THE POPES OF THE RENAISSANCE

Martin V	1417-1431	Innocent VIII	1484-1492
Eugenius IV	1431-1447	Alexander VI (Rodrigo Borgia)	1492-1503
Nicholas V	1447-1455	Pius III	1503
Calixtus III (Alfonso Borgia)	1455-1458	Julius II (Giuliano della Rovere)	1503-1513
Pius II	1458-1464	Leo X (Giovanni de' Medici)	1513-1521
Paul II	1464-1471	Adrian VI	1521-1523
Sixtus IV (Francesco della Rovere)	1471-1484	Clement VII (Giulio de' Medici)	1523-1534

BIBLIOGRAPHY

THE TWO most readable popular introductions to the Italian Renaissance are *The Renaissance: A History of Civilization in Italy from 1304 to 1576 A.D.* by Will Durant; and *The Horizon Book of the Renaissance* by the editors of *Horizon* magazine, J. H. Plumb and nine contributing scholars.

Casual readers uninterested in delving deeply into the period might enjoy the few good historical novels about it. In my life as a literary critic I have found only five of these. They are: *A Cardinal of the Medici*, by Mrs. Hicks Beach, which is about Ippolito de' Medici, a bastard of Giuliano who grew up at the court of Urbino; *The Dwarf*, by Pär Lagerkvist, which is a grimly sardonic fantasy about guile, treachery and murder; *Web of Lucifer*, by Maurice Samuel, which is about the career of Cesare Borgia; *The Mercenary* and *Medusa's Children*, both by Charles Durbin, which are about the Baglioni.

In more than forty years of reading about the Renaissance I have read many periodical articles which cannot be listed here. Among the works consulted for this book are the following:

Ady, Cecilia M. *A History of Milan under the Sforza.* London, 1907.
————. *The Bentivoglio of Bologna: A Study in Despotism.* London, 1937.
————. *Morals and Manners of the Quattrocento.* Annual Italian Lecture of the British Academy. London, 1942.
————. *Lorenzo dei Medici and Renaissance Italy.* New York, 1955.
Alfani, Teseo. *Memorie Perugine 1505-1527.* In Archivio storico italiano. Firenze, 1851.
Allen, A.M. *A History of Verona.* New York, 1910.
Amettler y Vinas, J. *Alfonso de Aragon en Italia y la crisio religiosa del siglo XV.* Gerona, 1903-28.
Armstrong, E. *Lorenzo de' Medici and Florence in the Fifteenth Century.* New York, 1897.
Baron, Hans. *The Crisis of the Early Italian Renaissance: Civic Hu-*

manism and Republican Liberty in an Age of Classicism and Tyranny. Princeton, 1966.

Beccadelli, Antonio (il Panormita). *De Dictis et Factis Alphonsi Aragonum.* Amsterdam, 1746.

Bellonci, Maria. *The Life and Times of Lucrezia Borgia.* New York, 1954.

Beuf, Carlo. *Cesare Borgia: The Machiavellian Prince.* New York, 1942.

Bishop, Morris. *Petrarch and His World.* Bloomington, 1963.

Boccaccio, Giovanni. *The Fates of Illustrious Men.* Translated and abridged by Louis Brewer Hall. New York, 1965.

Breisach, Ernst. *Caterina Sforza.* Chicago, 1967.

Bridge, John S. *A History of France from the Death of Louis XI.* Oxford, 1924.

Brinton, Selwyn. *The Gonzaga—Lords of Mantua.* London, 1927.

Burckhardt, Jacob. *The Civilization of the Renaissance in Italy.* Translated by S. G. C. Middleton. Translation first published 1878.

Cambridge Modern History. Vol. 1 (The Renaissance). London, 1912.

Cartwright, Julia. *Beatrice d'Este, Duchess of Milan 1475–1497, A Study of the Renaissance.* London, 1899.

———. *Isabella d'Este, Marchioness of Mantua 1474–1539: A Study of the Renaissance.* New York, 1903.

———. *The Perfect Courtier: Baldassare Castiglione, His Life and Letters, 1478–1529.* New York, 1927.

Castiglione, Baldassare. *The Book of the Courtier.* Translated by Charles S. Singleton. Garden City, 1959.

Cellini, Benvenuto. *The Life of Benvenuto Cellini Written by Himself.* Edited and translated by John Addington Symonds. London, 1887.

Chabod, Federico. *Machiavelli and the Renaissance.* London, 1958.

Chamberlain, E.R. *The Count of Virtue: Giangaleazzo Visconti, Duke of Milan.* New York, 1966.

Cheyney, Edward P. *The Dawn of a New Era 1250–1453.* New York, 1936.

Chubb, Thomas Caldecot. *Aretino, Scourge of Princes.* New York, 1940.

Cipolla, Carlo M. *Guns, Sails and Empires: Technological Innovation and the Early Phases of European Expansion, 1400–1700.* New York, 1966.

Cleugh, James. *The Divine Aretino.* New York, 1966.

Clough, Cecil H. *The Relations between the English and Urbino Courts, 1474–1508.* Studies in the Renaissance, XIV. New York, 1967.

Collison-Morley, Lacy. *Naples Through the Centuries.* London, 1925.

———. *The Story of the Sforzas.* London, 1933.

Commines. *The Memoirs Of Philip de Commines, Lord of Argenton.*

Edited, with Life and Notes, by Andrew R. Scoble. 2 vols. London, 1856.

Cornforth, John. "The Gonzaga Palaces of Mantua," *Country Life* (London), Jan. 19, 1967.

Creighton, Mandell. *A History of the Papacy during the Period of the Reformation.* 4. vols. Boston, 1887.

———. *Historical Essays and Reviews.* London, 1902.

Cronin, Vincent. *The Florentine Renaissance.* New York, 1967.

Deiss, Joseph Jay. *Captains of Fortune: Profiles of Six Italian Condottieri.* New York, 1967.

Delaborde, H. Francois. *L'Expédition de Charles VIII en Italie: Histoire Diplomatique et Militaire.* Paris, 1888.

Della Casa, Giovanni. *Galateo, or The Book Of Manners.* Translated by R. S. Pine-Coffin. London, 1958.

Dennistoun, James. *Memoirs of the Dukes of Urbino.* 3. vols. London. 1909.

Elliott, J. H. *Imperial Spain 1469–1716.* New York, 1964.

Fabretti, Ariodante. *Biographie dei Capitani venturieri dell' Umbria scritte ed illustrate con documenti.* Montepulciano. 1842–46.

Fazio, Bartholomeo. *Fatti d'Alfonso d'Aragona, Primo Re di Napoli di Questo Nome.* Venice, 1580.

Ferguson, Wallace K., and others. *The Renaissance.* New York, 1962.

———, and others. *Facets of The Renaissance.* New York, 1963.

Ferrara, Orestes. *The Borgia Pope: Alexander VI.* New York, 1940.

Forrer, L. *Biographical Dictionary of Medallists.* London, 1904.

Freedberg, S. J. *Painting of the High Renaissance in Rome and Florence.* 2. vols. Cambridge, 1961.

Frolliere, Girolamo di. *La guerra del sale; ossia, Racconto della sostenuta dai Perugeni contro Paolo III. nel 1540.* In Archivio storico italiano. Firenze, 1851.

Funck-Brentano, F. *The Renaissance.* New York, 1936.

Gail, Marzieh. *Avignon in Flower: 1309–1403.* Boston, 1965.

Gardner, Edmund G. *Dukes and Poets in Ferrara.* New York, 1904.

———. *The King of Court Poets: A Study of the Work, Life and Times of Lodovico Ariosto.* London, 1906.

Gilbert, Felix. *Machiavelli and Guicciardini: Politics and History in Sixteenth-Century Florence.* Princeton, 1965.

Gilmore, Myron P. *The World of Humanism 1453–1517.* New York, 1952.

Glasfurd, Alec. *The Antipope (Peter de Luna 1342–1423): A Study in Obstinacy.* London, 1965.

Grassi, Paride de. *Il diario di Leone X.* Roma, 1884.

Gregorovius, Ferdinand. *History of the City of Rome in the Middle Ages.* London, 1909.

———. *Lucrezia Borgia: A Chapter from the Morals of the Italian Renaissance.* 1874. Translation: London, 1948.

Guicciardini, Francesco. The History of Guicciardini: Containing The Warres of Italie and Other Partes, Continued For Many Years Under Sundry Kings and Princes, Together With The Variations and Accidents Of The Same. Reduced into English by Geoffray Fenton. London, 1599.
———. History of Italy and History of Florence. Translated by Cecil Grayson. Edited and abridged by John R. Hale. New York, 1964.
———. Selected Writings. Edited and introduced by Cecil Grayson. Translated by Margaret Grayson. London, 1965.
———. Ricordi. Translated by Ninian Hill Thomson. New York, 1949.
Gundersheimer, Werner L. (ed.). The Italian Renaissance. Englewood Cliffs, N.J., 1965.
Hale, J. R. Machiavelli and Renaissance Italy. New York, 1960.
———. Renaissance. New York, 1965.
Hale, John, Roger Highfield and Beryl Smalley (eds.). Europe in the Late Middle Ages. Evanston, 1965.
Hay, Denys. The Italian Renaissance in its Historical Background. Cambridge, 1961.
———. Editor. The Age of the Renaissance. New York, 1967.
Heywood, William. A History of Perugia. London, 1910.
Hazlitt, W. Carew. The Venetian Republic: Its Rise, its Growth, and its Fall, 1421–1797. London, 1900.
Hicks, David L. The Education of a Prince: Lodovico il Moro and the Rise of Pandolfo Petrucci. Studies In The Renaissance, VIII. New York, 1961.
Huizinga, Johan. The Waning of the Middle Ages. New York, 1949.
———. Men and Ideas: History, the Middle Ages, the Renaissance. New York, 1959.
Hutton, Edward. Sigismondo Pandolfo Malatesta, Lord of Rimini: A Study of a XV Century Italian Despot. London, 1906.
Ilardi, Vincent. The Italian League, Francesco Sforza and Charles VII (1454–1461). Studies in the Renaissance, VI. New York, 1959.
Jacob, E. F. (ed.). Italian Renaissance Studies. London, 1960.
Jones, P. J. The Malatesta of Rimini: A Contribution to the History of the Papal States in the Later Middle Ages. Unpublished thesis in the Bodleian Library. Oxford, 1949.
Klaczko, Julian. Rome and the Renaissance: The Pontificate of Julius II. New York, 1903.
Lane, Frederick C. Venice and History. Baltimore, 1966.
Larner, John. The Lords of the Romagna: Romagnal Society and the Origins of the Signorie. London, 1965.
Latour, Anny. The Borgias. New York, 1966.
Lavin, Peter. Renaissance Italy 1464–1534. New York, 1966.
Machiavelli, Niccolò. The Historical, Political and Diplomatic Writings of Niccolò Michiavelli. Translated by Christian E. Detmold. 4 vols. Boston, 1882.

——. *History Of Florence*. London, 1901.
——. *The Letters of Machiavelli*. Edited and translated by Allan Gilbert. New York, 1961.
——. *The Prince and the Discourses*. Introduction by Max Lerner. New York, n.d.
Matarazzo, Francesco. *Chronicles of the City of Perugia 1492–1503*. Translated by Edward Strachan Morgan. London, 1905.
Mathew, Arnold H. *The Life and Times of Rodrigo Borgia, Pope Alexander VI*. London, 1926.
Mattingly, Garrett. *Renaissance Diplomacy*. Cambridge, 1955.
Mazzeo, Joseph Anthony. *Renaissance and Revolution: The Remaking of European Thought*. New York, 1965.
Meiss, Millard. *Painting in Florence and Siena after the Black Death: The Arts, Religion and Society in the Mid-Fourteenth Century*. Princeton, 1951.
Michelet, Jules. *Renaissance*. Paris, 1857.
Mitchell, R. J. *The Laurels and the Tiara: Pope Pius II 1458–1464*. New York, 1963.
Mollat, G. *The Popes at Avignon: 1305–1378*. New York, 1963.
Morgan, Charles H. *The Life of Michelangelo*. New York, 1960.
Muir, Dorothy. *A History of Milan under the Visconti*. London, 1924.
New Cambridge Modern History. Vol. 1. (The Renaissance 1493–1520). Cambridge, 1957.
Noyes, Ella. *The Story Of Ferrara*. London, 1904.
Oman, Sir Charles. *A History of the Art of War in the Sixteenth Century*. New York, n.d.
——. *The Sixteenth Century*. New York, n.d.
Pasolini, Count Pier Desiderio. *Catherine Sforza*. New York, 1898.
Pastor, Dr. Ludwig von. *The History of the Popes from the Close of the Middle Ages*. London, 1906.
Piccolomini, Aeneas Sylvius. *Memoirs of a Renaissance Pope: The Commentaries of Pius II*. An abridgment translated by Florence A. Gragg. Edited by Leonora C. Gabel. New York, 1959.
Pontieri, Ernesto. *Per La Storia del Regno di Ferrante I d'Aragona Re di Napoli*. Naples, n.d.
Prescott, William H. *History of the Reign of Ferdinand and Isabella the Catholic*. Philadelphia, 1882.
Prezzolini, Giuseppe. *Michiavelli*. New York, 1967.
Purcell, Mary. *The Great Captain: Gonzalo Fernandez de Cordoba*. Garden City, 1962.
Ranke, Leopold von. *The History of the Popes during the Last Four Centuries*. London, 1908.
Ridolfi, Roberto. *The Life of Girolamo Savonarola*. New York, 1959.
——. *The Life of Niccolò Machiavelli*. Chicago, 1963.
——. *The Life of Francesco Guicciardini*. London, 1967.
Roeder, Ralph. *The Man of the Renaissance*. New York, 1933.

Roover, Raymond de. *The Rise and Decline of the Medici Bank, 1397–1494.* Cambridge, 1963.

Roscoe, William. *The Life and Pontificate of Leo X.* London, 1846.

Roth, Cecil. *The Last Florentine Republic.* London, 1925.

Sabatini, Rafael. *The Life of Cesare Borgia.* Boston, 1924.

Schevill, Ferdinand. *History of Florence from the Founding of the City through the Renaissance.* New York, 1936.

———. *The Medici.* New York, 1949.

———. *Siena: The History of a Medieval Commune.* New York, 1909.

Sellery, George Clarke. *The Renaissance: Its Nature and Origins.* Madison, Wisconsin, 1962.

Shellabarger, Samuel. *The Chevalier Bayard: A Study in Fading Chivalry.* New York, 1928.

Sismondi, J. C. L. *History of the Italian Republics in the Middle Ages.* Edited by William Boulting. London, n.d.

———. *A History of the Italian Republics: Being a View of the Origin, Progress and Fall of Italian Freedom.* Introduction by Wallace K. Ferguson. Garden City, 1966.

Sizeranne, Robert de la. *Beatrice d'Este and Her Court.* London, 1924.

———. *Le Vertueux Condottiere: Federigo de Montefeltro, Duc d'Urbino, 1422–1482.* Paris, 1927.

Speroni, Charles. *Wit and Wisdom of the Italian Renaissance.* Berkeley and Los Angeles, 1964.

Symonds, John Addington. *The Life of Michelangelo.* London, 1892.

———. *Renaissance in Italy.* London, 1875 – 1886.

———. *Sketches in Italy and Greece.* London, 1874.

Symonds, Margaret and Lina Duff Gordon. *The Story of Perugia.* London, 1908.

Taylor, Rachel Annand. *Leonardo the Florentine: A Study in Personality.* New York, 1927.

———. *Invitation to Renaissance Italy.* New York, 1930.

Thompson, James Westfall and others. *The Civilization of the Renaissance.* New York, 1929.

Urquhart, William Pollard. *Life and Times of Francesco Sforza, Duke of Milan.* Edinburgh and London, 1852.

Vallentin, Antonia. *Leonardo da Vinci: The Tragic Pursuit of Perfection.* New York, 1938.

Vasari, Giorgio. *Vasari's Lives of the Artists: Biographies of the Most Eminent Architects, Painters and Sculptors of Italy.* Edited by Betty Burroughs. London, 1960.

Vaughan, Herbert M. *Studies in the Italian Renaissance.* New York, 1930.

Venturi, Lionello. *The Sixteenth Century: From Leonardo to El Greco.* New York, 1956.

Vermiglioli, Giovanni Battista. *La Vita e le Imprese militari di*

Malatesta IV Baglioni, narrazione . . . con note, illustrazione e documenti. Perugia, 1839.

Vespasiano. *Renaissance Princes, Popes and Prelates.* The Vespasiano Memoirs: Lives of Illustrious Men of the XVth Century. Translated by William George and Emily Waters. Introduction by Myron P. Gilmore. New York, 1963.

Villari, Pasquale. *Life and Times of Girolamo Savonarola.* New York, n.d.

Woodward, William Harrison. *Vittorino da Feltre and Other Humanist Educators.* New York, 1963.

Yriarte, Charles. *Cesare Borgia.* London, 1947.

GEORGE ALLEN & UNWIN LTD

Head office:
40 Museum Street, London, W.C.1
Telephone: 01-405 8577

Sales, Distribution and Accounts Departments
Park Lane, Hemel Hempstead, Herts.
Telephone: 0442 3244

Athens: 7 Stadiou Street
Auckland: P.O. Box 36013, Northcote Central, N.4
Barbados: P.O. Box 222, Bridgetown
Beirut: Deeb Building, Jeanne d'Arc Street
Bombay: 103/5 Fort Street, Bombay 1
Calcutta: 285J Bepin Behari Ganguli Street, Calcutta 12
Cape Town: 68 Shortmarket Street
Delhi: 1/18B Asaf Ali Road, New Delhi 1
Hong Kong: 105 Wing on Mansion, 26 Hankow Road, Kowloon
Ibadan: P.O. Box 62
Karachi: Karachi Chambers, McLeod Road
Madras: 2/18 Mount Road, Madras 6
Mexico: Villalongin 32, Mexico 5, D.F.
Nairobi: P.O. Box 30583
Pakistan: Alico Building, 18 Motijheel, Dacca 2
Philippines: P.O. Box 157, Quezon City, D-502
Rio de Janeiro: Caixa Postal 2537-Zc-00
Singapore: 36c Prinsep Street, Singapore 7
Sydney, N.S.W.: Bradbury House, 55 York Street
Tokyo: C.P.O. Box 1728, Tokyo 100-91
Toronto: 81 Curlew Drive, Don Mills